The Spartan *Scytale* and Developments in Ancient and Modern Cryptography

Also available from Bloomsbury

Athens and Sparta by Stephen Todd
Authority and History: Ancient Models, Modern Questions
edited by Juliana Bastos Marques and Federico Santangelo
Demagogues, Power, and Friendship in Classical Athens
by Robert Holschuh Simmons

The Spartan *Scytale* and Developments in Ancient and Modern Cryptography

Martine Diepenbroek

BLOOMSBURY ACADEMIC
LONDON • NEW YORK • OXFORD • NEW DELHI • SYDNEY

BLOOMSBURY ACADEMIC

Bloomsbury Publishing Plc, 50 Bedford Square, London, WC1B 3DP, UK
Bloomsbury Publishing Inc, 1385 Broadway, New York, NY 10018, USA
Bloomsbury Publishing Ireland, 29 Earlsfort Terrace, Dublin 2, D02 AY28, Ireland

BLOOMSBURY, BLOOMSBURY ACADEMIC and the Diana logo
are trademarks of Bloomsbury Publishing Plc

First published in Great Britain 2024
Paperback edition published 2025

Copyright © Martine Diepenbroek, 2024

Martine Diepenbroek has asserted her right under the Copyright, Designs and Patents Act, 1988, to be identified as Author of this work.

For legal purposes the Acknowledgements on p. x constitute
an extension of this copyright page.

Cover design: Terry Woodley
Cover image © Anadmist/iStock

All rights reserved. No part of this publication may be: i) reproduced or transmitted in any form, electronic or mechanical, including photocopying, recording or by means of any information storage or retrieval system without prior permission in writing from the publishers; or ii) used or reproduced in any way for the training, development or operation of artificial intelligence (AI) technologies, including generative AI technologies. The rights holders expressly reserve this publication from the text and data mining exception as per Article 4(3) of the Digital Single Market Directive (EU) 2019/790.

Bloomsbury Publishing Inc does not have any control over, or responsibility for, any third-party websites referred to or in this book. All internet addresses given in this book were correct at the time of going to press. The author and publisher regret any inconvenience caused if addresses have changed or sites have ceased to exist, but can accept no responsibility for any such changes.

A catalogue record for this book is available from the British Library.

Library of Congress Cataloging-in-Publication Data
Names: Diepenbroek, Martine, author.
Title: The Spartan scytale and developments in ancient and modern cryptography / Dr Martine Diepenbroek.
Description: New York : Bloomsbury Publishing Plc, 2023. | Includes bibliographical references and index.
Identifiers: LCCN 2023017939 (print) | LCCN 2023017940 (ebook) | ISBN 9781350281325 (hardback) | ISBN 9781350281318 (paperback) | ISBN 9781350281288 (pdf) | ISBN 9781350281295 (ebook)
Subjects: LCSH: Cryptography–Greece–Sparta (Extinct city)–History. | Cryptography–History. | CIphers–History. | Military intelligence–History.
Classification: LCC Z103.4.S73 D54 2023 (print) | LCC Z103.4.S73 (ebook) | DDC 355.4/1–dc23/eng/20231002
LC record available at https://lccn.loc.gov/2023017939
LC ebook record available at https://lccn.loc.gov/2023017940

ISBN: HB: 978-1-3502-8132-5
PB: 978-1-3502-8131-8
ePDF: 978-1-3502-8128-8
eBook: 978-1-3502-8129-5

Typeset by RefineCatch Limited, Bungay, Suffolk

For product safety related questions contact productsafety@bloomsbury.com.

To find out more about our authors and books visit www.bloomsbury.com
and sign up for our newsletters.

Contents

List of Figures	vi
List of Tables	vii
Preface	viii
Acknowledgements	x
Notes on Texts and Translations, with Link to Online Appendices	xi
Introduction	1
1 Structure of Ancient Greek Armies and Military Communication	7
2 Sparta and Secrecy in Non-Spartan Sources	23
3 The *Scytale*	47
4 Cryptography and Steganography in Aeneas Tacticus' *How to Survive Under Siege*	85
5 Roman Views Towards the Spartan *Scytale*	101
6 The Development of the Principle of the Transposition Cipher System of the *Scytale* in Ciphers from the Renaissance to the Twenty-First Century	121
Conclusion	145
Notes	151
Bibliography	183
Index	227

Figures

1	*Scytale* with strip of writing material wrapped about it	63
2	Text: 'Enemy attacks at dawn tomorrow', written on *scytale*	64
3	Strip of writing material with text unwrapped from *scytale*	64
4	Text: 'Enemy attacks at dawn tomorrow' written across complete strip of writing material	65
5	Complete strip of writing material cut into pieces to show partial and complete letters	65
6	Reconstruction of Aeneas Tacticus' water clock	95
7	Five tablets with the letters of the ancient Greek alphabet used for Polybius' fire signalling method	96
8	Reconstructions of Aeneas Tacticus' wooden disk	99
9	Encrypting text with a Caesar cipher with a right shift of three	118
10	Decrypting text with a Caesar cipher with a right shift of three	118
11	Caesar cipher with a right shift of three applied to ancient Greek alphabet	118
12	Reconstruction of Alberti's cipher disk	123
13	Jefferson wheel cipher	131
14	Polybius square	134
15	ADFGX cipher table	135
16	ADFGX cipher table with rows and columns marked with letters	135
17	M-94 cipher cylinder	137
18	Rotors on Enigma machine	138
19	Plaintext message written in grid (modern substitution cipher)	138
20	Encrypted text (modern substitution cipher)	139
21	Encrypted text divided into groups of letters (modern substitution cipher)	139
22	Ciphertext cut into strips (modern substitution cipher)	141
23	DTRIP cipher M-138-A	143

Tables

1	Communication network among Greek soldiers	16
2	Communication network among Greek commanders	16
3	Trithemius' *Tabula recta* scheme for encryption and decryption	127
4	Bellaso's encryption table	129
5	Scheme to illustrate Bellaso's encryption method	130
6	Vigenère table	133
7	Scheme to illustrate Vigenère encryption method	133

Preface

It may well be that ciphers in classical antiquity were more advanced than the literature would lead us to expect [. . .].

Leighton 1969, 153.

The 21st century will see transposition regain its true importance.

Bauer 2007, 100.

I first became acquainted with ancient communication security (cryptography and steganography) after reading Dan Brown's *The Da Vinci Code* in which the Caesar cipher and the Spartan *scytale* are mentioned. To find out more about these methods for communication security, I started doing some research. Soon, I found out that many Greek and Roman authors from Homer, in the eighth/seventh century BCE, to Ausonius, in the fourth century CE, discussed how to secure confidential information, mainly in the context of warfare, but also in love letters. I also found out that the topic of ancient communication security was still mostly unexplored. Therefore, I decided to dedicate my Master's dissertation to the topic of ancient cryptography.[1] Later, I was lucky enough to get the chance to continue my research into this fascinating topic by doing a PhD in Classics and Ancient History at the University of Bristol (2015–21). My doctoral thesis with the title 'Myths and Histories of the Spartan *Scytale*', was a response to Kelly's article 'The Myth of the *Scytale*' (1998), in which he argues against the practical use of the *scytale* in Antiquity. This book, based on my doctoral research, is to reassess the extant evidence concerning the cryptographic Spartan device known as the *scytale*, and to challenge the view promoted by modern historians of cryptography that see the *scytale* essentially as a simple 'stick' that would have served little practical use as a vehicle for secret communication in the ancient world. This study will seek to demonstrate that the cryptographic principles employed in the *scytale* show an encryption and coding system that is no less complex than some twenty-first-century transposition ciphers. Moreover, it will be shown that the *scytale*-system was as complex and secure as other known ancient ciphers, including the substitution code used in the so-called 'Caesar cipher' discussed in chapter five. The work draws salient comparisons with a selection of modern transposition ciphers and their historical predecessors, to illustrate the relative sophistication of the Spartan *scytale* as a practical device for secret communication. This helps to establish the conceptual basis that the *scytale* would have offered its ancient users a secure method for such secret communication, particularly over long distances, albeit only theoretically since evidence for the use of the *scytale* as a cryptograph in Greek military history remains inaccessible.

Acknowledgements

My thanks and appreciation to everyone who has helped me to make the research and the creation of this book possible. First, many thanks to my supervisors and advisors at the University of Bristol: Professor Patrick Finglass, Professor Genevieve Liveley, Professor Neville Morley and Dr Isabella Sandwell.

About a month after finishing my PhD in January 2021, I lost access to academic libraries and archives, which made working on this book difficult. Luckily, in May 2022, the University of Johannesburg's Department of Languages, Cultural Studies and Applied Linguistics (division Classical Cultures and Mythologies) offered me a position as Association Research Fellow, and in July 2022 I was promoted to the position of Postdoctoral Research Fellow. With these new academic positions, I regained access to the sources that I needed to finish this book. Therefore, many thanks and appreciation also go to the University of Johannesburg's Department of Languages, Cultural Studies and Applied Linguistics.

Then, I would like to thank other colleagues, friends and family members for proofreading previous versions of the work. Special thanks to Professor Rose Mary Sheldon, Dr Nicholas Cross and Eugene Teitelbaum. Your suggestions and comments were most welcome and valuable. You have all helped me in so many ways to finish this work.

Finally, I would also like to thank the Bloomsbury Publishing team, especially my editors Ms Lily Mac Mahon and Ms Zoe Osman, and the experts provided by Bloomsbury who commented on earlier versions of the manuscript. Thank you all for your invaluable help and patience.

Notes on Texts and Translations

The following list provides an overview of Greek and Latin translations and commentaries used for this work. Translations of original text come from the Loeb Classical Library Series unless otherwise indicated. Full bibliographical details of all consulted works can be found in the bibliography.

	Dissoi Logoi	Laks and Most 2016
	Sylloge Tacticorum	Charzelis and Harris 2017
Aeneas Tacticus	*How to Survive Under Siege*	Barends 1955; Hug 1877; Hunter and Handford 1927; Illinois Greek Club 1923; Whitehead 1990.
Aeschylus	*Agamemnon*	Sommerstein 2008
Alberti	*De Componendis Cifris*	Williams, March et al. 2010
Ammianus Marcellinus	*Roman History*	Rolfe 1950; Seyfarth 1970
Apollodorus	*The Library*	Frazer 1921
Archilochus of Paros	*Fragment* 185	Gerber 1999a; Swift 2019
Aristarchus	*Scholia to the Iliad*	Schmidt 1920; Erbse 1971
Aristophanes	*Birds*	Henderson 2000; Sommerstein 1987
	Lysistrata	Henderson 2001; Sommerstein 1990
Athenaeus of Naucratis	*The Learned Banqueters*	Douglas Olson 2009
Aulus Gellius	*Attic Nights*	Rolfe 1946; Holford-Strevens 2019a; 2019b
Ausonius	*Epistles*	Evelyn-White 1921
Cardano	*De Subtilitate*	Forrester and Henry 2013
Caesar	*The Alexandrian War*	Way 1955
	The African War	Way 1955
	The Civil War	Damon 2016
	The Gallic War	Edwards 1917
	The Spanish War	Way 1955
Cassius Dio	*Roman History*	Cary and Foster 1914
Cicero	*Letters to Atticus*	Shackleton Bailey 1999 (4 volumes)

Cornelius Nepos	*On Great Generals*	Rolfe 1929; Watson 1866
Diodorus Siculus	*Library of History*	Oldfather 1950
Euripides	*Children of Heracles*	Kovacs 1995
	Suppliant Women	Kovacs 1998
Frontinus	*Stratagems*	Bennett and McElwain 1925
Herodian	*History of the Empire*	Whittaker 1970
Herodotus	*Histories*	Godley 1920; 1922; 1925; Holland and Cartledge 2013
Homer	*Iliad*	Murray and Wyatt 1924; 1925; 1999
Isidore of Seville	*The Etymologies*	Barley, Lewis et al. 2006
Johannes Tzetzes	*Chiliades*	Untila, Berkowitz et al. 2015
Julius Africanus	*Kestoi*	Illinois Greek Club 1928
Justin	*Philippic History*	Watson 1853
Nicophon	*The Birth of Aphrodite*	Edmonds 1957; Kassel and Austin 1989; Storey 2011a and b
Ovid	*Amores*	Goold 1977; Jestin and Katz 2000
	Heroides	Goold 1977; Jacobson 1974
	Ars Amatoria	Mozley 1929
Philo of Byzantium	*Compendium of Mechanics*	Thévenot, Boivin et al. 1693; Author's translation
Photius	*Lexicon*	Sosin 2018a and b
Pindar	*Olympian Odes*	Race 1997
Plato	*Greater Hippias*	Fowler 1926
Pliny the Elder	*Natural History*	Jones and Andrews 1980
Plutarch	*Life of Agesilaus*	Perrin 1916
	Life of Alcibiades	Perrin 1917
	Life of Artaxerxes	Forster Smith 2010; Perrin 1926
	Life of Lysander	Flaceliere and Chambry 1971; Perrin 1917
	Moralia	Babbitt 1931
Polyaenus	*Stratagems of War*	Shepherd 1793; Krentz and Wheeler 1994
Polybius	*Histories*	Paton, Walbank et al. 2011
Porphyry of Tyre	*Life of Pythagoras*	Guthrie 1987
Procopius	*Secret History*	Dewing 1935

Suetonius	*Lives of the Caesars:*	
	The Deified Augustus	Rolfe 1914
	The Deified Julius	Rolfe 1914
	Tiberius	Rolfe 1914
Tyrtaeus	*Fragments*	Gerber 1999b
Theophrastus	*Nomoi*	*Biblioteca Apostolica Vaticana*, 2306; Aly 1943; Sbordone 1950; Keaney 1974; Szedegy-Maszak 1981
Thucydides	*History of the Peloponnesian War*	Gomme, Andrewes, and Dover 1981; Hammond 2009; Hornblower 1996; 2010; Lattimore 1998; Rhodes 2014; Smith 1919
Xenophon	*Cyropaedia*	Miller 1914
	Hellenica	Brownson 1918; 1921; Warner and Cawkwell 1979.

Appendices for this title are available online at the following link: https://bloomsbury.pub/spartan-scytale

Appendix 1: Terminology Concerning Cybersecurity and Espionage
Appendix 2: Graeco-Roman and Medieval Sources on the Spartan *Scytale* in Alphabetic Order Per Author
Appendix 3: Graeco-Roman Sources on Cryptography and Steganography
Appendix 4: Medieval, Renaissance and Early Modern Sources on Cryptography and Steganography Referring to Graeco-Roman Sources

Introduction

Greek warfare in the Classical period has long been seen as a practice following unwritten rules in which the gods played an important role in soldiers' lives, and in which there was a distinct dislike of tricking your enemy, and communicating in secret. However, in recent years this view of a fair and structured Greek warfare has changed.[1] In fact, the ancient Greeks used trickery and deceit freely in war from very early times, starting with the trick of the Trojan horse (Homer, *Odyssey*, 4.21; 8.512; Virgil, *Aeneid*, 2.1–56; 2.228–253).[2] Next to this, communication in secret was not uncommon to Greek armies either. In this way spies or soldiers at posts away from headquarters could communicate with the main force. And finally, because of the fear of interception of confidential information by the enemy, concealing messages was necessary too. This concealing of information is known as cryptography and steganography, and it was among the common practices of ancient intelligence networks – especially in times of war. An example of a type of secret messaging that was probably used in ancient Greece is the Spartan *scytale*, which will be analysed in detail in this book.

Cryptography and steganography

Cryptography and steganography form part of contemporary studies of mathematics and computer science, but also play significant roles in studies of military history, both ancient and modern. Scholars working in these fields have written numerous works in which ancient methods of cryptography and steganography are referred to in passing as the early (which, in these studies, typically signifies 'primitive') precursors to modern cryptographic methods.[3] Steganography, from the Greek words στεγανός (*steganos*) meaning 'covered' or 'concealed' and γράφειν (*graphein*) meaning 'to write', is the practice of concealing a message within another message, an image, or an object, without giving the idea that a secret message is hidden in it.[4] In other words we can say that steganography is 'the practice of undetectably altering a work to embed a secret message'.[5] The hidden message that is created in this way is called a 'steganogram'.[6] In modern terminology two basic types of steganography are distinguished: technical steganography and linguistic steganography. Technical steganography includes every method of steganography in which a tool or device is used to conceal a secret message. This can be anything except text.[7] Ancient examples of technical steganography include the use of hiding places and the use of invisible ink (chapter four and five). Linguistic steganography can be described as 'any form of steganography in which language is used.'[8] There are several forms of linguistic steganography, which can be divided into two basis categories: open codes and semagrams. An open code is a non-secret text in which certain letters, words or sentences form a secret message.[9] Semagrams, from the Greek word σημα (sema) meaning 'sign', 'signal', 'mark' or 'symbol', are divided into two categories: text semagrams and real semagrams. A text semagram works in the same way as an open code. Again letters, words and/or sentences in a text are used to form a message. However, in the case of a text semagram, this is usually done by using a different type of script for the parts of the text that form the intended message or by marking these parts using dots or stripes, as mentioned by Aeneas Tacticus (*How to Survive Under Siege*, 31.1–3; chapter four). The second type of semagram is called a 'real semagram'. A real semagram is an object that represents a message without using text.[10] For example, a picture of a blue sky can mean 'everything is okay' while a picture of a dark grey sky can mean 'danger'. An ancient example of a real semagram is transmitting messages by using torches, as is described by Polybius (*Histories*, 45.6–12; chapter four). Hereby the torches represent letters.

A cryptogram is more complex than a steganogram. Cryptography, from the Greek words κρυπτός (kryptos), meaning 'hidden from' or 'secret', and γράφειν (graphein), meaning 'to write', is the practice of techniques for securing communication by enciphering a text.[11] In cryptography an original message, called plaintext, is converted into a disguised message, called ciphertext.[12] This encrypted message is called a cryptogram.[13] Cryptography works with inputting and outputting either cipher or code. A code works by converting words or phrases into other words or phrases. Ciphers, by contrast, encrypt messages at the level of individual letters, or small groups of letters.[14] There are two fundamental types of ciphers found in the ancient world: transposition and substitution ciphers. In a transposition cipher the normal sequence of letters of a plaintext is rearranged. Thus, alphabetic letters are not typically substituted by any other letters, numbers or symbols.[15] In substitution ciphers the letters of a plaintext message are substituted with other letters, characters, or symbols that are not necessarily found in the original text. The sequence of ciphertext letters that is used for such encryption and decryption is known as a ciphertext alphabet.[16] Examples of cryptography in Antiquity include the Spartan *scytale*, and the Caesar cipher.[17]

The Spartan *scytale*

According to Plutarch and Aulus Gellius – writing in the second century CE – the *scytale* was a device used for secret messaging by the Spartans in the fifth and fourth centuries BCE. Their descriptions show us how the device would have worked (Plutarch, *Life of Lysander*, 19.5–6; Aulus Gellius, *Attic Nights*, 17.9.6–16). What Plutarch and Gellius describe is a simple, yet ingenious device for sending secret messages, whereby only two *scytalae* (literally 'sticks') of the same size, and a piece of parchment or papyrus were needed. Even though the two authors discuss an ingenious system, we will see in this work that there is no clear evidence for the use of the *scytale* as a cryptographic device by the Spartans. In fact, extant evidence for the use of the *scytale* points to other uses of the device (chapter three). Moreover, there is only one potential and indirect Spartan reference to the *scytale*. According to Polyaenus (second century CE), the seventh-century BCE poet Tyrtaeus – being an Athenian by birth, but living and working in Sparta (Lycurgus, *Against Leocrates*, 1.106; Plato, *Laws*, 629a4; *Suda*, entry '*Tyrtaeus*')[18] – referred to the practice of the *scytalae* being used for identification purposes of fallen soldiers on the battlefield with *scytalae* fasted to their arms (Polyaenus, *Stratagems of War*, 1.17). This potentially makes the passage the only Spartan reference to a *scytale*. And, this obviously is not a reference to the *scytale* as a cryptographic device, but a reference to one of the other many purposes of the *scytale* (as we will see in chapter three). Also, since the source is indirect (Polyaenus referring to Tyrtaeus) we cannot say with certainty if – and what – Tyrtaeus wrote on the *scytale*. So, there may not be any Spartan references to the *scytale*. However, even though the *scytale*-system may have been (partially) invented by Plutarch (as we will see in chapter three), the system is the earliest known theoretical transposition cipher in history, and it formed the basis for modern transposition ciphers used up to the present day (chapter six).

Modern views on the Spartan *scytale*

Modern historians of cryptography seem to have overlooked the importance of the effect of the *scytale*-system on later forms of cryptography and steganography, regardless of its use as a Spartan cryptographic device. Instead, they see the *scytale* as a simple toy cipher that can never have been used for serious secret communications.[19] Next to this, there are no modern works on cryptography and steganography that focus in depth and detail upon the ancient history of the *scytale*, nor on the topic of ancient communication security in general. Furthermore, none of these modern studies offer a comprehensive account of all the extant ancient sources in which secret communication is mentioned. Although David Kahn's extensive 1967 work *The Codebreakers* is an excellent source, this work still does not give a complete overview of all original Graeco-Roman sources on cryptography and steganography. Other important general studies on the history of cryptography also simply offer overviews of general cryptographic and steganographic history. Examples from Antiquity up to the Middle Ages are briefly mentioned as an embryonic or primitive phase in the evolution of secret communication technologies, and are followed in each case by a more extensive discussion of secret communication from the early Renaissance until the modern day. The focus of the studies is typically the use of cryptography in the First and Second World Wars, often presented as a technical apogee. In this modern scholarship, this leads to the undervaluation, underappreciation and misunderstanding of the relative sophistication of cryptographic devices known from ancient Greek and Roman sources (if these sources are discussed or referred to at all).[20] Whitiak, for example, claims that the original sources show us that Greek historians were familiar with a range of steganographic methods for secret communication.[21] However, ancient historians such as Herodotus only referred to reports of stories and events in which secret messages may have played a role. There is no evidence that Greek historians were personally or directly familiar with such stratagems, and they even potentially invented these stories themselves, as we will see in chapter two and three.

When looking at modern historical works, Gardthausen's very thorough survey of writing in ancient Greece, *Griechische Paleographie* (1911–13), has a short section on basic principles of cryptography and steganography, but Gardthausen does not engage directly with any of the extant sources on cryptography and steganography from Antiquity. There is also Galland's 1945 work *An Historical and Analytical Bibliography of the Literature of Cryptology*, which is a 'register of the most important works that have been written, not only on the subject of cryptography, but also on its manifestations in related fields'.[22] Yet, this work does not critically analyse Greek and Roman sources on cryptography in detail either, let alone any sources. This is an obvious result of the purpose of the book: it is a bibliography of all sources on cryptography in several contexts, including military and commercial uses, and popular culture, rather than being a detailed work on ancient cryptography.[23] Next to this, Galland's work – written in 1945 – is outdated. The work that comes closest to a complete overview of sources on classical cryptography is Sheldon's *Espionage in the Ancient World: An Annotated Bibliography of Books and Articles in Western Languages* (2008). Although this study offers an excellent summary and catalogue of modern sources dealing with the history of cryptography, as the title implies, this book gives no substantive overview of *ancient* sources on the theme. The commentaries on, and translations of, ancient sources typically discuss passages on secret communication very briefly, if they are discussed at all.

This book aims to make a significant and original contribution to the existing scholarship on the topic of ancient cryptography by filling a gap in the current literature, and thereby casting new light upon some of the (incorrect) assumptions and (mis)readings of the ancient sources prevalent in the field, in addition to offering new knowledge of the Spartan *scytale* as the first theoretical transposition cipher in history. To achieve this a number of themes will be analysed in this work. Chapter one starts with an introduction to the role of communication within the structure of Greek armies. Chapter two is dedicated to the earliest examples of communication security in Greek sources, namely in the works of Homer and Herodotus. The chapter will also look into how the Spartans are depicted in Herodotus' work. At the end of chapter two we will make a connection to chapter three by discussing how Greeks after Herodotus – especially the Athenians in the fifth and fourth centuries BCE – saw the Spartans, in a time when anti-Spartan sentiments must have been high after the Athenian defeat in the Peloponnesian War (431–404 BCE). Chapter three is then dedicated to an analysis of ancient and modern sources on the Spartan *scytale*, to give an overview of the various meanings of the word '*scytale*'. In this chapter it will be shown that original Greek sources from the fifth and fourth centuries BCE do not discuss the *scytale* as a cryptographic device. Our sources for this use come from Plutarch and Aulus Gellius, who were active in the second century CE. Yet, it will also be shown that the *scytale* is still the earliest known theoretical transposition cipher in history, even though there is no clear evidence for its use as a cryptographic device by the Spartans in the fifth and fourth centuries BCE

– a point that has previously been overlooked by scholars. Modern scholars also believe that *scytalae* could not have been used for secret messaging, only because Aeneas Tacticus (a military author who wrote the earliest known book on cryptography) never discussed the device. Yet, in chapter four, I will show that it is too simple to state this, since there are a number of reasons why Aeneas Tacticus never discussed the *scytale* – the main reason being that he was far more interested in steganographic (hidden) messages than in cryptographic (enciphered) messages. Unlike the Greeks, the Romans believed that the Spartans used *scytalae* for secret messaging. Yet, interestingly, the Romans never adopted the *scytale*-system in their own secret communications. In chapter five, I will discuss the reasons why the Romans never adopted the device. The main reasons for this are – as we will see – that they were more interested in steganographic than in cryptography, like Aeneas Tacticus, and that letter writing in the Roman world differed from letter writing in the Greek world. Finally, in chapter six, the importance of the theoretical *scytale*-system to modern communication security will be shown. In the chapter a number of early modern and modern cryptographic and steganographic methods will be discussed that are based on the *scytale*-system. In this way it will be shown what influence the *scytale*-system, as the earliest known theoretical transposition cipher in history, has had on communication security systems throughout the ages. In doing so, I would like to shed new light on the 'simple' Spartan *scytale*: a system that has been far more useful than scholars in recent years have stated.

1

Structure of Ancient Greek Armies and Military Communication

Wars in ancient Greece from the beginning of the Graeco-Persian Wars (499 BCE) to the end of the Peloponnesian War (404 BCE) changed in scope, scale and character. Throughout the Archaic and Classical period Greek armies became more 'international', with mercenaries from different regions and countries joining the armies, and with the addition of new units, like the cavalry. With the addition of new units and people from different regions and countries – who spoke different languages – being added to the Greek armies, communication within the armies changed as well. And with increasing numbers of men and states involved in warfare, clear communication between all parties – and in fact, the right parties – became increasingly necessary. Also, alliances changed over time, and rapidly. One's ally could be the enemy soon after. Therefore, Greek armies had an increasing need for normal, but also secret communication, since any army obviously does not want the enemy to understand their internal communication. In fact, Greek military communications date back to the Classical period – at least to the fifth century BCE when it played a vital role during the Peloponnesian War. To set the scene for the rest of the book, this chapter will analyse communication in ancient Greek armies through the army's structure, to start making links to the use of secret communication in the following chapters. The chapter is divided into two parts. It starts with a discussion on how ancient Greek authors saw Greek warfare, a practice portrayed as being led by standard rules in which the gods decided everything. This 'practice of unwritten rules' has led scholars to believe for a long time that Greek warfare was fair, open and structured. However, as we will also see, the idea of tricking the enemy in a number of ways was certainly not unknown to the Greeks. Secondly, the structure of the Greek military in the fifth and fourth centuries BCE will be discussed, whereby there is a focus on the role of communication within the structure of Greek warfare.[1]

The unwritten rules of Greek warfare

The earliest references to Greek military protocols can be found in Euripides' works, like the *Children of Heracles* in which Eurystheus' argues that his death would be an unholy act – since he did not die on the battlefield – and that his faith was in the hands of the gods (Euripides, *Children of Heracles*, 1010–1017). In the *Suppliant Women* we also see this idea of the influence of the gods, as well as the customs concerning death and burial of soldiers in no less than four passages (Euripides, *Suppliant Women*, 16–19; 301–313; 523–527; 669–672).[2] This 'practice of unwritten rules' has led scholars to believe for a long time that Greek warfare was fair, open and structured with hoplite armies facing each other on the battlefield.[3] In a collection of essays published in 1968, Vernant, Detienne and De Romilly speak of Greek warfare as an *agôn*: a contest, conceived like a tournament with ceremonies and rules.[4] Mitchell (1996) speaks of 'rules of combat', and Connor (1988) describes the ritualisation of Greek warfare.[5] Yet, the structure of Greek warfare was not as clearcut as these scholars seem to believe. In fact, trickery and deceit for one's own benefit are as old as humanity. However, in many societies it was – and still is – seen as immoral to deceive your enemy. In Graeco-Roman literature we find examples of how despicable the ancient Greeks thought this deception was (Herodotus, *Histories*, 1.212.2; Thucydides, *History of the Peloponnesian War*, 4.86.6; 4.126; Xenophon, *Hellenica*, 6.5.16). Yet, the clearest example of the Greek aversion to tricking your enemy can be found in Euripides' *Rhesos*, where it is claimed that: 'No brave man thinks it right to kill his enemy in secret, but meets him face to face' (Euripides, *Rhesos*, 510–511).

Even though some Greek sources show that tricking your enemy in war was seen as immoral, other sources show the opposite, as will be shown in this book. To start with perhaps the most famous example, we have the story of the Trojan horse (Homer, *Odyssey*, 4.21; 8.512; Virgil, *Aeneid*, 2.1–56; 2.228–253). This story fits in perfectly in this book on the development of communication security, since a modern Trojan horse (in computing) is a piece of malware that also misleads users of its true intent, like the Greeks fooled the Trojans by letting them take the original Trojan horse into their city.[6] Because of this fear of 'hacking', or rather the interception of confidential information by the enemy, communication and communication security are of major importance to both the modern and the ancient world. Indeed, as Gerolymatos points out, the gathering of intelligence and spying on one's enemies is essential for any government to determine the political and military direction of the state, especially in times of conflict when essential information on enemies can obviously facilitate the war effort.⁷ As Chester G. Starr argues: '... modern superpowers need to be able to assess swiftly the potentialities of other states within a framework of rapidly technological change.'⁸

Since Antiquity, individuals in all civilisations have been trying to encipher confidential correspondence (mainly in a military context, according to our available sources⁹), while others have been trying to decipher these messages. In fact, the sixth-century CE Procopius of Caesarea already described the practice of secretly communicating and spying as an old one, that went all the way back to the ancient Near Eastern kingdoms (Procopius of Caesarea, *Secret History*, 30.12–13).¹⁰ Indeed, intelligence activities have always been an integral part of statecraft.¹¹ Gaining information about the enemy's situation and whereabouts could be achieved by reconnaissance when one, or a few, individuals were sent out openly to check on the enemy's force, or by espionage whereby disguised or otherwise hidden agents worked in the enemy's territory, or even for the enemy's forces.¹² These agents or spies had to find ways to send information to headquarters. This was dangerous work. The Athenians, for example, tortured and executed spies (Athenaeus of Naucratis, *The Learned Banqueters*, 2.66d; Aeschines, *Against Ctesiphon*, 3.244; Demosthenes, *On the Crown*, 18.133). Yet, the intelligence work was also of the utmost importance to improve your own chances of victory in war.¹³

So, where we first saw a dislike of deception in warfare, we now see a positive view towards the use of intelligence in warfare. The earliest Greek example of a reconnaissance mission goes as far back as Homer's *Iliad*. In book ten we read how Odysseus and Diomedes set out at night to check on the Trojans' camp (*Iliad*, 10.204–459).¹⁴ And in the *Odyssey*, Helen tells us how Odysseus, disguised as a slave, entered Troy secretly and came back to the Greek camp with useful information (Homer, *Odyssey*, 4.242–258).¹⁵ Later, Xenophon argues that there was nothing more profitable in war than deception, since the greatest advantages in war were achieved in this way (*Hipparchicus*, 5.9–11). And, while deceiving your friends was wrong, deceiving your enemies was not a problem.¹⁶ For example, Plato approves of lying to your personal enemies and opponents (Plato, *Republic*, 382c), while Aeneas Tacticus even recommends catching invaders by surprise preferably when they are drunk (*How to Survive Under Siege*, 16.10–22; 16.5–6). And Isocrates argues that it is appropriate for right-thinking men to gain an advantage over their enemies in any conceivable way in warfare (*Plataicus*, 14.23). Many Greek commanders must have followed this advice, since, as Krentz argues, the historical records show us that in Archaic and Classical Greece clever commanders deceived their enemies whenever they could.¹⁷ To give but one example, the Athenian general Demosthenes is described as a man who was a genuine tactician with a special gift for surprising the enemy in modern scholarship. Already in 1928, Woodcock claimed that scholars had underestimated the achievements of Demosthenes, in a work in which he stresses Demosthenes' pioneering use of military intelligence – as did True in 1956, Pritchett in 1971 and Roismann in 1993.[18] Yet, it was not just famous heroes or generals who set out to spy on the enemy. The most insignificant people in ancient Greece also played a crucial role in gathering intelligence. Slaves often seemed to be good recruits, as they were used to sending secret messages, they had little to lose, were used to obscurity, and were believed to live lives of duplicity anyway (Aeneas Tacticus, *How to Survive Under Siege*, 31.28–29; Aulus Gellius, *Attic Nights*, 17.9.18–27; Herodotus, *Histories*, 5.36; Polyaenus, *Stratagems of War*, 1.24).[19]

Military structure and communication in ancient Greece

War in the ancient Greek world was an 'act of communication', as Naiden points out.[20] When ancient Greek societies and their script developed, their military institutions developed too. Cherry already argued in 1962 that progression from the earliest communities to modern states is: 'one long story of improved means of communication.'[21] Since the Classical period of Greek history, there has been a need for long- and short-distance communication, as well as battlefield signalling to control large empires. As Assange puts it: '. . . armies are the essential building blocks of states, because otherwise one state just takes over another.'[22] Within the Greek armies it were the *hoplites* that made up most of the army and that played a major role in warfare in the Classical period. Around 800 BCE a significant increase in population in Greece allowed urbanised culture to flourish, leading to the rise of the Greek city-state (*polis*), and marking the end of the 'Dark Ages'.[23] Along with the rise of the city-states we see the emergence of the *hoplites* and a new style of warfare: the hoplite phalanx.

Hoplites were infantrymen who formed the central element of warfare in Archaic and Classical Greece.[24] Every Greek city-state had its own hoplite army that consisted of citizens who fought for their state as and when necessary.[25] This inevitably reduced the potential duration of campaigns, as citizens would need to return to their jobs, especially in the case of farmers. The exact origin of the hoplite armies is a topic of discussion among historians. According to Connolly, the first hoplite armies were established during the eighth or seventh century BCE when the 'heroic age was abandoned' and a far more disciplined system in warfare was introduced.[26] Based on archaeological discoveries of the earliest monumental *polyandrion* (a communal burial of male warriors) at Paros, Zafeiropoulou and Agelarakis argue that we find the first hoplites in the last quarter of the eighth century BCE.[27] Krentz gives a much later date. He argues that the ideology of hoplitic warfare did not develop until after 480 BCE when 'non-hoplite arms began to be excluded from the phalanx'.[28] However, the fact that other soldiers began to be excluded from the phalanx after 480 BCE does not mean that there were no hoplites before this date. In fact, the Chigi vase – dated to c. 650 BCE – provides us with the earliest known representation of the hoplite phalanx formation, which shows that hoplite armies were known in the mid-seventh century BCE. We also know that Argos suffered a crippling blow when the Spartan hoplite army – led by King Cleomenes I – defeated them at the Battle of Sepeia in 494 BCE.[29]

Together with the emergence of the hoplite army, a new military formation developed called the *phalanx*, which were rows of shoulder-to-shoulder hoplites. The phalanx was not the complete army, it was only the formation or the mass of infantry or cavalry that would deploy in line during battle. Hoplites would lock their shields together, and the first few ranks of soldiers would project their spears out over the first rank of shields. In this way the phalanx presented a shield wall and a mass of spear points to the enemy, making frontal assaults much more difficult.[30] The phalanx formed the core of ancient Greek armies and battles from the time the hoplite armies developed (eighth/seventh century BCE).[31] Since the hoplites were protected by shields around them, they were relatively safe as long as everyone stayed in formation. This importance of holding the formation can be found in the earliest sources (Tyrtaeus, *Fragments*, 10.15; 11;12; Xenophon, *Hellenica*, 5.1.12).[32] Staying in formation was fairly easy, since battles between two phalanxes usually took place in open, flat plains. Rough terrain would have defeated the purpose of the phalanx. Therefore, the two opposing sides would find the most suitable piece of land where the conflict could be settled.[33] The two sides would then advance at a walking pace, although it is possible that they picked up speed during the last several yards as Phiher and Ramsey argue.[34] Osborne even suggests that the soldiers: '. . . gradually picked up speed and ultimately broke into a run.'[35]

However, because of the nature of the formation, it is logical that soldiers usually tried not to run until they came into the reach of the enemy's missiles (Xenophon, *Hellenica*, 4.3.17), while the Spartans did not run at all (Xenophon, *Constitution of the Lacedaemonians*, 13.8; Plutarch, *Lycurgus*, 22). According to Herodotus, the Athenians at the Battle of Marathon in 490 BCE were the first Greeks to run towards the enemy (*Histories*, 6.112). So, if the hoplites of the phalanx were to pick up speed towards the latter part of the advance, it would have been for the purpose of gaining momentum against the enemy in the initial collision but without losing cohesion, as Hanson argues.[36] A battle would then rely on the men fighting in the front line, while those in the rear maintained forward pressure on the front ranks with their shields. It essentially became a pushing match in which, as a rule, the largest phalanx – the phalanx with the most rows of men – would almost always win, with few recorded exceptions (Thucydides, *History of the Peloponnesian War*, 4.96.4).[37] However, it goes too far to argue that a battle between two hoplite phalanxes was simply 'a bloodless pushing match' as Grossman argues.[38] In fact, as Crowley points out, at the Battle of Coronea in 394 BCE when the Thebans fought against the Spartans, men on both sides fought, killed and were killed, and it could have been rather chaotic and noisy, showing the importance of clear communication among the troops (Xenophon, *Hellenica*, 4.3.19).[39]

Hoplite armies played a major role in Greek warfare for the first time in history during the Graeco-Persian Wars. When we analyse the events in this war, we will see how important communication between all the Greek armies involved in it must have been. The Graeco Persian Wars were the result of attempts by the Persian king, Darius the Great, and then his successor Xerxes I, to subjugate Greece. Various Greek city-states made their submission to the Persians, but others did not, most notably Athens and Sparta. The first Persian invasion of Greece began in 492 BCE, with the Persian general Mardonius subjugating Thrace and Macedon before several mishaps forced an end to the rest of the campaign, as Sprawski points out.[40] Only two years later, in 490 BCE was a second Persian force sent to Greece, this time across the Aegean Sea, under the command of Datis and Artaphernes (Herodotus, *Histories*, 6.98). In the same year, some of the allied Greek forces, consisting of the Athenians and Plataeans, fought against the Persians at the Battle of Marathon, the first large battle in the Graeco-Persian Wars in which Sparta did not play a role.[41] To face the Persians in battle, the Athenians had to summon all available hoplites. Raising such a large army had denuded Athens itself of its defenders. As a result, a Greek defeat at Marathon would have meant the complete defeat of Athens, since no other Athenian army existed.[42] However, with clever strategy the Greek alliance defeated the Persians.[43] The Greeks enveloped them, and attacked. The Persian army broke in panic towards their ships, and large numbers were slaughtered (Cornelius Nepos, *Miltiades*, 5; Herodotus, *Histories*, 6.112; Plutarch, *Aristides*, 5.112). This Persian defeat at Marathon marked the end of the first invasion of Greece, and ended the Persian efforts in Greece for the time being.

The Battle of Marathon was the first engagement between an alliance of Greek hoplites and a non-Greek army, in which the potential of the hoplite phalanx was shown for the first time.[44] The fighting style of the hoplites had developed during wars between the Greek city-states; each city-state fought in almost the same way in battle against other Greeks. Therefore, the advantages and disadvantages of the hoplite phalanx had not been obvious before.[45] Interestingly, the Battle of Marathon was the first time where a hoplite phalanx faced more lightly armed (Persian) troops, and this revealed how effective the hoplites could be in battle. The phalanx formation was still vulnerable to flanking cavalry, but used in the right circumstances, it could be a 'potentially devastating weapon' if used well.[46] To create this 'devastating weapon' it was of the utmost importance to maintain cohesion within the hoplite ranks, and to achieve this, clear communication and following prearranged orders immediately was essential. Ancient Greek writers refer to maintaining communication and cohesion among the troops on the battlefield – as well as the consequences of losing control of this. As long as there was cohesion and communication among the troops, everything went in an orderly fashion, but as soon as these advantages were lost, the situation turned into chaos. Xenophon mentions men who were well-prepared attacking those who were unprepared, and men in good order fighting against those in disorder (Xenophon, *Hellenica*, 7.1.16, see also 5.1.12), while Thucydides mentions enemies being attacked when scattered (Thucydides, *History of the Peloponnesian War*, 5.9.2). Yet, there are also examples of Greeks pretending to be unorganised on purpose to confuse the enemy. According to Plato, when the Spartans fought the Persians in the Battle of Plataea (479 BCE) it looked like they refused to stand and fight and instead retreated. However, when the formations of Persians broke up – expecting victory on their side – the Spartans turned around, fought back and won the battle (Plato, *Laches*, 191C). Because this was part of the Spartans' plan, they were still organised and ready to fight, while the Persians became disorganised, and therefore vulnerable.[47] This shows that effective communication is of the utmost importance in warfare. As Aeneas Tacticus already pointed out in the fourth century BCE: 'In regard to . . . messages, there are all sorts of ways of sending them, but a private arrangement must be previously made between the sender and the receiver' (How to Survive Under Siege, 31.1).

This private arrangement, or in fact the information that is needed to encipher and decipher a message, is called the 'key' in cryptography.[48] In every situation in Greek warfare, all parties had to communicate before and during battles to understand the situation and know how to react to this (Polybius, *Histories*, 10.43). Yet, clear communication, and exactly following the prearranged orders, was not always easy in the heat of battle. Xenophon, for example, mentions a man who could not see more at night than in the midst of battle (*Anabasis*, 4.6.12), and argues that it is extremely hard to find men who would stand firm when they see their comrades flee (*Hellenica*, 5.7.24). We can also find instances of panic in battle among the Greeks when units were isolated and overwhelmed by missile troops (Thucydides, *History of the Peloponnesian War*, 2.79.6, 3.98.1, 4.96.6, 7.43.7); instances in which troops did not exactly know what to do (Herodotus, *Histories*, 7.103; Thucydides, *History of the Peloponnesian War*, 6.69, 6.72); and even situations in which men refused to follow orders (Herodotus, *Histories*, 9.53–55; Thucydides, *History of the Peloponnesian War*, 5.71–72).[49] To keep everything in control and to show that the commanders were in charge, two tactics were used. First, there was the element of the psychological motivation of the soldiers, for example by the use of battle cries (Polybius, *Histories*, 1.34.2–3), as well as the noise of whistles and trumpets (Polybius, *Histories*, 2.29.6–8).[50] Secondly, there was punishment: men were punished for not following orders (e.g. Herodotus, *Histories*, 9.53–55; Plutarch, *Apophthegmata Laconica*, 210f; *Aristides*, 21.3; Xenophon, *Anabasis*, 2.2.13, 2.6.10, 3.4.49; *Hellenica*, 3.5.7, 5.1.33, 6.2.19).[51] If everyone understood what he had to do, followed all given orders, and used the right prearranged signs, a Greek army had the largest chances of success (Thucydides, *History of the Peloponnesian War*, 5.66.4). Obviously, clear communication from the commanders to the hoplites in the aforementioned ways was necessary to keep cohesion within the troops.[52] Yet, Greek armies not only consisted of hoplites. There were a number of other units too, including cavalry and the navy. First, the hoplites were usually accompanied by other light armed infantry men, coming from the poorest economic classes who could not afford a full hoplite panoply. These men were divided into various groups, depending on their jobs. The *psiloi* usually had no specific training and went to the battlefield with rudimentary weapons like javelins and stones in their ordinary clothes.[53] Next to the *psiloi*, there were a smaller number of *toxotai* (archers), often coming from Crete.[54] Crete was the only area in Greece where young men were systemically trained as archers. Therefore, Cretan archers were employed as mercenaries by other Greek city-states from the earliest times.[55] Next to infantry men, cavalry had always existed in Greek armies, but whereas a full hoplite armour was already too expensive for many people, even fewer people could afford to buy full body armour and a horse. This limited the cavalrymen to the very wealthy class of the *hippeis*, a class that was often involved in local politics too.[56]

With more units being added to the armies and with the alliances of Greek states, more and more people became involved in the army's communication networks. Also, with mercenaries being added to the troops, there was the risk of people who did not speak the same language. Therefore, communication on the battlefield was both verbal and non-verbal to make sure that everyone could understand the orders. Another reason for the use of non-verbal communication was the simple fact that it must have been extremely hard to hear every order correctly during battle. Plutarch and Thucydides, for example, tell us that men could not hear their officers in the chaos of an unexpected battle (Plutarch, *Dion*, 30.5–6; Thucydides, *History of the Peloponnesian War*, 4.34.3). A solution for this may be found elsewhere in Thucydides' work, where the historian tells us that pipes were used to ensure Spartan soldiers marched in step (Thucydides, *History of the Peloponnesian War*, 5.70).[57] Also, the Spartans devised manoeuvres in which the soldiers only had to follow their commanders, without any talking being necessary (Xenophon, *Constitution of the Lacedaemonians*, 11.5–6). For this method to be successful, commanders had to rely on their soldiers all the time. Therefore, drilling the troops was not uncommon in ancient Greece since it kept everything in order (Diodorus Siculus, *Library of History*, 11.86.4; Xenophon, *Hellenica*, 4.1.15, 7.5.3). The Spartans were particularly well trained, with many men in different ranks fighting for the same cause, as Thucydides shows (*History of the Peloponnesian War*, 5.66.2–4).

In 480 BCE the second Persian invasion of Greece took place, led by King Xerxes, the son of Darius.[58] During this invasion, again different-sized Greek allied forces appeared throughout the campaign.[59] Like during the first invasion of Greece, during the second Persian invasion there was again a Greek victory due to cunning tactics and the forming of alliances. In the autumn of 481 BCE a congress of city-states met at Corinth to form a confederate alliance of about thirty city-states (Herodotus, *Histories*, 7.145–160).[60] And even though the Greek city-states were at war with each other at the time of the second Persian invasion, they joined forces against Persia once more (7.145).[61] The Greek alliance during the Graeco-Persian wars allowed for a diversification of the joined forces, rather than simply the mustering of a large hoplite army. Amongst the allies, each state had its own strength. The Athenians, led by Themistocles, had successfully built a huge fleet in 483–482 BCE to combat the Persian threat.[62] Athens was, therefore, able to form the core of a navy, whilst other cities, like Sparta, provided the army. This alliance thus removed the constraints on the type of armed forces that the Greeks could use, one that mainly contained hoplite soldiers until then.[63] The combination of an army and a navy let by capable generals proved to be useful and successful. Eventually, the Greeks were able to lure the Persian fleet into the Straits of Salamis, and in the Battle of Salamis in 480 BCE the Persians were defeated (Herodotus, *Histories*, 8). A year later, in 479 BCE, the united Greek forces defeated the Persian army completely at the Battle of Plataea (Ctesias, *Persica*; Herodotus, *Histories*, 9).

The eventual triumph of the Greeks over the much larger Persian army was achieved by alliances between many city-states, on a scale and scope that was never seen before in Greek history. For the Greeks to achieve this, communication networks were necessary. Greek soldiers communicated horizontally through a network. In this arrangement, each soldier was at a node, and communicated freely with those nearest to him (see Table 1). Hereby, it was possible to have partial connections with one person being connected to one or two others (Table 1, left). This is what we see amongst loosely organised troops, like raiding parties. In the second system there are full connections whereby everyone in the network was able to contact everyone else (Table 1, right). This is what we see in well organised units, like the Spartan hoplites. Networks of Greek soldiers made use of watchwords or prearranged codes to communicate with each other (Xenophon, *Anabasis*, 1.8.16). As Naiden argues, this shows that the men were drilled, knew when to speak or when to keep silent, and when to follow orders.[64] Officers would communicate vertically through an arrangement consisting of a hub and spokes. The chief commander would have been at the hub, and his subordinates would have been at the spokes (see Table 2). Hereby, there are three topologies: a simple hub with spokes (Table 2, left); an extended hub with spokes (Table 2, centre); and an asymmetrical hub with spokes (Table 2, right).[65]

Table 1 Communication network among Greek soldiers.
Author's illustration based on: Naiden 2017, 66.

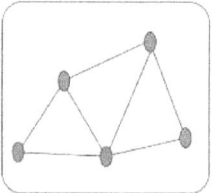
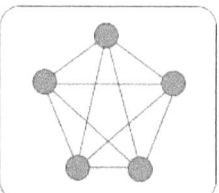

Table 2 Communication network among Greek commanders.
Author's illustration based on: Naiden 2017, 67.

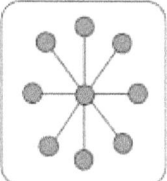
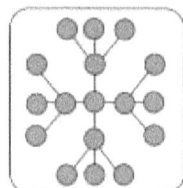
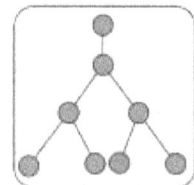

The enemy was not left out of the communication either. Greek slingshot pellets were often inscribed with insulting remarks.[66] And uniforms and armour were used to intimidate the enemy. The Spartans, for example, used the same typical hoplite equipment as other Greek city-states.[67] Yet, a degree of typical uniformity in Spartan military dress is attested by Xenophon. From the time of Lycurgus (the mythical ninth-century BCE founder of Sparta), it would have been compulsory for Spartan hoplites – Xenophon argues – to wear a red cloak (*phoinikis*), and a bronze shield which sometimes had a lambda insignia (*Λ*; 'L' for Lacedaemon) to scare the enemy off, sometimes even before the battle (*Hellenica*, 4.3.8; *Constitution of the Lacedaemonians*, 11.3). It has been assumed that the *phoinikis* was a distinctive military cloak used in battle. However, it would have been 'suicidal to hamper one's movements in hand-to-hand combat by donning any sort of cloak.'[68] Therefore, the *phoinikis* could have been a tunic worn in battle instead of a cloak, as Van Wees suggests. By Xenophon's time, red tunics were worn by hoplites across Greece, making any differences trivial between Spartans and other Greek soldiers.[69] However, another possibility is that a *phoinikis* was indeed a cloak, but that it was taken off before battle commenced. This latter view would be supported by the fact that various ancient authors specifically use the word *phoinikis* when discussing a red cloak often worn by the Spartans (e.g. Aristophanes, *Acharnenses*, 320; Plutarch, *Life of Aemilius Paulus*, 18; Xenophon, *Constitution of the Lacedaemonians*, 11.3). So, maybe Sekunda is correct when mentioning the 'distinctive crimson Spartan cloak.'[70] Yet, it was a cloak that was most likely not worn during battles, and probably not solely worn by the Spartans. Still, the connection between the *phoinikis* and Sparta shows us how communication could work. The distinctive red cloak became a symbol for Spartan strength, used to scare off the enemy. In fact, two other stories strengthen this idea. On one occasion during the Persian War, the Spartans swapped uniform with the Egyptians. The Persians, thinking they were fighting Greeks (especially Spartans), immediately fled (Frontinus, *Stratagems*, 2.3.13; Polyaenus, *Stratagems of War*, 2.16). Yet, this could also work the other way around. On another occasion the Spartans used the shields of their Sicyonian allies. These shields, marked with the letter sigma (*Σ*) for 'Sicyon', did not intimidate the enemy who stood fast and fought (Xenophon, *Hellenica*, 4.4.11).

After the Graeco-Persian Wars ended, the ambitions of various city-states dramatically increased, and Sparta and Athens became the two pre-eminent powers. This led to the start of the Peloponnesian War in 431 BCE between the Delian League (led by Athens) and the Peloponnesian League (led by Sparta). Building on the experience of the Persian Wars, the diversification of warfare mainly dominated by hoplite armies continued, something permitted by increased resources. We see, for example, an increased emphasis on the role of the navy, sieges, mercenaries and even economic warfare: stealing crops from the enemy, and devastating its lands.[71] Set-piece battles during this war proved indecisive. Instead, there was increased reliance on naval warfare, and strategies of attrition, such as blockades and sieges.[72] As Kagan argues, during the Peloponnesian War, conflict transformed from the previously known formalised forms of warfare, into an all-out struggle between city-states, complete with atrocities on a large scale, shattering religious and cultural taboos, devastating vast swathes of countryside and the destruction of complete cities, which again provided the need for communication methods and networks to develop further.[73] At the Battle of Aegospotami in 405 BCE, the Spartan general Lysander seized the Hellespont – the source of Athens' grain – with the Spartan navy. The remaining Athenian fleet was thereby forced to confront the Spartans, and were decisively defeated (Plutarch, *Life of Lysander*, 9; Xenophon, *Hellenica*, 2). A year later Athens surrendered, thereby ending the war in 404 BCE.[74]

Following the defeat of the Athenians in 404 BCE at the end of the Peloponnesian War, the Greek city-states fell under Spartan hegemony. Although the Spartans did not attempt to rule all of Greece directly, they prevented alliances of other Greek cities, and forced the city-states to accept governments deemed suitable by Sparta.[75] Yet, the Spartan hegemony was unstable and short lived.[76] The Persians then sensed an opportunity to sow disunity in Greece and sponsored a rebellion of Athens, Thebes, Corinth and Argos against Sparta. This led to the Corinthian War (395–387 BCE).[77] This war ended in 387 BCE when the Persians switched to supporting the Spartans. In return for helping the Spartans, the Persians demanded control over the Greek cities of Ionia again, while the Spartans would not interfere with Persian business in Asia Minor (Xenophon, *Hellenica*, 4–5).[78] Spartan hegemony lasted for another sixteen years until the Spartans were defeated by the Thebans and their allies at the Battle of Leuctra in 371 BCE.[79]

The Spartan army was different from other Greek armies. From its earliest days (*c.* 750 BCE) the Spartan army had been well-structured and divided into a number of units.[80] During the Peloponnesian War, the structure of the Spartan army evolved even further to address the resultant shortages in manpower due to previous battles and sieges, and to create a more flexible system which allowed the Spartans to send smaller detachments on campaigns or garrisons outside their homeland.[81] From a short analysis of the structure of the Spartan army in the late fifth century BCE, we see how complex this organisation was. According to Xenophon, the basic Spartan army unit throughout the fifth century BCE remained the so-called *enōmotia*, made up of thirty-six men in three files (rows) of twelve, under a commander called an *enōmotarches*. Two *enōmotiai* formed a *pentēkostys* of seventy-two men under a *pentēkontēr*, and two *pentēkostyai* were grouped into a *lochos* of 144 men under one *lochagos*. Four *lochoi* together formed a *mora* of 576 men under a *polemarchos* – the largest unit known in the Spartan army (*Constitution of the Lacedaemonians*, 11).[82] Six *morai* composed the Spartan army on campaign, to which were added contingents of allies. These allies were not only allied states. Spartan society was divided into three classes: the Spartiates (full citizens); the *perioikoi* (literally the 'dwellers nearby'), who were a group of people that lived in several dozen cities within Spartan territories which were dependent on Sparta; and, finally, the helots.[83] All groups played a role in military service, at least from the Classical period onward. The Spartiates were at the core of the Spartan army. They participated in the citizen assembly (known as the *apella* or *ekklesia*) and provided the hoplites in the army (Pausanias, *Description of Greece*, 3.12.10; Plutarch, *Lycurgus*, 4–6; Thucydides, *History of the Peloponnesian War*, 5.77.1; Xenophon, *Hellenica*, 3.3.8).[84] From the class of Spartiates also came the leaders of the army, including the two men at the top: the Spartan kings. The army was led by the two kings of Sparta, who would typically lead the full army in every battle.[85] A select group of 300 men served as royal guards. They were the so-called *hippeis* (cavalrymen) who accompanied the officials.[86] These units were accompanied by allies and other cavalry detachments, that acted as advance guards and scouting parties, and by provisionary troops.[87] During the fifth century BCE Sparta suffered from severe casualties in the various wars in which they were involved, and as a result the number of Spartiates gradually dwindled, which also meant a decline in available military manpower. This is where the other two classes of Spartan inhabitants came in: the *perioikoi* and the helots. Many of the *perioikoi* were originally merchants, craftsmen and sailors, but from the fifth century BCE, they also served as light infantry and auxiliaries on campaigns.[88] In the same period, helots were introduced to accompany Spartan hoplite warriors on the march to carry their heavy gear and armour.[89] Sometimes the Spartans also used helots to fight. They could either be used as light armed troops in skirmishes, or even as hoplites.[90] During the Peloponnesian War – a time in which the Spartans did not always have enough manpower – battle engagements became more fluid. Light troops became increasingly used, and tactics evolved to meet these changes in all Greek armies, not just the Spartan army. As already mentioned, for the Spartans one of these tactics may have been the use of the *scytale* to allow communication amongst commanders secretly (chapter two). Finally, next to the army, based on the land, the Spartan navy became important during the Peloponnesian War. As we have already seen, the Spartans were a land-based force throughout their history. Yet, during the Graeco-Persian Wars (499–449 BCE), they contributed a small navy of twenty *triremes*, and Sparta provided the overall fleet commander.[91] During the Peloponnesian War, eventually the Spartan navy developed further. In fact, it was the creation of a navy that enabled Sparta to overcome Athens.[92] However, the Spartan engagement with the sea would be short-lived, and did not survive the turmoils of the Corinthian War. In the Battle of Cnidus of 394 BCE, the Spartan navy was decisively defeated by a joint Athenian-Persian fleet, marking the end of Sparta's brief naval supremacy.[93]

By discussing a series of major events in Greek warfare from the eighth to the fourth century BCE, and by analysing the Spartan army, we have seen how the structure of Greek armies has developed over time. Because of the enlargements of the scope and scale of armies, and therefore, wars, there was a growing need for clear communication systems. It is in the period from the outbreak of the Peloponnesian War in 431 BCE to the end of Spartan hegemony at the Battle of Leuctra in 371 BCE, that communication networks expanded further. This was because armies were becoming more and more diverse, and this period we see one city state taking over hegemony from the other. This is also the era in which commanders were away from home and would, therefore, have needed devices to enable secure confidential long-distance communications during operations in the field. According to Plutarch and Aulus Gellius – writing in the second century CE – the Spartans used the so-called *scytale* for this purpose: a stick around which a strip of papyrus or parchment was wrapped on which a commander could write a classified message that was then sent back to Sparta (Plutarch, *Life of Lysander*, 19.5–7; Aulus Gellius, *Attic Nights*, 17.9.6–16).[94] Plutarch adds to this how Spartan commanders like Pausanias, Lysander, Alicibiades, Clearchus and Agesilaus used this device (*Life of Alcibiades*, 38; *Life of Agesilaus*, 10.5; 15.4–6; *Life of Artaxerxes*, 6.2–5; *Life of Lysander*, 16–17.1, 19–20). This will be discussed in chapter three where we will also see that there is in fact no evidence from the fifth and fourth century BCE that *scytalae* were used by the Spartans for the purpose of secret communication. In other words, there is no evidence to back up Plutarch's and Gellius' accounts. However, it will be shown that the *scytale* as discussed by these two later authors is still the earliest known theoretical transposition cipher in history, that formed the basis for later communication security systems (chapter six), something that scholars seem to have overlooked previously. Yet, first we will discuss the earliest examples of secret communication known from Greek warfare: a story from Homer's *Iliad* (6.168–178) and four stories from Herodotus' *Histories* (1.123, 5.35, 7.239, 8.128) in the following chapter (chapter two). We will see that Homer's story is the earliest reference to trickery and deceit in Greek warfare – even before the trick with the Trojan horse – and that it links the Greeks to trickery and deceit in warfare more in general. As we will see, Herodotus' work in turn gives us the earliest known examples of secret hidden communication sent during wars. Thus, Herodotus also links the Spartans to secret communication. This idea of 'secretive Spartans' is something that we see downplayed in post-Herodotean Athenian sources from the time of the Peloponnesian War. According to Plutarch and Aulus Gellius, it is in this period that we also see the Spartan *scytale* used for secret messaging (chapter three).

2

Sparta and Secrecy in Non-Spartan Sources

As we have seen in chapter one, warfare in ancient Greece developed over time from the early Archaic period to the end of the Classical period. Since alliances changed regularly, clear communication was necessary, both regular and secret. In fact, the Greeks deceived and surprised their enemies in several ways: by tricks, ambushes and surprise attacks, by spying, but also by actions that misled the enemy.[1] This concealing of information is known as cryptography and steganography, and it was among the common practices of armies, especially in times of war.[2] The earliest examples of secret communication in warfare come from the ancient Near East. According to Herodotus, the use of this type of communication was common there, but stood in contrast to what he describes as open clear communication in Greece (1.123–124; 5.35; 8.128–129). Later, in Herodotus' *Histories*, we also see that the author links the Spartans to such covert messaging, as some of the first Greeks to adopt this practice from Near Eastern states (7.239). Herodotus does not necessarily describe the Spartans' sending of secret messages as a negative practice. Yet, interestingly, during and after the Peloponnesian War, this link between Sparta and secrecy becomes negative. This is the time when the Athenians started depicting the Spartans as a strange, barbaric people with 'non-Greek' practises, in a period when anti-Spartan sentiments were high in Athens. Hereby, one type of secret messaging becomes linked to the Spartans: the so-called *scytale* that will be discussed in chapter three. Before moving to the *scytale*, in this chapter we will first discuss the oldest examples of cryptography and steganography known from ancient Greek sources, and analyse how these sources have influenced later Athenian sources from the fifth and fourth century BCE. The chapter is divided into three parts. First, there will be an analysis of the story of Bellerophon from Homer's *Iliad* (book 6, *passim*). Modern historians of cryptography tend to see this story as the oldest example of cryptography in Greek history. However, as I will show, the story is nothing more than a message sent in private between two individuals. Yet, it will also be shown that the story fits into the larger theme of communication security during warfare, since, with the story, Homer anticipates later Greek examples of trickery and deceit. Secondly, the actual earliest examples of steganography will be discussed: four secret letters that can be found in Herodotus' *Histories* (1.123–124, 5.35, 7.239, 8.128–129). Historians of cryptography tend to present Herodotus' stories as clear historical facts, attributing the direct influence of the secret messages that Herodotus discusses to the success of subsequent historical events. The case, however, is more complex, as we will see in this chapter. Finally, it will be shown that one story (Herodotus' story about the Spartan Demaratus sending a secret message to Sparta to warn his fellow Greeks about Xerxes' invasion of Greece) influenced ideas about the Spartans being 'secretive' in post-Herodotean Athenian sources.

The earliest examples: Homer's story of Bellerophon

Extant evidence for the ancient application of cryptography first appears in the second millennium BCE in Egypt and Mesopotamia.[3] In this context, ancient historians suggest that the replacing of standard writing signs for non-standard signs was most likely intended not to hide confidential information, but to impart some magical prestige and authority to a scribe's writing.[4] In fact, there are no examples of cryptography and steganography known from Egypt and Mesopotamia that appear to have had the primary purpose of sending confidential information for strategic purposes.[5] Our earliest evidence shows that instead of the Mesopotamians or Egyptians, it was the Greeks and Romans who first started to use encrypted communications for securing confidential information.[6] Some historians of cryptography believe that the first extant example of secret communication designed for strategic rather than magical effect from Greek and Roman sources, can be found in Homer's *Iliad* (6.166–170, 178).[7] Here, in an embedded story narrated by the grandson of the mythical hero Bellerophon, we read about how a secret message was once used to arrange a murder. In this first and sole reference to letter writing in the *Iliad*, we hear how Bellerophon, being a guest-friend at the court of King Proetus of Tiryns, is accused by the king's wife of attempting to rape her. Proetus, not wanting to kill a guest protected by the strict rules of *xenia* (hospitality or guest friendship) could not punish Bellerophon himself. Therefore, he instead invented a pretext and sent Bellerophon to his father-in-law Iobates, king of Lycia, sending with him a tablet with 'baneful' or 'evil signs' (σήματα λυγρα; *semata lygra*; 6.168; see also σῆμα κακόν; *sema kakon*; 6.178) requesting Iobates to kill Bellerophon.

Thus: '[Proetus] shunned killing him [Bellerophon], for his heart shrank from that; but he sent him to Lycia, and gave him fatal tokens, scratching in a folded tablet signs many and deadly, and ordered him to show these to his father-in-law [Iobates], so that he might perish' (6.166–170). And a little further on Homer continues: '[Iobates] had received from him [Bellerophon] the evil token from his son-in-law [Proetus]' (6.178).

Murray and Wyatt translate σήματα λυγρά (*semata lygra*) as 'deadly signs', probably referring to the fact that Bellerophon was carrying his own death sentence, and σῆμα κακὸν (*sema kakon*) as 'an evil token' in line 6.178.[8] Already in Antiquity there was discussion about what Homer precisely meant by his references to 'baneful signs' and 'an evil token' in this context. The earliest preserved comments on the passage are those of the third-century BCE grammarian Zenodotus of Ephesus and of the late third/early second-century BCE grammarian Aristarchus of Samothrace. According to Aristarchus, the words 'baneful signs' (σήματα λυγρά; *semata lygra*) did not mean alphabetic 'letters' as previous scholia critics, including Zenodotus, had assumed (Aristarchus, *Scholia to the Iliad*, lines 6.168–169a). Aristarchus proposed instead that King Proetus drew or inscribed pictorial images on a tablet which his father-in-law Iobates would understand and act upon, but which Bellerophon (a stranger and non-family member) would not be able to comprehend (6.166–170). Again, in his commentary on line 6.178 Aristarchus similarly insists that Homer must have meant signs instead of letters.[9]

In other words, Aristarchus believed that Proetus must have engraved signs, images or symbols on the tablet instead of writing alphabetic letters. As Schmidt points out, Aristarchus may well have been inspired to suggest the idea of signs being used in this context (instead of alphabetic letters) after seeing ancient Egyptian hieroglyphics.[10] Yet, although Aristarchus may well have believed that the mythical Greek Proetus wrote in a sort of proto-Greek, quasi-Egyptian, pictogram-based script, resembling ancient hieroglyphics, it remains unclear whether Aristarchus understood Proetus to have used these pictogram 'signs' as a way of encoding his message to Iobates, or whether this was assumed to be the usual means of written communication between members of this (mythical) ancient Greek family.[11] It remains unclear for many modern scholars what exactly was supposed to have been written on Bellerophon's tablet, and whether or not some kind of code was employed in this communication. Powell, for example, speaks of 'inscribed signs' that were very simple marks known to be made on folded tablets from Mesopotamia and Anatolia, and he argues that Homer's words σήματα λυγρά (*semata lygra*) could certainly not have referred to any known script.¹² Bellamy instead presumes that the signs were straightforwardly alphabetic signs instructing Iobates to act,¹³ while Bowra sees the text on Bellerophon's tablet as: '... something mysterious and rare, an echo from a far Mycenaean past, not fully understood [and] a dark element in a remote legend.'¹⁴

Chadwick sees the text on the tablet as 'exotic', 'magical' and a 'reference to a dim past', and Van Oldenburg Ermke speaks of 'deadly and ominous signs'.¹⁵ Yet, the example is not as clear-cut as some historians of cryptography assume. There is nothing in Homer's text to exclude the possibility that the tablet in question contained a written message using conventional symbols or letters. In fact, various scholars since the nineteenth century suggested that the words ἐν πίνακι πτυκτῷ (*en pinaki ptykto*; 6.169) in Homer's text should be translated as 'sealed tablet', since seals and sealed tablets were common in correspondence in the Near East since the fourth millennium BCE.¹⁶ The words being translated as 'folded' or 'folding tablet' indicates a diptych like the one found in the Bronze Age shipwreck at Uluburun and like the ones still in use in Roman times.¹⁷ This idea of a folded tablet further supports the argument that the message was not written in any form of code.¹⁸ The fact that the letter was folded would have granted Proetus the necessary protection and security he needed to ensure that his letter to Iobates remained unread by its intermediary Bellerophon. Thus, the references to 'baneful' or 'evil signs' in Homer (σήματα λυγρά; *semata lygra* (6.168); and σῆμα κακὸν; *sema kakon* (6.178)) could simply refer to the fact that Bellerophon was carrying his own death warrant within the message he unwittingly carried between Proetus and Iobates.

Indeed, we can already see this idea being suggested in Antiquity: Apollodorus, for example, writing in the first or second century CE, claimed that Proetus sent Bellerophon to Iobates with a simple letter providing clear written instructions that he was to kill Bellerophon (*Library*, 2.31). However, the example of Bellerophon's letter as a potential candidate for the first literary reference to a (fictional) coded letter is complicated further when we consider that the story of this secret communication is in a period of ancient history in which Greek literacy is only just emerging. Alphabetic literacy had arrived in Greece in the eighth century BCE, around the time that Homer composed his work.¹⁹ In fact, Bellerophon's tablet is the only indication in the *Iliad* in which Homer shows any explicit knowledge of the art of writing.²⁰ This leads Bellamy to conclude that the σήματα (*semata*) inscribed on Bellerophon's letter offer evidence of Greek alphabetic writing systems already being in use in the eighth century BCE in Archaic Greece.²¹ Although this may be this case, in general in ancient Greece, the habit of writing, and the specific practice of letter-writing as a mode of communication, appears to have remained restricted down to the end of the fifth century BCE, since the majority of written sources can be dated to this period, a point that will be discussed further later in this chapter.[22] Therefore, it is debateable whether the custom of communicating via written missive or letter (encrypted or otherwise) was a concept with which Homer and his archaic Greek audience would have been familiar. This seems unlikely, since in the story of Bellerophon we find the only reference to writing in Homer's entire work. Ceccarelli is slightly more cautious than Bellamy, therefore, when suggesting that Homer referred to some kind of alphabetic writing given the unequivocal reference to these two kings communicating through the medium of a folded tablet, but also that we can extrapolate little more from this story.[23] Indeed, Steiner and Rosenmeyer focus judiciously upon the importance of the tablet as a token of guest friendship instead of the murderous message that was sent between Proetus and Iobates, and differentiate between the singular and plural forms of the word σῆμα (sema) in this context.[24] According to these two scholars, the tablet (or letter) itself was a σῆμα (sema) or 'token' (singular) of guest friendship, something known from both literary (Euripides, *Medea*, 613; Pollux, *Onomasticon* 9.71)[25] and archaeological records.[26]

The symbols inscribed on the tablet or letter were therefore the σήματα (semata) or 'linguistic signs' conveying Proetus' message to his father-in-law Iobates.[27] This is something we can potentially also see in Murray and Wyatt's translation of the words σῆμα κακὸν (sema kakon) as 'evil token' in their rendering of line 6.178 of the *Iliad*: 'evil' since the tablet contained an instruction to murder Bellerophon, and a 'token' since the tablet or letter was a token sent from Proetus to Iobates.[28] Since we do not and cannot know anything concrete in this case about the character of the text or symbols on the tablet, it cannot be said with any confidence that the case of Bellerophon's letter as described in Homer's *Iliad* is an example of ancient code-writing or cryptography. What we see here is nothing more than an example of a private message sent from Proetus to Iobates in a sealed tablet or letter. Yet, when we take a look at the further context of the Bellerophon story, we see how it fits into the main theme of this work – trickery and secret communication in warfare – in a number of ways. First, we can link Proetus and Iobates to the internationalisation of Greek warfare. According to other stories, Proetus, pursued by his brother Acrisius, once fled to Lycia. There he found shelter at the court of King Iobates, and he soon married his daughter Anteia. With the help of the Lycians, he managed to return to Greece, and occupied Tiryns (Apollodorus, *Library*, 2.2.1, 2.4.1; Pausanias, *Descriptions of Greece*, 2.16.2, 2.16.4, 2.25.7). Here we see an example of both the internationalisation of warfare (a Greek in Lycia with foreign soldiers), and the changing of alliances over time (brothers fighting each other). When we return to the story of Bellerophon and bear in mind that Proetus spent time at the court of Iobates in Lycia, we can say that the text on Bellerophon's tablet was most likely written in a non-Greek language because of the Near Eastern context of the passage and the background of Proetus and Iobates, serving ostensibly as a token of guest friendship but also communicating a more sinister ('baneful' or 'evil') message: Bellerophon's death sentence.

Secondly, we can link the story of Bellerophon to the bigger picture of trickery and deceit in Greek warfare in general, and in the *Iliad* more specifically. Both Proetus and Iobates were bound to the rules of guest friendship. Proetus – in trying to rid of Bellerophon – sent him away with a covered death sentence. After receiving the message, Iobates, who was also bound to the rules of guest friendship, sent Bellerophon on a number of quests to kill monsters like the Chimaera, and wage war against tribes including the Solymi (who inhabited Anatolia), the Amazons and Carian pirates (Apollodorus, *Library*, 2.3.2; Hesiod, *Theogony*, 319ff.; Homer, *Iliad*, 6 *passim*; Hyginus, *Fables*, 157; Pausanias, *Description of Greece*, 2.4.1). As the message on the tablet was a covert death sentence, so were the quests a kind of covert suicide missions. In both cases Bellerophon did not know the actual reason why he was sent away to perform these tasks. In other words, the Greek Bellerophon was being tricked by the Greek/Near-Eastern Proetus and Iobates.

Thirdly, there is the place of the Bellerophon story within the *Iliad* that should be considered. It anticipates the stories of further trickery among the Greeks. Bellerophon's story is told by his grandson, the Trojan hero Glaucus (Homer, *Iliad*, 6 *passim*). Glaucus then meets the Greek hero Diomedes on the battlefield near Troy. Diomedes asks him about his origins, and Glaucus then replies with the story of Bellerophon and his exploits (*Iliad*, 6.85–261). Later, in book ten we read how the same Diomedes, together with Odysseus, set out at night to spy on the Trojans' camp (*Iliad*, 10.204–459). And, of course, it was the Greeks who conquered Troy by means of the Trojan horse (*Odyssey*, 8.512). With this trick of the Trojan horse, it is in a way as if the Greeks were now tricking the Near-Eastern people (the Trojans) in return. Finally, since letter writing was still uncommon in Homer's day, and very few people could read and write, this written message was already a type of secret communication. This is a very practical point that we also see throughout Herodotus' early fifth-century work the *Histories*, and especially in four secret messages that the author discusses (1.123–124, 5.35, 7.239, 8.128–129).

Secret communication in Herodotus' *Histories*

When we take a look at Herodotus' *Histories* – written in the early fifth century BCE – we immediately see that written forms of communication were still rather uncommon in Greece in Herodotus' day, as they were in Homer's time (eighth/seventh century BCE). In the whole of Herodotus' work, we can find only eleven instances of written communication.²⁹ These can be divided into eight references to letters (1.123, 1.125, 3.40, 3.42, 3.128, 5.35, 6.4, 7.239), and three references to other written messages (1.187, 5.35, 8.22).³⁰ Of these eleven instances, we find six references to letters written and sent in a Near Eastern context (1.123, 1.125, 1.187, 3.128 (twice), 6.4),³¹ four references to letters written and sent in a partially Greek context (3.40, 3.42, 7.239, 8.128),³² and only one message sent between Greeks (8.22). We must keep in mind that Herodotus still lived in a mainly oral-based society in which his, and other, stories were handed down verbally from one generation to the next.³³ Just as Homer drew extensively on a tradition of oral poetry, sung by minstrels, so Herodotus appears to have drawn on a tradition of story-telling and oral histories he chanced upon in his travels.³⁴ These oral histories often contained folk-tale motifs and demonstrated a moral, yet they also contained substantial facts relating to geography, anthropology and history.³⁵ By the end of the fifth century/beginning of the fourth century BCE, literacy was most likely more widespread in the Greek world than before this date, and exchanges of letters took place regularly, it seems, judging by the large number of inscriptions that have survived from this period.³⁶ Yet, until the first reading culture appears in Athens in the fourth century BCE (and perhaps even later), in ancient Greece, letters and long-distance communication were often related to the Near East and their tyrannical regimes, and believed to be fraught with dangers (Apollodorus, *Epitome*, 3.7, 5.19; Hellanicus (*FGrHist* 4 frag. 178a); Pausanias, *Descriptions of Greece*, 10.31.2; Plato, *Apology*, 41b; Herodotus, *Histories*, e.g. 1.99–100).³⁷ Herodotus' *Histories* follows this pattern by referring to only eleven written messages, only one of which concerned direct intra-Greek communication in a Greek context (8.128–129). Herodotus seems to have been aware of both the advantages and disadvantages of writing over oral communication, because, as O'Toole states: 'writing fixed a message in time and space, a written document that seemed objective and straightforward could also be full of paradoxes.'³⁸

In the generation after Herodotus, we see these disadvantages of writing appearing again in Plato's *Phaedrus* where Socrates complains that writing represented no true wisdom, but only its semblance and, even worse, once something had been put into writing it could fall into the wrong hands (Plato, *Phaedrus*, 275B-275E). Like Socrates, Herodotus knew that writing was full of ambiguities. Since a written document could not be cross-examined as a person could, it could have been used not to inform but to deceive.[39] We see this deliberate deception, for example, in the story of Themistocles cutting messages into rocks for the Ionians. Around the time of Xerxes' invasion of Greece (480 BCE), the Persians and the Athenians were vying for the help of the Ionians. As descendants of Greek settlers who had colonised Asia Minor, but were now living under Persian rule, the Ionians were in between the two camps and had to choose a side. At first, most Ionians sided with the Persians, but the Greeks sought their aid on the grounds of common ancestry. Themistocles used the ambiguity of writing to enlist the help of the Ionians. He sent men to the places where Ionian ships put in for resupply, and he had them cut written messages into the rocks there, urging the Ionians to abandon Xerxes and join the Greek side (Herodotus, *Histories*, 8.22, 8.55). As O'Toole argues, this was a clever plan: either the Ionians who read the messages would be persuaded to rebel against the Persians, or Xerxes himself would see the messages and distrust his allies, withholding them from the order of battle. Herewith, an important point was made: writing could send a deliberately confusing message as well as a direct one. In other words, a message was not always as straightforward as it appeared to be (Herodotus, *Histories*, 8.22, 8.55).[40] Sending deliberately confusing – or even secret – signs or messages could be useful when enemies were nearby, something that Herodotus knew, since in the *Histories* we can find at least sixty-nine instances of trickery and deceit.[41] In fact, most of these eleven instances of written communication in Herodotus' work are either deceptive or ambiguous. And four of these eleven messages are clear examples of purposefully hidden confidential messaging: that is, steganography (1.123, 5.35, 7.239, 8.128).[42] One obviously had to be careful when committing anything to writing, since if a letter or a document were intercepted, its secrecy would be lost. Moreover, in times of war, one could not be certain who to trust: even a friend or a trusted messenger could be working for the enemy (6.4).[43] In such cases sending hidden messages was useful, as the following examples show (1.123, 5.28, 7.239, 8.128). One crucial caveat must be made here before we discuss the examples. Herodotus tells the stories as if they have actually happened. However, as O'Toole argues, Herodotus was often unable to resist a good story just for the story itself.[44] Therefore, we cannot say with certainty how much – if any – of these and other stories actually took place. In fact, we might even speak of the mirage of Herodotus' *Histories*. Yet, the historicity of the examples is fairly irrelevant here, since I analyse the contents of the stories to show how these examples of secret messaging fit into Herodotus' greater narrative.

The first instance of steganography that Herodotus tells us about occurs in book one.[45] According to Herodotus, political intrigue and feuding among the Persians once prompted the Median general, Harpagus, to plot against his king, Astyages, seeking revenge for the murder of Harpagus' son by the king. Harpagus, therefore, plotted to assist the Persian prince Cyrus against Astyages in a *coup d'état*. Having garnered support from some Median nobles, Harpagus sent word to Cyrus through a message hidden in the body of a hare, since he desired to make his intent known to Cyrus while the plot obviously had to remain a secret, since all roads were guarded, as Herodotus tells us (1.123–124).[46] After receiving the gift, cutting the hare open and reading the message, Cyrus acted upon Harpagus' advice to rally the Persians against the Medes. Interestingly, the secretive and deceitful uses of writing in this case did not end there. Instead, Cyrus resorted to a second subterfuge to accomplish the revolt. In a ruse to enlist the help of the otherwise loyal army, he wrote out a document containing instructions to the soldiers. He read from this document aloud, pretending that it had come from King Astyages without letting anyone see it. This bogus royal document ordered the troops to assemble fully armed, and it appointed Cyrus as their leader, with instructions that the army had to obey him in everything. Thus, thanks to an apparently authoritative charter, Cyrus won the army to his side and seized the throne (1.125–127).[47] Herodotus finishes his story by stating that in this way King Astyages was deposed from his sovereignty after ruling cruelly for thirty-five years (1.130).

Lateiner suggests that Herodotus promoted cases such as the story of Harpagus and Cyrus – in which an otherwise defenceless individual attempted to outwit or out-manoeuvre a powerful tyrannical autocrat – because of personal experience. As a young man, Herodotus may have taken part in the political struggles against the Persian ruler Lygdamis, who ruled over Herodotus' birthplace Halicarnassus in the early fifth century BCE.[48] With this story in mind, Lateiner argues that Herodotus had a strong aversion to despotic regimes.[49] However, it is not as black and white as Lateiner argues. The *Histories* is certainly not a work of a personal grudge against the Persians; rather it has a much broader theme of recording the ancient traditions, politics, geography and clashes of various cultures that were known in Greece, Western Asia and Northern Africa at that time. Moreover, the story about Herodotus' early life comes from the *Suda*, a tenth-century Byzantine encyclopaedia of the ancient Mediterranean world, thus written about 1500 years after Herodotus lived. So, even though

Herodotus may have disliked of even fought against Lygdamis, he certainly did not always see Persia as 'the enemy.' There is even a passage in book one where Herodotus seems to be in favour of the Persians (1.131–140). When we return to our story of Harpagus and Cyrus, we see that Harpagus holds a personal grudge against Astyages for killing his son. After the king killed his son, Harpagus took several years to plan his revenge by sending gifts to Cyrus and meeting secretly with Median nobles before the actions took place (book one). Therefore, the story is not simply an example of Herodotus' aversion against despotic regimes, as Lateiner believes. It is better to say – as Hamel argues – that in this story we see a struggle for dominance between Cyrus and Astyages, with the help of Harpagus.[50]

The second example of steganography appears in book five, in a passage on Histiaeus of Miletus (5.35). Histiaeus was a Greek ruler of Miletus in the late sixth century BCE. He was chosen as tyrant of Miletus by Darius I, king of Persia, who had subjugated Miletus and the other Ionian states in Asia Minor, and who generally appointed Greeks as tyrants to rule the Greek cities of Ionia in his territory.[51] According to Herodotus, Histiaeus took part in Darius' expedition against the Scythians (c. 513 BCE). After the successful campaign, Darius considered Histiaeus to be a loyal servant. Therefore Histiaeus was offered a reward and, on request, he received part of the conquered territory. Although this request was granted, Histiaeus' ambitions alarmed Darius' advisors, and Histiaeus was, therefore, further 'rewarded' by being compelled to remain in Susa as Darius' 'Royal Table-Companion'.[52] However, Histiaeus was unhappy having to stay in Susa, since he was in a way imprisoned, and made plans to return to his position as king of Miletus by instigating a revolt: the Ionian Revolt.[53] During the time Histiaeus was residing in Susa, Histiaeus' nephew and son-in-law Aristagoras was left in control of Miletus (book five). In Histiaeus' view, Darius had to send him back to Miletus to deal with this revolt and, after his arrival there, Histiaeus would take control of the area again. In this way, Darius was betrayed (5.30–35). To send word to Aristagoras urging him to start the revolt, Histiaeus shaved the head of his most trusted slave and tattooed a secret message on it.[54] Histiaeus then waited for the slave's hair to grow back, and subsequently sent the man to Aristagoras in Miletus, instructing him to let Aristagoras shave his head again for the message to become visible (5.35.2–4).[55] As in the previous example, the message was delivered, and Aristagoras could start the revolt.

According to Ceccarelli, the story of Histiaeus' message fits in well with Herodotus' negative view towards autocratic rulers in the Near East, since the example shows how in that area slaves could be mutilated to send messages.[56]

However, tattooing slaves was common in the ancient Greek world too. Marking your slaves was a way to punish them and to show that they were your property.[57] To give a few examples, in Aristophanes' *The Wasps* (844–850; 1372–1375), and *Women at the Thesmophoria* (773–784), we read about slaves whose bodies were punctured, punctuated and tattooed. As DuBois argues, a slave girl's pubis was once covered with black pitch used to prepare writing tablets.[58] So, one could literally write on a body of a slave, the body hereby being seen as a worthless object.[59] Tattooing involves pricking the flesh with iron needles and then pouring ink into the wounds.[60] As Petronius says, this is so that the wounds prepared by the iron absorb letters – making tattooed messages permanent (*Satyricon*, 106). If text were written on a slave's back or on his head (as in Herodotus' story) the bearer could not even see it himself. In this way the slave was forever marked by his master, showing his master's power over him, even if a slave was later freed.[61]

However, we cannot be certain if any of these events concerning the slave and the secret message did in fact happen. Yet, the Ionian Revolt did take place, and it formed the start of the Graeco-Persian war. In this war, the Greek city states came together on a large scale to form an alliance against the Persian invaders for the first time in history. So, maybe we can say with caution that Herodotus' story of Histiaeus, Aristagoras and the slave, shows that, according to Herodotus, secret messages could have played a role in revolts against the Persian invaders. However, according to O'Toole, what we see in the story is only Herodotus' inability to resist a good story for the story itself.[62] And with this story, Herodotus makes a graphic point about the uses of secret writing, in a Greek world that was still getting used to the very idea of writing.[63] Histiaeus was communicating with his son-in-law Aristagoras, while both were in Asia Minor. So, here we see the first reference of Greeks using secret communication, yet still in a Near Eastern context. The story is also an example of trust and betrayal. Even though Histiaeus was appointed by Darius as ruler of Miletus, he was later 'imprisoned' at the Persian court and, therefore, tried to escape and seize power over Miletus again. So, as in the first example, the instigator of the rebellion again had personal reasons to take revenge.

The third secret letter can be found in book seven of the *Histories*. According to Herodotus, when the Spartan King Demaratus was in exile at Xerxes' court in Persia, he wanted to send word to the Spartans to inform them about Xerxes' invasion of Greece (480 BCE). Since Demaratus was afraid that the message would fall into the wrong hands, he wrote the message under the wax of a wax tablet. The seemingly blank tablet reached Sparta, and the Spartans were initially confused about what to do with an ostensibly blank tablet until Gorgo, the wife of King Leonidas, suggested that they should look for a hidden message and scrape off the wax. In this way the message was discovered and the Spartans were warned about Xerxes' invasion (7.239).[64] Herodotus does not tell us why it was Gorgo who discovered the message or how she discovered it, but according to Herodotus, because of Demaratus' letter, the Spartans were warned in time, informed the other Greeks, and together they defeated the Persians at the Battle of Salamis (7.239, 8).[65] This is significant since Demaratus had to rely on the ingenuity of the Spartans to discover the secret message. Interestingly, with Demaratus' letter to the Spartans, Herodotus literally introduces letters into the Greek world with a physical written message being sent from Persia to Sparta. Herodotus' story also obviously implies that the Spartans were able to read and write.[66] Archaeological and epigraphic evidence support this view of Spartan literacy.[67]

In fact, it is highly likely that there were once many more (now lost) Spartan written documents and inscriptions related to a variety of private and public events. Many Spartan documents would have been written on perishable materials such as wood, leather or papyrus that have not survived. Millender, therefore, argues on the basis of the available evidence that we should not assume that the Spartans wrote very little, but that we should instead consider the existence of a great number of 'now lost inscriptions' from Sparta.[68] In fact, it has been argued that literacy skills, however basic, were even necessary for a full Spartan citizen, because of the Lacedaemonians' frequent conduct of warfare and diplomacy.[69] The evidence discussed above therefore proves that the Spartans were certainly not illiterate, even if the true extent of literacy in Sparta as, indeed, in the ancient Greek world as a whole, is still much debated.[70] However, later in the fourth century BCE, the Spartans were depicted as 'illiterate', 'foolish' and secretive by other Greek – especially Athenian – sources, as we will discuss in the final part of this chapter. This view of the Spartans leads some modern historians to incorrectly describe Sparta as the most secretive of all Greek states.[71] Yet, it is important to reiterate that here we are dealing with Athenian sources on Sparta from the period during and after the Peloponnesian War, with the Athenian defeat, when anti-Spartan sentiment would have been high.[72] Therefore, this idea of 'secretive Spartans' is a stereotypical one. The Spartans were not so different from the other Greeks or more secretive than others. In fact, in the story of Histiaeus and Aristagoras, we see a Greek communicating with another Greek to start a rebellion, while in the story of Demaratus we see a Greek who wanted to warn his fellow Greeks about Xerxes' planned invasion of his homeland.

The final instance of a secret letter occurs in book eight of Herodotus' work. This story is set at the siege of Potidaea in 479 BCE,[73] after the battle of Salamis. Timoxenus, *strategos* of the Scionians, betrayed his city Scione (near Potidaea) by trading messages with the Persian commander Artabazus through letters hidden under the feathers of arrows that were shot into an agreed-upon place (8.128.1). The messages were wrapped around the shaft of the arrow that was subsequently covered in feathers to make the message invisible, just as the message on the slave's head was covered by his hair (5.35.2–4).[74] Timoxenus' treachery was discovered only when Artabazus missed his aim. Instead of his steganographic arrow falling in the spot agreed upon, Artabazus accidentally shot a Potidaean soldier. His fellow soldiers who came to aid the wounded man found the letter on the arrow and Timoxenus' betrayal became known (8.128–129.1). In this example we see a Greek (Timoxenus) betraying his fellow Greeks by aiding the Persian army in Greece. While in the story of Histiaeus and Aristagoras we saw two Greeks in a Near Eastern context communicating in secret, here we see a Greek and a Persian communicating with each other in a partially Greek context (Greek-Persian). Herodotus may have disapproved of Timoxenus' betrayal, but he discusses the passage in a neutral way. We cannot, therefore, say with certainty what he thought of the matter. Yet, he discusses how the leaders of the army responded to it. According to Herodotus, the people who came to aid the wounded man and found the letter, took the letter to one of their generals. The generals read the letter and perceived that Timoxenus was a traitor, but they decided not to condemn Timoxenus with a charge of treason, for fear that the people of Scione would thereafter all be called traitors (8.128).

In the previous three stories (Harpagus and Cyrus; Histiaeus and Aristagoras; Demaratus to the Spartans), a secret plot was not discovered. Yet, in this example Timoxenus' betrayal was discovered when a secret letter fell into the wrong hands. And here, we get to the point of the spreading of literacy in the ancient world once more. As Svenbro argues, the fact that the soldiers handed over the letter to their general, may simply have been a sign of respect for their leaders. However, it is more likely that they gave the letter to someone who could in fact read.[75] As generals, Timoxenus and Artabazus had a better education than the soldiers. They could read and write and, therefore, they could communicate with each other fairly secretly, since many people around them could not read and write. Although Herodotus does not discuss what he thought of Timoxenus' betrayal, maybe we can say that the story is used as a warning for those who communicate secretly: when communicating in secret, you have to be very cautious and you should be aware that there is always the risk of discovery.

As Fabule argues, one can see a pattern in the four steganographic messages found in Herodotus' work: 'the pattern reflects the following scenario: under the thumb of some potentate, a leader (foreign tyrant, a general, or client-king) sends a cunningly disguised secret message, that related information detrimental to his overlord.'[76] Fabule is correct in stating that the four instances of steganography in Herodotus' work are unique, since there is a pattern. However, the pattern in fact does not simply reflect the scenario that Fabule presents. The four secret messages are unique because the messages have three features in common that cannot be found in this combination elsewhere in Herodotus' *Histories* in connection with other messages or in other instances of trickery and deceit.[77] First, all four instances are examples of long-distance communication sent when roads were guarded. The steganographic methods used for sending the messages were purposefully chosen instead of cryptographic methods and designed to raise as little suspicion as possible among third parties. Secondly, there is no intra-Greek exchange of messages. Messages were either sent between a Greek and a non-Greek (Timoxenus and Artabazus), between non-Greeks (Harpagus and Cyrus), or in a non-Greek setting (Histiaeus and Aristagoras in Asia Minor; Demaratus as exile in Persia). Thirdly, all four instances do indeed deal with resistance against a despotic ruler.

Here two points must be made. First, the word 'tyrant' has a negative meaning in the modern world. Yet, it must be pointed out that *tyrannos* in Greek can simply be translated as an absolute ruler, someone who had unlimited powers to rule the state, often seen in the ancient Near East in Herodotus' days, as something opposed to the democratic state in Greece (especially Athens). Yet, in Herodotus' days the rule of a *tyrannos* in the Near East was seen as a bureaucratic autocracy and was marked by an institutional harshness and distance between ruler and ruled.[78] Secondly, in the four stories we see various reasons to dispose of despotic rulers, and the stories contain an element of gaining personal advantage. In two out of four instances we can see that individuals who hold a personal grudge against a ruler wanted to dispose him (Harpagus and Cyrus; Histiaeus and Aristagoras). While in the third example it is unclear what exactly the reasons for betrayal are (Timoxenus and Artabazus). Only in the fourth story, the story of Demaratus' letter to the Spartans, can we see that an entire nation (first Sparta, and then all of Greece) was urged to respond to the Persian invasion of Greece. Even in this story we may see an element of gaining personal advantage, since Demaratus may have informed the Greeks about Xerxes' invasion to gain the favour of the Spartans (and perhaps all the Greeks) again. When we take a look at Herodotus' narrative as a whole, we see this element of gaining personal advantage return regularly. In fact, the work is full of stories about characters who used various forms of trickery and deceit either to gain power as despotic leaders (negatively portrayed) or to deceive these leaders (1.47–49, 1.60, 1.63, 3.72, 3.85–88, 3.154–60, 8.24–25). We can also find various examples of political treachery (1.205.2, 4.78.2, 5.37.1, 3.65.6, 9.85) and of military deceit that Herodotus appears to have admired for its effectiveness or intellectual ingenuity (1.21, 1.91.1, 1.212.2, 2.100.2, 3.72, 4.146.3, 4.160.4, 4.201–202, 6.77–79, 8.27.3–4, 9.90.3).[79] Such acts of deception necessarily had to be hidden from what Greek sources (including Herodotus) call the 'King's Eyes and Ears', apparently a sort of ancient 'secret service', most likely in the form of a group of high ranking officials through whom (in the view of the Greeks) the Persian king received all sorts of information on agitation throughout his kingdom (Aeschylus, *The Persians*, 979; Herodotus, *Histories*, 1.114.2; Xenophon, *Cyropaedia*, 8.2.10–12, 8.6.17–18).[80] This type of official institution is known from a number of ancient (Near) Eastern Empires, including Assyria, Egypt, Persia, India and China.[81] That fact that the Greeks potentially saw the Persian 'King's Eyes and Ears' as some sort of secret police or intelligence agency becomes most clear from a passage in Xenophon's *Cyropaedia* where the author tells us that Cyrus had men spying for him (8.2.10–12). As becomes clear from the passage, according to Xenophon, Cyrus obviously had a number of men spying for him, since one man cannot keep an eye on everything on his own. Another interesting detail is that people could have become aware of someone around them who was a spy. And – as Xenophon mentions – then they would know that they must very careful when this person was around. In a way this implies that when a spy was exposed, someone else had to take his place. Therefore, Cyrus had numerous 'eyes' and 'ears' working for him. And in fact, anyone could act as a spy, since Cyrus listened to every person who claimed to have heard or seen anything worthy of attention. In other words, as Oppenheim argues:

> Secrecy, of course, is the prime requisite for these servants of the king so that unexpectedly and swiftly his arm can strike those who fail in what the king considers their duty, or those who act directly against his interests. The traumatic effect produced by the activities of such a 'secret service' provides the psychological basis for the concepts behind these expressions.[82]

Xenophon's explanation of the Persian secret service – with its large numbers of spies – at first sight seems plausible in view of the large size of the Persian Empire. However, the larger Cyrus' spying network was, the bigger the chance that it was exposed. Therefore, it is perhaps more plausible to follow Herodotus, who mentions that Cyrus appointed one person as the 'King's Eye' (the person in charge), and various other men as this person's assistants (*Histories*, 1.114.2). In fact, later in Xenophon's work, he also suggests a smaller number of spies (a handful of 'King's Eyes and Ears', the officials, who had some assistants: *Cyropaedia*, 8.6.16).

We cannot know what Herodotus thought of the 'King's Eyes' since he discussed it in a neutral way. Yet, the passage shows that Herodotus saw a connection between Near Eastern states and kings spying on their people. Indeed, this idea of spying and eavesdropping on one's subordinates in Near Eastern states can also be found in Herodotus' discussion of how Deioces the Mede had spies and eavesdroppers throughout his lands (*Histories*, 1.100.2).

Through its association with these closed societies and non-democratic Near Eastern states, later ancient sources attribute to Sparta a similar sort of secret service, known as the *krypteia* (Aeschylus, *The Persians*, 979; *The Suppliants*; Aristotle, *On the Universe*, 398a; Herodotus, *Histories*, 1.114.2, 8.8.1–2; Justin, *Epitome of the Philippic History of Pompeius Trogus*, 3.3; Plato, *Laws*, 1.633b-c, 6.763b).[83] Significantly, as Bowie and Briant point out, descriptions of the 'King's Eyes and Ears' can only be found in Greek sources, not in Persian sources.[84] The same is the case for our sources on the Spartan *krypteia* and the *scytale* (chapter three): all sources are non-Spartan and, accordingly, unreliable and liable to (anti-Spartan, pro-Athenian) bias. Therefore, as an organisation, the *krypteia*'s mandate and practices have been debated since Antiquity and must be considered with a large pinch of salt (Plato, *Laws*, 1.633c; Plutarch, *Life of Cleomenes*, 28, *Life of Lycurgus*, 28).[85]

Furthermore, the stories on the 'King's Eyes and Ears' and the four stories on secret messages, show us an important feature of Herodotus' work: his love of, and gift for, narrating history in the storyteller's manner. In this regard, he inserts not only amusing short stories but also dialogue and even speeches by the leading historical figures into his narrative, thus beginning a practice that would persist throughout the course of historiography into the Classical world.[86] In other words, Herodotus writes with the purpose of explaining; that is, he discusses the reason for, or the causes of, an event. So, what we see in the four stories on secret communication are some Greek and Persian individuals who played the right role in the narrative at the right time. For example, the events in which Cyrus took control of the Persian Empire, and of the Ionian Revolt, led to the point in the story in which Demaratus warned the Greeks at the right time about Xerxes' planned invasion.

As Gould argues, Herodotus' means of explanation does not necessarily posit a simple cause; rather, his explanations cover a host of potential causes and emotions.[87] Herodotus attributes these causes to both divine and human agents. And the causes are not perceived as mutually exclusive, but rather as mutually interconnected, something that is true of Greek thinking in general, at least from Homer onward.[88] Interestingly, this idea of causes attributed to both divine and human agents is something that we do not see in the four stories on secret communication. Here there is no godly intervention. Instead, clever individuals try to outmanoeuvre the rulers against whom they hold a personal grudge, at least in the stories of Harpagus and Cyrus, and Histiaeus and Aristagoras. The individuals in the stories alone are responsible for their actions. It is almost as if Herodotus tells us that the gods did not approve of plotting, while Greek mythology is full of examples of the gods plotting against each other. Yet, stating this goes too far. It is better to say that the four examples show us that clever individuals could achieve whatever they wanted with good planning, without godly intervention and with a bit of luck (Timoxenus' betrayal was discovered when an arrow accidentally missed the agreed upon spot). Therefore, it is incorrect to state that Herodotus believed that everything was related to fate and humans had no choice in what happened in their lives, as De Ste. Croix and Lang argue.[89] I agree with Gould, who instead, argues that:

> Herodotus' sense of what [cause and effect] is not the language of one who holds a theory of historical necessity, who sees the whole of human experience as constrained by inevitability and without room for human choice or human responsibility, diminished and belittled by forces too large for comprehension or resistance; it is rather the traditional language of a teller of tales whose tale is structured by his awareness of the shape it must have and who presents human experience on the model of the narrative patterns that are built into his stories; the narrative impulse itself, the impulse towards 'closure' and the sense of an ending, is retrojected to become 'explanation'.[90]

So, throughout Herodotus' work (including in the four stories on secret messaging) we see stories of individuals who take matters into their own hands, hereby using their own experiences.

Obviously, personal experience is different for everyone and, because of this, there can be a number of versions of a story. This is what we see in the work of Hecataeus of Miletus (Hecataeus of Miletus, FGH 1, F.1). Yet, even though Hecataeus is critical towards the use of history and myth, he too failed to completely separate the two, as Murray points out. His book actually seems to have been a collection of heroic myths and genealogies of heroes, designed to reduce them into a pseudo-historical account by rationalising them.[91] In fact,

Herodotus mentions Hecataeus in his *Histories*, on one occasion mocking him for his naive genealogy and on another occasion quoting Athenian complaints against his handling of their national history (2.143, 6.137). We have to be cautious when following Murray in this, since only very few fragments of Hecataeus' work have survived. Still, throughout ancient literature we see a very narrow dividing line between history and myth, including in Herodotus' *Histories*. When we take a look at his work, we see that Herodotus is neither a mere gatherer of data nor a simple teller of tales, instead he is both. While Herodotus is certainly concerned with giving accurate accounts of events, this does not preclude for him the insertion of powerful mythological elements into his narrative, elements which will aid him in expressing the truth of matters under his study.

Thus, to understand what Herodotus is doing in the *Histories*, we must not impose strict demarcations between the man as mythologist and the man as historian, or between the work as myth and the work as history. As Romm argues, Herodotus worked under a common ancient Greek cultural assumption that the way events are remembered and retold in myth and legend produces a valid kind of understanding, even when this retelling is not entirely factual.[92] For Herodotus, then, it would have taken both myth and history to produce truthful understanding. We cannot say with certainty how much – if any – of the stories on secret messaging are true, but to Herodotus this was irrelevant: the stories simply played an explanatory role in his narrative that was partly based on facts and partly on myth.

Contrary to Hecataeus, who wrote on the mythical Greek past as if it were history, Herodotus recorded events that had occurred in living memory, and included the oral traditions of Greek history within the larger framework of oriental history.[93] To do so, Herodotus used a number of oral and written sources that he used to fit into his work in the most suitable way.[94] For example, Athenian tragic poets provided him with a worldview of a balance between conflicting forces, upset by the hybris of kings, and they provided his narrative with a model of episodic structure.[95] Here again we see our four secret messages reappear. In the four stories, the hybris of kings and leaders led them to feel that they were invincible. Yet, the stories show us otherwise. Harpagus and Cyrus managed to overthrow Astyages; Histiaeus and Aristagoras managed to fool King Darius and start an uprising; Demaratus fooled Xerxes by sending word of the latter's upcoming invasion to Greece; and finally, Timoxenus and Artabazus perhaps became overconfident and did not pay attention when shooting their arrows. Artabazus hit a man, and thereby, their betrayal was discovered.

Homer was another inspirational source for Herodotus.⁹⁶ Like Homer, who drew extensively on a tradition of oral poetry, so Herodotus appears to have drawn on an Ionian tradition of story-telling, collecting and interpreting the oral histories he chanced upon in his travels. These oral histories often contained substantial facts relating to geography, anthropology and history, all compiled by Herodotus in a style and format that was used to show his audience the causes of the war between the Greeks and the Persians.⁹⁷ Yet, they also contained folk tale motifs and demonstrated a moral. One moral that we find throughout the work seems to be that individuals are responsible for their own actions, and that they can achieve whatever they want with persistence, practice and a bit of luck, but also caution. This is something that we clearly see in the four secret message stories. In every example a few individuals try to outmanoeuvre others who are higher in rank. And, with caution – without too much hybris, as we see in the story of Timoxenus and Artabazus – they can be victorious (Harpagus and Cyrus; Histiaeus and Aristagoras; Demaratus for the Spartans).

Spartan society according to non-Spartan sources

With Herodotus' story of Demaratus message to the Spartans about Xerxes' planned invasion of Greece, Herodotus links Sparta to messaging, secrets and Persia (Herodotus, *Histories*, 8.128–129). Yet, the author discusses the stories without judging either Demaratus or the Spartans in general. Still, in this way Herodotus' work introduces a contradiction that we see playing out in several post-Herodotean sources: that is, on the one hand, the Spartans are stereotyped as uncivilised, stupid and semi-literate, while on the other hand they are associated with cunning secrecy and deception, including the use of secret *written* communications, and the *krypteia*. Greek sources after Herodotus (mainly from the fifth and fourth centuries BCE) distance themselves from the use of such strange and secretive stratagems and devices.⁹⁸ These sources mainly come from Sparta's most famous opponent Athens in the period during and after the Peloponnesian War, when anti-Spartan sentiments must have been high. Aristophanes, for example, in his comedy *Birds* depicts the Spartans as barbarians in a passage in which he opposed this barbarism to Athenian civilisation. Before Athens became civilised, the poet states, Athenians would even have behaved like these barbaric Spartans, a thing they luckily, so it seems, did not do anymore in his days (1280–1285). More differences between Athens and Sparta can be found in book one of Thucydides' *History of the Peloponnesian War*. Contrary to

Athens, with its elaborately decorated temples and public edifices, Sparta, the Athenian historian argues, was built in an overly simplistic (read 'non-Athenian') way, while Lacedaemon (Sparta) was composed of rural villages as opposed to the cities found in Attica (1.10).

Thucydides argues that Athens' military power just before the Peloponnesian War alarmed the Spartans, who became afraid of losing their own empire to the Athenians and made the outbreak of the war inevitable (1.23, 1.79, 1.68–71, 1.75–78, 1.88). Plutarch adds to this that war seemed so important to all of Spartan society that even Spartan mothers urged their sons to come back from war either *with* their shields (that is, victorious), or *on* them (that is, dead), but never *without*, since the latter would mean a soldier had retreated or even deserted (*Moralia*, 241–242). With these warlike customs came the idea (among non-Spartans) of the Spartans being uneducated. According to Plato, the sophist Hippias of Elis complained about the Spartans not being able to count, let alone be able to understand and appreciate his lectures (in this case an astronomy lecture), in a discussion with Socrates (*Greater Hippias*, 285c). With these statements comes the underlying idea of the 'civilised citizens' in Athens as opposed to 'simple' and 'uneducated' folk in Sparta.

Together with these negative stereotypical views of the 'illiterate' Spartans comes a further connection that seems to have been made between Sparta and secrecy. Thucydides, for example, discusses the secrecy of the Spartan government (*History of the Peloponnesian War*, 5.68.2, 7.424). The number of Spartans was unknown to the other Greeks, and therefore, Thucydides reasons, the Spartans were secretive. They supposedly monitored their citizens and kept the state under close surveillance in other ways. Various other non-Spartan sources, for example, discussed the 'eyes and ears' of the Spartan kings, or *krypteia* (Plato, *Laws*, 1.633b-c, 6.763b; Plutarch, *Life of Cleomenes*, 28.4; *Life of Lycurgus*, 28.1–7).[99] However, there are no Spartan sources on the *krypteia*, as there are no Persian sources on the 'King's Eyes and Ears'. This stereotypical view of the Spartans leads some modern historians to describe Sparta as the most secretive of all Greek states.[100] Finally, from Plutarch and Aulus Gellius (based on Theopompus) we learn that the Spartans in the fifth and fourth centuries BCE probably used a method for secret communication known as the *scytale* (chapter three).[101] However, it is of the utmost importance to reiterate that all known sources on Sparta discussed here are non-Spartan or even anti-Spartan, and that the idea of 'secretive Spartans' is a stereotypical one. It raises an important caveat to be taken into consideration when analysing the extant evidence for the use of hidden, encrypted and coded communications in the ancient Greek world. That is, the ancient Greek, and especially Athenian, sources from the fifth and fourth centuries BCE tend to be biased in their discussions of the Spartan practice of using secret communication, as opposed to open communication in democratic Athens, in a period when anti-Spartan sentiment would have been high in Athens.

Yet, in fact our sources show us that the Spartans were not so different from other Greeks, no more secretive than others, nor untrustworthy. Herodotus argues that the Spartans are more like the Persians and the Egyptians than they are like the other Greeks, but primarily in their constitution (*Histories*, 6.58–60). Here it must be kept in mind that Sparta was one of the few *poleis* in Greece ruled by kings.[102] The section quoted here discusses kingship, and rituals related to the death of the king. There is not a reference to Sparta emulating the Persian spying regime, or that the *krypteia* was considered the same. Yet, the passage shows that Herodotus linked Sparta to the Near Eastern kingdoms, and we have seen that he wrote about Greeks writing and sending secret messages in a Near Eastern context. Moreover, in passage 1.152, Herodotus tells us that the Spartans refused to aid the Ionians (their fellow Greeks) in the Greek struggle against the Persian occupation (1.152), while in the next passage Cyrus (according to Herodotus) argued that one should never be afraid of a people (in this case the Spartans) who perjured themselves and deceived each other (1.153.1). This may show biases surrounding Persia as being particularly 'non-Greek,' and the Spartans as being untrustworthy and different from other Greeks. Moreover, like the Persians, the Spartans used non-Greek methods of secret communication (7.239). Yet, it is important to reiterate once more that all known sources on Sparta discussed here are non-Spartan or even anti-Spartan.

This raises an important caveat to be taken into consideration when analysing the extant evidence for the use of hidden, encrypted and coded communications in the ancient Greek world. That is, the ancient Greek and especially Athenian sources tend to be biased in their discussions of the 'non-Greek' practice of using cryptography and steganography, especially sources from the fifth and fourth centuries BCE (including Aristophanes and Thucydides): the period during and after the Peloponnesian War, and the Athenian defeat (when anti-Spartan sentiment would have been high). The Athenian influence upon the picture of supposed Spartan illiteracy matters because Athens prided itself on its own sophisticated literacy. The first book culture in the world – with various Athenian sources offering multiple references to book sellers and reading – developed in Athens in the second half of the fifth century BCE (Aristophanes, *Frogs*, 52f; Euripides, Fragment 369 in *Tragicorum Graecorum Fragmenta*; Plato, *Apology*,

26d-e).[103] Large numbers of inscriptions from this period and later sources suggest that written documents also seem to have been widely used in Athens, and potentially in other cities as well, from the fifth and fourth century BCE onwards in public, private, monumental, commemorative and administrative contexts.[104] Indeed, in contrast to Athens, with its seemingly common use of written documents for political, business, social, education and all kinds of other activities, the extant Athenian sources include Spartan *illiteracy* as part of the stereotypical idea of Sparta being different from other city-states (especially Attica), and Athenians certainly supposed that Spartan society possessed a very low level of literacy in comparison with their own. Hereby, according to (Athenian) tradition, the Spartans had no historical records, literature, or written laws, as this was expressly prohibited by an ordinance of the lawgiver Lycurgus, who supposedly lived and set up the Spartan Constitution (the Great Rhetra) in the ninth century BCE (Cicero, *On the Republic*, 2.10; Plutarch, *Comparison of Lycurgus and Numa*, 4; *Life of Agesilaus*, 31; *Life of Lycurgus*, 7, 13, 29; Thucydides, *History of the Peloponnesian War*, 1.18).

Perpetuating these stereotypical, mythical ideas about Sparta having unwritten laws and the Spartans being mostly illiterate, Isocrates, in his *Panathenaicus* (c. 340 BCE) claimed that the Spartans were even more backward than barbarians. He argued that, while some barbarians had been pupils of more civilised cultures (such as Athens), and even occasionally their teachers, the Spartans had fallen so far behind civilised Greek culture and learning that they would not even know how to instruct themselves 'in letters' (meaning, in this context, in reading and writing) anymore (*Panathenaicus*, 209). As Harris argues, the word that Isocrates (and other Greeks) used to describe the supposed illiteracy of the Spartans also seems to have meant 'ignorant', 'uneducated' or 'uncultured'.[105] Interestingly, we also see this in Xenophon's *Memorabilia* where the author seems to have meant a lack of culture when using the word (*agrammatos*) to describe the Spartans (4.2.20). Aristotle even uses the word when speaking about animals, whereby the word meant 'unable to utter articulate sounds', which again seems to refer to the idea of an *agrammatos* (either human or animal) being uncivilised (*The History of Animals*, 1.1.488a33).[106] And indeed, as Havelock points out, Greeks in the Classical period seem to have distinguished, with relatively broad strokes, between 'literate/educated' and 'illiterate/uneducated' people.[107] In fact, the Romans also seem to have adopted this view. In the Roman period the idea of 'not knowing letters' (*litteras nescire*) still seems to have referred more to a lack of culture than to actual illiteracy (Cicero, *On the Orator*, 2.6.25; Seneca the Elder, *Suesoriae*, 7.13; Seneca the Younger, *On Benefits*,

5.13.3).¹⁰⁸ The idea of the Spartans being both illiterate and uneducated, as an enduring Athenian stereotype, is further supported by an account of Plutarch, who stated that it was Lycurgus who had originally decreed that, in order to develop themselves physically, the Spartans had to give up on their mental or intellectual development (*Life of Lycurgus*, 16). Finally, as Boring argues, it is not until the beginning of the second century BCE that evidence for literacy in Sparta becomes more abundant and Athenian authors appear to accept that their Spartan neighbours might be more educated and cultured than previously understood or accepted.¹⁰⁹

This prevailing (Athenian) mythology concerning the relative lack of culture of the Spartans in the Classical period (although grounded in the tradition that decreed the Spartans did not have written laws and upon the Spartan focus on physical rather than intellectual development) resulted in a predominant trend for other Greeks (especially Athenians) to see the Spartans not only as barbaric and illiterate, but also (perhaps even consequently) as secretive and different. With this mythical idea in mind, Campbell states that the Spartans were famous, or better still notorious, for their (physical) military deeds, while Melville and Melville argue that during the siege of Plataea the Spartans only used clumsily built and incomplete blockades since the Spartans were unable to build anything better.¹¹⁰ Yet, as Rundle Clark points out, myth belongs to a way of thinking in which logical sense is irrelevant. Myths do not necessarily represent real life.¹¹¹ The same applies to stereotypes. The reality of Spartan literacy, therefore, is not necessarily represented by the prevailing myths and stereotypes. The Spartans in the fifth and fourth centuries BCE were obviously not completely illiterate, nor were they entirely ignorant or uneducated. Herodotus describes the Spartans' sending and receiving of messages (Demaratus' letter; Herodotus, *Histories*, 7.239), and Plutarch argues that, although the Spartans did not learn to read and write for leisure (as the Athenians did), the Spartans did learn some literacy basics for *practical* reasons (*Moralia: The Ancient Customs of the Spartans*, 4).

Indeed, as Thomas argues, the purpose of learning to read and write must be relevant to its users and to the contexts in which such literacy skills may be used, otherwise literacy cannot take root in a society, while Powell adds that writing in Antiquity was never a scientific device, as we see it now. Instead, it was a tool only designed for practical ends by practical people.¹¹² Obviously, the practical reasons to learn to read and write are always different for everyone depending on the context of their situation and background. For the Spartans, for example, being able to read and write their names, as well as being able to read and write other simple messages in a variety of practical contexts (such as those relating to inscriptions) would probably have been sufficient, as illustrated by the simple votive inscriptions found at the 'Menelaion' and other Spartan archaeological sites. Thus, although some non-Spartan sources seem to perpetuate the belief that the Spartans were illiterate, barbaric, uncivilised and uneducated, a range of other ancient sources signal a connection between Spartans and literacy in the context of messaging or keeping records. In these contexts, these sources typically and significantly highlight the use of some kind of *scytale* as will be discussed in chapter three. According to these sources, the *scytalae* could have been used in a variety of contexts and for a variety of purposes. These would have included giving a messenger formal authentication, as we find in Pindar's odes (6.90–92).

The 'illiterate' Spartans were, it seems, perfectly able to read and to write and to use their skills in literacy (however basic) to communicate effectively in a variety of *practical* contexts. Indeed, we see this apparent contradiction between (Athenian) stereotype and (Spartan) reality already reflected in Herodotus' treatment of the Spartans. According to Herodotus, writing around 440 BCE, Demaratus, as we have seen, sent a secret letter to the Spartans to warn them about the Persian invasion around 480 BCE (7.239), hereby making a salient connection between Spartans and their characteristic secrecy. However, all these accounts also (necessarily) assume a connection between the Spartans and letter writing, that is, an acknowledgement of their literacy. For a Spartan, then, having basic literacy skills would have been just as useful as knowing how to use a spear or sharpen a sword.[113]

3

The *Scytale*

In chapter two we have seen that Herodotus discussed how Greeks in a Near Eastern context first came in contact with the practice of sending and hiding secret confidential information (Herodotus, *Histories*, 5.28, 7.239, 8.128). Here, we have also seen the Spartans being linked to this practice for the first time (8.128). In the second century CE, about 700 years after Herodotus lived, we see Plutarch and Aulus Gellius linking the Spartans to one particular method of secret communication: the *scytale*. According to the authors, the *scytale* was a method used for sending confidential messages over long distances between the *ephors* in Sparta and generals in the field during wars (Plutarch, *Life of Lysander*, 19.5–7; Aulus Gellius, *Attic Nights*, 17.9.12–13). However, there is no straightforward evidence that the *scytale* was used for the purpose of secret messaging. In fact, there is more evidence from the fifth and fourth century BCE that *scytalae* (pl. of *scytale*) were used for other purposes.[1] In this chapter this evidence for the use of *scytalae* will be discussed. The chapter is divided into three parts. We start with a discussion on original Greek sources on the *scytale*. Herewith, it will be shown that *scytalae* – in various contexts – are regularly related to Sparta in ancient sources (Aristophanes, *Birds*, 1280–1285; *Lysistrata*, 985–992; Athenaeus of Naucratis, *The Learned Banqueters,* 10.451d; Diodorus Siculus, *Library of History*, 8.27; 13.106.8–9; Nicophon, *The Birth of Aphrodite* (*The Fragments of Attic Comedy* 1 (Fragment 2)); Pindar, *Olympian Odes*, 6.90–92; Photius, *Lexicon*, entry: σκυτάλη (I and II); Plutarch, *Life of Agesilaus*, 10, 15; *Life of Alcibiades*, 38; *Life of Artaxerxes*, 6; *Life of Lysander*, 19, 20; Polyaenus, *Stratagems of War*, 1.17; Theophrastus, *Nomoi*, fragment from *Biblioteca Apostolica Vaticana*; *Vat. Gr. 2306*; Thucydides, *History of the Peloponnesian War*, 1.131.1; Xenophon, *Hellenica*, 3.3.8, 5.2.33–37). Secondly, we will analyse the use of the *scytale* as a cryptographic device used by the Spartans as discussed by Plutarch and Aulus Gellius. We will see that the *scytale*-system may have been (partially) invented by Plutarch. However, the system is still the earliest known theoretical transposition cipher in history, that formed the basis for modern transposition ciphers used up to the present day.² However, modern historians of cryptography seem to overlook the importance of the system, and instead they see the *scytale* as a simple toy cipher that can never have been used for serious secret communications.³ We will see in the third part of this chapter that this undervaluation of the *scytale* as an important theoretical transposition cipher may have been the result of misinterpretations of Plutarch's and Aulus Gellius' original sources by later scholars (Plutarch, *Life of Lysander*, 19.5; Aulus Gellius, *Attic Nights*, 17.6).

The *scytale* in Greek sources

The first thing that strikes us when we undertake a comprehensive survey of the extant sources which discuss the *scytale* – used by all Greeks – is the wide variety of different devices and artefacts to which the label *scytale* seems to apply. The second significant discovery we make is the fact that, although most ancient Greek sources discuss the *scytale* in the context of messaging or communication of some kind, very few sources directly or unambiguously link the *scytale* to any type of *secret* communication.⁴ To get a better understanding of how *scytalae* were discussed in Greek sources, this section analyses sources on the *scytale* from the seventh century BCE to the ninth century CE.

In a passage from *The Learned Banqueters*, Athenaeus of Naucratis, who wrote in the late second/early third century CE, reports that Apollonius of Rhodes had referred to the *scytale* as a Spartan cryptograph in his *Treatise On Archilochus*, on the seventh-century BCE poet Archilochus of Paros (Athenaeus of Naucratis, *The Learned Banqueters*, 10.451d). Based on this passage some modern historians of cryptography (who do not believe that *scytalae* were used for secret messaging) see Archilochus as the first ancient writer to incorrectly refer to the *scytale* as a means of secret communication.⁵ Yet, this claim cannot be made with any certainty. Archilochus' original work has not survived, nor has Apollonius of Rhodes' *Treatise on Archilochus*, which is the reputed second-hand (third century BCE) source for this attribution to Archilochus. The reference to the *scytale* only appears third hand in a work by Athenaeus of Naucratis, written in the late second/early third century CE. Ceccarelli argues that Athenaeus here describes an obscure and enigmatic mode of writing related to the Spartans, as Apollonius and potentially Archilochus did as well.⁶ Yet, this interpretation cannot be derived from Athenaeus' passage, since nothing in the text indicates that *secret* messages were meant in this context. Instead, Athenaeus mentions that the poet

Achaeus of Eretria uses 'obscure language' and expressed himself 'in an enigmatic fashion' (Athenaeus of Naucratis, *The Learned Banqueters*, 10.451d).

As becomes clear from Athenaeus' text, when Achaeus wanted to refer to a white thong from which a silver oil-flask was hanging, he refers to it as an 'inscribed Spartiate' rather than as a 'Spartan message-staff'. And Apollonius of Rhodes, discusses the Spartans wrapping message-staffs in white thongs and wrote what they wanted on them, in his work *On Archilochus*. What exactly Achaeus of Eretria, Apollonius, or in fact Athenaeus, mean in this passage in unclear. In this passage, Apollonius may be referring to the *scytale* as a cryptographic device, but he probably only refers to a sort of normal messaging for which the sticks were used. However, it is plausible that Archilochus might well have discussed the *scytale* as a cryptograph in Apollonius' source or any other source because he appears to do the same in a fragment from Archilochus, that has survived in the work of Herennius Philo ('ἀχνυμένη σκυτάλη; achnymene scytale'). Here, Archilochus does appear to have had some cryptographic form of the *scytale* in mind (*On the Different Meanings of Words; Greek Iambic Poetry: From the Seventh to the Fifth Centuries BC*; Fragment 185). According to this source, he described the *scytale* as a sort of messenger-stick as a type of authentication, used to give the speaker the right to speak, an idea also suggested by Bowie.[7] Gerber translates the Greek words 'ἀχνυμένη σκυτάλη' (*achnymene scytale*) as 'a grieving message stick'.[8]

Quite what a 'grieving' stick of any variety might look like is hard to imagine here, but the word 'grieving' potentially refers to one of the *scytale's* functions, namely to identify fallen soldiers on the battlefield (Diodorus Siculus, *Library of History*, 8.27; *Excerpta Constantiniana* 4; Polyaenus, *Stratagems of War*, 1.17). Yet, another possibility is that the word ἀχνυμένη (*achnymene*) in this context should not be translated as 'grieving' or 'mourning' but as 'vexing' or 'annoying'.[9] This invites the interpretation that the messenger-stick in question is puzzling or perplexing in some way, perhaps because the message it contains is encrypted or encoded and therefore difficult to read for anyone without the means to decode its cipher. This is an intriguing possibility but is far from clear-cut as a description of the *scytale* as an ancient cryptographic device. In this context the *scytale* could have been a messenger stick, a baton bearing incisions and functioning as an *aide-mémoire* for the messenger, or the vehicle for a Spartan non-secret message.[10] What is more, many of Athenaeus' sources were fictitious and anecdotal, making it difficult to use him as a reliable source here, which, significantly, while first arguing that Athenaeus certainly described a useful obscure and enigmatic mode of writing related to the Spartans in this passage (see above).[11] Sheldon may be in error too when arguing that based on this passage from Athenaeus, we can say that Athenaeus made up the idea of the Spartan *scytale* as a cryptograph, and that, therefore, Apollonius of Rhodes made it up too.[12] It seems more plausible to say that if the idea of the Spartan *scytale* as a cryptographic device in this case was made up, it was made up by Athenaeus, not Apollonius. Moreover, on the basis of the evidence that is available to us, we may logically only say that Apollonius referred to the *scytale* in the context of messaging and communication before Athenaeus did so; and that Archilochus probably referred to the *scytale* in the same context earlier still, in a now lost passage. The assumption that these early references to the *scytale* unambiguously indicate its use in *secret* messaging and communication would seem to be unjustified.

According to Polyaenus (second century CE), the seventh-century BCE poet Tyrtaeus – being an Athenian by birth, but living and working in Sparta (Lycurgus, *Against Leocrates*, 1.106; Plato, *Laws*, 629a4; *Suda*, entry *Tyrtaeus*)[13] – referred to the practice of *scytalae* as being used for identifying fallen soldiers on the battlefield with *scytalae* fastened to their arms. This potentially makes the passage the only Spartan reference to a *scytale* (Polyaenus, *Stratagems of War*, 1.17). In this example, *scytalae* were not used for the purpose of securing confidential details but were instead used for identification purposes – the ancient equivalent of name badges or military tags. We can find the same story in Diodorus Siculus' *Library of History* (8.27.2). Identifying the dead on a battlefield was not easy without the men carrying some form of identification. In the carnage following a hoplite battle, such identification could at times be impossible.[14] Xenophon, for example, described the chaotic aftermath of a hoplite battle at Koroneia (394 BCE; Xenophon, *Agesilaus*, 2.14).

As Vaughn describes it, the image of tangled bodies and weapons on a field reeking of carnage is clear here. The corpses had to be separated and catalogued somehow, regardless of the condition of the actual remains. Therefore, Greek forces were accustomed to knowing who, and how many men, went to battle, to recover their dead and to administer funeral rites.[15] In Athens, for example, lists of men going to war were available in the so-called *katalogos*: the state register of all men in military service. The *katalogos* was posted in Athens by tribe, each list being affixed to the statue of the eponymous hero of that tribe (Aristotle, *Athenian Constitution*, 53.7, cf. 26.1; Aristophanes, *Peace*, 1181–1184, *The Knights*, 1369–1372).[16] As Vaughn argues, each *taxiarch* (officer) would have kept the service lists for his own tribe and made out the muster rolls for each campaign from that service list. Such lists were used to call roll at the beginning of an expedition and were in the possession of the *taxiarch* during the campaign. They would have been the primary source against which to check the names of the missing and dead (Aristophanes, *Peace*, 354; Andocides, *On the Mysteries*, 45; Lysias, *Against Alcibiades*, 15.5).[17] However, others argue that there is no evidence for such roll calls, and that close friends identified most of the bodies.[18] An extra problem in the retrieval and subsequent identification of the dead was that after a battle the victorious army had control of the battlefield and enjoyed a monopoly over the fate of the dead. The exchange of bodies was predicated on the benefaction of the winning party.[19] As Vaughn points out, the winning party would often start to collect their own dead, hereby viewing and plundering the bodies of the enemy. We already see this in Homer's *Iliad* where Nestor told the Argive forces to slay the enemy and then plunder the corpses (6.70–71). The defeated army would retreat and check the muster rolls again – if these were indeed used – or they would ask around if anyone was missing.[20] Then they would send a herald to ask permission to collect their fallen soldiers. By the time the defeated force was allowed to retrieve its men, virtually all possible identifying tokens, shields, helmets and cloaks would have been stripped by the winning party. In other words, the dead men were returned to their own side completely nude, and thus without specific identifying markings.[21] It could take several days before the defeated party was finally able to collect the dead. By the time they were ready for collection, the wounded and mutilated corpses would have been outside exposed to the physical elements and animals, making identification even harder (Menander, *Apsis*, 69–72; Plato, *Republic*, 10.614B; Plutarch, *Alexander*, 77.3; Thucydides, *History of the Peloponnesian War*, 4.101.1; Xenophon, *Anabasis*, 6.4.9).[22]

But, as we already have already seen, the Spartans seem to have had a solution for this identification problem: *scytalae* as name tags (Aelian, *Various History*, 6.6; Diodorus Siculus' *Library of History*, 8.27.2; Polyaenus, *Stratagems of War*, 1.17; Plutarch, *Lycurgus* 27.1–2; *Moralia*, 238d). Soldiers would wrap a *scytale* around their left wrists, so that their relatives and comrades would know who they were.[23] Boring suggests another possibility for how *scytalae* were used for identification. A *scytale* could have been cut in half or one could have taken two *scytalae* of the same size, with the soldier's name being written on both halves. One half could then be given to the soldier to be identified on the battlefield if necessary, while the other half was kept in Sparta and served as a sort of register of participants in any given battle or expedition. Those soldiers who failed to return home – and who could not be found on the battlefield – could later be identified with these sticks.[24] Whether these stories are true, we cannot know. Yet, the practicality of using simple markers like *scytalae* and the uniformity of hoplite battle throughout Greece, should suggest similar practices outside of Sparta. However, there seems to be no evidence for this.[25]

The Theban poet Pindar certainly refers to the *scytale* in a non-cryptographic messaging context in the fifth century BCE. It becomes clear from his sixth *Olympian Ode* that a *scytale* was used as a sort of messenger-stick, like heralds or bards would have, whereby the stick would give the bearer the chance and right to speak, as we have already seen in the passage on Archilochus (Pindar, *Olympian Odes*, 6.91–93). In Pindar's passage, the *scytale* is not used for sending secret messages; on the contrary, in the passage a singer holding the *scytale* or messenger stick is thereby given the opportunity to praise an Olympian victor.[26] Although Race translates the word σκυτάλη (*scytale*) as 'message stick', he then in a note refers to the Spartans' use of the *scytale* as a cryptographic device.[27] This dual reference (by Race) seems to suggest that Pindar's singer may have meant to communicate a secret message here, but this is not confirmed by the text. While Boring seems to believe that Pindar did indeed mean a secret *scytale* message here, he argues that although Pindar said nothing about the *scytale* being used for secret communication in this passage, it shows his awareness of the existence of the common use of *scytalae* for the purpose of secret communication.[28] However, it seems clear that the *scytale* in Pindar's ode has no cryptographic associations and is simply the referent for a symbolic stick or staff.

The comic poet Aristophanes, who was active in the late fifth to early fourth century BCE, provides our first Athenian source for the *scytale*. Aristophanes used the word twice in his plays. The word first appears in his *Birds*, where a herald tells the Athenian Peisetairos that once upon a time, before Athens became civilised, all Athenians would behave like the barbaric Spartans (Aristophanes, *Birds*, 1280–1285). So, according to the poet, the Athenians would wear their hair long, never bathe themselves, and brandish batons (*scytalae*) to threaten their enemies or simply to show their anger or excitement. Indeed, the first-century BCE grammarian Didymus points out in his ancient commentary on the *Birds*, that a *scytale* was simply a stick carried about by Spartan commanders, which may have been used to strike an enemy or person of lower rank (*Didymi Chalcenteri Grammatici Alexandrini*, Fragment 1283–1284).[29] It is likely, then, that Aristophanes wanted his audience to think that the Spartans were carrying big phallic sticks for no reason other than to look fashionably rugged and manly. Indeed, as Boring, Piccirilli and Sommerstein point out, Aristophanes probably refers here to a distinctive type of walking-stick with a twisted and knobbed end that is known from ancient Sparta, rather than referring to the Spartan cryptographic practice of sending *scytale* messages.[30] According to the scholarship on this topic, Spartans often used such walking-sticks, as did upper-class Athenians who aped Spartan ways, in comedy and in real life.[31] Thus, the passage is not a reference to *scytalae* being used for sending messages (secret or otherwise) per se. However, according to Sommerstein, the passage might show that the Athenians were familiar with *scytalae* in the context of their use for communicating 'official Spartan dispatches', whether these were secret dispatches or not.[32] Hornblower, who does believe that *scytalae* were used as cryptographic devices, points out that sticks in ancient Greece (*scytalae*), gave their bearer clear and visible power over other people, for example, to violate one's subordinates, but also to show symbolic power (as sceptres do for kings and queens).[33] The use of the *scytale* as a cryptographic device, he states, clearly illustrates that the Spartans had this feeling of the physical and symbolic power that the sticks would give their bearers, and that they knew how to use them.[34] Although Piccirilli did not discuss the *scytale* as a cryptographic device, he seems to agree with Hornblower on this point of physical and symbolic power, when arguing that the *scytale* was the weapon *par excellence* of an archaic fighter, and a symbol of strength, a point similarly made by Eliade.[35] Nevertheless, it is impossible to determine from this source whether or not the *scytale* in Aristophanes' *Birds* refers to a staff or baton, a walking stick, or a 'dispatch stick'. Yet it seems unlikely, in either case, that any secret messaging is associated with its function in this context. A second passage in which Aristophanes used the word *scytale* (twice) can be found in the *Lysistrata* – which, like *Birds*, is set in Athens (Aristophanes, *Lysistrata*, 985–992). In this passage the Athenian magistrate Cinesias asks a Spartan messenger what he has hidden under his cloak. The messenger assures him that he is not hiding a weapon but is instead carrying a 'Spartan walking stick' (*scytale*). Cinesias, whom the herald is addressing, then assures him that he understands the problem, since he sometimes has a 'Spartan walking stick' too (Aristophanes, *Lysistrata*, 985–991). The tone of the passage clearly suggests that the messenger is trying to hide a phallus, which he and Cinesias here euphemistically call a 'Spartan walking stick'. As in the *Birds*, Aristophanes here mocks the unsophisticated (barbaric) Spartans. And again, this is not a reference to secret communication. Boring, therefore, seems in error when arguing that this passage offers evidence of the *scytale* being used for the purpose of secret communication.[36] Yet, although the herald in this case may be trying to hide an erect phallus, the reference to the *scytale* in this context might also be a reference to a walking stick (as in the previous passage) or to an official messenger stick (used as a sort of authentication device) as suggested by Anderson and West.[37] And again, although it is impossible to determine from this source whether or not the *scytale* in Aristophanes' *Lysistrata* refers to a staff or baton, a walking stick, a 'dispatch stick', or a phallus, it seems unlikely that any secret messaging is associated with its function. Sheldon mentions a variation to the authentication system in which a commander on the battlefield took one half of the stick and a government at home kept the other half. When it was time to send a message, a messenger was given one half so that it would establish his identity when he arrived at the other point.[38] Although Sheldon does not believe that *scytalae* were used for sending secret messages, what she discusses here in fact resembles how *scytale* messages were sent: both parties had one stick (or in this case one half of a stick), and messages were sent by a messenger carrying the *scytale* (the scytale in this case meaning only the message without the stick as Plutarch tells us (see below)) back and forth. Another theoretical possibility is that both secret and non-secret messages were sent in this way with a *scytale*.

Although Jeffery does allow for the possibility that the Spartans used *scytalae* for the purposes of secret communication, there are some flaws in her argument. In her 1990 publication *The Local Scripts of Archaic Greece* she suggests that writing messages on leather rolls, and then winding them round a stick for transport had once been common practice in Archaic Greece, and that it is likely that in using the *scytale* for secret communication the Spartans were merely retaining this practice.[39] However, the practice that Jeffery describes seems to be the opposite of how the Spartans actually used *scytalae* for sending secret messages. In Jeffery's example, a message is first written on some writing material, like a strip of parchment, and only then wrapped around a *scytale* for easy transport.[40] However, in using the *scytale* for sending secret messages, the ancient evidence suggests that the Spartans first wrote their message on the writing material that was *already* wrapped around the *scytale*, and then *unwrapped* it before it was sent away (possibly wound around yet another *scytale* rod for transportation). To decode the encrypted message, the recipient rewrapped the material around a second (or third) *scytale* rod (which would have needed to be the same diameter as the original to make easy decryption possible).[41] Therefore, Jeffery might be correct in theorising that the Spartan *scytale* retains some element of an archaic Greek tradition involving the transportation of messages written on strips of leather and wrapped around a ceremonial staff of some kind, but there are crucial differences in the two practices. Indeed, it is noteworthy that Jeffery's theory aligns the Spartan *scytale* with an *archaic* (that is, an early, relatively primitive) practice for messaging in ancient Greek societies, perpetuating the Athenian stereotype of Sparta as a relatively primitive, backwards and uncivilised society. It thereby potentially obscures the idea that the Spartan *scytale* might represent a development and evolution upon this earlier Greek tradition for messaging, downplaying the possibility that the *scytale* might also have been used for other, more sophisticated, types of (secret) communication.

Although the earliest sources on the *scytale* are highly ambiguous, offering little concrete evidence on whether the *scytale* was used for secret communication, the Athenian historian Thucydides, in the second half of the fifth century BCE, ostensibly offers a slightly clearer picture. In chapter 1.131.1 of the *History of the Peloponnesian War*, Thucydides discusses how the Spartans summoned their general Pausanias home, because of misbehaviour, by sending him a *scytale* message (Thucydides, *History of the Peloponnesian War*, 1.131.1). Smith, in his translation of Thucydides' work, translates the word 'σκυτάλην' as 'scytale message', while Hammond translates it as 'dispatch-stick'.[42] Both scholars then align these references to the Spartan practice of using a *scytale* as a cryptograph, whereby Smith explicitly describes the *scytale* as a special staff used to send cryptographic messages.[43] Rhodes and Lattimore simply use the word '*scytale*' in their translations.[44] Rhodes adds that the *scytale* stick was not used as a cryptograph in this context, but for easy transport of a dispatch instead, while Lattimore aptly points out that it is unclear how the *scytale* as a message stick would have worked, or how a stick (as opposed to a bag, say) would have made transporting a written message easy.[45] Yet, in a commentary on Thucydides, Gomme, Andrewes et. al. argue that in the letters and situations that Thucydides describes, it must be assumed that secret communication (in this case *scytale* messages) was commonly used.[46] However, although it is clear that the Spartan *scytale* discussed in Thucydides' passage conveyed some kind of official dispatch and message, and although it is plausible that a coded letter – a *scytale* message – was sent (because of the politically and military sensitive content and intent of the letter), since the passage is not a complete and clear description of the use of the *scytale* as a cryptographic device, we cannot tell whether the *scytale* in this case was used for the purpose of secret communication.

The Athenian playwright Nicophon (late fifth to early fourth century BCE) referred to a *scytale* in his play *The Birth of Aphrodite*. Very few fragments from this comedy have survived, but one noticeably short fragment in which the word *scytale* appears, is collected in Edmonds' *The Fragments of Attic Comedy* 1 (Fragment 2). The fragment is only one sentence long and very few commentaries and translations are available in which this passage is discussed. Edmonds, in his 1957 translation in *The Fragments of Attic Comedy*, translates the sentence as: 'Let go the stick [*scytale*]-and-parchment and to hell with you!'.[47] The translation of the words 'σκυταλίου < > καὶ τῆς διφθέρας (*scytaliou* [...] *kai tes diphtheras*') as 'stick-and-parchment' suggests a reference to the Spartan practice of either wrapping letters or dispatches around a *scytale* for transport, as Jeffery suggests, or to the practice of using them to communicate secret messages.[48] However, Storey, in his 2011 translation of *Fragments of Old Comedy*, translates the sentence as: 'Why don't you take your hands off the ["my"?] staff and jacket and go to hell?'.[49] This implies that the person who was being cursed was holding the other person's cloak. However, the word ἱμάτιον (*himation*) was commonly used to describe a cloak or coat in ancient Greece instead of the word σκυτάλην' (*scytale*; Aristophanes, *Ecclesiazusae*, 333; Demosthenes, *In Timocratem*, 24.114; *De Falsa Legatione*, 19.314; *Inscriptiones Graecae*, 22.1524.205).[50] Also, according to Herodotus, paper or parchment was sometimes referred to as 'skin' as it was made from animal skin, an argument in favour of Edmonds' translation of a 'stick-and-parchment (Herodotus, *Histories*, 5.58). Since the passage is only one line long and completely out of context, it is extremely hard to reconstruct what Nicophon may have meant. Kelly presumes that nothing in the passage directly refers to *scytalae* being used as cryptographic devices and, therefore, asserts that Nicophon does not have secret communication in mind here.[51] However, absence of evidence is not evidence of absence, and nothing about the *scytale* in this source can be said with any certainty based on the evidence provided.

In a passage on judicial procedures in Sparta, potentially written by Theophrastus, a pupil of Aristotle, it becomes clear that *scytalae* were regularly used for yet another purpose: to keep records during commercial, financial and contractual processes (*Biblioteca Apostolica Vaticana*; Vat. Gr. 2306).[52] This does not preclude their use in these contexts as tools for secret (or private) communication, but clearly their form and function here is very different to the encoding required for a full cryptographic function. Keaney and Szedegy-Maszak – in their translations of Theophrastus' work (based on the works of Aly and Sbordone) – therefore, simply use the word '*scytale*'.[53] Again it shows that *scytalae* – in this case, it seems, 'sticks' of some kind – were used for a range of different purposes, and that we must examine context closely to ascertain whether any encryption or secret communication was implied.

The use of *scytalae* for record keeping can again be found in Diodorus Siculus' *Library of History* (first century BCE), and in the *Excerpta Constantiniana*: a Byzantine encyclopaedia written in ancient Greek in Constantinople in the tenth century CE.[54] The passages from Diodorus Siculus and the *Excerpta Constantiniana* on the *scytale* are based on the now lost work of the fourth-century BCE author Ephorus, who wrote a universal history of the Greek and non-Greek world. In the sources we see the word *scytale* once as well as the word *scytalida* ('little stick;' σκυταλίδα). In the first passage it is discussed how the Spartans, when going into battle, wrote their names on *scytalida* (little sticks) that they fastened to their arms in order that their relatives and comrades could identify them if they died on the battlefield, a practice that we already saw in our discussion of Tyrtaeus

(Polyaenus, *Stratagems of War*, 1.17). In Ephorus' second passage on the *scytale*, it is discussed how the Spartan general Lysander, when campaigning against the Athenians, sent his man Gylippus back to Sparta with booty and 1500 talents of silver (Diodorus Siculus, *Library of History*, 13.106.8–9; *Excerpta Constantiniana* 4). In the bags Lysander had put *scytalae* indicating the amount of money per bag. Gylippus, who did not know about this, took money out of the bags for himself. The *ephors*, who instead knew about the *scytalae* in the bags, soon discovered Gylippus' crime and condemned him to death. In this case, *scytalae* are used to indicate the amount of money in bags. However, Oldfather presumes that there were also secret *scytale* dispatches in the bags and refers to this as a customary Spartan practice. According to Oldfather, even if Gylippus had found the dispatches, he would not have been able to read them as they would have been encrypted.[55] However, Diodorus does not explicitly mention any dispatches in this case. He simply states that the *scytalae* indicated the amount of the money in the bags. Nevertheless, Oldfather's interpretation points to an intriguing possibility: that the Spartans employed a form of encryption to help ensure the security of important financial transfers and transactions. The financial 'tagging' use of *scytalae* allegedly described by Theophrastus, Ephorus, and described again by others, may well have included a cryptographic element too, but if so, this is not described in the surviving sources.

The broad semantic range and ambiguity of the term '*scytale*' as it appears in various ancient contexts, as we have seen above, makes it difficult to determine sometimes whether a writer is referring to a simple staff or baton, a walking stick, a 'dispatch stick,' a cryptographic device or, in at least one instance, a phallus. From another group of sources, it seems that there was yet another meaning attached to the term *scytale* in Antiquity, which merits our particular consideration and analysis here. In a passage from Photius' *Lexicon*, written in the ninth century CE (but recording much earlier lexical definitions), Photius gave various meanings of the word *scytale* (Photius, *Lexicon*, entry: σκυτάλη (I) and (II)). According to Photius, the principal meaning of the word *scytale* was 'a thick-ended rod' or a 'whip' ('βακτερία ἄκρο πάχη ἢ φραγέλλιον'; Photius, *Lexicon*, entry: σκυτάλη (I)). However, Photius then adds a secondary meaning, discussing how the Spartans used *scytalae* for their secret communication in a description that is remarkably similar to those of Plutarch and Aulus Gellius, and is clearly derived from these sources (Photius, *Lexicon*, entry: σκυτάλη (II); Plutarch, *Life of Lysander*, 19.5–7; Aulus Gellius, *Attic Nights*, 17.9–15; and see below 'The scytale in practice'). However, in a third definition of the word *scytale*, Photius also described how – according to Dioscorides in his now lost first-century CE work *On Customs* – the

Spartans used *scytalae* to set up contracts (Photius, *Lexicon*, entry: σκυτάλη (II)). A money lender in Sparta would divide a *scytale* into two pieces and write the same contract onto the two *scytalae*, thereby creating two copies. One copy would be given to a witness while the other copy stayed with the money lender (Photius, *Lexicon*, entry: σκυτάλη (II)). According to Photius, Aristotle had already described this practice as occurring among the Ithacans in his now lost *Constitution of the Itacans* (entry: σκυτάλη (II)). Diels and Oehler (and Sheldon later, following Oehler) seem to misinterpret this source when arguing that this passage shows that, according to Aristotle, the Ithacans used *scytalae* for secret communication like the Spartans did.[56] However, since Aristotle's original work is lost, we cannot say with certainly what he wrote on the *scytale* in the original source, nor does the passage show that the Ithacans and the Spartans used *scytalae* in the same way. Moreover, the use of *scytalae* to set up contracts as discussed by Photius was clearly not the same as the Spartan practice of using the *scytale* as a cryptographic device and clearly no secret communication per se is involved in this ingenious scheme.

The *scytale* in practice

If *scytalae* were used for the purpose of secret communication, the most likely period in which the Spartans used them was from the late fifth to the early fourth centuries BCE, especially the period between the outbreak of the Peloponnesian War (431 BCE) and the Battle of Leuctra (371 BCE). In this period Spartan commanders were away from home and would, therefore, have needed such devices to enable long-distance communications during their operations in the field.[57] Interestingly, Plutarch and Aulus Gellius write on the *scytale* much later: in the late first to late second century CE. However, both authors drew upon much earlier sources. In this section, we will first discuss Plutarch's and Aulus Gellius' sources on the *scytale* as a Spartan cryptography, before moving on to their descriptions of the device.

The range of Plutarch's sources is considerable and the scholarship on how Plutarch makes use of his sources is equally extensive. But it has been suggested that Plutarch's description of the *scytale* is likely to have been based on a work of the fourth-century BCE Greek historian and rhetorician Theopompus of Chios, who wrote the historical work *Hellenica*.[58] This work seems to have been an important source for Plutarch's *Life of Lysander*, where we can find his description of the *scytale*.[59] Indeed, Plutarch referred to Theopompus directly at least twice in *Life of Lysander*, and may well have used more material from the historian, that remains unattributed (Plutarch, *Life of Lysander*, 17.2–3; 30.2). Only fragments of Theopompus' work have survived, none of which refer directly to the *scytale* (*Fragments of Old Comedy*, 3). However, we know a few significant details from a short biography written by Photius (Photius, *Lexicon*, 176 = T 2).[60] Theopompus was born around 378/377 BCE, and both he and his father Damasistratus were allegedly exiled from their home in Chios for '*lakōnismos*' (that is, for 'sympathising with Sparta'). There is good reason to believe, therefore, that the Greek Theopompus (and his father) would have had closer dealings with Sparta than many other Greeks of the time and would have had particular (perhaps even unique) opportunities to witness, or to hear first-hand, about the Spartan *scytale* and its use. We also know, by comparing Plutarch's reworking of passages from Theopompus that have been preserved, that Plutarch accurately and reliably preserved the details of the original in his paraphrase, although not repeating his source word for word (Plutarch, *Moralia* 210d and Theopompus F22 = Athenaeus of Naucratis, *The Learned Banqueters*, 14.657b-c). If, as seems likely, Plutarch used Theopompus as his source on the Spartan *scytale*, it would make Plutarch's late first/early second-century CE description of the *scytale* and its use in the fifth and fourth centuries BCE a more reliable source. For, although Plutarch himself would not have witnessed the use of the *scytale*, and we must therefore treat his testimony as to its use as a cryptographic device with some caution, recognition of Plutarch's own historical sources helps to lend authority to his account, and lends weight to the argument that the *scytale* was, indeed, used for cryptographic communications by the Spartans.

Like Plutarch, Aulus Gellius (writing in the late second century CE) identified a considerable number of earlier sources for his work, from both well-known and less well-known authors. Aulus Gellius was a well-educated figure who seems to have conducted extensive research on a large variety of topics for his work *Attic Nights*.[61] However, by far the most influential historical source for Aulus Gellius is Plutarch himself, who is quoted in no fewer than eleven passages including in chapter seventeen, in which we find Aulus Gellius' description of the Spartan *scytale* (1.1.1, 1.3.5, 1.4.31, 1.26.4–8, 2.8–9, 3.5–6, 4.11, 11.16, 15.10.1, 17.11, 20.8.7).[62] Like Plutarch, Aulus Gellius likes to illustrate his work with biographical narratives and anecdotes, and his *Attic Nights* features all the same Greek, Spartan and Roman characters that Plutarch wrote about (such as Pericles, Themistocles and Alcibiades).[63] The reasons for Plutarch's great influence upon Aulus Gellius' writing are therefore clear. However, as Cavazza observes, Aulus Gellius depends on his sources, but still has a mind of his own: 'he does not merely weigh up other people's ideas, he judges them, filters them, and [..] he not only quotes his sources but corrects them.'[64] Gellius does this, typically, by taking multiple sources for each chapter.[65] However, he does not always tell us which sources he has consulted, and even when he does, we can never be sure whether he has consulted a source at first or second hand.[66] Similarly, even when he is clearly quoting from an older source text, Gellius does not always record that source.[67]

Theopompus also appears in *Attic Nights* only once, and in a similarly trivial context.[68] Yet, as Cavazza shows, even if Aulus Gellius was consulting Theopompus at first hand for his account of the *scytale*, he would not necessarily name him as a source. In fact, although Gellius did not identify his sources for his passage on the *scytale* (*Attic Nights*, 17.9.6–16), he will certainly have drawn upon earlier sources for his description here too. These sources include both Plutarch's description of the *scytale*, given the close similarity of Plutarch's and Aulus Gellius' accounts, and Plutarch's own original source(s) on the topic, which is most likely Theopompus.[69]

Interestingly, Theopompus' historical work is used as a source by Plutarch and Aulus Gellius, rather than military sources, like Xenophon's works. If the historian Theopompus knew about the *scytale* being used as a Spartan cryptography, it may seem odd that Xenophon as a military man did not discuss the device. Xenophon was a military man with a clear interest in innovation, who wrote military protocols (see e.g. *Hellenica*, 3.2.22). Also, Xenophon had a positive view towards the use of intelligence in warfare.[70] Moreover, despite being born an Athenian citizen, Xenophon came to be associated with Sparta, the traditional opponent of Athens. Experience as a mercenary and a military leader, service under Spartan commanders in Ionia, Asia Minor, Persia and elsewhere, exile from Athens, and friendship with King Agesilaus II, endeared Xenophon to the Spartans.[71] Considering Xenophon's interest in military innovation, his admiration of Spartan military systems and his close relationship with Agesilaus, we may wonder why Xenophon did not discuss the *scytale* as a Spartan cryptograph, even though he mentions the device three times in his *Hellenica* (3.3, 5.2.34–35, 5.2.37). The reason for this is the context in which the word '*scytale*' appears in Xenophon's work.

In *Hellenica* 3.3, Xenophon discusses how a conspiracy led by Cinadon became known to the Spartan *ephors* (Xenophon, *Hellenica*, 3.3.4–5). To prevent the conspiracy from happening, upon hearing about this, the *ephors* decided to send Cinadon together with some of his fellow conspirators away from Sparta to the town of Aulon on an errand. Cinadon had to bring back to Sparta certain

Aulonians and Helots whose names were written in an official dispatch (a *scytale*; *Hellenica*, 3.3.8–9). The *scytale* here apparently refers to an official Spartan dispatch, rather than a device for secret communication. Therefore, it is aptly translated as 'official dispatch' by Brownson, and as 'despatches' by Warner and Cawkwell.[72] It is notable in this context, however, that the dispatch under discussion appears to have been remarkably simple indeed in terms of the text of its message. In fact, it seems to have simply comprised certain 'names.' What we do not see is evidence for the *scytale* being used in this source or this context for the purposes of secret communication.

The other two references to *scytalae* in Xenophon's work can be found in book five. In the first reference, Leontiades addressed the Spartans, proposing a new alliance between Thebes and Sparta. With this alliance, according to Leontiades, if the Thebans ever found themselves in need of help from their allies, they would only have to send a short message – a *scytale* – to Sparta and help would immediately come (*Hellenica*, 5.2.34–35). Because of the non-secret context here, and the two different states involved, Brownson translates the word σκυτάλη (*scytale*) as 'brief message,' and Warner and Cawkwell translate it as 'short message.'[73] Once again, it is notable in this context that the dispatch under discussion appears to have been simple and short. We see here further evidence of the stereotype of the Spartans as semi-illiterate and able only to read and write short messages. Once again, what we do not see is evidence for the *scytale* being used for the purposes of secret communication. The same applies to the second reference to a *scytale* in book five of Xenophon's work, in which Xenophon described how the Spartans, after the speech of Leontiades, sent *scytalae* to various allied states (*Hellenica*, 5.2.37). In this context the term σκυτάλη (*scytale*) has again been translated by Brownson as 'official dispatches' and simply as 'despatches' by Warner and Cawkwell, and it seems unlikely that these *scytalae* were secret or encrypted messages because of non-Spartan parties being involved.[74] Another passage must be discussed here. At 1.1.23, Xenophon mentions a letter from the Spartan vice-admiral Hippocrates to the *ephors* in Sparta about chaos among the Spartan troops (*Hellenica*, 1.1.23). In the original Greek we find the word ἐπιστολέως (*epistoleos*) for 'letter', instead of the word σκυτάλη (*scytale*).[75] However, as we will see in the description of the scytale (see below) sometimes only the wooden sticks are indicated by using the term σκυτάλη (Plutarch, *Life of Lysander*, 19.5–6), while at other times the sticks and the secret messages were both indicated by the term (Aulus Gellius, *Attic Nights*, 17.9.6–16). More importantly, the message sent from Hippocrates to the *ephors* was sent during the Peloponnesian War between Athens and Sparta, making it plausible that there was some form of encryption in the message, a point that it strengthened by the fact that the message was intercepted by the enemy, as Xenophon tells us (ἁλίσκομαι; aliskomai). However, we cannot say with certainty that this was a *scytale* message. It seems that Xenophon did not see the *scytale* as a Spartan cryptography, or at least not in these stories. In fact, *scytalae* were used for a variety of purposes, including the sending of secret and non-secret messages, as is discussed in the section above ('The scytale in Greek sources'). Moreover, even though Xenophon wrote a lot on military tactics, and had a positive view towards deceiving the enemy, he did not describe the workings of actual methods for secret communication, as e.g. Aeneas Tacticus (*How to Survive Under Siege*, 31) or Aulus Gellius did (*Attic Nights*, 17.9).

Let us now turn to Plutarch's and Aulus Gellius' descriptions of the *scytale* as a Spartan cryptograph. Their passages do not prove that *scytalae* were used in practice for secret communication. However, the ingenious rearrangement of the letters that they describe as the key feature of *scytale* communication makes the *scytale* a candidate for the earliest known theoretical transposition cipher in history. According to Plutarch, writing in the late first/early second century CE:

> When the ephors send out an admiral or a general, they make two round pieces of wood exactly alike in length and thickness, [...] and keep one themselves, while they give the other to their envoy. These pieces of wood they call '*scytalae*'. Whenever [...] they wish to send some secret and important message, they make a scroll of parchment long and narrow, like a leather strap, and wind it round their '*scytale*' [...]. After doing this, they write what they wish on the parchment [...]; and when they have written their message, they take the parchment off, and send it, [...] to the commander.
>
> Plutarch, *Life of Lysander*, 19.5–6

Aulus Gellius' later second-century CE description is remarkably similar to Plutarch's:

> The ancient Lacedaemonians, when they wanted to conceal and disguise the public dispatches sent to their generals, in order that, in case they were intercepted by the enemy, their plans might not be known, used to send letters written in the following manner. There were two thin, cylindrical wands of the same thickness and length, smoothed and prepared so as to be exactly alike. One of these was given to the general when he went to war, the other the magistrates kept at home under their control and seal. When the need of more secret communication arose, they bound about the staff a thong of moderate thickness, but long enough for the purpose, in a simple spiral, in such a way that the edges of the thong

which was twined around the stick met and were joined throughout. Then they wrote the dispatch on that thong across the connected edges of the joints, with the lines running from the top to the bottom. When the letter had been written in this way, the thong was unrolled from the wand and sent to the general, who was familiar with the device. But the unrolling of the thong made the letters imperfect and broken, and their parts and strokes were divided and separated. Therefore, if the thong fell into the hands of the enemy, nothing at all could be made out from the writing; but when the one to whom the letter was sent had received it, he wound it around the corresponding staff, which he had, from the top to the bottom, just as he knew that it ought to be done, and thus the letters, united by encircling a similar staff, came together again, rendering the dispatch entire and undamaged, and easy to read. This kind of letter the Lacedaemonians called σκυτάλη.

Aulus Gellius, Attic Nights, 17.9.6–16

What Plutarch and Aulus Gellius (following Plutarch) describe is a simple but ingenious device for sending secret messages, whereby only two *scytalae* (literally 'sticks') of the same size, and a piece of parchment or papyrus were needed. When a Spartan commander was going to war, the *ephors* would take two *scytalae*. They gave one to the commander to take with him and kept the other one in Sparta. The following example shows how this worked according to Plutarch's and Aulus Gellius' descriptions, and how the strip of writing material may have looked during the subsequent steps in the process. For this example, the text 'Enemy attacks at dawn tomorrow' will be used.

1 – First, a strip of papyrus or parchment is wrapped about the *scytale*. In this way small rectangular columns are created. Since the wrapping was done by hand, it is likely that the edges of the strip overlapped each other. Therefore, the columns were not all the same in size.

Figure 1 *Scytale* with strip of writing material wrapped about it. Author's illustration.

Perrin, on the one hand, translates the word βιβλίον (*biblion*) as 'parchment' in the Loeb version of Plutarch's *Life of Lysander*, as Poe already did in his 1841 work *A Few Words on Secret Writing*.[76] Smith, Kahn and Mollin, on the other hand, seem certain that parchment was used instead of papyrus.[77] However, both papyrus and leather parchment were typically used as writing materials in Antiquity, so there seems to be no particular significance attaching to the use of either as the medium for the *scytale*'s encrypted messages. It seems plausible that leather parchment would offer a more robust material for messages that might need to be sent over long distances, over difficult terrain and in conflict situations, a context in which the *scytale* was used (Plutarch, *Life of Lysander*, 19.5; Aulus Gellius, *Attic Nights*, 17.9).[78] Yet, while on campaign, one obviously had to be able to write and send messages simply and quickly, so where papyrus was readily to hand this would presumably have offered a convenient alternative medium.

2 – In the second step, the text was written on the strip of writing material. In Figures 2 and 3 (below), the text is written from left to right and top to bottom on two lines.

Figure 2 Text: 'Enemy attacks at dawn tomorrow', written on *scytale*. Author's illustration.

3 – As Plutarch describes in his account of the *scytale*, once the strip of writing material had been unwrapped from the *scytale*, all letters would have been rearranged and the recipient could not get any meaning out of it since the letters had no connection (*Life of Lysander*, 19.7). By unwrapping the strip, the letters would now appear per column, instead of per row. So, instead of reading E-N-E-M-Y, the first word of the message, one would now read E-D-N-A-E, etc. (see Figure 3). In Figure 3, every letter of the message has been written on a complete piece of material strip. In other words, no letters were written over the edges of the strip, meaning that when the strip was subsequently removed from the *scytale* stick, all the letters would have remained intact and would simply have been rearranged in their order of sequence.

| ED | NA | EW | MN | YT | AO | TM | TM | AO | CR | KO | SW | A | T |

Figure 3 Strip of writing material with text unwrapped from *scytale*. Author's illustration.

4 – However, according to Plutarch, the complete *scytale* was covered in the writing material (Plutarch, *Life of Lysander*, 19.6). This makes it more plausible that the sender of a message did not in practice write with all letters neatly contained upon complete pieces of the *scytale*'s material strip, but that the letters of the message would also have been written across the edges of the strip (Figure 4).

Figure 4 Text: 'Enemy attacks at dawn tomorrow' written across complete strip of writing material. Author's illustration.

Since Plutarch's description indicates the likelihood that the whole strip was used for writing, at least some of the letters on the strip would have been written whole and on a complete piece of strip. These letters would have remained intact and recognisable once the strip was unwrapped from the *scytale*. Yet, since some of the letters on the strip would have been written overlapping the edges of the strip, these letters would not have remained intact once the strip was unwrapped from the *scytale*. And indeed, according to Aulus Gellius, this is what happened in practice: the unrolling of the strip made the letters imperfect and broken (see Figure 4; Aulus Gellius, *Attic Nights*, 17.9.12–14). If the strip from Figure 3 was unwrapped from the *scytale*, the strip would look like the following image (Figure 5). In this figure the strip is cut into pieces to show the difference between the partial and complete letters.

Figure 5 Complete strip of writing material cut into pieces to show partial and complete letters. Author's illustration.

Although neither Plutarch nor Aulus Gellius mentions it, the message could have been written in either plaintext (normal non-encrypted text) or ciphertext (encrypted text), with the latter option making the message doubly secret and, therefore, doubly secure. However, nothing in their descriptions proves that the text was written in cipher. It will, therefore, be presumed that the *scytale* messages were written in plaintext. After a message was written on the strip of parchment or papyrus, the strip was then unwrapped from the *scytale* stick (Plutarch, *Life of Lysander*, 19.5; Aulus Gellius, *Attic Nights*, 17.9.6–10). By unwrapping the text strip from the *scytale* all letters in the original message were transposed to a different position, as Plutarch and Aulus Gellius described. Thus, according to Plutarch, when a general in the field received a *scytale* message: 'He, [could not] get any meaning out of it, — since the letters have no connection, but are disarranged' (*Life of Lysander*, 19.7). While Aulus Gellius additionally mentions partial and broken letters (*Attic Nights*, 17.9.12–13). This transposing of the letters in the message makes the *scytale* the first theoretical military transposition cipher known in history, an encryption technique whereby the normal sequence of letters of a plaintext (non-encrypted text) is rearranged.[79] As Singh states: '[A] form of transposition is embodied in the first ever military cryptographic device, the Spartan *scytale*.'[80] We can see from the reconstruction above just how challenging it would have been to attempt to reconstruct the original text from this scrambled ciphertext. It would certainly not be impossible, but without a *scytale* rod of the same size as the one used in the original encryption it would have been time-consuming. A good modern parallel might be the paper shredder, which offers one way of 'encrypting' or scrambling a confidential source text. With patience, skill and time, the original text can be reconstructed from the shredded strips of paper. The advantage of the *scytale* device, however, is that it offers the opportunity for that reconstruction to be managed much more quickly and easily.

Plutarch not only discusses the working of the *scytale*. He also discussed how and when he believed that the device was used.[81] In chapter 19.4 of *Life of Lysander* Plutarch describes how the Persian leader Pharnabazus complained to the Spartan *ephors* that Lysander was pillaging his territories for no purpose. Therefore, they subsequently sent a message by *scytale* to Lysander summoning him to come home or to be sentenced to death on account of this misbehaviour. Plutarch confirms that this was an example of a message created by *scytale*, which the *ephors* often used when they wanted to communicate on confidential matters with generals in the field (*Life of Lysander*, 20). Perrin translates the word *scytale* here as 'dispatch-scroll', as Plutarch observes that both the *scytale* stick and the message were known as a *scytale* since the thing measured (the message or letter) had the same name as the measure (the stick).[82] However, it is not clear from the context whether the secret message ('ἀπόρρητόν; *aporreton*') was encrypted or not. Lysander, being much disturbed upon receiving the dispatch, then went to Pharnabazus asking him to send another letter to the *ephors* stating that he had not misbehaved. Pharnabazus, however, fooled Lysander by sending the *ephors* two more letters: one written openly in which he stated that he had not been wronged by Lysander, and a second one written in secret in which he complained about Lysander's misbehaviour once more. Pharnabazus then sent Lysander back to Sparta with the second letter (20.1–6).[83] This second letter was not necessarily a cryptographic secret communication (19.4). Instead, it may simply have been written in secret without Lysander knowing about it (20.1–6). Since Lysander had seen Pharnabazus writing a letter in which the claims of serious misbehaviour and pillaging had been nullified, he felt confident going back to Sparta with Pharnabazus' letter, which he carried openly. After the *ephors* showed Lysander the 'secret' letter he understood that he had been misled and left the city (20.4; see also: Polyaenus, *Stratagems of War*, 7.19; Cornelius Nepos, *The Book on the Great Generals of Foreign Nations. Pausanias*, 4.3.4.).[84] The modern historians of cryptography Singh and Bauer believe that Plutarch's account indicates that another *scytale* message was sent to Lysander: a message warning the Spartans that Pharnabazus was planning an attack on the Greeks. They suggest that, thanks to this *scytale* message, Lysander was prepared for the attack and could repulse it.[85] This is another example of how incorrectly cryptographers see stories in original Greek and Roman sources as clear facts. However, Plutarch only mentions the letter that Lysander received from the ephors and the two letters that Pharnabazus subsequently wrote.[86] There is no indication that Lysander also received a *scytale* message informing him about a planned attack, let alone that a single *scytale* message prevented this attack. We cannot, then, take this as an unambiguous example of cryptographic secret communication.

However, Plutarch's writings elsewhere offer a more likely reference to the sending of a *scytale* message that is not merely secret but also encrypted. This can be found in his *Life of Alcibiades*.[87] According to Plutarch, at some point in his life, the same general Lysander was among the leaders of the Athenians (his enemies) when he received a message by *scytale* from the *ephors* urging him to kill the Athenian statesman Alcibiades (*Life of Alcibiades*, 38.1–4). Perrin once more translates the word *scytale* as 'dispatch-scroll.'[88] Yet, since Lysander was among his Athenian enemies when he received the *scytale* message from the Spartan *ephors*, there is reason to believe that this message would have been an encrypted message so as to prevent the Athenians from intercepting and reading it. However, this interpretation must be inferred from context only, and there is no concrete reference in the text describing this *scytale* as a secret *cryptographic* message here.

The third reference to the sending of a *scytale* message – again, secret according to Plutarch – can be found in Plutarch's *Life of Artaxerxes*.[89] According to Plutarch, when Cyrus the Younger started a war against his brother Artaxerxes II, he requested help from the Spartans. The Spartans accordingly sent a message by *scytale* to their general Clearchus ordering him to aid Cyrus (*Life of Artaxerxes*, 6.2–5; see also Xenophon, *Anabasis*, 1.1.9; 1.2.21; 1.4.3). Plutarch does not tell us much more about this event, which gives the impression that Clearchus was in Sparta or working for the Spartans at the time when Cyrus called the Spartans for help. However, the situation is more complex than it may seem at first glance. Plutarch's version of events stands in stark contrast to Xenophon's and Diodorus' versions. Xenophon knew Clearchus personally, while Diodorus may have been using another veteran of the campaigns as a source. Both authors describe Clearchus as an exile of Sparta after some transgressions in Byzantium. At the beginning of 402 BCE, Clearchus entered the service of Cyrus the Younger to aid Cyrus against his brother Artaxerxes II (Diodorus Siculus, *Library of History*, 14.12.7–9; Xenophon, *Anabasis*, 2.6.4). Cyrus supplied Clearchus with funds and instructed him to recruit as many mercenaries as possible (Diodorus Siculus, *Library of History*, 14.12.7–9, 14.19.8; Xenophon, *Anabasis*, 1.1.9). This is an interesting situation. We see a Spartan in exile working for the Persians yet still with the agreement of the Spartans, since they sent a *scytale* message to Clearchus in Byzantium urging him to aid Cyrus. Perrin simply translates the word as 'dispatch-roll'.[90] Yet, although the war between Cyrus the Younger and his brother Artaxerxes II was a war between two Persian brothers in which the Greeks only sent mercenary troops, the information communicated between the *ephors* in Sparta and Clearchus would still have been highly confidential, and of major importance to the Spartan campaign and strategy. Moreover, the message was sent to Clearchus over a long distance: from Sparta to Byzantium, and *scytale* messages were sent over long distances (Plutarch, *Life of Lysander*, 19.5–7; Aulus Gellius, *Attic Nights*, 17.9.12–13). If any enemies of the Spartans had intercepted this message, they could have decided to attack Sparta at the same time, knowing that most, if not all, of the Spartan troops would have been away at war in Persia at that time.

In such a context, it seems sensible to assume that the *scytale* message in question would have been encrypted. However, once again, this can only be inferred from the context, and is not an explicit description of the *scytale* as a form of secret communication here. A similar example can be found in Herodotus' *Histories* (7.239) where we see how Demaratus of Sparta was in exile at the court of Xerxes of Persia around the time of Xerxes' invasion of Greece in

480 BCE. Even though he was exiled, Demaratus sent a secret message to the Spartans to warn them about the invasion (see chapter two).

Finally, two further references to the sending of secret *scytale* messages are mentioned in Plutarch's *Life of Agesilaus*.[91] The first reference to a *scytale* can be found in chapter ten of Plutarch's *Life of Agesilaus*. Here, Plutarch describes how the Spartan commander Agesilaus received word from the *ephors* in Sparta requesting him to take control of the Spartan army and navy, while Agesilaus was on campaign in Lydia and Phrygia (*Life of Agesilaus*, 10.5; see also Xenophon, *Hellenica*, 3.4.27ff). Although the *scytale* message discussed here can be seen as an official request whereby Agesilaus was promoted by the *ephors*, it was also an example of a politically and strategically sensitive and important message sent from the *ephors* in Sparta to a commander in the field who was on campaign. Because of the sensitive content we might assume that the message would have been sent in encrypted form so that no one other than its intended recipient would have been able to read and act upon it.

We find a parallel scenario in chapter fifteen, where Plutarch discussed how Agesilaus received another *scytale* message from the *ephors* in Sparta while still campaigning in Asia. As soon as Agesilaus received the *scytale* message, he acted upon its contents (*Life of Agesilaus*, 15.5). As in the previous examples from Plutarch's *Lives,* confidential information is sent between the *ephors* in Sparta and commanders in the field during wars and revolts. Although Perrin translates the word σκυτάλη (*scytale*) simply as 'dispatch-roll' both times, given the campaign context, it is likely that all these messages would have been encrypted *scytale* messages.[92] Indeed, Plutarch's discussion of the sensitive contents of the messages sent between the *ephors* of Sparta and their commanders in the field show that *scytalae* could have been used for secret encrypted communication in warfare. Supporting this reading is the fact that Plutarch's accounts of the letters of Pharnabazus to the Spartans because of Lysander' misbehaviour (*Life of Lysander*, 19.1–7; 20.1–6) can also be found in Polyaenus' second-century CE work *Stratagems of War* (7.19), where again we see three letters: a secret *scytale* letter sent from the *ephors* to Lysander to summon him home, and the two conventional letters from Pharnabazus to the *ephors*. Significantly, only for the presumably encrypted *scytale* message does Polyaenus use the word σκυτάλην (*scytale*), while for the two non-encrypted letters he used the words ἐπιστολὴν (*epistolè*), βιβλιά (*biblia*) and γράμματα (*grammata*) respectively.[93] However, it must be borne in mind that Plutarch is not offering us an eye-witness testimony of the *scytale* as a Spartan cryptograph in these descriptions: Plutarch wrote about the sending of secret *scytale* messages in the second century CE, about

600–700 years after Lysander, Clearchus and Agesilaus – who allegedly received these encrypted *scytale* messages – lived. Therefore, we cannot know with certainty how much of Plutarch's and Aulus Gellius' (following Plutarch) stories are true. Perhaps Plutarch believed that the messages were sent in the secret way that he described (Plutarch, *Life of Lysander*, 19.5–7). And he may have had sources that are lost to us, including Theopompus' works. However, another possibility includes Plutarch invented the method to enhance his stories, and Aulus Gellius has later followed Plutarch (Aulus Gellius, *Attic Nights*, 17.9–5). Yet, with Plutarch's description we have the earliest theoretical transposition cipher in history: a cipher system that keeps reappearing and developing throughout the ages up to today. The fact that Plutarch gave us a description of the earliest known theoretical transposition cipher is something that has previously been overlooked by other scholars. So, we must give Plutarch some credit, even though the description of the *scytale* as a Spartan cryptograph, and the stories Plutarch tells us, may be (partially) invented by the author himself.

Misinterpretations of the Spartan *scytale* (1100–1800 CE)

Even though the *scytale*-system may have been (partially) invented by Plutarch, the system is the earliest known theoretical transposition cipher in history, and formed the basis for modern transposition ciphers used up to the present day.[94] However, modern historians of cryptography seem to overlook the importance of the system, and instead they see the *scytale* as a simple toy cipher that can never have been used for serious secret communications.[95] This undervaluation of the *scytale* as an important theoretical transposition cipher may have been the result of misinterpretations of Plutarch's and Aulus Gellius' original sources on the *scytale* as a Spartan cryptograph (Plutarch, *Life of Lysander*, 19.5; Aulus Gellius, *Attic Nights*, 17.6). These misinterpretations of the sources already started in the Late Middle Ages.

In the twelfth century CE, the word *scytale* appears in the work the *Book of Histories in Political Verse* (also known as the *Chiliades*), written by the Byzantine scholar Johannes Tzetzes.[96] Tzetzes gave us no less than seven meanings for the word *scytale*. Here we see a number of earlier sources coming together. The first meaning of the word (or in fact its derivation *scytos*), was 'a whip to punish schoolchildren' (*Chiliades*, 9.123). Photius also describes the *scytale* as a whip, although he does not specify whether it was used to punish schoolchildren or anyone else (Photius, *Lexicon*, entry: σκυτάλη (I). Tzetzes also suggest the use of the *scytale* as 'a rod [...] used to end and resolve anger and wrath' (*Chiliades*, 9.133). We see something similar in the works of Aristophanes and Didymus who refer to the *scytale* as a weapon (Aristophanes, *Birds*, 1280–1285; *Didymi Chalcenteri Grammatici Alexandrini*, Fragment 1283–1284).[97] The third meaning of the word *scytale* we find in Tzetzes' work is 'finger-bone' (*Chiliades*, 9.126). Tzetzes' source here is the seventh-century CE Byzantine physician Paul of Aegina, who used the word *scytale* in a section on bones in his medical encyclopaedia *Medical Compendium in Seven Books* (Paul of Aegina, *Medical Compendium*, 6.43).

According to Tzetzes, the fourth meaning of the word *scytale* is a square rod used by marble masons while the fifth meaning is 'any kind of rod (*Chiliades*, 9.128). Here the sources are unclear. Yet, we already find the meaning 'rod' in an inscription from Delos dating back to the second century BCE (*Inscriptions de Délos*, 442 B170), and again in the fourth-century CE work *Ethiopica* by Heliodorus of Emessa (Heliodorus of Emessa, *Ethiopica*, 9.15). Moreover, a mason using a rod, say to flatten out cement, is highly plausible. Tzetzes then refers to a *scytale* as a fish (9.124).[98] Tzetzes' final meaning of the word *scytale* is a Spartan secret message (*Chiliades*, 9.134–153). Here Tzetzes follows Plutarch and Aulus Gellius, but gives his own interpretation to the working and the appearance of the device (*Chiliades*, 9.134–153). According to Plutarch and Aulus Gellius, secret *scytale* messages were sent between the *ephor*s of Sparta and their commanders in the field (Plutarch, *Life of Lysander*, 19.5; Aulus Gellius, *Attic Nights*, 17.9.6–7). Yet, Tzetzes believes that anyone in Sparta could have used these *scytale* messages (*Chiliades*, 9.134). Although it is theoretically plausible that other Spartans used this method for secret communication too, Plutarch and Gellius do not mention this. Yet, according to the two ancient authors, *scytale* messages were sent over a long distance. So, if *scytalae* messages have been used by the Spartans, then maybe political Spartan envoys could have used the method too, but this is speculative. Tzetzes then continues to describe the stick. According to the author, the Spartans would use the shortest stick they could find, and only one stick (*Chiliades*, 9.136). Why Tzetzes suggests the use of the shortest stick is unclear, and again, this is a detail we cannot find in the works of Plutarch and Gellius. In fact, when we take another look at Plutarch's and Aulus Gellius' descriptions, we see that two parties sending *scytale* messages would have needed two sticks of the exact same size and diameter (Plutarch, *Life of Lysander*, 19.5; Aulus Gellius, *Attic Nights*, 17.9.12–13). The length of the stick is not mentioned here.

Then there is the material of the strip. According to Tzetzes, a thin piece of skin was used (*Chiliades*, 9.139). Here we see a resemblance to Plutarch's original work. Instead of skin, Plutarch mentions a thin strip of leather parchment, but obviously parchment is dried and prepared skin (*Life of Lysander*, 19.5–6).[99] Even more interesting is the next point. According to Tzetzes, the Spartans wrote their secret messages under the strip of skin (*Chiliades*, 9.138–140), instead of on the strip as we see in the works of Plutarch and Gellius, and in Erasmus' later work (see below). According to Tzetzes, the writing became visible again when the skin was unwrapped from the stick (9.140). This is already the opposite of what we see in Plutarch's and Gellius' works. Then we see that Tzetzes' method is in fact very different from Plutarch's original idea. We read that: 'However, [the message] could not be completely read / If someone rolled away the entire skin. / Then the rod would be examined, / To see if the skin had been rolled and fitted to the rod (*Chiliades*, 9.141–144).

So, part of the skin had to remain on the stick, and the stick had to be examined to read the entire message to see if the skin and the stick would fit together. Tzetzes does not clarify the passage, but it is plausible that he believed that one had to write partly on the skin, and partly on the stick. Perhaps he even had to idea to write on the inner side of the skin instead of the outer side. In that case, all the writing would have been invisible, even if the skin was wrapped around the stick. Then the skin and the stick were sent to the recipient separately and with great care (*Chiliades*, 9.148–149). The latter point may indicate that there was writing on the stick that had to be hidden from the enemy. When using Tzetzes' method, only one stick was needed, instead of two sticks as we saw in Plutarch's original method. Tzetzes finishes by stating that a Spartan *scytale* was 'a skin rolled onto a rod, bearing secret messages' (*Chiliades*, 9.153).

Erasmus in his early sixteenth-century work *Adages*, believes that both the stick and the leather thong wrapped around the stick together were called a *scytale* (*Adages*, ed. Mynors, vol. 33, 1991, p. 78, vol. 34, 1992, p. 50). Erasmus here, potentially confused Plutarch's and Aulus Gellius' descriptions of the *scytale* since, while Gellius mentioned that the letter that was sent to the general was called a *scytale* (*Attic Nights*, 17.9.6–16), Plutarch suggested that either the stick or the leather strap were both called *scytale* (*Life of Lysander*, 19.7).

Gerolamo Cardano in his 1550 work *De Subtilitate* simply mentions cylinders (*scytalae*) that were used for secret communication by the Spartans without giving any details as to how this worked and what materials were used for it. This may indicate that Cardano knew about Plutarch's and Aulus Gellius' descriptions but found it unnecessary to repeat them in his own work (*De Subtilitate*, 17.1036).

Yet, there is another possibility for the reason why Cardano does not refer to Plutarch and Gellius. According to the scholar, when using a *scytale* no writing would be visible (*De Subtilitate,* 17.1036). In other words, the complete message would become invisible. This is something we see in steganography, instead of cryptography. Yet, the *scytale* as described by Plutarch and Gellius is an example of cryptography, since the letters on the strip of writing material change place but are still visible. So, Cardano clearly has a different system in mind. Since Cardano does not describe the *scytale*, we cannot know with certainty what he means in this passage. Yet, maybe Cardano followed Tzetzes' idea of writing on the *scytale* and on the inner side of the strip, instead of writing on the outer side.

In 1557, Julius Caesar Scaliger published *Exercitationes*; this was a confutation to Cardano's *De Subtilitate,* containing 365 exercises for non-experts on a number of topics discussed in Cardano's work. In exercise 327, Scaliger rejects the use of the Spartan *scytale* method (*Exercitationes*, 327). He argues that the use of the *scytale* was far too simple, and, therefore, could not have been used for serious communication security. According to Scaliger, someone who found or intercepted a strip with partial and broken letters on it could simply try to put the edges of the strip together to find the letters. And, if he had found a few letters and knew how the method worked, he could easily have deciphered a secret message. Therefore, the method would certainly not have worked in the days of Cardano and Scaliger, and perhaps would not even have worked in ancient Greece, at least according to the author (*Exercitationes*, 327).[100]

In the seventeenth century, we see other interesting differences appear between Plutarch's and Gellius' original descriptions of the *scytale* and later works. In 1641, the natural philosopher John Wilkins discussed the *scytale* in his work *Mercury or the Secret and Swift Messenger*. According to Wilkins, when using a *scytale* as the Spartans did, one would have ended up with only partial and broken letters, an idea introduced by the fourth-century CE Roman poet Ausonius, Wilkins believes (*Mercury or the Secret and Swift Messenger,* pp. 38–39). Yet, Wilkins is incorrect here for two reasons. First, instead of Ausonius, it was Aulus Gellius who first introduced the partial and broken letters idea in his second-century CE description of the *scytale* (Aulus Gellius, *Attic Nights,* 17.9.12–13). Secondly, Ausonius does not explicitly mention writing only across the edges of the strip. He only states that the characters of the text become incoherent when unwrapping the strip from the stick, since then the normal sequence of letters is lost (Ausonius, *Epistles*, 28.23–27; see chapter five). Next to this, Wilkins argues that Plutarch tells us how the Persian leader Pharnabazus tricked the Spartan general Lysander with a secret *scytale* message (*Mercury or the Secret and Swift Messenger*, p. 39). Again, this is incorrect. In chapter 19.4 of *Life of Lysander*, Plutarch describes how Pharnabazus complained to the Spartan *ephors* that Lysander was pillaging his territories for no purpose. Therefore, the *ephors* subsequently sent a message by *scytale* to Lysander summoning him to come home or to be sentenced to death on account of this misbehaviour (*Life of Lysander*, 19.4–7). So, it was not Pharnabazus, but the *ephors* of Sparta who sent Lysander this message. The modern scholar Tomokiyo adds another incorrect detail. He argues that the idea of writing over the edges of the strip was in fact introduced by John Wilkins in his work *Mercury or the Secret and Swift Messenger*, without mentioning Plutarch and Gellius.[101]

Another interesting aspect that appears in the seventeenth century is the variety of inventors given for the *scytale* method. According to Moller (1695) and Crell (1697), it was not Plutarch who first discussed the system, but the Greek mathematician Archimedes who invented it. According to the two scholars, this theory was introduced by the German abbot Johannes Trithemius in his 1518 work *Polygraphia* (Moller 1695, *Disputatio historico-philologica de scytala Lacedaemoniorum*, § 18; Crell 1697, *De scytala Laconica*, § 22). However, Trithemius never actually mentions Archimedes or the *scytale* in his work. Following Moller and Crell, the invention of the *scytale* was also incorrectly ascribed to Archimedes by John Falconer in his 1685 work *Cryptomenysis Patefacta* (section 5, p. 91) and ultimately by Wolf (2004) and Gamer (2022).[102] Other scholars assumed that it was the Italian scientist Giovanni Battista Porta who first ascribed the *scytale* to Archimedes in his 1593 work *De Occultis Literarum Notis*.[103] Again this is incorrect. Even though Porta describes the *scytale* in book 1 of the work, he argues that he follows the works of Aulus Gellius and Johannes Tzetzes, while he says that others ascribed the *scytale* as a messaging system to Archimedes (*De Occultis Literarum Notis*, 1.12–13).[104]

Philip Thicknesse, writing in 1772, adds other interesting details to the use of the *scytale*. He refers to the *scytale* in relation to a practice in the Greek Orthodox Church whereby priests held a *kontakion* in their hands. The word *kontakion* derives from the Greek κοντάκι (*kontaki*), which means 'rod' or 'stick', and especially refers to the stick around which a scroll is wound.[105] According to Thicknesse, the *kontakion* was: '... a short staff, to which was made fast, and wrapped round, very long slips of parchment, consisting of a great number of pieces, on which were written, the prayers and offices to be performed by the priests' (*A Treatise on the Art of Decyphering, and of Writing in Cypher*, p. 99).

Indeed, a strip of writing material for *scytale* messages was wrapped around a stick in the same way, according to Plutarch and Aulus Gellius. Yet, interestingly, Thicknesse only describes text being written on the strip; he does not add anything about unwrapping the strip from the stick. Still, Thicknesse seems to believe that the *kontakia* (pl. of *kontakion*) were a form of code like the Spartan *scytale*, since he mentions a: 'curious [specimen which is] adorned with accents and letters, or rather half letters, for it is a perfect *scytale*.' (*A Treatise on the Art of Decyphering, and of Writing in Cypher*, p. 99). The half letters may correspond to what Plutarch and Gellius tell us about broken and partial letters (Aulus Gellius, *Attic Nights*, 17.9.6–16; Plutarch, *Life of Lysander*, 19.5–6). However, since there is no unwrapping of the strip from the stick, this example of wrapping a *kontakia* around a stick resembles the idea of a letter around a stick for easy transportation, as has been suggested by Jeffery, Lattimore and Rhodes.[106] Or maybe hymns were rolled up around the sticks after the service for easy archiving, like scrolls were put in piles in ancient archives.[107] Moreover, according to Thicknesse, the curious text he describes was found in the library of the French King Louis XV (reign 1715–74).[108] What kind of text this is, is unknown, since Thicknesse does not clarify this. Therefore, we cannot say with certainty that the curious text with partial and broken letters is in fact a *kontakion*. It makes more sense to simply say that it was a different kind of text.[109] *Kontakia* do not resemble ancient *scytale* messages since there is now evidence for unwrapping of the strip from the stick, as already mentioned.

We see the appearance of partial and broken letters in relation to the *scytale* again in a number of other sources. In 1676, the French scholar Georges Guillet de Guilletiere in his work *Lacédémone ancienne et nouvelle* mentions that the words were truncated and without connection. In fact, Guilletiere mentions that every letter of a text became partial and broken when the strip was unwrapped from the *scytale*.[110] Following De Guilletiere, we also see this idea of only ending up with broken letters in several other publications from the seventeenth to the twentieth century.[111]

Following these early modern scholars, we also see the idea of only ending up with broken letters in a number of nineteenth- and early twentieth-century sources, starting with Bonavilla and Aquilino's *Dizionario etimologico* (1821, 1831), and Jacob's *La cryptographie* (1858).[112] Then we have the *Encyclopedia Britannica* (1878), Edward Samuel Farrow's *Farrow's Military Encyclopedia* (1885), Martin's article 'Scytale' (1877), Ball's *Mathematical Recreations and Essays* (1892), William Shepard Walsh' article 'Secret Correspondence' (1891), and his work *Handy-book of Literary Curiosities* (1892), Kluüber's 1809 work

Kryptographik Lehrbuch der geheimschreibekunst, in Delastelle's *Traité élémentaire de cryptographie* (1902) and finally Lillian de la Torre's 1946 short story *The Stolen Christmas Box*.[113] In fact, only a handful of authors who discuss the *scytale* in the (early) modern period do not believe that every letter became partial and broken. Edouard Charton believes that most (but certainly not all) letters became partial and broken (*De la Cryptographie*; 1837), while Franz Xavier von Moshamm interestingly argues that one ended up with separate words (*Europäisches Gesandschaftsrecht*, 1805).[114] Cario and Langie in turn suggest one ended up with separate letters (*De la Cryptographie*, 1917; *Cryptographie*, 1919; *Cryptography*, 1922).[115] Finally, there are two questionable sources on the matter. Edgar Allan Poe, in his 1841 essay *A Few Words on Secret Writing* only mentions that the text became unintelligible when the strip was unwrapped from the *scytale* without mentioning partial and broken letters.[116] In the *Dictionnaire étymologique* (1803) it is not mentioned that the letters were broken when the strip was unwrapped from the *scytale*, instead it is only stated that the lines and words would return to their original position when rewrapping the strip around another *scytale*.[117] Whether the authors of the French dictionary and Poe followed the idea of partial and broken letters is, therefore, unclear. When we return to our original sources, we see that neither Plutarch, nor Gellius mentions anything about one ending up with separate words, let alone separate letters, as various scholars discussed in this passage suggest. Also, Gellius mentions that the unrolling of the strip from the stick made the letters imperfect and broken. However, he does not specifically state that every letter became imperfect during the unwrapping (*Attic Nights*, 17.9.12–13). In fact, Plutarch mentions that the complete *scytale* was covered in writing material, and that one had to use as much of the strip as possible (*Life of Lysander*, 19.6). In this way, some letters would have been written on a complete piece of strip, and, therefore, stay intact when the strip was unwrapped from the *scytale*. Other letters would have been written on the edges of the strip. These letters would become partial and broken with the unrolling of the strip. However, it seems incorrect to state that every letter definitely became partial and broken with this unrolling of the strip, as the various scholars state.

A final crucial point must be made here. All the authors mentioned in this section – from the twelfth to the nineteenth century CE – are certain that *scytalae* were used for secret messaging by the Spartans in the fifth and fourth centuries BCE. De Guilletiere even states that the Spartans invented cryptography.[118] And John Falconer adds that the Spartan *scytale* was the earliest method for secret communication known, and that the method was commonly used throughout the Greek world.[119] However, as we have established in chapter two, earlier examples of secret messaging can be found in the works of Homer (eighth/seventh century BCE), and Herodotus (fifth century BCE), and in sources from Egypt and the Near East. Moreover, it must once more be stated there is no clear evidence for the use of *scytalae* by the Spartans in the fifth and fourth centuries BCE, let alone throughout the Greek world. Plutarch and Gellius only provide us with the earliest theoretical transposition cipher in history (Aulus Gellius, *Attic Nights*, 17.9.6–16; Plutarch, *Life of Lysander*, 19.5–6). This view of the *scytale* certainly being used as a cryptography changed from about 1750, when several scholars changed to the complete opposite view: *scytalae* have never been used as devices for secret communication and could not have been used for this purpose either, since the method was far too simple.

The first argument against the *scytale* being used as a Spartan cryptograph, comes from Toustain and Tassin's 1750 work *Nouveau traité de diplomatique*, in which the two scholars describe the *scytale* not as a cryptographic device (to encrypt messages) but as a steganographic device instead (to hide messages).[120] In steganography a complete message is hidden in or under another message or object, while in cryptography the letters of the message itself are encrypted or encoded in some fashion. Toustain and Tassin appear to assume that the widespread use of the *scytale* as a 'dispatch stick' allowed for hidden messages to be sent, either within the *scytale* rod or beneath the *scytale* message (the term *scytale* referring, as Plutarch explains, to both carrier and text in this context: Plutarch, *Life of Lysander*, 19.5–7).[121] Yet, the *scytale* appears to have offered the ancient Spartans opportunities for both steganographic (hidden) and cryptographic (encoded) secret messaging, even if only theoretically. As this study demonstrates, in ancient Greece, messenger sticks (*scytalae*) were used for authentication purposes.[122] Theoretically, a messenger could have wrapped a secret letter around a *scytale* and, in that way, could have hidden the message in plain sight, a classic steganographic method. This idea is made clear in the work of the seventeenth-century scholars Panciroli and Forelius (quoting Panciroli), who argue that both the writing and the sending were completely secret, since the message was invisible.[123] The cryptographic element comes into play when the strip of writing material was unwrapped from the *scytale* and all the letters in the message changed position, and some letters would not even have remained intact if text was written over the edges of the strip, as Plutarch suggests (Plutarch, *Life of Lysander*, 19.7; Aulus Gellius, *Attic Nights*, 17.9.12–13). What is more, although some ancient writers do discuss the *scytale* in the wider context of secret messaging, there is no evidence to suggest that the *scytale* was used primarily or solely for steganographic (that is, hidden) messages as Toustain and

Tassin presume (e.g. Aristophanes, *Birds*, 1280–1285; *Lysistrata*, 985–992; Athenaeus of Naucratis, *The Learned Banqueters*, 10.451d; Diodorus Siculus, *Library of History*, 8.27; 13.106.8–9).

Following the ancient view of the *scytale* being used for several purposes, we see a second argument against the *scytalae* being used as a cryptographic device. This is the idea that the use of *scytalae* for secret messaging by the Spartans was far too simple, and that secret *scytale* messaging could easily have been deciphered by the enemy. We already saw this view in the sixteenth-century work of Julius Caesar Scaliger (*Exercitationes*, 327). Scaliger argues that one could simply try to put the edges of the strip together to find a few letters, and perhaps words. And if one had found these letters, one could easily have deciphered the *scytale* message. A number of eighteenth-, nineteenth- and early twentieth-century sources follow Scaliger on this point.[124] Finally, in the early twentieth century we see the idea of the *scytale* being a far too simple method to be any practical use in Étienne Bazeries' *Les Chiffres Secrets Dévoilés* (1901).

Even though all the authors discussed here believe that the method of wrapping and unwrapping a strip of writing material around a *scytale* was far too simple for practical use, they still believe that *scytalae* were used by the Spartans for secret messaging. Interestingly, only one early twentieth-century scholar disagrees with the idea of the wrapping around the *scytale* method being far too simple. Süß, in his 1922 article *Über Antike Geheimschriftenmethoden und ihr Nachleben*, instead argues that ancient systems for communication security – like the *scytale* – would have been far more advanced than the sources make us believe, and therefore they would have worked well and were not too simple for the time in which they were used.[125] The fact that only one scholar believes that the use of *scytalae* was not too simple shows the predominant view in scholarship.

A group of scholars who similarly challenge the idea of the *scytale* being used in Antiquity as a Spartan cryptograph, emerges in the last third of the twentieth century, starting with Anderson (1970), and followed by (among others) Kelly (1985, 1998), Sheldon (1987, 2003) and West (1988). Yet, these scholars go a step further: they believe that *scytalae* were never used for secret messaging because of a lack of clear evidence. These modern scholars are correct in arguing that there is no straightforward evidence that *scytalae* were used for secret messaging by the Spartans in the fifth and fourth centuries BCE. However, there are flaws in the arguments these scholars use. Also, erroneously, none of these scholars see the *scytale* as the earliest theoretical transposition cipher in history, nor do they acknowledge the impact the system that Plutarch tells us has about had on later transposition ciphers (see chapter six).

The twentieth-century scholars present three core arguments to substantiate their theory that *scytalae* were never used as devices for secret communication. The first and most important argument comes from Kelly and West, who both stress that the principal meaning of the word σκυτάλη (*scytale*) in ancient Greek is simply 'stick' or 'staff', and that such terminology is, in their view, incompatible with the *scytale* serving as a cryptographic device.[126] According to Kelly – who focuses on the principle meaning of the word being 'stick': '... it is ironic that writers should ever have thought that the Spartans sent secret or coded messages in the past. Throughout the long centuries of their history the Spartans were viewed by other Greeks as a conservative, tradition-bound people deeply interested in military matters, but not [...] in learning and culture.'[127] However, the fact that other Greeks saw the Spartans as conservative does not necessarily mean that the Spartans would never have used secret communication. On the contrary, Greeks in the fifth and fourth centuries BCE – especially the Athenians – saw the Spartans as a hostile 'other' people exhibiting strange practices. These included the use of secret communication, much like (the Athenians imagined) the Near Eastern states which had historically threatened and repeatedly tried to invade Greece (see chapter two).

After Kelly, West points out that: '... a cryptographic interpretation of [the] σκυτάλη has come to look increasingly implausible with a more widespread appreciation of the fact that in [Archilochus'] days a written message was in itself a relative novelty; [...] it is clear that Archilochus lived in a society still essentially oral.[128]

It is correct to suggest that the seventh-century BCE Greek poet Archilochus of Paros still lived in an essentially oral society, as was the case for Homer (eighth/seventh century BCE) and Herodotus (fifth century BCE; see chapter two). However, this again does not necessarily show that the Spartans could never have used the *scytale* for secret communication in the fifth and fourth centuries BCE. Sheldon argues – without references or further explanation – that: 'While [the *scytale*] may be [the first transpositional cryptograph], it cannot be dated to the Classical period and is almost certainly not Spartan. There is even serious doubt that it was a method of cryptography.'[129] In another source, she even argues that the description of the device from Plutarch and Aulus Gellius can only be seen as: '... the once standard, but now possibly defunct, definition of the Spartan *scytale*.'[130] Interestingly, Sheldon contradicts herself by stating in a later publication that the *scytale* never even existed. Instead, Sheldon argues, the *scytale* as a Spartan device for secret messaging was an idea made up by Apollonius of Rhodes (who referred to Archilochus' earlier work) who tried to define an unknown term he had stumbled across in a manuscript.[131] However, as we have seen in the examples in this chapter, the word '*scytale*' exists in ancient Greek, and has a number of meanings. The idea of the Greek word for *scytale* simply referring to a 'stick' and the understanding that its function, therefore, must be equally simplistic and primitive, is also widespread in the secondary scholarship on this topic. The notion that its description in ancient Greek as a 'stick' is incompatible with the *scytale* serving as a cryptographic device is reiterated by Strasser, who claims that Roman authors had promoted the erroneous assumption that '... such a "stick" or "rod" was used by the warlike Spartans.'[132] We also find this view expressed more recently by Coles and Landrum, who stress the basic simplicity of the *scytale*, which they describe as a rod around which a piece of leather was wrapped.[133] Indeed, the predominant view of the *scytale* as merely a 'toy cipher' in modern histories of cryptography may owe something to popular studies of secret codes, including those aimed at children.[134] D'Agapeyeff states that, to modern eyes, the *scytale* does not appear to be a secret method, but at a time when writing was still rather new, it must have been secure enough.[135] Significantly, D'Agapeyeff does not see the *scytale* as a complex cipher.[136] However, deciphering a *scytale* message was not as simple as D'Agapeyeff seems to presume. When we take another look at Plutarch's and Aulus Gellius' descriptions, on receiving a *scytale* message, one would have received a strip with some complete, but also partial and broken letters, and would not have been able to understand the intended messages properly without using a *scytale* of the exact same size and diameter themselves (Aulus Gellius, *Attic Nights*, 17.9.12–13). D'Agapeyeff similarly suggests that a *scytale* device entailed nothing more than a message wrapped around a cylinder made of wood. In keeping with the intended readership of his work, perhaps, he even suggests the use of pencils or cardboard tubes as toy *scytalae* that children can use to send each other secret messages for fun, clearly representing the *scytale* as a 'toy' and as a rudimentary device that would not have been used in the context of any kind of serious communication security.[137] Sheldon in turn, in her 1986 article 'Tradecraft in Ancient Greece', also stresses the simplicity of ancient Greek cryptographic devices and messages, like the Spartan *scytale*, arguing that they: '... would hardly deceive a modern military censor, but could well have fooled a simple-minded gatekeeper or a barbarian [...] in an age when reading and writing were uncommon.'[138]

Walker (2008) follows a similar line, and argues that in many ancient societies the use of encryption of the kind that the *scytale* could offer would have been unnecessary since the majority of people would have been illiterate anyway.[139] Mollin adds that in our modern world the primary goal of cryptography is to secure confidential information, while this was simply not the case in Antiquity. Instead, he argues, cryptography in Antiquity was only used to increase the level of mysticism in religious practices (see chapter two).[140] While this theory is persuasive in the case of cryptographic coding described in the contexts of ancient Egypt and Mesopotamia, it is not the case for the Spartan *scytale*.

The idea of the *scytale* system as being far from sophisticated and its use for official correspondence being impractical and unnecessary, can also, more recently, be found in Smart's 2018 study on modern cryptography, in which Smart illustrates this enduring notion of the *scytale* as an example of simple 'toy' cryptography, by explicitly excluding these and other ancient cryptographic devices from his history, arguing that these historical ciphers are nothing more than 'toy examples' that have no place in serious modern studies of the evolving history of cryptography.[141] This prevalent and enduring idea of the *scytale* as merely a 'toy cipher', I argue, is misleading and appears to prompt too many historians of cryptography to assume that the *scytale* method (whether or not it has historically been used) would have been far too simplistic to have been useful as a means of secret communication in real world military and tactical operations.

Although Kelly and West are broadly correct in stating that the principal meaning of the word *scytale* in classical Greek is 'stick' or 'staff', the Greek word actually has a wide range of meanings. It means 'stick' or 'staff', 'finger-bone' and 'serpent', and is also used in ancient sources to refer to Spartan identity tags, cash receipts and – in Aristophanes – as a euphemism for a phallus.[142] Kelly, West, Strasser et al., therefore, focus upon a narrow range of the available definitions. What is more, in themselves, the definitions of the *scytale* that these critics do accept ('stick' or 'staff') again do not necessarily mean that *scytalae* could never have been used as devices for secret communication or any other purpose. On the contrary, the method for using the *scytale* as a device for encrypted messaging as described by Plutarch and Aulus Gellius, is so detailed and obviously useful, that it is theoretically plausible that *scytalae* could have been used for this purpose in contexts where secrecy of communication was important (Plutarch, *Life of Lysander*, 19.7; Aulus Gellius, *Attic Nights*, 17.9.12–13). This is not to say that *scytalae* were always or only used for the purpose of secret, encrypted communication. The extant evidence certainly does not support this theory. *Scytalae* were clearly used for many different purposes, including the sending of diverse types of messages. Yet, when necessary, Plutarch and Gellius suggest that the *scytale* also offered its users an ingenious means of encryption.

Anderson, in the 1970 study *Military Theory and Practice in the Age of Xenophon*, and Debidour in the 2019 article 'Le secret de l'information et la cryptographie dans le monde gréco-romain' also argue that *scytalae* were never used as devices for secret communication, but instead as official messenger's equipment, as a sort of authentication device. This is the second argument put forward by historians of cryptography who do not see the *scytale* as a cryptographic device.[143] Although there is plenty of support for this type of usage as authentication in the extant evidence, it was not the sole purpose of the *scytale* and its only use in Antiquity. Hiding an encrypted message in plain sight and conveying it through hostile territories using the vehicle of an official piece of equipment or authentication device is entirely plausible, and there is nothing in Anderson's theory to preclude the use of the *scytale* for secret communication as part of its 'officially' recognised purpose. Indeed, such an officially sanctioned use would support and enhance the opportunities for secret messaging, enabling the *scytale* messenger and message to access protected areas. Anderson's theory was later adopted by West who adds to this argument that *scytalae* could also have been used by messengers as mnemonic aids. In West's theory slight incisions would have been made into the *scytalae*, which all had a different meaning to help a messenger to remember the message that he was supposed to deliver.[144] In support of her hypothesis, West points out that notched sticks used as mnemonic aids for conveying messages are attested all over the world. The sticks would be incised in the presence of the messenger, to whom the meaning of each notch was verbally emphasised.[145] In fact, the use of mnemonic tools to store and remember information dates to prehistory.[146] However, there is no evidence that this particular mnemonic technique was actually adopted anywhere in ancient Greece, and none of the extant sources discuss the *scytale* in this context.

West further points out that when the word *scytale* was first attested in the Greek world by Archilochus of Paros in the seventh century BCE, this world was still essentially oral and a written message was a novelty.[147] Although this is a valid – indeed, important – observation, reminding us that literacy and written communications in the ancient world are complex issues, we should not take a single reference to the *scytale* in a fragmentary archaic Greek source and extend the speculative definition of that reference to discussions of *scytalae* in ancient sources from later centuries.[148] We should acknowledge that ancient forms of cryptography will have gone through various stages of evolution and although it is quite possible – even plausible – that *scytalae* were once used both for authentication purposes and as mnemonic aids, this does not mean they were only ever used for such purposes, and again that they were never used as devices for secret communication. One of the central problems with the various theories proposed by Toustain and Tassin, Anderson, West, et. al., then, is that they attempt to limit the use of the *scytale* to a specific activity or function. Sheldon, for example, argues that a *scytale* could either have been used for authentication – as Anderson also suggests – or as a tool for secret communication, but not both, and she does not admit its use as a mnemonic aid.[149] Such arguments also tend to assume that the official purpose of the *scytale* was fixed and immutable, and that it could not be 'hacked' or put to use serving purposes other than those befitting its officially sanctioned role. These arguments also assume that such official uses were constant over time; that the use of the *scytale* in the seventh century BCE, for example, would have continued in the same way into the fifth century BCE and beyond. Yet, again, there was not one sole purpose for the *scytale*, or one primary use in Antiquity. A stick or staff can, and could, have been used for a variety of different purposes, including authentication, mnemonic aid and as a device for secret communication, even though the latter purpose is solely theoretical.

Alongside the first two objections to the use of the *scytale* as a cryptograph raised by modern historians of cryptography – the fact that it was simply a stick, and that it could only have been used as messenger authentication and/or as mnemonic aid – a third core objection to the use of the *scytale* as a cryptographic device concerns its absence from a major work on ancient secret communication. West points out that the fourth-century BCE Greek military strategist Aeneas Tacticus does not discuss the *scytale* in chapter 31 of his work *How to Survive Under Siege* which is dedicated to secret communication.[150] This point was later adopted by Whitehead, and by Strasser in support of their corresponding views that the *scytale* was not used by the Spartans as a device for cryptographic communication. We might expect Aeneas Tacticus to have mentioned the *scytale* if it were a device with which he was familiar, is what these scholars argue.[151] It is obviously possible that the *scytale* as a cryptograph was not known to Aeneas in the fifth century BCE, since it was invented by Plutarch about 700 years later. However, it goes too far to state that the *scytale* was never used for secret messaging, only because Aeneas Tacticus never discussed it. There are a number of other possible reasons that explain the absence of the *scytale* from his work, the most important one being that Aeneas seems to have had a much greater interest in hidden messages (steganography) than in encrypted messages (cryptography; see chapter four).

As part of the downplaying of the Spartan *scytale* as an effective cryptographic device useful in secret military communications, modern cryptographers instead typically posit the Roman Caesar cipher (see chapter five) as being a (and sometimes *the*) crucial conceptual milestone in the development of ancient and modern cryptography.[152] Indeed, as opposed to the Spartan *scytale*, modern cryptographers have acknowledged the Caesar cipher as a working and useful system in ancient cryptography, albeit a simple one. Modern historians of cryptography often (erroneously) present Caesar's professional use of the cipher as a historical fact, in marked contrast to their dismissive view of the Spartan *scytale* as little more than a toy.[153] However, as there is no clear evidence for the *scytale* being used in the way Plutarch and Aulus Gellius describe it, there is no clear evidence for the use of the Caesar cipher either, as will be discussed in chapter five.

Yet, there is perhaps the magic of Caesar's name to consider in explaining this discrepancy in the treatment of Spartan versus Roman encryption techniques. As a famous Roman general, Caesar is better known (including by historians of cryptography) than the Spartans and Greek *scytalae* are. This potentially explains why historians of cryptography seem to take a greater and more serious interest in the Caesar cipher than in the *scytale*. However, the Spartan *scytale* offers an example of ancient cryptography that is earlier and at least as sophisticated as the Caesar cipher, whether or not one of both methods were in fact used (see chapter five). We cannot go further than arguing that the use of the *scytale* method in fifth-century BCE Greece is theoretically plausible. However, the ingenuity and importance of the transposition system of the *scytale* cannot and should not be overlooked here, whether it was used by the Spartans in the fifth and fourth century BCE, or invented by Plutarch in the second century CE. In fact, some modern cryptographers see the *scytale* as a forerunner of modern transposition ciphers, as we shall see in chapter six.[154]

4

Cryptography and Steganography in Aeneas Tacticus' *How to Survive Under Siege*

As already mentioned in chapter three, the fourth-century BCE Greek military author Aeneas Tacticus never discussed the Spartan *scytale* in his influential writings on secret communication techniques in Antiquity. Modern historians of cryptography argue that the *scytale* cannot, therefore, have been used as a cryptographic device in the ancient Greek world since Aeneas Tacticus did not discuss it in his otherwise broadly comprehensive survey of classical stratagems and devices for secret communication.[1] Whitehead, in his translation of Aeneas Tacticus' work argues that the omission of the well-known Spartan *scytale* is no surprise, since it was not a cryptograph.[2] And Sheldon and West argue that Aeneas did not discuss it in his work because he was personally unfamiliar with the device.[3] In chapter three we have seen that there is no evidence for the use of *scytalae* as devices for secret communication by the Spartans in the fifth and fourth centuries BCE. Even though these scholars may be correct in stating that the *scytale* was not a cryptograph, because of the lack of evidence, it goes too far to state that *scytalae* were never used for secret communication only because Aeneas Tacticus never discussed the device. In fact, in chapter three we have also seen that the *scytale* system, as discussed by Plutarch and Aulus Gellius, is the earliest known theorical transposition cipher in history.

In this chapter it will be shown that there are a number of other reasons why Aeneas Tacticus did not discuss the *scytale*, even if the device was known to him. The chapter is divided into two parts. First, we will analyse the possible reasons why Aeneas Tacticus never discussed the *scytale* by analysing his work as a whole. Secondly, by analysing the methods for secret communication that Aeneas discusses instead of the *scytale*, we will see that the *scytale*, used for long-distance communication between Sparta and generals in the field, was not relevant for Aeneas' work, which focused on short-distance siege warfare. Rather, Aeneas chose to discuss those stratagems and devices for secret communication most suited to this military context.

Aeneas Tacticus' *How to Survive Under Siege*

Little is known about the life (and therefore of the direct military, cryptographic or steganographic experiences) of Aeneas Tacticus. Aeneas Tacticus, or Aineias the Tactician, wrote a treatise on tactics known as *How to Survive Under Siege* or *On the Defence of Fortified Positions* around 360–355 BCE.[4] A date around 360–355 BCE makes Aeneas Tacticus' work not only the oldest known military manual in history but also the oldest known work on cryptography and steganography.[5] Chapter thirty-one of the work is specifically dedicated to recommendations regarding the use of cryptographic and steganographic devices and methods during sieges, and it is here that historians of cryptography insist that we would expect to find a discussion of the *scytale* had its use as a cryptographic device been known to Aeneas Tacticus.[6] In the course of chapter thirty-one of his work, the author discusses twenty-one different methods for secret communication, offering us a detailed catalogue of methods for ancient communication security. Next to this, we know from Polybius, that in a now lost work Aeneas also discussed the use of fire signalling for secret communication (*Histories*, 10.44–46). The absence of the *scytale* from Aeneas' work is straightforwardly explained by West, Kelly and Whitehead on the grounds that it was not a cryptographic device known to Aeneas Tacticus, and therefore, not a cryptographic device at all.[7] Given Aeneas Tacticus' (presumed) extensive military experience, these scholars extrapolate from this that the *scytale* was, therefore, not a cryptographic device that was used in Greece in this period. Since there is no evidence that *scytalae* were used by the Spartans for secret messaging in the fifth and fourth centuries BCE, this may be correct. However, if the *scytale* were used by the Spartans in the way Plutarch and Gellius describe, there are other reasons that might explain the absence of a discussion of the *scytale* in Aeneas Tacticus' work, a point that has not been picked up by scholars previously.

First, it is possible (though perhaps not probable) that Aeneas simply did not know of the *scytale*'s potential or actual use by the Spartans as a cryptographic device at the time of writing *How to Survive Under Siege* as cryptographers suggest.[8] This period also matches with the timeframe in which Plutarch later maintains that key Spartan figures, including Lysander and Agesilaus, received coded messages by *scytale* (*Life of Lysander*, 20.1-6; *Life of Agesilaus*, 10.5; 15.4-6). Aeneas Tacticus wrote his work *How to Survive Under Siege* in the mid-fourth century BCE. So, it is just possible that the military use of the *scytale* for secret communication by the Spartans in the early fourth century BCE was not yet known by other Greeks, since the Spartans would obviously not have wanted the secret of the *scytale* to be written about at the time when the device was in actual use for secret communication.⁹ Secondly, it seems that Aeneas Tacticus did not have much knowledge of Sparta. From the textual evidence supplied by *How to Survive Under Siege*, it appears that Aeneas Tacticus' military experience is confined to the geographical limits of parts of the Peloponnese and the western coast of Asia Minor (10, 11). Aeneas Tacticus never mentions Sparta or a Spartan in his work.¹⁰ Yet, thirdly, we should consider another point of view too in this case. Aeneas Tacticus – living and writing in the middle of the fourth century BCE (that is, after the Peloponnesian War) may well have seen Spartan devices like the *scytale* as thus unworthy of inclusion in his treatise. He might, therefore, have excluded such a device from his list of techniques for Greeks to survive during sieges even if he had been familiar with such stratagems.

Fourthly, Aeneas may have discussed the *scytale* as a cryptographic device in a now lost work. Only his work *How to Survive Under Siege* has been preserved completely. Yet, there are indications that Aeneas wrote other works too. From Polybius, for example, we know that Aeneas discussed a method for fire signalling in another work (Polybius, *Histories*, 10.44). Indeed, he may have discussed this method and/or the Spartan *scytale* in one of at least four other works on military strategy that are now lost.¹¹ The fifth reason Aeneas may have had for not discussing the *scytale* is a very practical one. According to Plutarch, the *scytale* would have been used by the Spartans for long-distance communication and field warfare, while Aeneas Tacticus instead focuses on surviving a siege in the closed quarters of a besieged town in his own work *How to Survive Under Siege*. In his work he shows the inhabitants of a *polis* whose city and homeland were endangered – especially those inhabitants who oversaw maintaining the *polis*' security – that there was the constant danger of treachery from *within* the city itself during sieges. The focus in *How to Survive Under Siege* is upon hiding messages to smuggle them in and out of the besieged *polis* and not upon encoding them to prevent them from being read and understood by hostile agents (either within or without the city walls). Indeed, this is a recurring theme throughout Aeneas Tacticus' whole work, in which he made clear that establishing secure and mutually comprehensible means of secret communication were of vital importance. The *polis*' inhabitants had to secure all forms of communication that went in and out of the city (*How to Survive Under Siege*, 4.1–4, 5.1, 9.2, 10.6, 10.11, 10.18–19, 10.25–26, 11.3–6, 12, 18.3–6, 18.8–11 (see also Polyaenus, *Stratagems of War*, 2.36), 18.13–21, 20, 22.5, 22.7, 23.7–11, 29.3–10).¹² Given the significant risk of citizens within the *polis* conspiring and communicating with the enemy, it was vital for the commanding forces to be able to communicate between themselves secretly and securely in Aeneas Tacticus' view. All methods for secret communication that Aeneas Tacticus discussed in chapter thirty-one of the work are therefore related to this theme of internal treachery, and to his idea of an enemy who is always nearby. As the sources discussed in chapter three demonstrate, if *scytalae* were used, they would typically have been used for long-distance communication rather than for the sort of local communications that concerned Aeneas Tacticus. He therefore might well have known about the use of the *scytale* for long-distance communication, but he would not have seen it as a fit subject for his own work, with its particular focus on local communication in a time of siege.

A final reason – and in fact the most important reason – for excluding the Spartan *scytale* from the treatise may have been that Aeneas Tacticus was simply more interested in steganographic practices than cryptographic ones. Out of twenty-one methods for secret communication we can only see two examples of cryptography (31.30–31, 31.31). This fits in perfectly with the aim of Aeneas Tacticus' chapter thirty-one which is to teach inhabitants of a *polis* how to hide messages from enemies that were always nearby. Coded yet unhidden messages would obviously have attracted too much attention in such situations, hereby making steganographic methods of communication preferable over those that were purely cryptographic.

In chapter thirty-one of *How to Survive Under Siege*, Aeneas discusses twenty-one[13] different methods for secret communication that can be divided into fifteen examples of steganography, 31.4–5 (3x), (31.6, 31.7, 31.8, 31.9–9b, 31.10–13, 31.14, 31.15, 31.15–16, 31.23, 31.25–27, 31.28–29, 31.31–32), two examples of cryptography (31.30–31, 31.31), and a further four examples that are a combination of cryptography and steganography (31.1–3, 31.16–22).[14] Of the examples he offers of cryptographic devices and of crypto-steganographic combinations, there are three examples of transposition ciphers (31.16–19, 31.20, 31.21–22), and three examples of substitution ciphers (31.10–13, 31.30, 31.31). As Whitehead points out, this makes the collection the fullest accumulation of cryptographic and steganographic devices known from Antiquity. So, it is certainly striking that the *scytale* is not included within this catalogue, especially since secret communication was clearly a subject of enormous fascination for Aeneas Tacticus.[15] Other scholars argue that there was no clear categorisation in the methods for secret communication discussed in his work; the author simply discussed a sample range of methods covering,[16] as Liddel argues: 'a variety of (a) means of physical transference of written objects,

(b) means of concealment and (c) of the materials used for writing.'[17] However, as my own classification above makes clear, Aeneas Tacticus is clearly far more knowledgeable about and interested in steganographic devices for hidden secret communication than in encrypted messaging (i.e. cryptography). That is, his main focus in *How to Survive Under Siege* is upon hiding messages so as to smuggle them in and out of the besieged *polis* because of a constant danger of treachery from within a city during sieges, and not upon encoding messages so as to prevent them from being read and understood by hostile agents (either within or without the city walls), a point that previous scholars have not picked up upon before.[18]

Various methods of secret communication discussed in the work seem to have been Aeneas Tacticus' own inventions, especially the use of *astragali* (knucklebones) and its variations (31.16–22), while other methods have clearly been based on reports and descriptions found in historical sources. These sources included Herodotus' *Histories*, as well as other unspecified oral and/or written sources.[19] Yet, when Aeneas Tacticus used one of these secondary sources he then nuanced the method for secret communication discussed in the source with his own ideas, presumably since he believed that his own alternatives based on his own first-hand tried and tested experiences, perhaps were improvements upon the original method.[20] Again, we can only speculate, but it may be that Aeneas Tacticus omits the *scytale* from his list because he has no direct experience of using it in military practice in the field. Indeed, in this context, is makes perfect sense that Aeneas Tacticus did not devote any specific attention to the Spartan *scytale* in his treatise.

Aeneas Tacticus' methods for cryptography and steganography

A careful cataloguing of the several types of secret communication that Aeneas Tacticus discusses in his treatise indicates that he was most familiar with simple steganographic devices for secret communication, and preferred these over encrypted messaging for siege contexts. In chapter 31.14 of *How to Survive Under Siege*, he discusses a straightforward strategy of secret communication involving the concealment of writing under the wax of a wax tablet. According to Aeneas, a non-encrypted secret message would be written on the base of a tablet and then wax was poured over it, and a second, open message would be written on the top film of wax. When this tablet was delivered, the recipient – who knew or anticipated that a message was written under the wax – would scrape off the wax to read the message hidden underneath and send any reply in the same way (31.14). This example is clearly based upon the story of Demaratus' message to the Spartans derived from Herodotus' *Histories* (7.239; see also Aulus Gellius, *Attic Nights*, 17.9.6; Julius Africanus, *Kestoi*, 53; Justin, *Epitome of the Philippic History of Pompeius Trogus*, 2.10.13; Polyaenus, *Stratagems of War*, 2.20).[21] However, Aeneas did not simply follow Herodotus' earlier account verbatim. After discussing how the person in his example (probably Demaratus[22]) sent a secret message to the Spartans following the details of his Herodotean source closely, Aeneas Tacticus suggests that a message was sent back in the same way (31.14), as if this were a useful practical way of secret communication that had taken place between two parties.

He then adds two other possibilities, as if to show that he could improve on his sources by supplementing them with ideas of his own. First, we see the possibility of writing a message on the base of a boxwood tablet, and then whitewash the tablet and paint a picture over it to render the writing invisible. To make the writing visible again a recipient had to place the tablet in water to dissolve the paint (31.14–15). His second alternative suggestion is to use a hero's plaque (an image of a hero usually left in a shrine) for the same purpose (31.15–16). Clearly, Aeneas considered that his alternatives would have worked more effectively as practical steganographic devices than the original method described by Herodotus (whether or not Herodotus' story is in fact true). It is plausible that Aeneas Tacticus (quite sensibly) believed that a seemingly empty tablet in transit would have attracted too much suspicion if it fell into the wrong hands. Aeneas based another example of secret steganographic communication on Herodotus. In 31.28–29, Aeneas discusses the Herodotean story of Histiaeus' message to Aristagoras tattooed on a slave's head. This example from Herodotus again fits in well with the broader theme of Aeneas Tacticus' work on sieges, since here we are dealing once again with a hidden message being smuggled out of a besieged city (Herodotus, *Histories*, 5.35.2–4; see also Aulus Gellius, *Attic Nights*, 17.9.18–27; Polyaenus, *Stratagems of War*, 1.24). Indeed, this case is included as an example of the importance of the use of trustworthy messengers for secret communications during a siege, which is a recurring theme in Aeneas' work (*How to Survive Under Siege*, 9.2, 10.6, 10.11, 10.25–26, 22.5, 22.7, 31). Unlike his reworking of the Demaratus story reported by Herodotus, however, here Aeneas Tacticus includes the names (Histiaeus; Aristagoras) and places (Miletus) that Herodotus had supplied in his version, thereby lending credibility and authority to his own account.

Aeneas also discusses seven further examples of steganographic messages that could be sent hidden in or under clothing, footwear, armour, jewellery and even in a dog collar. Four examples are based on Aeneas' sources (31.6, 31.23, 31.25–27, 31.31–32), while three examples were his own suggestions (31.4–5, 31.7, 31.9). Amongst his simple suggestions are to hide a message under a breastplate (31.8), or to sew a letter into a bridle-rein (31.9–9b). One could also hide a letter in between layers of clothing (31.23; see also Julius Africanus, *Kestoi*, 53; Philo of Byzantium, *Compendium of Mechanics*, D.78 (102.37–39)). Aeneas then discusses how a message was once sent bound to a wound on a man's leg (31.6), and how in Epirus and Thessaly it was the custom to take a dog away from his home, hide a secret message in its collar, and then send it back home (31.31–32; see also Julius Africanus, *Kestoi*, 53).[23]

A slightly more complicated method compared to these is found in 31.7, where Aeneas Tacticus suggests writing messages on pieces of lead that could be rolled up and worn as women's earrings (31.7). Significantly, the lead being rolled up made it possible to send a closed and sealed message hidden in plain sight. This makes the method a noticeably clear example of Aeneas Tacticus' interest in hiding messages rather than encrypting them. Another slightly more complicated method can be found in 31.4–5. Here, Aeneas discusses the sending of secret messages by using a messenger without the messenger knowing about it (see also Julius Africanus, *Kestoi*, 51; Philo of Byzantium, *Compendium of Mechanics*, D. 81 (102. 45–50) in: Thévenot, Boivin, et al. 1693, *Veterum Mathematicorum Opera*, 102). Before sending out the messenger the sender had to insert a secret letter into the messenger's sandals.[24] He would then send the messenger to the recipient with a non-secret letter to provide a cover for his actual mission. The recipient could reply in the same way if requested.[25] These seven examples show Aeneas' interest in steganographic messages that were hidden in simple ways almost in plain sight by using commonly known household objects.

In chapter 31.10–13 Aeneas Tacticus discusses some no less simplistic, though rather more laborious, ways of sending secret messages by using an oil-flask and a bladder (31.10–13). So, according to him, one could inflate a bladder and write on it with ink mixed with glue. Once the writing was dry one had to deflate the bladder, press it into a flask, and inflate it again. Hereby, the glue would stick the bladder to the insides of the flask. Then one had to fill the flask (or technically the bladder lining it) with oil. In this way, the bladder would become (nearly) invisible. Upon receiving the flask, the recipient had to pour out the oil, re-inflate the bladder and read the text.[26] He could then wipe off the text with a sponge and reply in the same way (31.10–13). This particular method of steganographic communication is not only laborious but demands access to a panoply of domestic supplies. Indeed, such a method for securing the secret communication of hidden (though not encoded) messages would have been highly impractical on a battlefield (the context in which a *scytale* was used) since both parties would have needed a flask, bladders, ink, glue and oil, etc. However laborious, the method might have been useful as a means of securing a secret communication in a siege defence, and therefore offers us a salient reminder that this is the specific context of Aeneas Tacticus' work. His predominant focus in his treatise on *How to Survive Under Siege* is upon providing his readers with a catalogue of devices and stratagems suitable for secret communication under siege conditions. His priorities are upon smuggling concealed messages in and out of the *polis* or city, and he focuses upon concealment rather than encryption as the priority in securing these communications. In fact, so confident is Aeneas in the security of these various steganographic devices that he has comparatively little to say about the risks of these messages being intercepted and read by hostile agents. There are only two examples in *How to Survive Under Siege* in which Aeneas appears to take seriously such a risk and to mitigate against it by sending a hidden (steganographic) message that is also, for extra security, encrypted or encoded (a cryptographic message) in some way, as will be discussed later in this chapter (31.1–3).

One more method for steganography that Aeneas discusses is known from Polybius. Polybius tells us that Aeneas discusses a method for fire signalling (Polybius, *Histories*, 10.44). Fire signals are a specific type of steganography known as 'real semagrams'. A real semagram is an object that represents a message without using text.[27] For example, a picture of a blue sky can mean 'everything is okay' while a picture of a dark grey sky can mean 'danger'. In our case, the fire signal represents the message. Interestingly, Aeneas' method for fire signalling (discussed by Polybius) is in fact an example of long-distance communication instead of short-distance communication within and around a besieged city. So, maybe Aeneas had an interest in sending secret messages over long distances on the battlefield too. Yet, he may have decided to discuss it in another work (now lost to us), since he believed that it did not fit in with the theme of *How to Survive Under Siege*.

From accounts of Near Eastern, Greek (and later Roman) history starting in the Archaic period, for example, we know that both normal (that is, non-encrypted) and simple encoded or encrypted messages could be sent over long distances by means of fire signals, as discussed in a wide range of classical sources.[28] Thus, to take just one salient example from this extensive list, Aeschylus, in his *Agamemnon*, describes how Clytaemnestra received a message from

Agamemnon returning from Troy by means of beacon signals that were fast and efficiently sent from one station and one hilltop to the next (Aeschylus, *Agamemnon*, 281–316). As it was only possible to send one prearranged message using this archaic system of fire signalling, parties needing to communicate on urgent matters faced significant limitations, as Polybius points out (*Histories*, 10.43). Aeneas Tacticus, accordingly, invented a method for fire signalling in which water clocks and torches were used, whereby a series of messages could be sent back and forth between distant mountain tops. Aeneas' system is discussed in a now lost work on military preparations, but its basic design has been handed down to us via Polybius:

> Aeneas, [...] the writer of the treatise on tactics, wished to correct this defect, and did in fact make some improvement; but his invention still fell very far short of what was wanted, as the following passage from his treatise will show. "Let those who wish," he says, "to communicate any matter of pressing importance to each other by fire-signals prepare two earthenware vessels of exactly equal size both as to diameter and depth. Let the depth be three cubits, the diameter one. Then prepare corks of a little shorter diameter than that of the vessels: and in the middle of these corks fix rods divided into equal portions of three fingers' breadth, and let each of these portions be marked with a clearly distinguishable line: and in each let there be written one of the most obvious and universal of those events which occur in war; for instance in the first 'cavalry have entered the country', in the second 'hoplites', in the third 'light-armed', in the next 'infantry and cavalry', in another 'ships', in another 'corn', and so on, until all the portions have written on them the events which may reasonably be expected to occur in the particular war. Then carefully pierce both the vessels in such a way that the taps shall be exactly equal and carry off the same amount of water. Fill the vessels with water and lay the corks with their rods upon its surface and set both taps running together. This being done, it is evident that if there is perfect equality in every respect between them, both corks will sink exactly in proportion as the water runs away, and both rods will disappear to the same extent into the vessels. When they have been tested, and the rate of the discharge of water has been found to be exactly equal in both, then the vessels should be taken respectively to the two places from which the two parties intend to watch for fire signals. As soon as any one of those eventualities which are inscribed upon the rods takes place, raise a lighted torch, and wait until the signal is answered by a torch from the others: this being raised, both parties are to set the taps running together. When the cork and rod on the signalling side has sunk low enough to bring the ring containing the words which give the desired information on a level with the rim of the vessel, a torch is to be raised again. Those on the receiving side are

then at once to stop the tap, and to look at the words in the ring of the rod which is on a level with the rim of their vessel. This will be the same as that on the signalling side, assuming everything to be done at the same speed on both sides.

Polybius, *Histories*, 10.44

According to Polybius, Aeneas Tacticus discussed how communicating parties could send messages by using water clocks and torches. Both parties would fill large vessels of the same size with a cork at the bottom with water. Then they would take a rod graduated in sections, each clearly marked off from the next also with a cork attached to the bottom of the rod. In each section there would be written the most evident and ordinary events that occurred in war (e.g. 'Enemy approaching with ships from the west'). The rod was placed into the vessel. When the two parties wanted to send a message, they would first wave torches to attract each other's attention. Then they would pull out the corks from the vessels to let the water run out. In this way the rods would sink. When the intended message on the rod had reached the top of the vessel, the sending party would wave a torch again to let the receiving party know that they had to pull the cork back into the vessel and check the intended message. If all worked well, the receiving party could then read the message. What Polybius and (we infer from the attributions to Aeneas Tacticus here) what Aeneas also described, was a highly inventive mode of long-distance communication. Indeed, it has been described as the earliest form of telegraphy used in the world and the most sophisticated system for secret communication discussed by Polybius (see Figure 6).[29] It is suggested by the second-century CE author Polyaenus that the Carthaginians used a similar method successfully (*Stratagems of War*, 6.16). Polyaenus implies that by sending (secret) fire signals the Carthaginians were always provided in the most rapid way with what they needed in their warfare.[30] Experiments carried out by Woolliscroft in 2001 have shown the Carthaginian system to be feasible (and potentially also Aeneas Tacticus' similar system, as reconstructed by Polybius).[31] Although at first, doubts were raised as to whether the ancient Greeks and Romans would have had the engineering skills to build and use such a system, Woolliscroft showed the potential and usefulness of these ancient fire signalling systems.

However, there are two significant downsides to Aeneas Tacticus' method. First, it would have been extremely difficult to let the two water clocks run exactly parallel, as Woolliscroft argues: 'It is in fact surprisingly difficult to make water run out of two vessels at exactly the same rate and even tiny inaccuracies become more serious the longer the clock is left running.'[32] Because of this it is hard to believe that Aeneas' mechanism ever functioned well. What is more, with

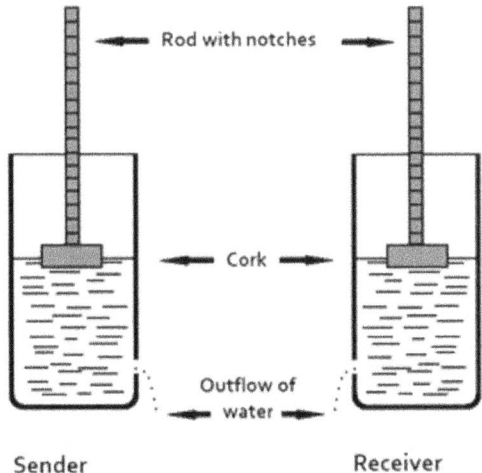

Figure 6 Reconstruction of Aeneas Tacticus' water clock as described by Polybius (Polybius, *The Histories*, 10.43). Author's illustration based on Aschoff 1984, 47–8.

this method it remains the case that only prearranged messages could be transferred between the communicating parties, something that Polybius acknowledged. He states that it would have been impossible to communicate by using Aeneas Tacticus' method if anything unexpected occurred (Polybius, *The Histories*, 10.45.1–5).

Polybius, therefore, believed Aeneas Tacticus' method to have been a slight advance over the earliest and simplest beacon signals, yet the system was still quite rudimentary, as, he argues, still only a series of prearranged messages could be sent. Therefore, Polybius decided to improve upon this method, like Aeneas improved the methods that he knew from Herodotus. Polybius developed a more sophisticated system of fire signalling that was capable of dispatching with accuracy any kind of message. Thus, Polybius describes how to take five tablets and write on these tablets all letters of the (Greek) alphabet from *alpha* to *omega*, and use two sets of five torches. The dispatcher of the message would then raise the first set of torches on the left side indicating which tablet was to be consulted (one-five). Then he would raise the second set of torches on the right to indicate what letter on the tablet the receiver should write down:

> We take the alphabet and divide it into five parts, each consisting of five letters. There is one letter less in the last division, but this makes no practical difference. Each of the two parties who are about to signal to each other must now get ready five tablets and write one division of the alphabet on each tablet, and then come to an agreement that the man who is going to signal is in the first place to raise

two torches and wait until the other replies by doing the same. This is for the purpose of conveying to each other that they are both at attention. These torches having been lowered the dispatcher of the message will now raise the first set of torches on the left side indicating which tablet is to be consulted, i.e. one torch if it is the first, two if it is the second, and so on. Next he will raise the second set on the right on the same principle to indicate what letter of the tablet the receiver should write down.

Polybius, The Histories, 10.45.6–12

Like Aeneas Tacticus, Polybius still uses torches, but replaces the water clocks with tablets on which the letters of the Greek alphabet were written (see Figure 7). One could then send messages letter by letter, whereby each fire signal represented one letter. Although Polybius' method was still extremely laborious, it was clearly a significant improvement over Aeneas Tacticus' method, since in Polybius' system no water clocks were involved that had to run parallel. What is more, when using Polybius' system, every possible alphabetic message could be sent between communicating parties, instead of only a series of prearranged messages. This is made possible by using Polybius' alphabetic tablets that form the basis for what is known in modern cryptography as the 'Polybius square'. Some historians of cryptography (erroneously) believe that this modern square has been invented by Polybius himself (see chapter six).[33]

Both the Spartan *scytale* and the systems for fire signalling discussed by Aeneas and Polybius could be used to send short messages over a long distance. However, when using the *scytale* (at least in theory), the Spartans could quickly send any (short) message at the moment it had to be sent. With Aeneas' method for fire signalling this was not possible, since only a series of prearranged messages could be sent. And, even though one could send any possible message with Polybius' method, it was most likely still too complicated and laborious when a message had to be sent quickly.

1	2	3	4	5
α 1	ζ 1	λ 1	π 1	φ 1
β 2	η 2	μ 2	ρ 2	χ 2
γ 3	θ 3	ν 3	σ 3	ψ 3
δ 4	ι 4	ξ 4	τ 4	ω 4
ε 5	κ 5	ο 5	υ 5	

Figure 7 Five tablets with the letters of the ancient Greek alphabet used for fire signalling, as discussed by Polybius (*The Histories*, 10.45.6–12). Author's illustration based on Savard 1998-9.

Aeneas Tacticus' only two suggestions for the use of cryptography can be found in passage 31.30–31. In this passage Aeneas Tacticus suggests that, instead of marking a slave's head (another reference to Herodotus) with easily recognisable words or letters, one could instead write by replacing vowels with dots (31.30–31), or any other letter or symbol (31.31).[34] The encoded messages created here by using this very basic form of encryption through partial substitution, would help to add an additional layer of security should the messenger/slave be intercepted by hostile agents and his head shaved to reveal the message on his scalp.[35] Aeneas Tacticus' methodology here represents the first known substitution cipher recommended for use in warfare. Yet, it is important not to overlook the fact that it is presented by Aeneas Tacticus as a secondary device, an insurance policy of sorts, to support his primary stratagem recommending a steganographic approach as the foundation to successful secret communication.

The only two examples of methods that involved a combination of cryptography and steganography can be found at the start of chapter 31 of *How to Survive Under Siege*. In passage 31.1–3, Aeneas discusses how a message could be written by marking letters in a book or document with dots and the book or document with the message then hidden in baggage. The recipient had to make a transcript of all the marked letters to understand the message (31.1–2). As an alternative, Aeneas suggests that instead of using a book or document as the vehicle for the message, one could simply write a letter and then add the markings (31.3), which obviously had to be as inconspicuous as possible by placing them far apart and making them as small as possible (31.3).[36] Clearly marked letters in a text would have attracted suspicion especially for trained people who would have been trying to uncover their enemy's secrets, especially if there were a pattern in the text, such as every third letter being marked, for example. One, therefore, had to avoid clear marking and patterns when using this technique. The combination of cryptographic and steganographic encryption here, as in the previous case, makes the method more secure. However, Aeneas Tacticus is clearly less confident in the protection offered by encryption than he is in the protection offered by concealment. Although he has recommended numerous steganographic techniques that work (so he suggests) on their own, here he once again recommends that the coded message or text is also hidden and concealed in a bag to secure its transmission. His personal preference for secure secret messaging falls clearly on the side of steganography rather than cryptography.

A possible explanation for Aeneas' comparative lack of confidence in cryptographic devices, may be traced to his account in his treatise of the use of *astragali* (also known as knucklebones or *talus* bones) to send secret messages

(31.16–22).³⁷ As becomes clear from his description, one could pierce twenty-four holes into an *astragalus* to represent the twenty-four letters of the Greek alphabet. Only knucklebones of hooved animals – like sheep or goats – were useful for this purpose since these are almost square or rectangular and, therefore, have four more or less flat sides onto which the Greek alphabet naturally fell into four neat groups of six letters.³⁸ Whenever someone wanted to communicate a message by using an *astragalus*, this person had to draw a thread through its holes. In other words, he would 'sew' a message through an *astragalus*, and this transposing of letters would compose a simple transposition cipher (31.16–19).³⁹ The unthreading obviously took place in the reverse order, since the decoding necessarily started by unthreading at the end. Consequently, all the letters of the message appeared in reverse order. Therefore, to understand the intended message properly, the recipient had to turn the letters back into their normal order. Because of its size, a message sent using an *astragalus* could not have been much longer than one or two words or a very short sentence. The message 'Enemy attacks at dawn' could, for example, have been abbreviated to 'EAAD'. Yet, the use of such a small object must have made the use of *astragali* for this form of secret communication very time consuming and very difficult in practice. One would easily end up with a ball of thread whereby it was no longer possible to find the correct holes, making the use of *astragali* rather troublesome for the sender, and even more so for the receiver, as Whitehead, and Hunter and Handford point out.⁴⁰

Therefore, it is questionable whether the method may have functioned well. It seems plausible that Aeneas found out for himself that using the *astragali* for secret communication was laborious, since he described the method not only as the most secret, but also the most difficult (or 'troublesome' as Whitehead translates it: 31.16).⁴¹ Since the method was rather complicated and very time consuming, Aeneas Tacticus accordingly suggests two simpler variations. Instead of an *astragalus* one could either use a rectangular piece of wood (31.20) or a wooden disk (31.21–22) in which one would then pierce twenty-four holes as in the bone *astragalus*. When using the disk, one had to prick holes in the centre of the disk too. Whenever a letter occurred twice in a row, one had to pull the thread through one of the holes in the centre in between the two other letters (31.22). Figure 8 shows two possible reconstructions of what this disk might have looked like. Diels' suggestion (Figure 8; left) is that the letters *alpha* to *omega* are written clockwise in their normal order at the edge of the disk. Diels incorrectly describes this as a reconstruction of an *astragalus*, yet it clearly represents Aeneas Tacticus' wooden disk.⁴² Figure 8 (right) shows Welskopf's reconstruction in which the first four letters – *alpha, beta, gamma* and *delta* – can be found at the top, bottom and left

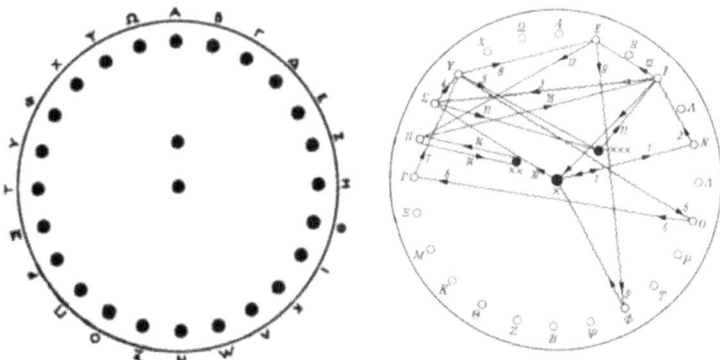

Figure 8 Reconstructions of Aeneas Tacticus' wooden disk, used instead of an *astragalus*. Author's illustration based on Diels 67 (left), and Welskopf 44 (right).

and right side of the disk as on a compass, where north, south, east and west are marked. The rest of the letters can be found right opposite each other on the disk, starting at the top with a letter on the right side, then a letter on the left side and so on.[43] Yet, it is more plausible that the letters were 'written' in alphabetical order to avoid making this already complex method yet more complex.

Aeneas mentions that the extra holes in the middle were added to prevent suspicion from being raised (31.21), though what exactly he meant by this is unclear. Translations and commentaries seem to have overlooked this point. It might be that there is an omission in the text here, but another intriguing possibility is that one could have pulled a thread through the holes in the middle in order to wear the disk as a necklace, in the same way as the lead earrings described as a steganographic device in the treatise were designed to be worn as jewellery (31.7). Indeed, this interpretation fits in well with Aeneas Tacticus' wider approach to such devices and stratagems in *How to Survive Under Siege*.

As we have seen in this chapter, Aeneas clearly places greater emphasis upon the value of *hidden* devices used for short distance communication than upon devices for *encoded* communication used over either short or long distances. And in this light, it is easy to see why the example of the *scytale* – an encoded message carried in plain sight, as Plutarch and Gellius tell us – would not fall within his list of recommendations for secret communications at a time of siege. So, even though the *scytale* is only a theoretical cipher, we can still see why Aeneas would not have discussed it. We can reasonably conclude, then, that the absence of the Spartan *scytale* from Aeneas Tacticus' treatise does not in itself offer sufficient evidence to support the theory forwarded by Whitehead, West, and Sheldon that the *scytale* was unknown to him, and therefore, was not really a form of ancient cryptography at all.[44] Instead, when we look at another body of evidence on *scytalae* we get the opposite view. According to the Romans, *scytalae* were certainly used by the Spartans for secret messaging in the way Plutarch and Aulus Gellius tell us (see chapter five).

5

Roman Views Towards the Spartan *Scytale*

It is highly likely that the Romans would have been familiar with Aeneas Tacticus' work *How to Survive Under Siege* and that this text would have served an educational purpose as a manual for army commanders.[1] Indeed, the treatise seems to have been intended as a pragmatic guide for commanders in the field.[2] Although the Romans would not have learned much about the *scytale* by studying Aeneas Tacticus, they would certainly have encountered descriptions of the *scytale* form other Greek sources, discussed in chapter three. In contrast to the Greek sources, Roman sources on the *scytale* show that they accepted that the device had been used by the Spartans for secret communication in centuries past (Cicero, *Letters to Atticus*, 10.10.3; Cornelius Nepos, *The Book on the Great Generals of Foreign Nations. Pausanias*, 4.3.4; Ausonius, *Epistles*, 28.23–27). In fact, it was Aulus Gellius, a Roman, who wrote a full description of the *scytale* as a cryptographic device in the second century CE (*Attic Nights*, 17.9.6–16). Perhaps the *scytale* system seemed far too simple for the Romans, and it is possible that they therefore never used it. Yet, we might question why the Romans do not appear to have adopted scytalae for their own military use given their familiarity with literary descriptions of the *scytale* as a sophisticated cryptographic device with particular benefits for use in military contexts. In this chapter we will analyse the reasons why the Romans never used the device for sending secret messages, as well as discuss other forms of secret communication that seemed more useful to them. The chapter is divided into two parts. First, we will analyse the topics of secrecy and letter writing in Roman society. Hereby, Roman sources on the *scytale* will be analysed as well. Secondly, we will discuss several other forms of secret communication known to the Romans, including the Caesar cipher: a method that is in fact seen as a useful cryptographic device in modern cryptography instead of the *scytale*.[3] By doing so, we will see that the Romans preferred other ways to secure their messages over the *scytale* system, very much like Aeneas Tacticus also had his reasons for not discussing the device.

Secrecy and Roman letter writing

By the end of the first century BCE, letter exchange was widely practised in elite Roman society. Indeed, participation in letter exchange was an essential element of Roman aristocratic culture.[4] With this emergence of the widespread practice of letter writing, there came, from the first century BCE onward, an understanding of, and need for, secret and veiled communication in letters, precisely because there was an awareness that letters were not always private. In fact, maintaining confidentiality and cautiousness in correspondence seems to have been expected of the correspondents.[5] This, for example, is why Ovid urged lovers to be as secretive as possible when sending each other letters (*Ars Amatoria*, 3.625). In modern times the postal system protects the relative privacy of letters.[6] However, in Antiquity individuals had to make their own arrangements for the sending of their letters. In ancient Greece, the extant evidence suggests that official despatches were often sent by a physical messenger.[7] This messenger then delivered an 'oral' message: a message written to be read out (Aeneas Tacticus, *How to Survive Under Siege*, 22.3, 22.22; Herodotus, *Histories*, 6. 105-106; 9. 12; Polyaenus, *Stratagems of War*, 5.26.1; Thucydides, *History of the Peloponnesian War*, 1.131.1).[8] The messengers used an official messenger stick as a sort of authentication device. This is one and, possibly the original, use of the Spartan *scytale* stick (Archilochus, *Fragment* 185; Aristophanes, *Lysistrata*, 985-992; Pindar, *Olympian Odes*, 6.90-92). In contrast to this method of official despatch communication across the Greek world, in the Roman world, letter writing, including the sending and reading of official despatches, appears to have become more of a private matter, with sealed letters sent from one individual to another (Cicero, *Against Catiline*, 3.5.12; Ibid., *Letters to Brutus*, 2.5 = 5.4; Ibid., *Letters to Friends*, 5.11.77, 6.3.8; Ovid, *Amores*, 2.15.15-18; Suetonius. *The Deified Augustus*, 50).[9] For the Romans to have their letters delivered, some individuals could have used the imperial postal system (the *cursus publicus*; Suetonius, *The Deified Augustus*, 49). Yet, this system was mainly used for official governmental and military correspondence, since only those with official authorisation could use it. This made the use of this postal system not easily accessible to other individuals.[10] A second option – in fact the only option for most people – was to give the letters to someone who was travelling in the direction of the intended recipient.[11] The fact that it was not always easy to find a trustworthy messenger is something that we already saw as a recurring theme in Aeneas Tacticus' *How to Survive Under Siege* (chapter four). This is also known from dozens of references in Roman letters, many of which can be found in Cicero's correspondence (*Letters to Atticus*, 1.16.16, 2.39.5; Ibid., *Letters to Friends* 11.20.4, 11.26.5).¹² Cicero, for example, even mentions at least twice that he opened his brother's letters (*Letters to Atticus*, 5.11.77, 6.3.8). Moreover, the Romans (especially Cicero) seem to have been aware of other issues related to the delivery of letters.¹³ Letters, for example, could fail to reach their destination (*Letters to Atticus*, 2.8.1, 4.15.3; Ibid., *Letters to Quintus* 3.7.6; Ibid., *Letters to Friends*, 2.10.1, 12.19.1), their delivery could be delayed (*Letters to Atticus*, 2.8.1), or they could be misdelivered (*Letters to Atticus*, 4.15.3).

Some historians further suggest that privacy in letter writing would have been compromised in the Roman world because letters were often expected to be read out loud by the intended recipient and addressee (in contrast to the messenger declaiming the message, as was common in the Greek world).¹⁴ Obviously, one could not control who might be listening in on this process, either intentionally or unintentionally. Yet, at least the idea of sealing letters, and sending them from one person to the another, shows that in Roman letter writing, as opposed to Greek, there was more of an idea of a shared individual (yet, not always private) space between the two communicating parties. Cicero, in his second Philippic oration, describes a letter as a private conversation between absent friends (*Second Philippic Oration Against Marcus Antonius*, 2.7) while Henderson, in his discussion of Cicero's letters to his brother Quintus, even speaks of a 'private republic' in which the brothers communicated.¹⁵ Therefore, the Romans would have found the use of the *scytale* a wholly alien and inconvenient method of communication, secret or otherwise. Wax tablets seem to have been more commonly used among the Romans for writing (as opposed to papyrus and parchment for the Greeks and the Greek speaking world).¹⁶ Indeed, one can assume that most, if not all, of the secret letters discussed by Ovid, Cicero, Pliny the Elder and Ausonius and analysed in this chapter were written on wax tablets, as Ovid suggests (*Amores*, 1.11, 1.12, 2.5.17, 3.496; *Ars Amatoria*, 2.396, 3.621–624; *Metamorphoses*, 9.450–665.) Also, wax tablets were often favoured over papyrus since text could be erased and the tablets reused. This more common use of wax tablets for writing among the Romans would have made the theoretical use of the *scytale*, with its strips of papyrus or parchment, something rather alien and impractical. In addition, like Aeneas Tacticus, the Romans apparently had a greater interest in steganographic messages and devices to hide messages, than in cryptographic messages and devices to encipher a message: Caesar with his cipher being the only exception (see below).

Twenty-first-century readers of Greek sources on the *scytale* may struggle to identify precisely what a Greek writer meant when he referred to a Spartan *scytale* since the word had a variety of meanings, as has been discussed in chapter three.

It is particularly hard to determine whether any secret communication or encryption was envisaged. Modern readers in particular, are often dependent upon translators to guide them as to which meaning is intended from a wide range of possibilities suggested by the term '*scytale*'. In this context, Roman writers offer some interesting (though ultimately limited) insights, leading some modern cryptographers to believe that the Romans erroneously helped to promote the myth that the *scytale* was genuinely a Spartan cryptographic device (Cicero, *Letters to Atticus*, 10.10.3; Cornelius Nepos, *The Book on the Great Generals of Foreign Nations. Pausanias*, 4.3.4; Aulus Gellius, *Attic Nights*, 17.9.6–16; Ausonius, *Epistles*, 28.23–27). Strasser, for example, argues that: 'Roman authors – beginning with Cicero [...] – considered the Spartan *skytale* a cryptographic device. Their – apparently erroneous – assumption that such a 'stick' or 'rod' was used by the warlike Spartans, as far back as the fifth century BC, would make the *skytale* the first cryptographic tool. It was supposed to be an ingeniously simple system [...]'.[17] As already mentioned, there are a number of Roman authors who discussed the *scytale*. Their descriptions and understanding of the *scytale* as a device for secret communication are not as straightforward as Strasser suggests. This is related to the fact that our Roman authors do not have first-hand knowledge of the Spartan *scytale* but draw their knowledge from some of the same Greek sources that we have considered in chapter three.

In Roman sources we first find the Spartan *scytale* in Cicero's work (first century BCE). Indeed, he even uses the Greek word σκυτάλη (*scytale*). Although Cicero's reference to the *scytale* may simply have been an allusion to the need for an increased attention to security and privacy in the context of letter-writing in general, rather than a call for Romans to emulate the Spartans in more widely adopting a system of cryptographic messaging for important communications. In one of his *Letters to Atticus*, Cicero writes about another letter that he had himself received from Mark Anthony, which Cicero describes as a *scytale Lakoniken* (10.10.3). This 'Laconian despatch', as Shackleton Bailey translates it, seems to be a message created or communicated by Spartan *scytale*.[18] In the original Latin text, the words 'Laconian despatch' are written in Greek instead of Latin, something that Cicero often did in his correspondence.[19] It is possible that what Cicero meant by this was that he had received a secret message from Mark Anthony, but the context does not make it clear whether the Laconian despatch in question is a coded missive or merely some other form of private communication. The Dutch scholar Erasmus, in his early sixteenth-century work *Adages*, suggested that the 'Laconian despatch' indicated a private letter that was hard to understand and concerned either a mysterious subject or unwelcome news, very much like Homer's story of Bellerophon who was carrying his own death sentence without knowing (Desiderius Erasmus, *Adages*, 77; Homer, *Iliad*, 6.168–178). Shackleton Bailey similarly seems to understand that Cicero's reference to receipt of a *scytale* message merely referred to receipt of a very private letter. In his translation of Cicero's text, the meaning 'despatch' is supplied for the word *scytale*, favouring a more mundane interpretation of the 'Laconian despatch' here and distancing this reference from any allusion to its cryptographic Spartan origins.[20] However, Cicero's references to secrecy, concealment and clandestine behaviour in this letter (10.10.3) suggest that the *scytale* in question here might well be understood as conveying a secret and coded message, whether from Mark Anthony to Cicero, or from Cicero to Atticus. Indeed, the fact that we read about the arrival of the original *scytale* despatch here in another kind of 'despatch' (Cicero's own letter) offers the intriguing possibility that the Latin letter itself might be read as secret or even coded communication: a Roman version of a Laconian despatch. The opening lines of the letter ('Habes σκυτάλην Λακωνικήν – Habes scytale Laconiken'), literally meaning 'you have a Spartan *scytale*' further invites this intriguing interpretation.[21] Yet, unfortunately, despite the fact that Cicero's letter includes references to dates and numbers, and also includes Greek letters alongside Roman alphabetic writing, there is no way we can attempt to identify or to decode any possible coded (*scytale*) message here. Nor can we find any substantive evidence to support Donderer's argument that Cicero regularly used coded communications, made on the grounds of a reference to communicating 'through signs' in another letter to Atticus (13.32.2).[22] Thus, the 'Erasmian' reading of Cicero's 'Laconian *scytale*' remains the safest and most persuasive interpretation: for Cicero, a *scytale* meant not a secret or encrypted communication per se, but a private letter conveying a message that was perhaps hard to understand, and concerned unwelcome news. We cannot, therefore, take Cicero's letter(s) as evidence for any Roman use of the *scytale*, although his writing does offer evidence of Roman familiarity with the key principles of the *scytale* as a device for communication.

Cornelius Nepos, also writing in the first century BCE like Cicero, was the first author who used the Latin equivalent of the word *scytale*, namely, *clava*. He did so in *The Book on the Great Generals of Foreign Nations*, in a chapter on the Spartan general Pausanias (4.3.4). In this chapter we see Cornelius Nepos tell the story of how Pausanias, whilst campaigning in Asia, was summoned home by the Spartan *ephors* by means of a *scytale* (or *clava*) message because of his misbehaviour (4.3.4–5), a story also told by Thucydides (*History of the Peloponnesian War*, 1.131.1) and Plutarch (*Life of Alicibiades*, 19–20). In their translations of Cornelius Nepos' work, Watson uses the Greek word '*scytale*', while Rolfe translates the Latin word '*clava*' into English as 'staff'.[23] Like the word '*scytale*' in Greek, the word '*clava*' has a range of different meanings in Latin, ranging from 'stick' to 'a weapon for exercising, used by young men, and especially by soldiers'.[24] Yet there is nothing in the lexicon that suggests that the '*clava*' has any part to play in the sending (or encrypting) of messages. Rolfe's rendering of 'staff', therefore, is a legitimate translation, but it is highly misrepresentative of the function that the 'staff' or 'stick' in this context is performing. Watson's *scytale* (a re-translation or re-coding of the Latin not into English but into transliterated Greek) is a much better equivalent. However, neither the Latin text, nor the translation, nor the fact that Cornelius Nepos is basing his description upon one of Thucydides' Greek stories, can help us to decipher whether Cornelius Nepos regards the *scytale* that is sent in this story, to summon back the errant Pausanias, to be a regular 'Spartan despatch' or just the conveying of a secret message.

In a letter to his friend Paulinus (who may have been his lover), the fourth-century CE Latin poet Ausonius suggests various ways to send secret letters to each other to make sure that their secret love affair was not revealed (*Epistles* 19.7–8, 26, 28).[25] Ausonius claimed that he knew of countless methods for cryptography and steganography from the ancient Greeks and Romans before him (28.28–29), including tracing letters with milk as invisible ink (28.21–22) and the use of the Spartan *scytale* (28.23–27).[26] Ausonius' description of the *scytale* is very similar to Plutarch's and Aulus Gellius' descriptions: 'Imitate the Spartan *scytale*, writing on strips of parchment wound about a rounded stick in continuous lines, which, afterwards unrolled, will show characters incoherent because sequence is lost, until they are rolled again about just such another stick' (28.23–27). Ausonius describes the *scytale* as a stick around which a strip of parchment was wound on which a message was subsequently written. The strip was then unwrapped from the *scytale* and sent to the intended recipient whereby all letters changed placed, and therefore, the message turned into gibberish until it was wrapped about a *scytale* of the same diameter again (28.23–27). Plutarch also mentions strips of papyrus, like long and narrow leather strips (*Life of Lysander*, 19.5), while Aulus Gellius speak of thongs; in this context probably strips of leather parchment (*Attic Nights*, 17.9.9). In Ausonius' description of the *scytale* we again find these strips of parchment referred to (*Epistles*, 28.23–24). Unlike other Roman authors, in Ausonius' Latin text we find the transliterated form of the word '*scytale*' used for the first time, instead of the use of the Greek word σκυτάλη or the Latin word *clava*, and the cryptographic associations of the *scytale* are thereby set out as unambiguous. We can only speculate as to the cause of this change, but it seems that the influence of Ausonius' primary Greek sources Plutarch and Aulus Gellius may help to explain this new appreciation of the *scytale* not merely as stick or staff but as a cryptographic device.

Roman systems for secret messaging

It has already been established in the first part of this chapter, that the Romans accepted the Spartan's practical use of the *scytale*, but also that they themselves never seem to have adopted the system for number of reasons. One of the main reasons for this is the apparent Roman interest in steganographic (hidden) messages over cryptography (coded) messages, as we will see in the following examples.

In many of the works of the Augustan love poet Ovid – especially in the *Amores*, *Ars Amatoria* and *Heroides* – we find a range of suggestions for lovers to secretly communicate with each other. Significantly, no equivalent references to secret communication by lovers can be found in the earlier Greek context. This suggests that the Greeks and Romans may have had different concerns about, and interests in, cryptographic and steganographic messaging, in the contexts of both private discourse and official (including military) communication. This apparent Roman interest in steganographic over cryptographic modes of secret communication is illustrated by the variety of stratagems described by Ovid. In Ovid's work, the use of secret signs between lovers in their efforts to try to communicate with each other, especially at banquets and public gatherings, are a favourite theme with the author (*Amores*, 1.4.15–28, 1.4.55–58; *Ars Amatoria*, 1.91, 1.137f., 1.341ff.; *Heroides*, 1.31–36, 17.77, 17.88). A clear example of Ovid's steganographic tricks can be found in *Ars Amatoria* book 3, where Ovid suggests that a slave could carry a secret letter under her clothing or concealed in her sandals: '*When a confidant can carry a written tablet. Concealed by a broad band on her warm bosom? When she can hide a paper packet in her stocking. And bear your coaxing message 'twixt foot and sandal?*' (3.621–624).

Similar suggestions for lovers to secretly communicate with each other are found in the elegies of Ovid's near contemporaries, the poets Propertius and Tibullus, indicating that such secret signals between lovers at dinner-parties and other such public occasions formed a stock theme for the Augustan elegists (Propertius, *Elegies*, 3.8.25–26; Tibullus, *Elegies*, 1.2.21–22, 1.6.19, 1.8.1f., 6.19.20).[27] Yet, as in Ovid, none of these cases of private secret communication are examples of cryptography or steganography in the full sense, since no *written* secret messages are involved. Rather, these are simply suggestions for secret *signing*. Yet, Ovid does refer to secrecy and secret letters sent between lovers in some of his works (*Amores*, 2.15.15–18; *Ars Amatoria*, 2.596, 3.483–398, 3.627–630; *Heroides*, 4.3–5). In the earliest example, from *Amores* 2.15.15–18, Ovid reminds lovers of the need to seal secret missives written on wax tablets in order to keep their secrets safe (*Amores*, 2.15.15–18). This example tells us little more than the fact that wax tablets were among the material media used by the Romans for their letter writing. Moreover, nothing in this example indicates that Ovid suggested that lovers should write their messages to each other in code.[28] However, potential references to coded writing can be found in two other Ovidian works. In *Ars Amatoria* 2.596 Ovid speaks of letters written 'in a secret hand.' And in *Heroides* 4.3–5, Ovid refers to secret or mysterious marks in letters (*arcana notis*). Goold translates the Latin here as 'secret characters'.[29] However, this does not necessarily indicate coded or encrypted writing. The *arcana notis* could easily relate to Ovid's suggestion in the *Ars Amatoria* 3.485 and 3.493 that lovers let their secret messages be written by someone else (such as a slave or confidante) to disguise their handwriting and thus the identity of the sender. It is also feasible that the 'secret characters' referred to here have been written in a kind of 'invisible ink.'

Remarkably, we do not have any evidence for the use of invisible ink as a form of secret communication in Greek or Roman warfare, while it would have been an easy-to-use method. Moreover, the oldest description of the use of invisible ink is provided by the Greek military engineer Philo of Byzantium in his third-century BCE work *Compendium of Mechanics*. Philo suggests making invisible ink by mixing crushed gallnuts with water (*Compendium of Mechanics*, 102). When someone wrote with this 'ink' and then waited for the ink to dry, the text had become invisible. To make the text visible again a sponge soaked in vitriol (an acid which is also known as iron sulphate) had to be rubbed over the writing.[30] In the surviving part of Philo's work we cannot find out where and how vitriol could have been found. Yet, from the Greek physician Dioscorides (first century CE) and Pliny the Elder we know that vitriol could have been found in the vicinity of copper ore deposits in Cyprus. Here vitriol is formed as white dripstones in caves and mine tunnels (*Natural History*, 34.32).[31] Whitiak considers that Ovid, and later Pliny the Elder and Ausonius, would have been inspired by Philo.[32] However, Ovid – followed by Ausonius in the fourth century CE – suggests the use of fresh milk and moistened flax for this purpose (Ovid, *Ars Amatoria*, 3.267–630; Ausonius, *Epistles*, 28.21–22). And Pliny the Elder suggests the use of the milky juice of a plant known as the Mediterranean Spurge or Goat's Lettuce (*Natural History*, 26.39 (62)). Ashes or linseed oil could be used to make the text visible again (Ausonius, *Epistles*, 28.21–22; Ovid, *Ars Amatoria*, 3.627–628). There is no mention of gallnuts, water, or vitriol here. This makes sense since Ovid, Pliny and Ausonius wrote about straightforward ways to contact your lover with simple everyday materials, while Philo wrote a mechanical treatise for a specialised audience.

Whitiak further suggests that the Romans might have used various readily available substances including fruit juice (e.g. lemon juice) and urine as their invisible inks and used them as suited to various contexts.[33]

However, it is not until the eighth century CE that Europe first discovered lemons via merchants from the Middle East.[34] Yet, it has been suggested that the citron could be the fruit described in Pliny's *Natural History* (12.7.15), which he calls the *malum medicum*: the medicinal fruit.[35] Also, depictions of citrus trees appear in later Roman mosaics from North Africa.[36] Yet, although we find that lemon juice in particular has been used on a large scale in steganography in modern warfare, up to and including the Second World War, we do not have any extant ancient sources mentioning the use of such substances as invisible inks (in any context), so it is difficult to assume with any confidence that any substances other than the fresh milk, regular ink, or 'Goat's Lettuce sap' would have been used by the Romans for secret messaging.[37] When using any of these substances, Ovid, Pliny and Ausonius clearly had in mind secret communication through a letter written on a papyrus or paper-like medium, and not a wax tablet. Ovid has adapted his steganographic methodology to suit the medium of the message in each case. Indeed, in his *Ars Amatoria*, Ovid even suggests that lovers can write a secret message on the human body, either in normal ink (3.625–626), or, once again, in invisible ink (3.628). The latter suggestion, that the lovers use a kind of invisible ink to write on a human body, would have made the message doubly secret since it would have been hidden under clothing and written in invisible letters.[38] However, there is no indication in this example, or in any of Ovid's other examples of secret messaging, that such 'secret signs' are to be written in any kind of code: this is simply another example of hidden *steganographic* messaging.

Despite the ingenuity and variety of Ovid's descriptions of secret communication in his poetry, all his examples involve steganography, and there is nothing at all to indicate any interest in cryptographic methods of messaging. In fact, this pattern of a marked preference for steganographic over cryptographic methods of communication appears to mark a wider trend among our extant Roman sources, and discussions of encrypted or encoded communications are comparatively rare.[39]

Let us first have a look at the Roman use of fire signalling (see chapter four). Tactical signals had been employed by the Romans in battles since the time of the Republic (*c.* 509 -27 BCE). In fact, fire signals in wartime can be found in Roman military records (Appian, *Spanish Wars*, 6.15–90-92; Caesar, *The Gallic War*, 2.20; Ibid., *The Civil War*, 3.65; Suetonius, *Life of the Caesars: Tiberius*, 65).[40] To employ these tactical fire signals, the Romans had access to earlier Greek and Carthaginian systems, known from Aeneas Tacticus, Polybius and Polyaenus (Polybius, *Histories*, 10.43–46; Polyaenus, *Stratagems of War*, 6.16.2).[41] Yet, as with so many aspects of Roman culture, while Greek examples formed the basis for the fire signalling systems, there were differences between the ways in which the Romans employed fire signals and the way in which the Greeks did so. First, for the Romans, fire signals and signalling stations had another purpose than for the Greeks. From the fourth/early third centuries BCE, the time the empire started expanding, fire signals were used on a large scale to control it. The Romans started building watchtowers with fire signalling stations throughout the empire, and especially at the borders to facilitate easy communication between these stations throughout Roman territories.[42] When we return to the Spartan *scytale*, we see why the Romans would have found its use wholly alien, because of the context in which the *scytale* was used. If *scytalae* were used in the way Plutarch and Aulus Gellius describe, then they were used to send short messages quickly from Sparta to the battlefield and back. Hereby, secrecy was of the utmost importance. However, Roman fire signalling stations had a different purpose. They appeared throughout the empire to control everything and everyone, especially at the borders. There was no need to do so secretly, as was the case with the Spartan *scytale*. Instead, it was well-known that the stations were used to keep things in order in plain sight. However, there is evidence for the use of fire signalling stations to send secret messages.

This brings us to the second way in which Roman fire signals were used differently from their Greek predecessors. As we have seen in chapter four, with fire signals only one or a few prearranged messages could be sent between communicating parties. Therefore, the Romans often used fire signals as part of the larger communication system. In 134 BCE, for example, at Numantia (Spain), the Roman general Scipio Aemilianus operated a combined system of relays, posts, messengers and fire signals (Appian, *Spanish Wars*, 6.15–90-92).[43] According to Vegetius, the Romans used daylight signalling by means of smoke, and night signalling by means of fires, signal flags, semaphore and military horns (*Concerning Military Matters*, 3.5).[44] There is one documented case in Roman history in which a fire signal as part of a larger communication system conveyed intelligence. This was a signal that announced the fall of the Roman soldier Sejanus, who lived from about 20 BCE-31 CE (Tacitus, *Annals*, 4.1).[45] Originally, Sejanus had been a friend and confidant of the Roman Emperor Tiberius. Yet later, Sejanus betrayed the emperor, and was therefore condemned to death. The order to kill the man was given when Tiberius was residing on Capri. Tiberius ordered that he should receive a message about the outcome of the mission as quickly as possible. According to Suetonius, Tiberius waited on a cliff top for the distant bonfire signals, announcing all possible eventualities, which he had ordered to be sent in case his couriers were delayed (Suetonius, *Tiberius*, 65). So, fire signals were the fastest way to convey a message in this case; before the couriers arrived with more detailed information, Tiberius was already aware of the situation. In other words, the signal was for the emperor's private use, and was used as a back-up system.

When a secret message was used by means of *scytale*, the context was again different. In the case of the *scytale*, when one party had to inform the other party, they would write a message and send a messenger with a *scytale* to the other side. Hereby, only a few people were involved: the two parties communicating with each other and the messenger. These three people formed the entire communication network, while the Romans often used larger communication systems, with more people and methods of communication involved, as we see in the example of Tiberius giving orders to kill Sejanus. Since the Romans often combined communication systems into a larger network, they may have found the *scytale* system unsuitable.

From the first-century CE civil engineer, author, soldier and senator Frontinus, we know that the Romans were familiar with other forms of trickery and secret messaging, that were again used in contexts different from when the Spartans used the *scytale*. In a passage on sending and receiving secret messages, Frontinus discusses eight situations from the Roman past in which messages or people were sent in secret. What we see in Frontinus' first two stories are situations in which individuals pass into enemy territory to convey a message in person to friends or allies at the moment when a message had to be conveyed, rather than situations in which secret written messages are sent between communicating parties that had made arrangements beforehand (*Stratagems*, 3.13.1–2). When using *scytalae*, however, arrangements had been made between the *ephors* in Sparta and officers in the field. Moreover, while *scytalae* were used to encrypt messages, what we see in these examples is once more the greater Roman interest in hiding messages (steganography) instead of encrypting them. We have already seen this discussion of Aeneas Tacticus in chapter four. In fact, some of the examples we see in Frontinus' work are clearly based on the work of Aeneas, for example the writing on skin (3.13). Whereas Frontinus suggested using skin, Aeneas used a bladder (*How to Survive Under Siege*, 31.10–13). This bladder in fact can be found in Frontinus' next story, where he discusses inflated bladders used to help men float when crossing a river (3.13.6).

Another one of Frontinus' suggestions based on the work of Aeneas is to write on lead plates. Where Aeneas Tacticus suggested to write messages on pieces of lead that were rolled up to be worn as women's' earrings, Frontinus argues that the Roman consul Hirtius often sent letters inscribed on lead plates that were 'delivered' by a soldier (3.13.7). Frontinus provides us with three other stories in which secret messages were sent, according to him. These suggestions cannot be found in Aeneas' work, yet they would not be out of place in there, since the situations can be related to smuggling messages in an out of a besieged city. Frontinus tells us the story of how people stuffed a message under the tail of a mule while passing the picket-posts (3.13.4). This simple hiding of messages in, or under, another object can be compared to Aeneas Tacticus' suggestions for hiding messages in or under clothing, footwear, armour, jewellery, and even in a dog collar (*How to Survive Under Siege*, 31.4–5, 31.6, 31.7, 31.9, 31.23, 31.25–27, 31.31–32). In fact, whereas Aeneas argues how it was the custom in Epirus and Thessaly to take a dog away from his home, hide a secret message in its collar, and then send it back home (*How to Survive Under Siege*, 31.31–32), Frontinus tells us about the use of carrier pigeons by the Roman senators Hirtius and Brutus (*Stratagems*, 3.13.8). Frontinus' examples show us once more the greater Roman interest in hiding messages instead of encrypting them. When someone wanted to hide a message completely the *scytale* method would obviously not have been useful, since with it the written message is still visible on the strip of writing material. Only if the messenger who was sent to deliver the *scytale* message hid the strip (for example in a bag or under his clothes), would the complete message have been invisible. For the Romans, instead, this hiding of messages would have made the message invisible, and therefore private, and secret, something that we also see in a passage by Herodian, written in the early third century CE (*History of the Empire from the Death of Marcus*, 7.6.5). This passage brings us back to the Roman idea that there was a certain level of privacy in sending sealed letters.

Later Roman sources also highlight the apparent Roman preoccupation with steganographic over cryptographic methods for secret communication. Indeed, although the fourth-century CE author Ausonius seems to have presented himself as an expert in secret messaging, his knowledge of such stratagems and devices is fairly limited, and largely focuses upon the sorts of steganographic methods seen in Ovid and the other Latin love elegists.⁴⁶ In this letter to his pupil Paulinus, Ausonius wrote that he knew 'countless codes of the ancients for concealing and unlocking secret messages' (*Epistles*, 28.28–29). However, despite this expansive claim to know 'countless forms' of secret communications, Ausonius only refers directly in his writing to a handful of the various methods that the Greeks and Romans used, discussing only Ovid's suggestion to use milk as invisible ink (28.21–22) and the Spartans' use of the *scytale* (28.23–27). In Ausonius' description of invisible ink, it clearly echoes Ovid, since Ausonius, like Ovid, suggests the use of fresh milk that would become completely invisible when it had dried. Only when rubbing ashes onto the paper would the text become visible again.⁴⁷

Here, it is significant that the language Ausonius uses to characterise this secret communication clearly emphasises *hidden* rather than coded or encrypted messaging. He refers to concealing or hiding ('*celandi*') and revealing or exposing ('*ostendere*') messages, rather than encoding them. Tellingly, Ausonius describes such secret communications as hidden rather than encrypted. Ausonius, therefore, highlights not only the scant variety of options for such 'clandestine' communication known by the ancient Roman sources with which he is familiar, but also the focus in those sources upon *steganographic* modes.

As we have seen, the Romans were familiar with a number of steganographic systems to hide messages, instead of encrypting them. In fact, the only cryptographic system that seems to have been used in Roman secret communications, according to our available sources, is the so-called 'Caesar cipher', named after Julius Caesar by modern cryptographers. Caesar seems to have used his cipher to communicate with his generals over long distances, similar to the theoretical Spartan use of the *scytale*. The Caesar cipher is often regarded as a simple substitution technique for encryption, whereby each letter of a plaintext is replaced by a letter that can be found a fixed number of positions down the alphabet.⁴⁸ In other words, in the ciphertext alphabet used for encryption and decryption there is always one shift of letters for the entire message, for example a right shift of three, as in the case of Caesar's use of the cipher. According to Cassius Dio this worked in the following way: 'It was his [Caesar's] usual practice, whenever he was sending a secret message to any one, to substitute in every case for the proper letter of the alphabet the fourth letter beyond, so that the writing might be unintelligible to most persons' (*Roman History*, 40.9.4). And Suetonius adds that:

> There are [...] letters [...] from [Caesar] to [Quintus] Cicero, and others to his friends, concerning his domestic affairs; in which, if there was occasion for secrecy, he wrote in cyphers; that is, he used the alphabet in such a manner, that

not a single word could be made out. The way to decipher those epistles was to substitute the fourth for the first letter, as D for A, and so for the other letters respectively.

Suetonius, *The Deified Julius*, 56.6

Finally, Aulus Gellius mentions the names of two of Caesar's correspondents with whom Caesar communicated in cipher: his generals Oppius and Balbus (*Attic Nights*, 17.9.1–2). Significantly, the term 'Caesar cipher' is a term that only appears in modern books on cryptography.[49] Caesar himself did not discuss the cipher (nor its potential name) in any of his surviving works. Yet, descriptions of the cipher (again without its potential name) come from Antiquity and can be found in the abovementioned passages of Suetonius, Aulus Gellius and Cassius Dio.[50] Dio argues that Caesar's secret letters were unintelligible to most – but not all – people (*Roman History*, 40.9.4). Suetonius in turn describes letters to Caesar's intimates on confidential affairs – in both a private context and in his capacity as a general – as having been written in cipher to prevent Caesar's enemies from reading the messages if they were intercepted (*The Deified Julius*, 56.6). From Suetonius' and Dio's descriptions it becomes clear that Caesar's encryption worked by substituting every alphabetic letter of a plaintext for the alphabet letter that could be found three places further down the alphabet (moving from the left to the right): e.g. 'A' became 'D', 'B' became 'E' and so on with the rest.

In addition to sending secret and/or encrypted letters to his generals, Caesar would also most likely have communicated in cipher with his scouts and spies: the *exploratores* and *speculatores*.[51] Indeed, communicating in cipher would have been especially important for Caesar's *exploratores* and *speculatores* since it was their task to find out everything about the enemy's strengths and whereabouts and communicate this highly sensitive information back to the central command, all without the enemy knowing about this. Such *exploratores* and *speculatores* often came up close to the enemy's camp, which made them vulnerable to being captured by the enemy. In fact, Caesar tells us that the Gauls sometimes captured his messengers (*The Gallic War*, 5.45–46) and intercepted at least one letter sent from Caesar's general Quintus Cicero to Caesar (5.39). If *exploratores* and *speculatores* were captured with letters to or from Caesar written in plaintext, then the enemy could easily have found out what was known about their forces. Therefore, it is likely that Caesar's *exploratores* and *speculatores* would have used the Caesar cipher when communicating with Caesar and his generals, and amongst each other.

Although Caesar never directly discusses the use of the Caesar cipher in his works, we can find dozens of references to the sending and receiving of important confidential despatches in them. There are nineteen references in total in Caesar's works to the sending of important confidential despatches from Caesar to his staff;[52] while Caesar's staff sent forty highly confidential reports back to him about the enemy's strengths and whereabouts.[53] In addition to this, Caesar mentions sixty-nine times that he sent word to some of his troops in general, or to specific people, without explicitly mentioning that he sent them a written message.[54] Then there are another sixty-seven potential references to secret letters, which are situations in which Caesar left some of his forces at a certain location, and then moved on to another place with only a small part of his forces joining him.[55] And, finally there are 140 situations in which Caesar sent troops away from himself or urged them to join him again.[56] This brings the total number of potential references and allusions to secret messages sent to Caesar to 128, and another 207 occasions in which secret messages could have been sent. Suetonius and Cassius Dio, therefore, seem to make a reasonable argument in saying that Caesar wrote in cipher whenever he had anything confidential to say (Suetonius, *The Deified Julius*, 56.6; Cassius Dio, *Roman History*, 40.9.3). Caesar's use of the cipher was important to him.

Indeed, the use of the cipher must have been especially important during periods of conflict – such as the Gallic War and even more important during the civil war in which Romans fought against other Romans.[57] In one passage (*The Gallic War*, 5.48) we read that Caesar's general Quintus Cicero was besieged by the Gauls. This Quintus Cicero was a younger brother of the orator Cicero. According to Caesar's own account, in order to let Quintus Cicero know that Caesar was about to send help, he decided to write Cicero a letter written in 'Greek letters' to prevent the Gauls from understanding the letter in case it was intercepted (5.48). This letter Caesar had delivered by a Gaul who worked for him. Cassius Dio presumes that Caesar simply wrote a letter in Greek to make sure that the Gauls could not understand the message (*Roman History*, 40.9.3–4). Cary and Foster also seem to adopt this idea in their translation of *Roman History* since they translate the text simply as '(Caesar) wrote … in Greek' without adding any critical notes to the text and/or referring to the Caesar cipher.[58] Adams and Harris too assume that Caesar must simply have written the letter in the Greek language, without using any codes.[59] However, a letter simply written in Greek in order to encrypt Caesar's message seems an inadequate interpretation of the situation in this case. Correspondence between elite Romans in this period would typically have been written in Greek as a matter of course, and Caesar knew that some of the Gauls had knowledge of the Greek language and script (*The Gallic War*, 1.19.1, 6.14).

Modern historians of cryptography Pieprzyk, Hardjono and Sebbery, therefore, seem to be in error when presuming that Caesar's letters, if written in Greek, would have been undecipherable to his enemies in Gaul.[60] So, it seems implausible that Caesar simply wrote the letter in Greek to prevent the Gauls from comprehending its contents. Singh, Bauer and Holmes assume that Caesar transliterated a message that was originally written in Latin, into Greek characters or letters. In this way a 'Greek' meaningless message was created.[61] This is plausible, in fact the use of different languages with different alphabets (Latin and Greek) would have made the messages even more secure. Caesar would in all probability already have communicated with Quintus Cicero using 'Greek letters' in his non-secret correspondence, and he would have changed to communication in cipher if an extra layer of security were needed. Moreover, since the two men would normally have communicated in Greek, and Cicero was besieged by the Gauls, Caesar could not (easily) have communicated to him that he had decided to change his method of secret communication by sending a message in Latin (in a Greek alphabet), instead of in Greek. In other words, Caesar's secret letter to Cicero was most likely a letter already written in Greek and encrypted in a Greek substitution cipher. It seems plausible then that the language for this secret communication was not simply Greek, nor Latin with a Greek substitution cipher, but, as Reinke describes it, 'cryptic Greek'.[62] That is, a coded letter written with a Caesar cipher using the Greek alphabet. Such an interpretation is also supported by Edwards' translation of *The Gallic War* in which he aptly translates '*Graecis litteris*' as 'Greek characters' instead of 'Greek letters'.[63] We can decode this story as a veiled account of Caesar's own cipher being used in the field, as suggested by Harris.[64] We can, therefore, gain fresh insights into the cryptographic principles on which the Caesar cipher operated. Furthermore, there is a 'quasi-Spartan' character to Caesar's use of this 'cryptic Greek', which invites us to recall the Spartan *scytale*. When unwrapping a *scytale* message from the stick, most letters turned into unintelligible partial characters from the Greek alphabet, or better 'cryptic Greek'. In the case of Caesar's secret letter to Cicero, the 'cryptic Greek' appears when the normal non-encrypted text is turned into encrypted text by changing every letter into the 'character' that could be found three places down the alphabet.

In modern cryptography, the Caesar cipher is still regarded as a simple substitution technique for encryption, whereby each letter of a plaintext is replaced by a letter taken from a fixed number of positions down the alphabet.[65] Caesar most likely always used a right shift of three in the ciphertext alphabet used for encryption and decryption of his confidential correspondence, something known as monoalphabetic encryption in modern cryptography since only one ciphertext alphabet is used to encrypt and decrypt the entire message.[66] Modern cryptographers, however, often presume that Caesar used a variety of possible ciphertext alphabets. Van Tilborg, for example, argues that Caesar shifted the alphabet over a number of places regularly to create new ciphertext alphabets, while Kahn and Oriyano presume that Caesar used up to two dozen ciphertext alphabets.[67] Although it might have been the case that, theoretically speaking, Caesar changed his shift regularly – which would have given him twenty-three possible ciphertext alphabets since he used the twenty-four-letter ancient Greek alphabet – it is highly unlikely that Caesar used more than one shift of letters or changed the shift regularly, since he would not have had the time nor the means to inform all of his units about this change of shift, especially not whilst on campaign.

Rather, as we have said, it is known from Suetonius and Cassius Dio that Caesar – whenever using the technique to create a ciphertext alphabet – substituted every alphabetic letter of a plaintext for the alphabet letter that could be found three places further down the alphabet (moving from the left to the right) with 'A' becoming 'D', 'B' becoming 'E' and so on. The Latin text in Suetonius' work reads: 'quae si qui investigare et persequi velit, quartam elementorum litteram, id est D pro A et perinde reliquas commutet' (*The Deified Julius*, 56.6). Rolfe translates this as: 'If anyone wishes to decipher these, and get at their meaning, he must substitute the fourth letter of the alphabet, namely D, for A, and so with the others.'[68]

Decryption of messages written in a Caesar cipher with a right shift of three obviously worked the other way around by substituting each letter in the ciphertext for the letter that could be found three places back to the left in the alphabet.[69] Rolfe in his translation of Suetonius' work, and Cary and Foster in their translation of Dio's work, each use the word 'substitute' to describe these operations in their respective translations.[70] Yet in Suetonius' work, we find the word '*commutet*', literally 'change', 'alter' or 'substitute', while in Dio's work we see the word 'ἀντεγγράφειν' (*antengraphein*) literally 'insert [one name instead of another]' (Suetonius, *The Deified Julius*, 56.7; Cassius Dio, *Roman History*, 40.9.3). Rolfe, and Cary and Foster, in using the word 'substitute' in their respective translations, unequivocally align Caesar's cipher with the simple substitution techniques used in modern Caesar ciphers. However, the system also reminds one of transposition in the technical sense, if the ciphertext alphabet and the plaintext alphabet are written out, one under the other. We can clearly see this in the diagrams below:

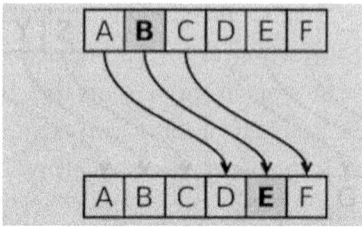

Figure 9 Encrypting text with a Caesar cipher with a right shift of three. Author's illustration based on Cheshire Library Science 2013.

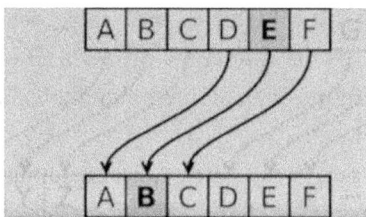

Figure 10 Decrypting text with a Caesar cipher with a right shift of three. Author's illustration based on Cheshire Library Science 2013.

In a simple substitution cipher, the characters of a plaintext are replaced by other characters, numbers, symbols, or a combination of those, as is the case in Caesar's substitution of plaintext letters for ciphertext letters.[71] This becomes especially clear when an encryption table is used, like the one presented in Figure 11.[72] And here, I have taken the insights from my study of Caesar's own account of using such a shift cipher for encrypted secret communication, to further suggest that the alphabet used for this shift – at least in the one case we can reasonably attribute to Caesar himself (*The Gallic War*, 5.48) – was not Latin but Greek (Figure 11).

Letter in plaintext	Α	Β	Γ	Δ	Ε	Ζ	Η	Θ	Ι	Κ	Λ	Μ
Letter in ciphertext	Δ	Ε	Ζ	Η	Θ	Ι	Κ	Λ	Μ	Ν	Ξ	Ο
Letter in plaintext	Ν	Ξ	Ο	Π	Ρ	Σ	Τ	Υ	Φ	Χ	Ψ	Ω
Letter in ciphertext	Π	Ρ	Σ	Τ	Υ	Φ	Χ	Ψ	Ω	Α	Β	Γ

Figure 11 Caesar cipher with a right shift of three applied to ancient Greek alphabet. Author's illustration.

Indeed, I suggest that if we look further back into history, and into the ancient Greek world, we can arguably see the embryo of this principle of a fractionating transposition cipher, particularly when we recall that the design of the *scytale* entailed that encrypted texts contained letters that were not merely 'transposed' (taken out of place by their unwrapping and re-wrapping around various diameters of a *scytale* rod) but also effectively 'substituted' by the incomplete lines, dots, dashes and other marks of incomplete letters.

The Caesar cipher is still mentioned in almost every book on twenty-first-century cryptography, where it is typically described as being a conceptual milestone in the development of modern cryptography.[73] Yet, none of these studies consider the significance (indirect or otherwise) of earlier Greek substitution and/or transposition ciphers including the theoretical system of the *scytale*, upon the development and deployment of the Caesar cipher. Such modern studies typically position Caesar's Roman technique for secret communication as the embryonic form of the modern cryptographic method, and ignore the fact that complex modes of encryption already existed in the Classical world and were in use centuries before the Caesar cipher.

It is impossible to trace a continuous line of evolution – or, indeed, any direct relationship – between the Spartan *scytale* and the development of the Caesar cipher. However, the system of the Caesar cipher nevertheless shares important conceptual principles with the encryption technique utilised in the Spartan system of the *scytale*, known form Plutarch and Aulus Gellius. When messages were unwrapped from the *scytale* the alphabetic letters physically changed place according to a variable 'shift' determined by the diameter of the *scytale* rod used, and in the alphabet(s) used for the encryption of the Caesar cipher we see a cipher with a right shift of three.[74] Although this later Roman cipher is less sophisticated (involving a regular, fixed, shift and not requiring any specialist equipment to supply its 'key') understanding the dynamics of its operation can help us to better appreciate the comparative complexity and security of the Spartan *scytale* system, thereby supporting the overarching argument of this book that the *scytale,* in theory, would have been potentially a more useful device for secret messaging than the Caesar cipher. In fact, it is the principle of the *scytale* method that keeps reappearing in later substitution and transposition ciphers that have been used from the Renaissance up to the present day, as we shall see in chapter six.

6

The Development of the Principle of the Transposition Cipher System of the *Scytale* in Ciphers from the Renaissance to the Twenty-First Century

As we have seen in chapter five, the Caesar cipher represents an important staging post in the history of cryptography. Yet, following the fall of the Western Roman Empire (*c.* 476 CE), the use of cryptography and steganography in Western Europe appears to have stagnated for almost a thousand years, from before *c.* 500 CE to *c.* 1400.[1] During the Middle Ages in Europe, the use of cryptography and steganography even became synonymous with the use of dark arts and magic, echoing the early Egyptian tradition of using hieroglyphs for 'mystical' secret communications.[2] However, via the Eastern Roman or Byzantine Empire, cryptography and steganography seem to have returned to Western Europe in the Late Middle Ages and Early Renaissance.[3] During this period we see more ciphers appear in which the basic transposition elements of the *scytale* can still be found. With this in mind, Süß, in his 1922 article 'Über Antike Geheimschriftenmethoden und ihr Nachleben', correctly argues that ancient methods for communication security could have been far more advanced than the literature would lead us to believe, and that these ancient systems would have influenced cryptographic and steganographic systems used from the Renaissance onwards.[4] In this chapter we will discuss such later systems for communication security in which we see the principle of the *scytale* reappear. The chapter is divided into two parts. First, we will analyse four cipher systems used in the period from *c.* 1400–1800. Secondly, we will discuss four other cipher systems that were used between *c.* 1800 and the present day. In doing so, it will be shown that we can see the basic operating principle on which the ciphertext encryption of the *scytale* was predicated, reappear throughout the ages from the Renaissance through into the twentieth and twenty-first century. Even though we cannot go further than arguing that the *scytale* is at least the first theoretical transposition cipher in history, we must not overlook the importance of the principle of this early transposition cipher, whether or not it was used by the Spartans in the fifth and fourth century BCE.

Renaissance and Early Modern communication security systems (c. 1400–1800)

The Caesar cipher is an example of a monoalphabetic cipher. In monoalphabetic ciphers only one ciphertext alphabet is used to encrypt and decrypt the entire message.[5] In Caesar's case this was most likely always a right shift of three, since Caesar did not have the time nor the means to inform all his units about a change in his cipher, as we have seen in chapter five. Obviously, systems for communication security changed and developed over time. Around 1466–1467 the Italian scientist Leon Battista Alberti introduced a polyalphabetic cipher in his work *De Componendis Cifris* (*A Composition of Ciphers*). In polyalphabetic ciphers, more than one ciphertext alphabet is used to encrypt and decrypt one entire message, as opposed to Caesar's monoalphabetic cipher with the right shift of three. Kahn attributes the invention of polyalphabetic ciphers to Alberti.[6] However, it can only be said with certainty that Alberti's cipher is the first *known* polyalphabetic cipher;[7] evidence for earlier polyalphabetic ciphers may be lost. Alberti's cipher certainly represented a major improvement on the Caesar cipher in using multiple alphabets for encrypting messages. However, Alberti introduced a new – or, rather, a radically old – cryptographic principle to increase the security and sophistication of his cipher. He worked with a cipher disk to encode his messages using a substitution of letters in the ciphertext alphabets. In Alberti's description of the working of the cipher disk, it is suggested that one had to position the two plates of the disk that contained letters relative to each other by turning them around, and in that way changing the position of the letters on the disks (14). The cipher disk that Alberti described consisted of two concentric circular plates, both made of copper, one placed on top of the other. On the bottom plate of the disk, called '*stabilis*', or 'stationary', the twenty capital letters of the fifteenth-century Italian alphabet were written followed by the numbers one to four (14–15). These letters and numbers were written down in their normal order, from A to Z and from one to four, and represented the plaintext (Figure 12).[8] On the upper plate of the disk, called '*mobilis*', or 'moveable', the twenty-three letters of the Latin alphabet used in the fifteenth century were written in lower case letters and in a random order, together with the ampersand symbol. These letters and the symbol represented the ciphertext (14).[9] Since the

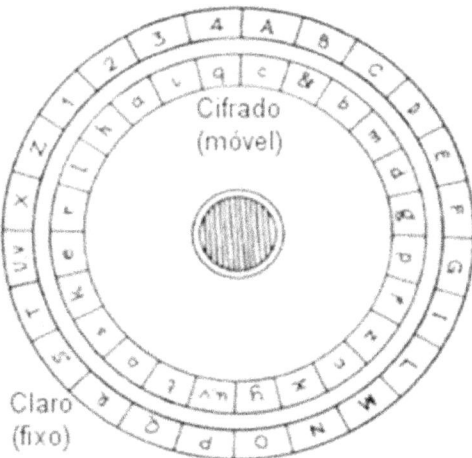

Figure 12 Reconstruction of Alberti's cipher disk. Author's illustration based on Facultad de Informática 2018.

two plates of Alberti's disk were only fixed in the middle with a pin, they could turn around. Hereby, the upper plate of the disk was used to turn, 'to move', while the other disk stayed in its original position.

When using Alberti's disk, both sender and recipient needed an identical cipher disk, just as the Spartans needed two *scytalae* of the same size and diameter to communicate easily with each other. In Alberti's model, ciphertext sender and recipient would then need to agree on the settings of the disk necessary to encipher and decipher messages. In this case, they had to choose a letter on the upper disk that Alberti used as a reference. Alberti called this letter the 'index' (14). In Alberti's example, the index letter was the lowercase letter 'k' on the upper disk, that was positioned opposite the capital letter 'B' on the bottom disk (14). Both sender and recipient had to place their disks in these settings to start encryption and decryption, and anyone who intercepted the message could not have deciphered it easily without having the 'key' to deciphering the messages.

In Alberti's case one would have needed both a cipher disk identical to the one used by Alberti to create the message, and the information about the index letters or the settings of the disk. In modern cryptography a key is the information needed to encipher and decipher a message.[10] Alberti's example, however, shows us that in earlier times, this 'key' could in fact be a physical object, like the cipher disk. The same applies to the Spartan *scytale*. The key to deciphering a *scytale* message is the use of a stick of the exact same size as the rod that was originally used to create the message. Moreover, just as the Spartans used the *scytale* for long-distance communication, so did Alberti use his disk, which becomes clear when he discusses how a receiver had to figure out the right settings of the disk to decipher the messages he had received (Figure 12): 'You [...], far away and receiving the message, have to look carefully in [the] reading [...]'.[11] Alberti's substitution coding essentially worked in the same way as Caesar's substitution technique, whereby every letter of a plaintext message on the bottom disk, was substituted by a ciphertext letter on the upper disk.

Yet, improving upon Caesar's fixed transposition principle, in which every letter was moved precisely three places along the alphabet, in Alberti's system, letters were transposed and changed places by regularly moving the upper disk relative to the bottom disk. At set intervals, Alberti rotated the upper disk to create a different setting or key (14). In this way another substitution of the letters took place. What is more, Alberti's system not only made use of letters that changed position, but also of the symbol of the ampersand (&) on the upper disk, and four numbers on the bottom disk. On the bottom disk, one could find the twenty letters of the Italian alphabet together with the numbers one to four (Figure 12). According to Alberti, these numbers were permuted into groups of two, three or four digits, e.g. twelve or 314. Numbers could also appear more often in a group, which gave various combinations such as eleven or 4,444. This gave Alberti 336 two-, three- and four-digit groups that each represented a 'standard' or common phrase or sentence. The numerical codes for these sentences could be found in a table, which Alberti had also created to accompany his disk (15–16). As Alberti states, number twelve, for example, meant: 'We have made ready the ships which we promised and supplied them with troops and grain' (16). Thus, sender and recipient also needed Alberti's codebook to completely decipher complex messages in addition to having identical cipher disks.

With the cipher disk but without the codebook anyone intercepting a ciphertext encrypted using Alberti's device could only have partially decoded the original message, making the codebook another part of the 'key'. Whenever number codes were contained within the ciphertext, for instance, the first phase of decoding would have seen numbers substituted with two to four alphabetical letters, producing seemingly senseless sequences of letters that would not form a word, such as 'xp' or 'dkge'. With Alberti's description of the codebook in mind, Kahn attributes the invention of enciphered code to Alberti.[12] Yet, evidence for earlier enciphered codes again may have been lost. Although the changing of letters into numerical values (as seen in Alberti's example) is a characteristic of substitution ciphers, the additional level of encryption can be compared to the encryption principles of the transposition system of the *scytale*, whereby partial

Greek letters were turned into gibberish when the strip was unwrapped from its original rod. Indeed, the similarities to be found between Alberti's disk and the Spartan *scytale* are highly suggestive. First, we see that the disk is rotated, as letters of a *scytale* message were transposed when the strip was unwrapped from its rod. Secondly, in both cases specific devices were needed to encipher and decipher the messages. If the Spartans (and maybe any other Greeks) wished to decipher their messages, they needed two *scytalae* of the same size and diameter to easily decode and understand each other's messages, while users of Alberti's disk would have needed both the disk and a codebook to decipher the messages completely.[13] Although, of course, Alberti's Renaissance disk is not in itself evidence that the Spartan *scytale* was also used for secret messaging, it helps to prove that such devices would have worked efficiently and would have offered the Spartans a potentially secure method of secret communication. And, just as Alberti used his disk for confidential communication so the Spartans would have used the *scytale* for the same purpose, even though only theoretically.

In Alberti's system the combination of plaintext and ciphertext letters changed after every couple of letters. In the most desirable situation, however, the combination of plaintext and ciphertext had to change after every letter. This step was made by the German abbot Johannes Trithemius. In 1518, two years after his death, Trithemius' work, *Polygraphia*, was published. This was a work that looked at a number of coding principles, including the *tabula recta* ('square table'). The *tabula recta* was a table containing twenty-four ciphertext alphabets, derived from the medieval Latin alphabet which consisted of twenty-four letters.[14] Compared to our modern twenty-six-letter alphabet, the letters 'J' and 'U' are missing. The letter 'W' is the final letter in this case, after the letters 'X' and 'Y'. On the first line of the table the alphabet could be found in its normal order, from 'A' to 'W'. Although the alphabet was written down in its normal order here, it was already a ciphertext alphabet. However, this first line was also used as the plaintext alphabet since there was no separate plaintext alphabet. On the next lines every letter kept shifting one place to the left. So, the second line started with the second letter, the 'B'; the first letter 'A' had moved to the last place in the row. The third line started with 'C' and ended with 'B', and so on (see Table 3). In this way twenty-four substitution alphabets were created. Encrypting a text by using the *tabula recta* worked in the following way: to start with, the first letter of the plaintext had to be found in the plaintext-alphabet, the upper row, e.g. a 'B'. This letter was then replaced by the ciphertext letter which could be found on the first line of the table at the place of this 'B', because the first line represented both a plaintext alphabet and a ciphertext alphabet. In this case this is also a 'B'. Then the second letter of the text had to be found in the plaintext-alphabet, e.g. an 'E'. This letter was replaced by the ciphertext letter, which could be found under the letter 'E' on the second line (F). In this way all the twenty-four alphabets in the table were used in one message.

Caesar probably used only one alphabet in a whole message, while Alberti used several alphabets; a new ciphertext alphabet was introduced after several words. After reaching the last line of the table, someone had to start again from the beginning. The use of the *tabula recta* was an improvement over Alberti's cipher disk. When the cipher disk was used a new cipher alphabet was introduced after several words. When using the *tabula recta,* a new cipher alphabet was introduced for each new letter. Trithemius did not mention anything about the context in which the *tabula recta* was used. Yet, interestingly, according to Bauer, the method could have been particularly handy for soldiers in the field. They could write up a *tabula recta* and destroy it after use, while it was more difficult to either carry a set of metal cipher disks or cut them out of a piece of paper or cardboard.[15] Here we see again a method used in a context of warfare over long distances, and therefore, a link to the Spartan *scytale*. And we also see the encryption principles of the transposition system of the *scytale* in the changing position of letters when creating a secret message by using the *tabula recta*. In the case of the *scytale*, we see partial Greek letters turned into gibberish when the strip was unwrapped from its original rod, while in this case, we see a meaningless text appear not only in the secret message itself, that is created by changing a letter into another letter, but also in the table that is used for the encryption. Thus, the letters of the alphabet changed position as the letters on the *scytale* did after unwrapping the strip from the rod.

In 1553, another Italian scientist Giovan (or Giovanni) Battista Bellaso made further significant refinements to Alberti's disk. These refinements which again help to illustrate the merits of the ancient Spartan *scytale* system of encryption and help to prove its practical utility as a method of secret messaging are described in Bellaso's *La Cifra del Sig. Giovan Battista Bellaso*.[16] In his system for encryption, Bellaso also used a table in which plaintext and ciphertext would have been found, like the *tabula recta*. However, he added something new to the system: keywords. As we have already seen, the 'key' is the information that someone needs to encrypt and decrypt a message.[17] Instead of using one particular setting of a disk, as Alberti did, Bellaso used complete words or a short sentence that could be easily remembered. Bellaso would then make a table with three rows: first the key; followed by the plaintext; and finally the ciphertext. The keywords were to be placed above the plaintext message. This key had to be repeated constantly, from the beginning until the end of the message (see Table 5). Now another table was used to encrypt the plaintext into ciphertext: Bellaso's encryption table (see

Table 3 *Tabula recta*. Author's illustration based on Trithemius' *Polygraphia*.

```
a b c d e f g h i k l m n o p q r s t u x y z w
b c d e f g h i k l m n o p q r s t u x y z w a
c d e f g h i k l m n o p q r s t u x y z w a b
d e f g h i k l m n o p q r s t u x y z w a b c
e f g h i k l m n o p q r s t u x y z w a b c d
f g h i k l m n o p q r s t u x y z w a b c d e
g h i k l m n o p q r s t u x y z w a b c d e f
h i k l m n o p q r s t u x y z w a b c d e f g
i k l m n o p q r s t u x y z w a b c d e f g h
k l m n o p q r s t u x y z w a b c d e f g h i
l m n o p q r s t u x y z w a b c d e f g h i k
m n o p q r s t u x y z w a b c d e f g h i k l
n o p q r s t u x y z w a b c d e f g h i k l m
o p q r s t u x y z w a b c d e f g h i k l m n
p q r s t u x y z w a b c d e f g h i k l m n o
q r s t u x y z w a b c d e f g h i k l m n o p
r s t u x y z w a b c d e f g h i k l m n o p q
s t u x y z w a b c d e f g h i k l m n o p q r
t u x y z w a b c d e f g h i k l m n o p q r s
u x y z w a b c d e f g h i k l m n o p q r s t
x y z w a b c d e f g h i k l m n o p q r s t u
y z w a b c d e f g h i k l m n o p q r s t u x
z w a b c d e f g h i k l m n o p q r s t u x y
w a b c d e f g h i k l m n o p q r s t u x y z
```

Table 4). To create this table the Italian alphabet was used, which consisted of twenty-two letters in Bellaso's day.[18] The alphabet was first cut into eleven pairs of letters, from 'A-B' to 'Y-Z'; subsequently the same alphabet was cut into two halves. The first half of the alphabet consisted of the letters 'A' to 'M'; the second half the letters 'N' to 'Z'. These two halves of the alphabet were written down next to the letter pair 'A-B' in their normal order. Now, the first half of the alphabet was written down next to all the letter pairs in the normal order, from 'A' to 'M'. However, the second half, which consisted of the letter 'N' to 'Z', was written down in another order every time. The letters 'N' to 'Z' shifted one place to the right every time. So, the first time the line started with the letter 'N', followed by the letters 'O', 'P', 'Q' and so on until the letter 'Z'. The second time the line started with the letter 'Z', followed by 'N', 'O', 'P', 'Q' and so on. This line ended with the letter 'Y'. The third line started with the letter 'Y', followed by the letters 'Z', 'N', 'O', 'P' and so on; and this line ended with the letter 'X'. These lines were subsequently placed under the first halves of the alphabet (letters 'A' to 'M') and next to every letter pair (see Table 4).[19]

In an example that Bellaso discusses himself, the text *'L' armata turchesca partira a cinque di luglio'* ('The armed Turkish forces will leave on the 5th of July') was encrypted with the key phrase *'virtuti omnia parent'* 'everything is obedient to virtue' as shown is Table 5. Above the plaintext, Bellaso wrote the keywords several times, until the complete message was covered. Now the encryption started. The first key letter, the 'V' indicated which alphabet had to be used to encipher the first plaintext letter. So, when we look at Bellaso's table (Table 5), the alphabet next to 'V-X' was needed. In this alphabet the first plaintext letter, the 'L', had to be found. Under the 'L' the letter 'S' can be found. Here the 'S' was the ciphertext letter. The second letter of the plaintext, the 'A', was connected to the second key letter: the letter 'I'. So, now the alphabet next to 'I-L' was needed. In this alphabet the letter 'Y' can be found under the letter 'A'. So, the plaintext 'A' was encrypted into the ciphertext 'Y'. In this way only the letters 'A' to 'M' could be encrypted into one of the letters 'N' to 'Z'. However, the method also worked the other way around. The third letter of the plaintext message, the 'R', can only be found in the lower line. The third letter of the key phrase, which is also an 'R', bring us to the alphabet next to the letter pair 'Q-R'. Above the 'R' we can find the letter 'B'. So, the plaintext letter 'R' was replaced by the cipher- text letter 'B.'[20]

So, in the Bellaso system, eleven ciphertext alphabets are created in which the letters of the second half of the alphabet are transposed one place to the right every time. All these second halves are then jumbled around and added to the first half to create not only an incomprehensible ciphertext, but also eleven incomprehensible ciphertext alphabets available for the encryption. Just as the letters of a *scytale* message turned into an incomprehensible anagram when the encryption took place as the strip was unwrapped from the *scytale* rod, so, in Bellaso's system two incomprehensible anagrams were created: one to create the table used for encryption and one for the encrypted message itself. Also, just as Bellaso used his method for his confidential long-distance communication, e.g. in warfare, so the Spartans would have used the *scytale* for the same purpose in the same context, according to Plutarch and Aulus Gellius.

Modern communication security systems (*c.* 1800 to the present day)

When moving on to the eighteenth century, we can again see the principle of *scytale*-style encryption appearing in so-called cipher machines, which were again, like the *scytale*, used in warfare. Based on Alberti's cipher disk, in the eighteenth century the first cipher machines appear. A cipher machine is a device that consists of a set of wheels or disks placed in a row, with each disk containing the letters of the alphabet arranged around their edge.[21] An example

Table 4 Bellaso's encryption table. Author's illustration based on Bellaso's 'La cifra'.

AB	a	b	c	d	e	f	g	h	i	l	m
	n	o	p	q	r	ſ	t	u	x	y	z
CD	a	b	c	d	e	f	g	h	i	l	m
	t	u	x	y	z	n	o	p	q	r	ſ
EF	a	b	c	d	e	f	g	h	i	l	m
	z	n	o	p	q	r	ſ	t	u	x	y
GH	a	b	c	d	e	f	g	h	i	l	m
	ſ	t	u	x	y	z	n	o	p	q	r
IL	a	b	c	d	e	f	g	h	i	l	m
	y	z	n	o	p	q	r	ſ	t	u	x
MN	a	b	c	d	e	f	g	h	i	l	m
	r	ſ	t	u	x	y	z	n	o	p	q
OP	a	b	c	d	e	f	g	h	i	l	m
	x	y	z	n	o	p	q	r	ſ	t	u
QR	a	b	c	d	e	f	g	h	i	l	m
	q	r	ſ	t	u	x	y	z	n	o	p
ST	a	b	c	d	e	f	g	h	i	l	m
	p	q	r	ſ	t	u	x	y	z	n	o
VX	a	b	c	d	e	f	g	h	i	l	m
	u	x	y	z	n	o	p	q	r	ſ	t
YZ	a	b	c	d	e	f	g	h	i	l	m
	o	p	q	r	ſ	t	u	x	y	z	n

of such an early cipher machine is Jefferson's cipher machine, or Jefferson's disk, invented by Thomas Jefferson in 1795 (Figure 13).[22] The system may have been used by commanders in the field during the American War of Independence (1775–83). Here we see another link to the *scytale* being used by Spartan commanders in the field during their military campaigns.[23] For Jefferson's cipher machine the modern twenty-six-letter English alphabet was used. The order of the letters was different for each disk and was usually scrambled in a random way as letters of *scytale* messages were scrambled when the strip was unwrapped from the *scytale*. Each disk was marked with a unique number. In the case of the Jefferson wheel cipher, these were the numbers one to thirty-six since Jefferson's device contained thirty-six disks. Every disk had a hole in its centre which allowed the disks to be stacked on an axle in the middle.[24] Again, we can see fundamental similarities with the Spartan *scytale* here. The axle can be seen as the *scytale* rod while the removable disks are similar to the strip of writing material that could be wrapped and unwrapped from the *scytale*. As text was written on the strip on the *scytale*, so text, in this case letters, was printed on the disks. Indeed, like the strips of leather or papyrus wrapped and unwrapped around the *scytale* rod, the disks on Jefferson's cipher machine were removable and could be mounted on the axle in any order desired. Since each disk was

Table 5 Scheme to illustrate Bellaso's encryption method. Author's illustration.

Key	V	I	R	T	U	T	I	O	M
Plaintext	L	A	R	M	A	T	A	T	U
Ciphertext	S	Y	B	O	V	E	Y	L	D

Key	N	I	A	P	A	R	E	N	T
Plaintext	R	C	H	E	S	C	A	P	A
Ciphertext	A	N	V	O	F	S	Z	L	P

Key	V	I	R	T	U	T	I	O	M
Plaintext	R	T	I	R	A	A	C	I	N
Ciphertext	I	I	N	C	V	P	N	S	H

Key	N	I	A	P	A	R	E	N	T
Plaintext	Q	U	E	D	I	L	U	G	L
Ciphertext	M	L	R	N	X	O	I	Z	N

Key	V	I
Plaintext	I	O
Ciphertext	R	D

marked with a unique number, the order of the disks, agreed upon between sender and recipient, was indicated by a row of numbers that represented the right order of the disks.[25] Whereas in the case of the *scytale* both parties needed a *scytale* of the same size and diameter to communicate with each other, in the case of Jefferson's method both parties needed Jefferson's cipher machine. Sender and receiver had to arrange the disks in the same predefined order. Once the disks had been placed on the axle in the agreed upon order, the sender rotated each disk up and down until a desired message was spelled out in one row.[26] Then the sender could copy down any row of text on the disks other than the one that contained the plaintext message. The recipient simply had to arrange the disks in the agreed-upon order, rotate the disks so that they spelled out the encrypted message on one row, and then look around the rows until he found the plaintext message, i.e., the row that is not complete gibberish. So, in the case of the Jefferson wheel cipher the message reappeared when the recipient had found the right row in the disk that corresponded with that of the plaintext. In the same way, when using the *scytale*, the encrypted ciphertext message became comprehensible only once the strip had been wrapped around the *scytale* again.

About a century later, we again see a cryptographic system based on the *scytale* appear in American warfare, namely, during the American Civil War (1860–65). In the sixteenth century the French diplomat, cryptographer and alchemist Blaise de Vigenère put the systems of Alberti, Trithemius and Bellaso together, and invented a system with a better key. In Vigènere's system the plaintext itself was used as the key (a so-called 'autokey').[27] Unfortunately, little is known about this original system. At the end of the eighteenth century we see a simpler variation to this method appear. This variation used standard alphabets and a short repeating keyword, instead of an autokey. It is known as the Vigenère cipher among modern cryptographers (Table 6), and it was used during the American Civil War.[28]

This simpler variation of the Vigenère cipher worked in the following way. For encrypting and decrypting messages someone needed a keyword or key phrase, like in Bellaso's example, and an encryption table like the *tabula recta* called the Vigenère table (Table 6). However, where the *tabula recta* consisted of twenty-three ciphertext alphabets, this table consisted of twenty-six ciphertext alphabets, since the modern twenty-six-letter alphabet was used. So, here the first ciphertext alphabet contained the letters 'A' to 'Z', whilst the second one contained the letters 'B' to 'A'. The last one contained the letters 'Z' to 'Y'. Above the first ciphertext alphabet, another alphabet was placed in its normal order. This alphabet represented the plaintext. Here we see a difference from the *tabula recta*, since as we have seen before, in the *tabula recta*, the first line of the table

Figure 13 Jefferson wheel cipher. Author's illustration based on NSA Picture Gallery 2018.

both represented the plaintext alphabet and the first ciphertext alphabet. On the left side of the table another alphabet was placed in its normal order. This is where the keys could be found. On the intersection of a plaintext letter from the top and a key letter, from the left side the correct ciphertext letter could be found. For example, at the intersection of the plaintext letter 'E' and a key 'X' you will find the ciphertext letter 'B'. For deciphering, the process was reversed. The key letter could again be found in the vertical column on the left and the ciphertext within the square, on the same line as the key. The plaintext could then be found on the top line, directly above the ciphertext letter. Thus, for example a key letter 'Z' and a ciphertext letter 'V', gives a plaintext letter 'W'. Just as the letters of a *scytale* message turned into an incomprehensible anagram when the encryption took place as the strip was unwrapped from the *scytale* rod, so, in the Vigenère table incomprehensible anagrams were created too, first by creating the table used for encryption and decryption, and secondly for the encrypted message itself. This is something that we already saw in the discussion of the works of Alberti, Trithemius and Bellaso, which reminds us once more of the fact that systems developed throughout the ages. Also, just as the Spartans could have used the *scytale* for long-distance communication during warfare, so the Vigenère table was used for this purpose during the American Civil War.

We can see the principle of the *scytale* again in Polybius' fire-signalling system that has already been discussed in chapter four. Both the *scytale* and Polybius' system could theoretically have been used in a context of warfare. A modern invention that is only based on Polybius' system is known as the 'Polybius square', a square which consists of five rows and five columns, giving twenty-five cells. In these cells the twenty-six letters of a modern alphabet are written in their normal order from left to right, and top to bottom (Figure 14). Hereby, following an idiosyncratic Latin rather than Greek tradition, the letters 'I' and 'J' are usually placed in the same block.[29] All rows and columns in the square have a number. In a basic square these are the numbers one to five for both rows and columns. Every letter in the square thus gets a coordinate. The letter 'A', for example, can be found in the first row on the first column, which gives the coordinate 1–1, written as '11'.[30] In this way, all the letters in the square have a coordinate between '11' (A) and '55' (Z). The coordinates can be compared to the place of the letters on Polybius' tablets.

A modern message that is sent by the use of a Polybius square, looks like a series of numbers. The message 'Send more troops before midnight', for example, would appear as the following numerical sequence:

43 15 33 14 32 34 42 15 44 42 34 34 35 43 12 15 21 34 42 15 32 24 14 33 24 22 23 44

Table 6 Vigenère table. Author's illustration.

```
  A B C D E F G H I J K L M N O P Q R S T U V W X Y Z
A A B C D E F G H I J K L M N O P Q R S T U V W X Y Z
B B C D E F G H I J K L M N O P Q R S T U V W X Y Z A
C C D E F G H I J K L M N O P Q R S T U V W X Y Z A B
D D E F G H I J K L M N O P Q R S T U V W X Y Z A B C
E E F G H I J K L M N O P Q R S T U V W X Y Z A B C D
F F G H I J K L M N O P Q R S T U V W X Y Z A B C D E
G G H I J K L M N O P Q R S T U V W X Y Z A B C D E F
H H I J K L M N O P Q R S T U V W X Y Z A B C D E F G
I I J K L M N O P Q R S T U V W X Y Z A B C D E F G H
J J K L M N O P Q R S T U V W X Y Z A B C D E F G H I
K K L M N O P Q R S T U V W X Y Z A B C D E F G H I J
L L M N O P Q R S T U V W X Y Z A B C D E F G H I J K
M M N O P Q R S T U V W X Y Z A B C D E F G H I J K L
N N O P Q R S T U V W X Y Z A B C D E F G H I J K L M
O O P Q R S T U V W X Y Z A B C D E F G H I J K L M N
P P Q R S T U V W X Y Z A B C D E F G H I J K L M N O
Q Q R S T U V W X Y Z A B C D E F G H I J K L M N O P
R R S T U V W X Y Z A B C D E F G H I J K L M N O P Q
S S T U V W X Y Z A B C D E F G H I J K L M N O P Q R
T T U V W X Y Z A B C D E F G H I J K L M N O P Q R S
U U V W X Y Z A B C D E F G H I J K L M N O P Q R S T
V V W X Y Z A B C D E F G H I J K L M N O P Q R S T U
W W X Y Z A B C D E F G H I J K L M N O P Q R S T U V
X X Y Z A B C D E F G H I J K L M N O P Q R S T U V W
Y Y Z A B C D E F G H I J K L M N O P Q R S T U V W X
Z Z A B C D E F G H I J K L M N O P Q R S T U V W X Y
```

Table 7 Scheme to illustrate Vigenère encryption method. Author's illustration.

Key	I	N	G	O	D	W	E	T	R
Plaintext	A	T	T	A	C	K	A	T	D
Ciphertext	I	G	Z	O	F	G	E	M	U

Key	U	S	T
Plaintext	A	W	N
Ciphertext	U	O	G

Since every coordinate contains two numbers – one for the row and one for the column – an encrypted text is created that is twice as long, as the non-encrypted text.[31] To decipher the message, the recipient would take a Polybius square, look for the coordinates in the square, and check which letters correspond to these coordinates – using the square as the 'key' with which to decrypt the encoded text. The Polybius square has reportedly been used for simple cryptographic communications in this way by the British Army in the Boer War, and by both

	1	2	3	4	5
1	a	b	c	d	e
2	f	g	h	i/j	k
3	l	m	n	o	p
4	q	r	s	t	u
5	v	w	x	y	z

Figure 14 Polybius square. Author's illustration based on Salomon 2003, 29.

the British and German armies in the First and Second World Wars.[32] Yet, the basic cryptographic operating principles upon which the Polybius square and its encryptions work can also be seen to be employed as the basis for other more sophisticated modern cryptographic methods. In the last year of the First World War, for example, the German military intelligence services used the Polybius square in their ADFGX and ADFGVX ciphers,[33] named after the only five, and later the only six, alphabetic letters that appeared in the ciphertext.[34] Messages encrypted with the ciphers were transmitted by Morse code so these six letters were chosen to minimise transmission errors, since the letters sound very different from one another in Morse code. In March 1918, the first of these cipher systems was introduced: the ADFGX cipher. This cipher used a Polybius square of 5x5. This square was filled with the twenty-six letters of the German alphabet in a random order, and the ensuing distribution pattern – the encryption key – shared between sender and recipient (Figure 15).[35] This scrambling of letters is a key characteristic of the modern Polybius square (Figures 14 and 15), something that we cannot see in the ancient accounts of Polybius' system in which the letters never seem to have changed position.[36]

The rows and columns of the Polybius square used for the cipher were then labelled with the letters 'A', 'D', 'F', 'G' and 'X' to produce a coordinate for each of the plaintext letters: in this case, for example, the plaintext letter 'Y', was encrypted as 'XF' (Figure 16).

In this way, a ciphertext was created that was twice as long as the plaintext, and that only contained the letters 'A', 'D', 'F', 'G' and 'X'. The plaintext message 'Send weapons quickly', for example, would have been substituted into the following ciphertext:

A	N	B	R	I
Q	E	U	H	P
K	L	O	W	D
S	C	V	X	Z
G	T	Y	F	M

Figure 15 ADFGX cipher table. Author's illustration.

	A	D	F	G	X
A	A	N	B	R	I
D	Q	E	U	H	P
F	K	L	O	W	D
G	S	C	V	X	Z
X	G	T	Y	F	M

Figure 16 ADFGX cipher table with rows and columns marked with letters. Author's illustration.

GA DD AD FX FG DD AA DX FF AD GA DA DF AX GD FA FD XF[37]

In June 1918, three months after the introduction of the first ADFGX cipher, the Germans added an extra row and column to the Polybius square that was used for the cipher to create a 6x6 grid to increase the level of sophistication of the method. Extending the grid meant that an extra letter was required to create the ciphertext. The letter V was chosen for this since this letter sounds different from the five other letters in Morse code. The newly created cipher was accordingly (and perhaps unimaginatively) called the ADFGVX cipher.[38] It worked in the exact same way as its predecessor the ADFGX cipher. The ADFGX and ADFGVX ciphers were the most advanced cipher systems that the German military intelligence used during the First World War.[39] In fact, despite being based on the encryption principles of the Polybius square, and sharing common features with an ancient Greek fire signalling device invented more than 2,000 years earlier, they turned out (according to military historians and modern cryptographers) to be amongst the toughest ciphers known in military secret communication until the end of the First World War.[40] The fact that we see the same basic technologies of secret communication also used in Antiquity, helps us to appreciate more fully the practical efficiency and value of those basic technologies and techniques. Indeed, the fact that ancient core principles of cryptography are still in use in some form in the twentieth- and even twenty-first-century methods for secret communication, demonstrates that these methods would and could have worked well in Antiquity, an idea that this book set out to consider more fully in the controversial context of the ancient Spartan *scytale*. And in fact, we can see the encryption principle of the *scytale* again in the tables used to create the Polybius square and the AGDFX and ADFGVX ciphers. Like we have seen in the tables of Trithemius, Bellaso and Vigenère, incomprehensible anagrams were created twice: first by drawing the table used for encryption and decryption, and secondly for the encrypted message itself. This principle obviously applies to the Polybius square and the AGDFX and ADFGVX tables as well. In the same way, the letters of a *scytale* message turned into an incomprehensible anagram when the encryption took place as the strip was unwrapped from the *scytale* rod. And once more, just as the Spartans could have used the *scytale* for long-distance communication during warfare, so the Polybius square was used by the British Army in the Boer War, and by both the British and German armies in the First and Second World Wars, while the ADFGX and ADFGVX ciphers were used in the First World War.

Cipher machines – such as the Jefferson wheel cipher invented in 1795 – did not become well known until an independent invention by the French commander Etienne Bazeries popularised their use in military contexts about a hundred years later, in 1891.[41] Indeed, a reinvention of the system – known as the M-94 cylinder cipher – was used by the United States Army from about 1922 to 1942 (Figure 17).[42] Like Jefferson's wheel cipher, Bazeries' device consisted of removable disks (in this case twenty-five of them)[43] – like the removable strip with writing material that could be wrapped and unwrapped from the *scytale* – and an axle in the middle, like the *scytale* rod. Similarly, both parties needed identical devices – both parties in the United States Army needed a M-94 cylinder to communicate with each other – just as for the Spartans both parties would theoretically have needed an identical *scytale* rod. And, it is my contention, just as the United States Army used the M-94 cylinder cipher for secret communication until halfway into the Second World War, so the Spartans could have used the *scytale* for secret communication in warfare.

Finally, there exists a superficial physical resemblance between an Enigma machine and the *scytale* rod, where the disks on the axle of the machine might

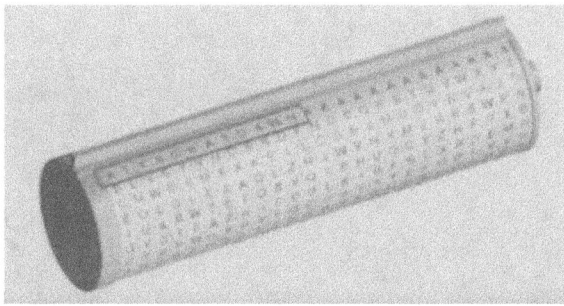

Figure 17 M-94 cipher cylinder. Author's illustration based on Kopal 2018, 941.

be compared to the strip of writing material that was wrapped about the *scytale* rod (Figure 18). However, the Enigma machine and the *scytale* system have nothing in common in terms of actual functionality, beyond their common use as cryptographic devices. Yet, it can be usefully kept in mind that, just as the Germans used the Enigma machine to attempt to secure their secret and confidential communication in warfare, so the Spartans would have used the *scytale* for the same purpose in the same context.

So far, we have seen several devices used for encryption and decryption that somehow resemble the Spartan *scytale*. Yet, the transposition cipher itself, like the transposition in the *scytale* method, developed as well in the early twentieth century. In the First World War, for example, the German military intelligence services used a transposition cipher in all their confidential correspondence, based on a principle similar to that used in the *scytale*.[44] In the 1920s, transposition ciphers were used by the Irish Republican Army, while during the Second World War various forms of transposition ciphers were used by both Axis and Allied powers: by Royal Air Force pilots, by Britain's Special Operations Executive (SOE) and by German troops operating in Latin America.[45] By the beginning of the Second World War, transposition ciphers had developed even further. In this period, combinations of transposition and substitution ciphers were used, by both the Axis and Allied Powers, and by resistance groups.[46] In simple modern transposition ciphers, the letters of a message are rearranged to generate an incomprehensible anagram, but remain *intact*, unlike the partial and broken letters that Plutarch and Aulus Gellius mention, a crucial point in this case.[47] Most modern transposition ciphers are created by the use of a grid composed of squares or cells.[48] The cryptographer inscribes one letter in each cell, writing from left to right (for most western languages), and from top to bottom (Figure 19).

With the text of the message written into the grid, a modern cryptographer still has the normal plaintext before her (Figure 19). To make the message

Figure 18 Rotors on Enigma machine. Author's illustration.

```
Q U I S S I M S C
I E S E X E O Q U
E M A D T E M I S
I C U R A U T V I
R S I S E T C O G
I T A Q U E M I N
L O C U M S I S P
R O G R E S S U S
V I D E Q U I D T
I B I I A M S I T
N E C E S S E E T T
C U R A U T O M N
I U M T I B I A U
X I L I A A D I U
N G A S E T I A M
I N F I M O R U M
```

Figure 19 Plaintext message written in grid. Author's illustration based on Reinke 1962, 116.

incomprehensible, a second step must be taken. In other words: the transposition must take place. To achieve this, a second rectangle is drawn in which the cryptographer re-transcribes the same message. However, now the letters in the columns, from top to bottom, are written horizontally from left to right, starting at the top left (Figure 20). So, instead of starting the first row with the letters Q-U-I-S, it now starts with Q-I-E-I, the letters that were first in the first column and that are now transposed to another row.

Now the cryptographer has the encrypted ciphertext: an incomprehensible anagram in which every letter has changed position. To make decryption even harder, the cryptographer can choose not only to write the letters of the columns as if they were the letters of the rows, but also to rearrange the order of the columns. This is called columnar transposition in modern cryptographic terms.[49] If columnar transposition is applied to a grid, a numerical key or a keyword shows

```
Q  I  E  I  R  I  L  R  V
I  N  C  I  X  N  I  U  E
M  C  S  T  O  O  I  B  E
U  U  I  G  N  I  S  A  U
I  A  C  G  D  I  C  R  M
L  A  F  S  E  D  R  S  Q
U  R  E  I  E  A  T  I  S
I  S  X  T  A  E  U  M  E
Q  A  S  U  I  A  E  M  I
E  E  U  T  E  S  S  U  M
S  T  B  A  T  O  M  O  M
T  C  M  I  S  I  S  E  O
I  D  I  R  S  Q  I  V  O
I  S  U  D  I  E  M  A  I
A  U  C  U  S  I  G  N  P
S  T  T  T  N  U  U  M  M
```

Figure 20 Encrypted text columns written from left to right in rows. Author's illustration based on Reinke 1962, 116.

```
QIEI    RILR    VINC
IXNI    UEMC    STOO
IBEU    UIGN    ISAU
IACG    DICR    MLAF
SEDR    SQUR    EIEA
TISI    SXTA    EUME
QASU    IAEM    IEEU
TESS    UMST    BATO
MOMT    CMIS    ISEO
IDIR    SQIV    OISU
DIEM    AIAU    CUSI
GNPS    TTTN    UUMM
```

Figure 21 Encrypted text divided into groups of letters. Author's illustration based on Reinke 1962, 116.

the intended recipient the right order of the columns. Another possibility for the cryptographer to make decryption harder is to divide the text into columns which can then be further rearranged (in Figure 21 the text is cut into three columns).

Indeed, in the same way as the *scytalae* rods must be perfectly matched cylinders, the interval between the successive letters of the plaintext in a columnar cipher must always remain constant. Indeed, as Bauer cogently points out, columnar transposition ciphers can be broken by using high-tech graph paper and scissors.[50]

This is, in fact, how modern cryptanalysts in the First World War would try to decipher some transposition ciphers: they would cut the text in the grids into strips, either horizontally or vertically. These strips were then juxtaposed (Figure 22). By sliding the strips up and down (or from side to side), the cryptanalyst would eventually have come to the point where she correctly surmised that one or more of the resulting trigraphs represented a clear text. The number of places that the cryptanalyst had to slide the strips relative to each other to get this clear text would have given her the interval that she was looking for. Then, when she had noted the interval between the letters of any one decoded trigraph, she would have applied this same interval to the other strips to establish the sequence of the letters in the rest of the dispatch, and she would eventually have arrived at the complete solution.[51] The deciphering of the encryption interval in this modern example is, perhaps, the equivalent of figuring out the exact diameter of a Spartan *scytale* in Antiquity.

In the early twentieth century we also see how cipher wheels keep developing. As we have already seen, in 1891, the French Major Etienne Bazeries developed a twenty-disk cylindrical cipher device, like the Jefferson wheel cipher.[52] In 1913, the American officer Parker Hitt (re)invented this basic cylinder cipher that made use of a ten-disk device based on Bazeries' system for the United States Army. Three years later, in 1916, Hitt then decided to flatten out the cylinder cipher into a strip cipher for ease of use.[53] Around the same time, in 1917, Major Joseph O. Mauborgne, invented a similar twenty-five-disk cipher device.[54] This work formed the basis for the cylindrical cipher device M-94 that was adopted by the United States Army in 1922.[55] This device consisted of: 'a central shaft on which is mounted a set of 25 rotatable alphabetical disks. On the rim of each disk is stamped a different, completely disarranged alphabet.'[56]

As in the case of the earlier cipher machines, and like the Jefferson wheel cipher, we are dealing here with a cylinder on which the disks could be stacked around the shaft in any order desired to create cryptographic messages. The fact that the M-94 worked in a similar fashion to the earlier cipher machines described above becomes clear from Kruh's description of the M-94:

The Development of the Principle of the Transposition Cipher System   141

QIEI	RILR	VINC
IXNI	UEMC	STOO
IBEU	UIGN	ISAU
IACG	DICR	MLAF
SEDR	SQUR	EIEA
TISI	SXTA	EUME
QASU	IAEM	IEEU
TESS	UMST	BATO
MOMT	CMIS	ISEO
IDIR	SQIV	OISU
DIEM	AIAU	CUSI
GNPS	TTTN	UUMM

Figure 22   Ciphertext cut into strips. Author's illustration based on Reinke 1962, 116.

After the encipherer [or sender] places the disks on the shaft in the prearranged order, he revolves one disk after another to align the first 25 letters of the message in a horizontal row. Then he selects at random any one of the other rows, which will form 25 letters of gibberish, as the ciphertext. He repeats this process in groups of 25 letters to the end of the message.[57]

The decipherer (or recipient) – who had knowledge of the correct order of the disks to decipher the message – would then have assembled the 'disks on the shaft' in the required order (turning each disk so that the ciphertext can be read across them), and would look for the line that contained the message: this was the line that was not complete gibberish.[58] About a decade later however, in 1933, the army decided to move from Mauborgne's M-94 cipher to Hitt's flattened strip cipher, and in 1934 the so-called M-138 strip cipher was officially adopted by the US military, followed by the improved version, the M-138-A, in 1938.[59] The M-138 and the M-138-A were 'flat strip cipher board' substitution ciphers that were (again) cryptologically equivalent to the Jefferson wheel cipher (similarly utilising 'different, sliding, mixed alphabets'), and to the previously discussed M-94 cipher.[60] Yet, in this case, paper strips were used in a flat device instead of the wheels on the M-94 cipher machine. When using the M-138-A, the cryptographer had a choice between 100 strips on which the alphabet was printed twice, every time in a different order. Thirty strips were selected to use each time, as opposed to the twenty-five disks on the M-94 (Figure 17).[61] The increasing number of strips obviously increased the security of the system. The

M-138-A cipher saw a great deal of use within the American military intelligence services – especially during the Second World War – and continued to be used until the 1960s.[62] In fact, even though electromechanical cipher machines (like Enigma) were introduced during the Second World War 'strip cipher systems continued in use by individuals, such as military attaches or units not authorised to use cipher machines', and even as 'standby equipment for [electromechanical cipher] machine users'.[63]

To encipher and decipher the strip cipher M-138-A, the cryptographer would have needed the right device for encryption and the strips should have been in the correct order to enable the cryptanalyst to understand the message (Figures 22–23), again just as, when enciphering and deciphering a *scytale* message, both sender and recipient would have needed *scytalae* of the exact same size and diameter to be able to properly and easily communicate with each other. In this context, it is significant that (according to Kruh), the US Army distributed its own flat strip cipher devices 'to at least six foreign governments including France, Italy and Russia, so they would maintain secure communications with United States Army personnel.'[64]

Although there are no direct connections between the Spartan *scytale* and twentieth-century ciphers (and a great many *operational* differences despite some ostensible *optical* similarities), just as twentieth-century cryptographers used (columnar) transposition ciphers, cylinders and strip ciphers for their secret and confidential communication in warfare, so – I argue – the Spartans could have used the *scytale* for the same purpose in the same context (at least theoretically). In fact, I suggest that the Spartan system that Plutarch and Gellius describe was arguably even more complicated than some of these transposition ciphers. For, when using the *scytale* the Spartan cryptanalyst would end up having many partial and broken letters in the code while, in these later ciphers, the letters retain their identity, but simply lose their position.[65] In other words, the cryptanalyst does not end up with partial and broken letters. When a twentieth-century cryptanalyst intercepted a secret message written in a modern transposition cipher, she could decipher the message by rearranging the order of the letters. However, when a Spartan intercepted an encrypted message written by use of a *scytale*, he would have had to deal with both whole and partial letters (Figure 5). He would therefore have needed a *scytale* of the exact same diameter as the one that was used to write the original message to quickly restore the original place of all the scrambled letters, both complete and partial. We can go another step further in the development of transposition ciphers based on the *scytale* system.

The Development of the Principle of the Transposition Cipher System   143

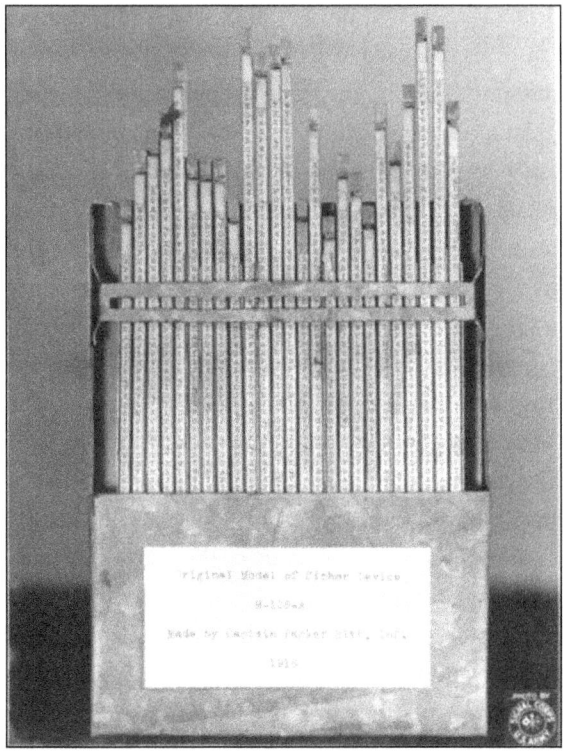

Figure 23 DTRIP cipher M-138-A. Author's illustration, based on Bauer 2017, 361–4.

During the First and Second World Wars, encryption by means of transposition ciphers was still done by hand. Cryptographers would use physical tables, grids and strips of paper to encipher and decipher their confidential correspondence. Since the 1970s and 1980s, however, as computer systems took over from handwritten correspondence, cryptography became electronic. Instead of physical tables, grids and strips of paper, computers were used to encipher and decipher messages. Interestingly, the principle of the Spartan *scytale* can still be seen in some modern digital transposition ciphers. For example, apart from the modern mathematical element, unknown to ancient societies, the basic principle of transposition encryption can still be found in the Advanced Encryption Standard (AES). This is a specification for the encryption of electronic data established by the United States National Institute of Standards and Technology (NIST) in 2001, and is still used worldwide. And ultimately, we see the scytale's basic encryption principle in the *New Scytale* algorithm. Here, literally, albeit digitally, a secret message is wrapped around a geometric form in the same way the Spartans could have wrapped *scytale* messages around *scytalae*.[66]

All forms of the ciphers and devices discussed in this chapter could have – and in several cases, were – used in warfare for encrypting and decrypting secret long-distance communication. The same applies to the Spartan *scytale*, which, according to Plutarch and Aulus Gellius was used for long-distance communications between the *ephors* in Sparta and officers in the field. Even though the *scytale* is only a theoretical cipher – perhaps invented by Plutarch in the second century CE – we should not overlook the fact that Plutarch provides us with a description of the earliest known transposition cipher in history. The historical cryptographic examples analysed in this chapter show the fundamental and enduring usefulness of relatively simple ciphers, supporting the main argument of this book that the *scytale* would similarly have been useful in the ancient world as a cryptographic device. The system of this transposition method keeps reappearing throughout the ages, up into the twenty-first century.

Moreover, as these various examples of the widespread use of ciphers using encryption techniques broadly analogous to those of the *scytale* attest, simple though a cipher may appear, it may not be easy to solve.[67] On this basis it seems naive for modern historians of cryptography to completely dismiss the ancient Spartan *scytale* as a 'toy' cipher, and to deny its value as a theoretical cryptographic device. In other words, as a report from the US Army Security Agency argues: 'It is very easy for us to condemn old devices in the light of later knowledge, and the M-94 looks childishly simple to us now, but let nobody underestimate the good purpose that it did serve at a period when something better than the old Cipher Disk and Playfair were badly needed.'[68]

In other words, systems develop throughout time as and when needed. A system that may seem simple nowadays has had a purpose as some point in the past. The same is true of Plutarch's Spartan *scytale* system, whether it was in fact used by the Spartans in the fifth and fourth centuries BCE or not. The system still formed the basis for techniques known up to the present day, ultimately in the *New Scytale* algorithm.

Conclusion

Greek warfare in the Classical period has long been seen as a practice following unwritten rules. This 'practice of unwritten rules' has led scholars to believe for a long time that Greek warfare was fair, open and structured with hoplite armies facing each other on the battlefield.[1] However, in recent years this view of fair and structured Greek warfare has changed.[2] In fact, it seems that the ancient Greeks freely used trickery and deceit in war, already starting in mythical times with the trick of the Trojan horse (Homer, *Odyssey*, 4.21, 8.512; Virgil, *Aeneid*, 2.1–56, 2.228–253). Next to tricking the enemy, the gathering of intelligence and spying on one's enemies was essential for the ancient Greeks too, to determine the political and military direction of the state, especially in times of conflict when essential information on the enemy can obviously facilitate the war effort.[3]

In chapter one we have seen how common warfare was in ancient Greece, and how it developed from the Archaic to the Classical period. Wars in ancient Greece from the beginning of the Graeco-Persian Wars (499 BCE) to the end of the Peloponnesian War (404 BCE) clearly changed in scope, scale and character. With increasing numbers of men and states involved in warfare, clear communication between all parties – and importantly between the right parties – became more and more necessary. One's ally could be the enemy soon after, since alliances changed rapidly. It is in the period from the outbreak of the Peloponnesian War in 431 BCE to the end of Spartan hegemony at the Battle of Leuctra in 371 BCE, that communication networks expanded further. Armies became increasingly diversified, with one state taking over hegemony from the other. It is also the period in which commanders were away from home and would, therefore, have needed devices to enable secure confidential long-distance communications during operations in the field. According to Plutarch and Aulus Gellius, the Spartans used the *scytale* for this purpose.

Next to this alleged use of the scytale, we saw in chapter two that the Spartans were also sometimes seen as different from other Greeks and as 'illiterate', especially by the Athenians. Here we examined a salient selection of the earliest examples of secret communication in the Classical world, particularly Herodotus' four examples of this, as described in his *Histories*. It has been demonstrated that these early examples of secret communication are associated with non-Greeks and their use characterised as un-Greek behaviour. Hereby, Herodotus' account of Demaratus' letter to the Spartans nicely illustrates the biased ancient Greek view of the Spartans as a society familiar with the use of secret communication (in contrast to the open modes of communication preferred by other Greeks), and that the Spartans may have learned about the use of secret communication from the Persians. Yet, this example also shows us that the 'illiterate' Spartans were perfectly capable of reading and writing.

The work in the first two chapters established the groundwork for the focus of the book and prepared the way for a detailed analysis of various ancient myths concerning the Spartan *scytale* in chapter three. Mindful of the absence of any direct Spartan sources on the *scytale*, and of the biases in non-Spartan sources, including the contradictory stereotyping of the ancient Spartans as both practitioners of secret written communications *and* as semi-illiterate, a comprehensive range of surviving non-Spartan sources have been analysed in detail. This analysis demonstrated that Greek sources vary widely in their discussions of the *scytale* and, although they were broadly consistent in associating the *scytale* with messaging, they typically did not associate it with secret messaging per se. In fact, we have seen that *scytalae* were used for a variety of purposes throughout the Archaic and Classical period of Greek history. Furthermore, these purposes changed and developed over time.

For example, one of the oldest purposes of the *scytale* was its use as an authentication device, known from the oldest Greek sources including Pindar's *Olympian Odes* (6.91–93), and a fragment by Herennius Philo (*On the Different Meanings of Words*, Fragment 185). Yet, in later times we see the *scytale* being used for other purposes including record keeping (*Biblioteca Apostolica Vaticana*; *Vat. Gr. 2306*), and to identify fallen soldiers on the battlefield (Diodorus Siculus, *Library of History*, 8.27; Polyaenus, *Stratagems of War*, 1.17).[4] One other purpose of the *scytale* is its use as a Spartan cryptographic device in the fifth and fourth centuries BCE, as argued by Plutarch (*Life of Lysander*, 19.5–7) and Aulus Gellius (*Attic Nights*, 17.9.6–16) in the second century CE. There is no evidence from the fifth and fourth centuries BCE that *scytalae* were in fact used for the purpose of secret messaging, and perhaps this purpose was even made up by Plutarch to enrich his stories. However, the fact that *scytalae* were used for a number of purposes that changed and developed over time, makes it theoretically plausible that secret messaging was one of these other practical uses of the device. This further development of devices and systems for communication security is something that keeps reappearing throughout the ages.

Having demonstrated the obvious potential of the *scytale* as a simple yet secure device for secret communication (even though only theoretically), chapter four considered the enigma of why the *scytale* was apparently overlooked by one of the most important classical Greek sources on practical ancient forms of secret communication: Aeneas Tacticus' *How to Survive Under Siege*. Even though *scytalae* are theoretical ciphers, it is too simple to state that they were never used for secret communication just because Aeneas never discussed the device. Whereas the *scytalae* would typically have been used for long-distance communication between Sparta and the battlefield, Aeneas Tacticus, in contrast, was more interested in short distance local communications during sieges. Next to this, Aeneas Tacticus – living and writing in a post-war period (after the Peloponnesian War) – may well have considered Spartan devices like the *scytale* as unworthy of inclusion in his treatise for Greeks. Finally, and perhaps most importantly, Aeneas Tacticus seemed to have been more interested in steganographic practices than cryptographic practices since the focus of *How to Survive Under Siege* is upon hiding messages to smuggle them in and out of a besieged *polis* and not upon encoding them to prevent them from being read and understood by hostile agents out in the field. The absence of the Spartan *scytale* from Aeneas Tacticus' treatise, therefore, cannot offer sufficient evidence to support the theory forwarded by Whitehead, West and Sheldon that the *scytale* was unknown to Aeneas Tacticus because it was not really an ancient cryptograph.

The Romans also seemingly never adopted the Spartan *scytale* for cryptographic communications in their own military contexts (chapter five), even though they were evidently familiar with descriptions of the device, and even believed it to be a Spartan cryptograph, unlike earlier Greek sources. Like Aeneas Tacticus, the Romans seem to have had a greater interest in steganography than cryptography, potentially because, in the Roman world, in general 'sealed' wax tablet letters were written and sent for communication. The use of the *scytale* with its sticks, and strips of papyrus or parchment, must have consequently seemed highly impractical and alien to the Romans, and helps to explain why the *scytale* model of secure and secret communication was not adopted by them.

Roman sources not only offer us concrete evidence that the *scytale* was perceived as a tool for secret cryptographic communication in the Classical world, but we also see that Roman, rather than Greek, sources give us the first solid confirmation for the operating principles of this cryptographic device. However, other evidence helps us to appreciate the practical utility of the *scytale* more fully as a tool for secret communication and to better understand its use and value as a cryptograph for the ancient Spartans. This is in the form of cipher systems from later periods, from the Renaissance right up to the twenty-first century. Throughout the ages, analogous principles to those employed by the *scytale* system have played a major role in the history of cryptography (particularly in military contexts), culminating in the *New Scytale* algorithm in which secret messages are digitally wrapped around a geometric form.[5] The fact that this core principle can still be found in the most recent and sophisticated examples of communication security demonstrates that it could have worked well in Antiquity too. Therefore, based on these comparisons, it can be concluded that it is naive for some modern historians of cryptography to dismiss the ancient Spartan *scytale* as a 'toy' cipher and to deny its historic value as a real cryptographic device.

To conclude, the aim of this work was to reassess the extant evidence concerning the cryptographic Spartan device known as the *scytale* and to challenge the view promoted by some modern historians of cryptography that see the *scytale* essentially as a simple 'stick' or staff that would have served little practical use as a vehicle for secret communication in the ancient world. It has been demonstrated that, even though there is no evidence that *scytalae* were used by the Spartans in the fifth and fourth centuries BCE, the cryptographic principles of this theoretical system should not be overlooked. The cryptographic principles employed in the *scytale* are potentially more complex and secure than other known ancient ciphers (especially the system used in the Caesar cipher). Indeed, we can draw favourable comparisons with a selection of historic ciphers in order to illustrate the relative sophistication of the Spartan *scytale* as a practical device for secret communication, at least theoretically.

Bauer argues that a summary of ancient Greek cryptography must, by necessity, be incomplete.[6] This is an important caveat since we only have access to a small sample of original extant material, only a tiny proportion of which survives, and which necessarily offers us only an incomplete picture of the role of cryptography in Antiquity. What is more, secret communication – by its very nature – is secret. Therefore, a great deal of information about ancient cryptography is concealed from, as well as unavailable to, modern eyes. One of the reasons that we know so little about the Spartan *scytale* and its actual deployment is because the Spartans were (at least, according to Athenian sources) a relatively 'secretive' society. Yet, Bauer's caveat has provided one of the core inspirations behind the shape and scope of this thesis. For, although it is itself also necessarily incomplete, this book includes the most comprehensive catalogue of classical cryptography from Graeco-Roman Antiquity (see Appendix 3) and represents the only study to date that seeks to understand the value and operating principles of the Spartan *scytale* by analysing its cryptographic potential through comparison with modern transposition cipher systems.

In setting out this research in this way, I hope to have unravelled some of the myths surrounding the Spartan *scytale*, and of classical Greek and Roman cryptography more widely. Yet, some secrets will most likely never be uncovered. On the one hand, information that is needed to decipher (ancient) secret messages may be lost forever, while on the one hand, systems for cryptography and steganography keep developing and keep being improved, making it harder for 'the enemy' to decipher a message every time.[7] This means that we can keep researching the history of cryptography in the entire (ancient) world, since: 'There will always be secrets – personal secrets, political secrets, military secrets – and there will always be those determined to uncover those secrets.'[8] In continuing this research, I hope not only that 'the 21st century will see transposition regain its true importance'[9], but that the twenty-first century will also see the ancient Spartan *scytale* – whether it was only a theoretical method, or in fact one actually used by the Spartans – regain its true importance in the history of cryptography.[10]

Notes

Preface

1 Diepenbroek 2015.

Introduction

1 Krentz, 1997; 2002; Pritchett 1971; Van Wees 2000.
2 Krentz 2009, 170. See for a list of deceptions in archaic and classical Greek warfare: Krentz 2009, 183–200.
3 Bauer 2013, 2017; D'Agapeyeff '1939; Dooley 2013; Kahn 1967, 1974, 1996; Singh 1999.
4 In the ninth edition of the *Encyclopaedia Britannica* (1878) cryptography and steganography are incorrectly seen as the same practice (p. 669).
5 Cox, Miller et al. 2007, 2. See also Johnson, Duric et al. 2001, 1; Kahn 1996, 1; Schaathun 2012, 15; Singh 1999, 5; Whitiak 2003, 1.
6 Cox, Kalker et al. 2003, 158.
7 Bauer 2007a, 9: Kipper 2004, 47–8.
8 Kipper 2004, 42.
9 Chatton 2010, 43 Bauer 2007a, 13–17; Kipper 2004, 43, Lunde, 2012, 42.
10 Bauer 2007a, 10; Kipper 2004, 42.
11 Bauer 2013, xix; Hodges 1985, 146; Reba and Shier 2015, 479–80; Reinke 1962, 113; Seyfarth 1970, 181; Smith 1955, 16.
12 Mollin 2005, 1; Reba and Shier 2015, 480.
13 Mollin 2005, 1.
14 Churchhouse 2002, 64.
15 Bauer 2007a, 382; Reinke 1962, 113; Singh 1999, 5.
16 Ibid.
17 Interestingly, the terms 'cryptography' and 'steganography' are relative neologisms. The term 'steganography' first appears in the title of Johannes Trithemius' 1499 book *Steganographia*. The term 'cryptography' first appeared in Toustain and Tassin's 1750 work *Nouveau traité de diplomatique*, and in fiction in Edgar Allan Poe's 1843 short story *The Gold Bug*. Also, ancient sources on steganography often pre-date the

ancient sources on cryptography, offering us some of our earliest examples of secret communication.
18 See also Gerber 1997, 102; Hanink 2014, 56; Zavaliy 2020, 53.
19 D'Agapeyeff 1939, 15, 135; Churchhouse 2002, 13; Gardner 1983, 56; Mollin 2005, 5; Piper and Murphy 2002, 22; Sheldon 1986, 46–7; Smart 2018, 3; Walker 2008, 150.
20 Cox, Miller et al. 2007; D'Agapeyeff 1939; Kahn 1967; 1996a; 1996b; Mollin 2005; Sheldon 2008, 54–148; Singh 1999; Whitiak 2003, 1.
21 Whitiak 2003, 1.
22 Galland 1945, v.
23 Galland 1945, v.

1 Structure of Ancient Greek Armies and Military Communication

1 This period and region are chosen since in the rest of the book the Spartan *scytale* will be discussed, a device that was said to be used in the fifth and fourth centuries BCE for a variety of purposes, including for (secret) communication among the Spartans.
2 See also Herodotus, *Histories*, 7.9; 7.136.2; Thucydides, *History of the Peloponnesian War*, 1.85, 3.9.1, 3.59.1l, 4.97.2–3.
3 Connor 1988, 18; Detienne 1968, 123; Krentz 1997 (*passim*); Krentz 2002, 23; Mitchell 1996, 87–105; De Romilly 1968, 211; Sage 1996, xvii; Van Wees 2000; Vernant 1968, 21.
4 Detienne 1968, 123; Krentz 2002, 23; De Romilly 1968, 211; Vernant 1968, 21.
5 Mitchell 1996, 87–105; Connor 1988, 18.
6 The modern term 'Trojan horse' is derived from this ancient Greek story that led to the fall of the city of Troy: Landwehr, Bull et al. 1993.
7 Gerolymatos 1986, 13.
8 Starr 1974, 1.
9 See chapter five for references on the use of secret confidential information in the context of love letters. Evidence for the use of secret confidential information in other contexts in Antiquity might be lost.
10 Sheldon 2008, 8.
11 Ibid.
12 Richmond 1998, 2.
13 Blome 2020, 47.
14 Interestingly, at the same time the Trojan soldier Dolon promises to check on the Greek camp, making this an act of counterintelligence (Homer, *Iliad*, 10.204–459).
15 See for example on trickster figures in Greek myth: Harris and Platzner 2012, 106–27, 174, 196, 267.

16 Against deceiving one's friends, see e.g. Xenophon, *Anabasis*, 3.1.10, 5.7.5–11, 7.6.21; *Symposium*, 4.10.
17 Krentz 2009, 178; Pritchett 1971.
18 Pritchett 1971; Roisman 1993, 11, 23–33; True 1956, 420–47; Woodcock 1928, 93–108.
19 Richmond 1998, 6.
20 Naiden 2017, 62.
21 Cherry 1962, 1144.
22 Aitkenhead 2012.
23 Martin 2013, 46.
24 Connolly 2006, 37; Sekunda 2000, 3. The word *hoplite* (ὁπλίτης) derives from *hoplon* (ὅπλον) meaning 'the arms carried by a hoplite' (Sekunda 2000, 3).
25 Every hoplite had body armour and three weapons: the *aspis* (a shield measuring between 80 and 100 centimetres (31–39 inches)), a *doru* (a spear of 6–9 feet long), and a *xiphos* (a short sword). Alexander the Great's Macedonian hoplites had much longer spears called *sarissas*. These spears were 18 feet long (Bowden 1993, 45–63; Campbell 2014; Farrington 2019, 7; Fink 2014, 32; Markle 1977).
26 Connolly 2006, 37–8.
27 Zafeiropoulou and Agelarakis 2005, 30–5.
28 Krentz 2002, 23.
29 See on the Battle of Sepeia Robinson 2011, 7–9.
30 Hanson 1991, 89–91.
31 Amyx 1988, 31–3; Benson 1989, 56–8; Connolly 2006, 37; Dunbabin and Robertson 1953, 179–80; Krentz 2002, 23; Murray 1993, 130; Zafeiropoulou and Agelarakis 2005, 30–5.
32 In close battle formation each hoplite would occupy approximately 45 centimetres of ground. In open formation this would have been approximately 90 centimetres (Asclepiodotus, *Tactics* 4.3; Goldsworthy 1997, 4).
33 Hanson 1991, 88–9.
34 Phiher 2012, 202; Ramsey 2016.
35 Osborne 2002, 98.
36 Hanson 1991, 88–9; 139–41.
37 Hanson 1991, 169.
38 The size of a hoplite army, and therefore the number of casualties, could vary a lot. See on this Grossman 1996, 12–13; Hanson 1991, 88–9; 139–41; Sacks, Murray et al. 2014, 361.
39 Still, casualties in hoplite battles were low compared to later battles, with about 5 per cent casualties on the winning side, and *c.* 14–15 per cent on the losing side (Crowley 2016, 56; Farrington 2019; Rosenstein 2015, 424; O'Halloran 2018, 80; Sage 2002, 95).
40 Sprawski 2011, 135–8.

41 At the time the Athenians sent messengers to the Spartans to ask for help, the Spartans did not immediately respond because of the *Karneios* (or *Carneia*), a religious festival (Herodotus, *Histories*, 6.106; see also Lebow 2008, 199; Fink 2014; Olson 2013, 157).
42 Holland 2006, 187–91.
43 Ibid.
44 Lendering 2019.
45 Holland 2006, 194–7.
46 Holland 2006, 344–52.
47 Naiden 2017, 63.
48 Piper 2002, entry 'cryptography'.
49 Communication could not only go wrong in the heat of battle when men got scared and confused, it also happened because of overconfidence. At the Battle of Cunaxa in 401 BCE, Cyrus' elite troops of 600 men left him to pursue the enemy. Later, when a counterattack began, Cyrus found himself virtually alone, and could not reach his troops in time. He had become a victim of a communication breakdown (Xenophon, *Anabasis*, 1.8.25). Another example is related to the Battle of Olynthus in 382 BCE, when the Spartan commander Teleutias came to the rescue of the *peltasts*. Teleutias became overzealous and went too fast. In this way, he lost touch with his troops, and could not reach them when a counterattack started (Xenophon, *Hellenica*, 5.3.3–6).
50 An interesting observation about the advantage of a coherent battle cry over a discordant one was made by Livy (*History of Rome*, 30.34.1). Contemporary studies by Koon and Danilov confirm such observations (Koon 2010, 56; Danilov 2007, 175–6).
51 How someone was punished depended on the crime he committed. Officers who arrived too late for battle faced fines (Herodotus, *Histories*, 9.77). Corporal punishment was used too, although it was largely forbidden in Athens. Yet, corporal punishment was often still seen as normal and acceptable too, especially if someone was found communicating with the enemy (Aristotle, *The Constitution of the Athenians*, 61.2; Lysias, *Speeches*, 13.67; Xenophon, *Hellenica*, 1.1.5).
52 Bar Kochva 1973, 137; Gaebel 2002, 241.
53 In naval expeditions the *psiloi* would serve as rowers for the fleet (Esposito 2020).
54 Pritchard 2018, 86–102.
55 Phang, Spence, et al. 2016, 113; see also Elliott 2021, 21; Elliott 2022, 83; Webber 2011.
56 There had been cavalrymen in Greek armies from as early as the Mycenaean period (1500–1100 BCE; Worley 1994). However, when hoplite armies appeared in the eighth/seventh century BCE, the cavalry gave up their prominent position, and moved to the side and the background in favour of the hoplites who dominated the battlefield. Gradually, and especially during the Peloponnesian war (431 BCE–404

BCE), cavalry became more important again, as we see in a famous example from Thucydides about Syracusan riders who harassed, and eventually destroyed, the retreating Athenian army during the Sicilian expedition of 415–413 BCE (*History of the Peloponnesian War*, 6.52).

57 Naiden 2017, 68.
58 See on the number of Greek and Persian soldiers Herodotus, *Histories*, 7.186; De Souza 2003, 41; Holland 2006, 233; Shahbazi 2012, 129.
59 Gillespie 2013, 30. Even though the Persians most likely had a larger army than the Greeks, the enormous number of men and the large differences between Greek and Persian forces (100,000 Greeks at most against 2–5 million Persians) were to boost the morale among the Greeks. See for the numbers of Greeks and Persian soldiers note 58.
60 Carras 2006, 376.
61 On internal conflict in Greece in this period, see Bradford 2011; Connolly 2006.
62 Holland 2006, 164–7; 214–19.
63 Ibid.
64 Naiden 2017, 67. Soldiers' talk could make or break the unity of voice and spirit in the ranks. There are examples of men encouraging each other to climb hills and attack (Xenophon, *Anabasis*, 4.2.11, 4.7.12; *Hellenica*, 1.2.16, 4.4.17), but also talk of rivalry within the troops (Herodotus, *Histories*, 9.26).
65 Naiden 2017, 66–7.
66 Anochin and Rolle 1998.
67 For more on Spartan military dress, see Bowden 1993, 45–63; Farrington 2019, 7; Fink 2014, 32.
68 Van Wees 2017, 218.
69 Ibid.
70 Sekunda 1998, 20.
71 Taylor 2021, 273.
72 As Carruthers argues, these changes had a major effect on Greek society: the number of casualties increased, and all of society was disrupted more (Carruthers 2014, 5).
73 Kagan 2004, xxiii-xxiv; see also Castleden 2008; Elliott 2021, 93.
74 Sekunda 1998, 7.
75 Jones 2016, 294–5. See also Jones, 2008.
76 For the reasons behind the short-lived Spartan hegemony, see Doran 2018, 37; Jensen 2000, 80. Jones 2008; Jones 2016, 294–5; Kennell 2011; Lane Fox 2006; Pomeroy 2002, 44; Whisker and Coe 2021, 64.
77 Lazenby 2012, 150. See also Warner and Cawkwell 1979.
78 Connolly 2006, 38; Davis 2001, 24; Fine 1983; Gabriel 2001, 182–3.
79 However, Athens was permitted to retain some of the territory it had regained during the Corinthian War (Xenophon, *Hellenica*, 5.1.31; Farrington 2019, 8; see also Ruzicka 2012; Tritle 2013).

80 From its earliest times (c. 750 BCE), the Spartan army was divided into units based on social divisions, which changed over time. See Gerber 1999b, 65; Hall 2013, 213; Andrewes 1956; Hall 2007; Kelly 1970; Stillwell et al. 1976; Cartledge 2015; Dunstan 2000; Pechatnova 2001; Saunders 2007; Scott and Figueira 2012; Xanthippos 200.
81 Sekunda 1998, 15.
82 See also Connolly 2006, 40; Sekunda 1998, 19.
83 Connolly 2006, 11, 38.
84 In academic literature before the Second World War, the *ekklesia* is often referred to as the *apella* (Tod 1911, 160). However, this word is never found in ancient sources in the correct political context. See on the *apella*: Croix 1972, 346–7; Holland and Cartledge 2003, 29.
85 Initially, both kings would go on campaign at the same time, but after the sixth century BCE, only one would do so, with the other one remaining in Sparta (Sekunda 1998, 4; see also Connolly 2006, 47; Figueira 2006).
86 Despite their title, the *hippeis* were an elite infantry unit until the end of the Peloponnesian War, when Sparta started utilising cavalry units of about sixty men attached to each *mora* (Connolly 2006, 40; see also Figueira 2006; Naiden 2021). The *hippeis* were selected every year by specially commissioned officials, the *hippagretai*, drafted from experienced men who already had sons as heirs. This was to ensure that their line would be able to continue (Connolly 2006, 41).
87 Sekunda 1998, 18; Connolly 2006, 44.
88 Connolly 2006, 11.
89 Martin 2013, 99.
90 The latter role gave helots a chance to buy their freedom. In fact, there was even class of military men made up entirely of freed helots, who got the status of Spartiates and got a grant of land after serving a period of time as a hoplite in the Spartan army. They were known as the *neodamodeis*: Connolly 2006, 38; Sekunda 1998, 16–17. See also: Cartledge 2002; Ducat 1990; Lévy 2003; Talbert 1989; Tonini 1975; Ray 2011, 12; Robbins 1833, 124.
91 A *trireme* is a type of ship that derived its name from its three rows of oars, each manned with one man.
92 This Spartan fleet was commanded by *navarchs* who were appointed for a strict one-year term, and apparently could not be reappointed. For the *navarchs*, see Sekunda 1998, 7.
93 The final blow would be given twenty years later, at the Battle of Naxos in 376 BCE. The Spartans periodically maintained a small fleet after that, but its effectiveness was limited. The last revival of Spartan naval power was under Nabis, who created a fleet to control the Laconian coastline with help from his Cretan allies.
94 For the dates, see Kelly 1985, 143.

2 Sparta and Secrecy in Non-Spartan Sources

1. Krentz 2009, 170. For a list of deceptions in archaic and classical Greek warfare, see Krentz 2009, 183–200.
2. Besides its use in a military context, other ancient uses of cryptography and steganography include its use in love letters, in inscriptions to increase the level of mysticism, and its use in magical and religious texts (Ausonius, *Epistles*, 28.21–22; Ovid, *Ars Amatoria*, 3.627–630; Pliny the Elder, *Natural History*, 26.39 (62). See also Pieprzyk, Hardjono, and Seberry 2013, 6; Waldstein and Wisse 1995; Wisse 1979, 1980, 1981, 1982, 1983, 1989, 1990).
3. Caubet 2008, 421; Kasten 2001, 2; Nemet-Nejat 1998; Pieprzyk, Hardjono, and Seberry 2013, 6; Waldstein and Wisse 1995; Wisse 1979, 1980, 1981, 1982, 1983, 1989, 1990. See also Porphyry of Tyre, *Life of Pythagoras*, 11–12. Modern cryptographers refer to cryptography being well-known from archaeological data since 2000 BCE without referring to any sources: e.g. Zapechnikov, Tolstoy et al. 2015, 146. They may be referring to the Egyptian and Mesopotamian uses of cryptography in this case.
4. Mollin 2005, 4–5; Pieprzyk, Hardjono, and Seberry 2013, 6; Waldstein and Wisse 1995; Wisse 1979, 1980, 1981, 1982, 1983, 1989, 1990.
5. Yet, it has been suggested that a cuneiform tablet from Seleucia on the Tigris (dating to 1500 BCE) containing an encrypted recipe for glass-making, is a clear attempt to protect confidential information: Caubet 2008, 421; Mollin 2005, 5.
6. However, evidence for the use of cryptography and steganography used for the purpose of securing confidential information in other ancient civilisations may be lost. In fact, it has been suggested that all ancient civilisations may have been familiar with the use of cryptographic and steganographic methods and devices to conceal their confidential correspondence: Al-Kadi 1992, 103; Pieprzyk, Hardjono, and Seberry 2013, 6.
7. Mollin 2000, 4.
8. Murray and Wyatt 1999, 287.
9. '*σημεῖα λέγει, οὐ γράμματα*'. Derived from Schmidt 1920, 58.
10. Schmidt 1920, 58.
11. On the origins of the Greek alphabet, see e.g. Garfield 2013; Keightley 1856; Keightley 1859; Maas 2012; Mure 1854; Powell 1997; Richardson 1984a; Richardson 1984b; Schmidt 1920; Schwab 2011; Steiner 1994.
12. Powell 1997, 27–8.
13. Bellamy 1989, 289–307, especially 290–4.
14. Bowra 1972, 12.
15. Chadwick 1976, 182; Van Oldenburg Ermke 1959, 103. See also Kirk 1962, 165, 184; Willock 1978, 245.

16 See e.g., Garfield 2013, 44; Keightley 1856, 126; Keightley 1859, 126; Maas 2012, 216; Mure 1854, 485; Powell 1997, 27; Richardson 1984a, 72–4; Richardson 1984b, 72–4; Schwab 2011, 202; Steiner 1994, 16.
17 See e.g., Garfield 2013, 44; Keightley 1856, 126; Keightley 1859, 126; Maas 2012, 216; Mure 1854, 485; Richardson 1984a, 72–4; Richardson 1984b, 72–4; Schmidt 1920, 65–6; Schwab 2011, 202; Steiner 1994, 16; for ancient diptychs, see e.g. Bowman 1975, 237–52; Pulak 1998, 188–224.
18 Spar and Jursa 2014, lxxxix.
19 Swiggers, 1996; Trapp 2003, 6.
20 Ceccarelli 2013, 56, 59; Chadwick 1976, 182; Rosenmeyer 2001, 39. One more passage in the *Iliad* might be a reference to writing: Homer, *Iliad*, 7.175–89. See also: Bowie 2013; Heubeck 1979, 127–8; Steiner 1994, 10–16.
21 Bellamy 1989a, 289–307, especially 290–4. See also Bellamy 1989b; Havelock 1982, 10; Steiner 1994, 4.
22 Novokhatko 2015, 11. From the fourth century BCE onwards, basic literacy and exchange of letters seems to have become widespread in the Greek world, although the topic of ancient literacy remains a highly contested one: Ceccarelli 2013, 185; Trapp 2003, 6. For the role of writing in Herodotus' time, see O'Toole 1991–2, 148–60. For literary and letter writing in ancient Greece, see Adams 2003; Boring 1979; Cartledge 1978; Goody and Watt 1968; Harris 1989; Harvey 1966; Millender 1996, 1999, 2001, 2002, 2009; Powell 1997; Street 1984.
23 Ceccarelli 2013, 60. See also Burkert 1983, 51–6; Cluzan 2008, 367–8.
24 Rosenmeyer 2001, 40–2; Steiner 1994, 15.
25 Müri 1976, 5.
26 Examples of archaeological evidence on tablets used as tokens of guest friendship, include terracotta plaques carrying painted names, potentially designed for guest friends as identification, or leaden plates carrying inscriptions referring to an agreement made between individuals: Gauthier 1972, 68 (note 18); Herman 1987, 62 (Figures 8a–d and note); Ladner 1979, 223–5; Steiner 1994, 31.
27 Rosenmeyer 2001, 40–2; Steiner 1994, 15.
28 Murray and Wyatt 1999, 287.
29 In thirty-two more situations it is not clear whether a written message was sent. In these examples we find the word ἀγγελία or ἀγγελίην, simply meaning 'message': 1.83, 1.114, 1.160, 2.114, 3.34, 3.53, 3.69, 3.77, 3.122, 5.14, 5.92G, 5.108, 5.117, 6.10, 6.28, 6.105, 7.1, 8.14, 8.99, 8.140A, 8.144, 9.14, 9.15. These messages could have been either oral or written. Since it is unclear whether a written message was meant in these situations, they will not be discussed here.
30 1.187: engravings on the tomb of the Babylonian queen Nitocris; 5.35: a message tattooed on a slave's head; 8.22: Themistocles engraving a message to the Ionians into a rock.

31 In 3.128, Herodotus mentions 'many letters' (βυβλία γραψάμενος πολλὰ); while in 6.4, Herodotus mentions the plural form 'letters' (βυβλία).
32 3.40: a letter from the Egyptian King Amasis to Polycrates of Samos; 3.42: a letter sent back from Polycrates of Samon to the Egyptian king Amasis; 7.239: Demaratus of Sparta sending a secret letter written under the wax of a wax tablet while he was being exiled in Persia; 8.128: Timoxenus, *strategos* of the Scionians, communicating with the Persian commander Artabazus.
33 Gould 1989, 76–8. For more on letters and letters writing in the ancient Near East, see e.g., Bellamy 1989a, 291–2; Ceccarelli 2013, 185; Luschan and Andrae 1943, 108–9; Mallowan 1966; Mylonas Shear 1998, 187–9.
34 For Homer as a source for Herodotus, see Rawlinson 1859.
35 For more on the structure of the *Histories*, see: Augustyn 2022; Immerwahr 1985, 426–41; Murray 1986, 190–1).
36 For literacy in ancient Greece, see Boring 1979; Cartledge 1978; Clanchy 1979; Goody 1986; Goody and Watt 1968; Harris 1989; Harvey 1966; Havelock 1963, 1982; Immerwahr 1990; Steiner 1994, 4; Street 1984; Swiggers 1996; Thomas 1989; Turner 1952.
37 Homer's story of Bellerophon's tablet, as we saw earlier, potentially appeals to this Near Eastern context of letters and letter-writing in terms of the readiness of ancient scholia critics to interpret Proetus' writing as a kind of Egyptian hieroglyphic text: Homer, *Iliad*, 6.166–170, 178; Bellamy 1989, 289; Ceccarelli 2013, 60; Rosenmeyer 2001, 39. Rosenmeyer further points out that the letter sent in Bellerophon's story encapsulates two major themes related to letter writing that can often be found in Greek literature: a deceitful letter and an association between letters and deceitful women, hereby again signposting the decidedly negative view towards letter writing in the Archaic period: Rosenmeyer 2001, 39–44; see also Bellamy 1989a and b; Ceccarelli 2013, 24, 60.
38 O'Toole 1991, 153.
39 O'Toole 1991, 153–4.
40 Ibid.
41 Hollmann provides us with a list of these sixty-nine instances of trickery and deceit in Herodotus: Hollmann 2005, 316–23; see also Hollmann 2011.
42 The three letters that did not involve trickery and deceit, are two letters sent between Amasis and Polycrates (Herodotus, *Histories*, 3.40–42), and a letter from Darius to Megabyzus instructing the latter to attack Paeonia (Herodotus, *Histories*, 5.14.1).
43 In the work of the fourth-century BCE military author Aeneas Tacticus, we see the danger of treachery and the importance of the use of trustworthy messengers in warfare (especially during sieges) as recurring themes: *How to Survive Under Siege*, 4.1–4, 5.1, 9.2, 10.6, 10.11, 10.18–19, 10.25–26, 11.3–6, 12, 18.3–6, 18.8–11 (see also Polyaenus, *Stratagems of War*, 2.36), 18.13–21, 20, 22.5, 22.7, 23.7–11, 29.3–10.

44 O'Toole 1991, 155. Modern cryptographers often incorrectly present this story as an historical account based on facts: Bauer 2013, 8; Singh 1999, 6.
45 Although modern historians of cryptography often present the stories as clear facts (e.g. Demaratus' letter to the Spartans, see Bauer 2013, 7–8; Bartlett 2002, 8–12; Singh 1999, 5), it cannot be said with certainty how much of each story is fact and how much is fiction. For the Spartans being depicted as having 'non-Greek' practices, see e.g. Cartledge 2009, 2013; Osborne 2011.
46 On Harpagus' motives for sending the message, and his role in the story as "described by Herodotus, see Gray 1995, 185–211, see also Polyaenus, *Stratagems of War*, 3.13.3.
47 On this passage, see also O'Toole 1991, 154.
48 Lateiner 1990, 231; see also Gould 2012, 674; Waters 1972, 138.
49 Lateiner 1990, 231.
50 Hamel 2012, 45.
51 Waters 2014, 83. See also Waters 1985.
52 Holland 2006, 153–4.
53 Chapman incorrectly suggests that Herodotus' work is the only account of the Ionian Revolt available to us (Chapman 1972, 546). In addition to Herodotus' work, we have, e.g. Aeschylus' *The Persians*, and Thucydides' *History of the Peloponnesian War*. On Histiaeus' role in Herodotus' account of the Ionian Revolt, see Blamire 1959; Chapman 1972, 546–68; Evans 1976; Lang 1968.
54 Sending the slave was a clever idea from Histiaeus' point of view. Slaves had little to lose, were used to obscurity, and were believed to live lives of duplicity. Therefore, they seemed useful as spies, as Richmond argues: Richmond 1998, 6.
55 Ceccarelli presumes that, according to Herodotus, Histiaeus tattooed the word '*revolt*' in plaintext on the slave's head (Ceccarelli 2013, 114). However, Herodotus does not disclose what Histiaeus' message said.
56 Ceccarelli 2013, 127.
57 Kamen 2010, 95 and note 1. On other purposes of tattooing, including decorative tattooing, see e.g. Fisher 1993; Kamen 2010; Jones 1987, 2000.
58 DuBois 1988a, 75. See also: DuBois 1988b, 1991, 2003, 2007; Kamen 2010.
59 DuBois 2003, 4; Jones 1987, 2000.
60 Kamen 2010, 98.
61 DuBois 1988a, 75–8, 2007; Kamen 2010, 95–8.
62 O'Toole 1991, 155.
63 O'Toole 1991, 155.
64 According to Justin, it was not the king's wife, but his sister who discovered Demaratus' message (*Epitome of the Philippic History of Pompeius Trogus*, 2.10.12). As Millender points out, Herodotus' account of the Spartans' reception of this message credits the Lacedaemonian authorities with the ability to read, and implies

Gorgo's familiarity with wooden writing tablets (Millender 2001, 142). See also Dvornik 1974, 57; Sheldon 1987, 28; Sheldon 2005, 42.

65 The passage in which Gorgo discovered Demaratus' secret message is the oldest known passage in which a woman took the initiative in deciphering a secret message. In Roman love elegy we find many examples in which the woman takes the initiative in sending secret messages (see Propertius, Tibullus, and especially Ovid [*Ars Amatoria*, passim.]).

66 Significantly, Harvey and Tigerstedt are unanimous in declaring that the Spartans could not read or write (Harvey 1966, 624; Tigerstedt 1965, 49, 111). Boring, although being slightly more cautious, seems to have adopted this view when stating that some Spartans might have been only able to write their name, while only very few Spartans could potentially have been able to write much more: Boring 1979, 1.

67 Powell 2017; Shipley 2002; Shipley, Cavanagh et. al. 2007; Todd 1933, 108–11; Cartledge 1978, 2003a and b; Christidis, Arapopoulou, and Chrite 2007; Hodkinson and Powell 2009; Hondius and Woodward 1919–21, 88–143; Kennell 2010; Powell 2017; Tod 1933, 108–11. See also: Bengtson 1975; Boring 1979; Millender 2001, 130–1; Peek 1974; Wolicki 2018, 21–30.

68 Millender 2001, 138.

69 Millender 2001, 159.

70 See, e.g.: Bodel 2001, 61; Cartledge 1978, 2001, 2013b; Harvey 1966, 585–635; Hodkinson and Powell 2009; 2010; Millender 2001; Mintz 2018; Schrader 2011, 501; Too 2001, 69.

71 Boring 1979, 94; Huxley 1983, 2.

72 Significantly, this idea of the Spartans being seen as a people using 'non-Greek' practices can even be found in Kasten 2001, 1–2.

73 For the date, see e.g. Burliga 2008, 92–3. See also Thucydides, *History of the Peloponnesian War*.

74 Godley 1925, 131; How and Wells 1928, 700. See also Aeneas Tacticus, *How to Survive Under Siege*, 31.25–27.

75 In this way, when messages were read out loud in ancient Greece, an audience was made up of a 'reader' and the 'listeners': Svenbro 2018, 55–6.

76 Fabule 2011, 36. For a concise list of exiled or alienated Greeks who, for their own purposes, solicited Persian assistance against their fellow-citizens, see Boedeker 1987, 191–2.

77 Ceccarelli 2013, 113.

78 Dewald 2003, 28–33; Ferrill 1978, 385–98.

79 Dewald 1993, 55–70; Hollmann 2005, 316–23; Hollmann 2011.

80 Bowie 2007, 160. The earliest references to officials called 'Eyes' and 'Ears' of Near Eastern kings, come from Egyptian sources datable to the second half of the second millennium BCE Thureau-Dangin 1922, 104 (tablet 7094) (letter from Amarna

81 For secret services throughout ancient (Near) Eastern Empires, see Oppenheim 1968; Brock-Utne 1945; Lods 1939; Schaeder 1934; Torzcyner 1937.
82 Oppenheim 1968, 175.
83 Cartledge 2003, 70; Ross 2012.
84 Bowie 2007, 160; Briant 2002, 343–4; Sheldon 2008, 79.
85 Africa 1968; Cartledge 2002; Ducat 2006; Figueira 2018; Gardner 2019; Jeanmaire 1913; Kennell 2010; Köchly 1835; Nafissi 2018; Richer 2018; Ross 2012; Wachsmuth 1844–6; Wallon 1850.
86 Augustyn 2022.
87 Gould 1989, 65. Yet, as Gould argues, it is notable, that the obligations of gratitude and revenge are the fundamental human motives for Herodotus, just as they are the primary stimulus for the generation of narrative itself (ibid.).
88 Gould 1989, 67–70.
89 De Ste. Croix 1977, 142; Lang 1967, 1984.
90 Gould 1989, 77–8.
91 Murray 1986, 188.
92 Romm 1998, 6.
93 Immerwahr 1985, 431.
94 On Hecataeus as a source for Herodotus, see Immerwahr 1985, 430, 440.
95 Herodotus' familiarity with Athenian tragedy is demonstrated in passages echoing Aeschylus' *The Persians*, including the epigrammatic observation that the defeat of the Persian navy at Salamis caused the defeat of the land army (*The Persians* 728 = *Histories* 8.68; Immerwahr 1985, 427, 432; Jebb 1976, 181–2 (notes 904–920)).
96 Rawlinson 1859, 6.
97 Murray 1986, 190–1.
98 See also Blösel 2018.
99 Cartledge 2003, 70, Cartledge 2013; Powell 2017, 25; Ross 2012.
100 Boring 1979, 94; Huxley 1983, 2.
101 Diepenbroek 2021, 2022; Kelly 1985; West 1988; Sheldon 2008.
102 Interestingly, the authority of the Spartan kings was severely circumscribed compared to other *poleis*. The actual power rested with the five elected *ephoroi*: Connolly 2006, 38.
103 O'Sullivan 1995, 115.
104 Harvey 1966, 624; Liddel 2018, 124; Rösler 2009, 436–7.
105 Harris 1989, 5–6.
106 Harris 1989, 6.
107 Havelock 1982, 41.
108 Harris 1989, 6.

addressed to the pharaoh; see also Hannig 2003, entry *jr . t* (p. 107) and *'nh* (p. 205; Law 2010, 111 (note 276)).

109 Boring 1979, 81.
110 Campbell 2006, 37; Melville and Melville 2008, 157–8.
111 Rundle Clark 1959, 263.
112 Powell 1997, 4; Thomas 2009, 13. See also Cartledge 1978.
113 Boring 1989, 63. A society in which most people cannot write more than their own name is known as a 'semi-literate' society: Havelock 1971, 14; Havelock 1982, 59; Turner 1973; Youtie 1971, 239–61.

3 The *Scytale*

1 In Kaufman's *Our Young Folks Plutarch* (1884; a series of Plutarch's stories for children), we find the plural '*scytales*' instead of '*scytalae*', pp. 138, 161.
2 On the development of the *scytale* system into modern transposition ciphers, see chapter six.
3 D'Agapeyeff 1939, 15, 135; Churchhouse 2002, 13; Gardner 1983, 56; Mollin 2005, 5; Piper and Murphy 2002, 22; Sheldon 1986, 46–7; Smart 2018, 3; Walker 2008, 150.
4 If some of the Spartans' contemporaries believed a *scytale* had only non-cryptographic uses, this would be to the Spartans' benefit. It would have been valuable disinformation.
5 Boring 1979, 40; Kelly 1998, 246; Sheldon 2003, 73; West 1988, 42.
6 Ceccarelli 2013, 238–9.
7 Bowie 2019, 284. See also Swift 2019.
8 Gerber 1999a, 201.
9 Liddell and Scott 2014, entry ἄχνυμαι.
10 Ceccarelli 2013, 32.
11 Ceccarelli 2019, entries: *Athenaios* (166), *Autokrates* (297).
12 Sheldon 2003, 73.
13 See also Gerber 1997, 102; Hanink 2014, 56; Zavaliy 2020, 53.
14 Vaughn 1993, 38.
15 Vaughn 1993, 38–9. Frequently, if it was neither practical nor feasible to bring the dead home for burial, they would be buried in regions which would treat them with respect; the Argive dead from Hysiai (*c*. 669 BCE), for example, were transported to Kenchreai so that they could be buried in allied territory (Pausanias, *Description of Greece*, 2.24.7; Vaughn 1993, 42).
16 Whately 2021, 65–6.
17 Vaughn 1993, 38–46.
18 Fink 2014, 60; Pritchard 2018, 107.
19 Vaughn 1993, 46.
20 Fink 2014, 60; Pritchard 2018, 107.

21 Vaughn 1993, 47–51.
22 Vaughn 1993, 47–51.
23 Whether anything was carved in, or written on, the *scytale*, like a letter or a mark, is unknown. Since these *scytalae* were pieces of wood, it is plausible that they were not taken by the enemy when they were plundering the battlefield, since they had no value. According to Plutarch, this idea of making identification tags came from the soldiers themselves who knew better than anyone else the real hazards of war, the likelihood of disfigurement, and the Spartan emphasis on proper identification of corpses for burial (Plutarch, *Lycurgus*, 27). According to Aelian, this identification principle worked well. He asserts that those Spartans who had especially distinguished themselves in battle were buried in their red cloaks, while others were laid among olive branches (Aelian, *Various History*, 6.6; Plutarch, *Lycurgus* 27.1–2; *Moralia*, 238d).
24 Either or both systems of identification are likely to have been used by the Spartans. Significantly, Boring sees it as a curious custom and wonders if, given the closeness of Spartan society and the relatively small numbers often involved in battles, such a device for identification of the dead would have been necessary (Boring 1979, 18).
25 Vaughn 1993, 56. The use of identification tags only reappears in a uniform way in the First World War – 2,500 years later.
26 In a similar performance context, Archilochus – in Fragment 185 – also appears to describe the *scytale* as a messenger stick, although here the speaker was about to tell a fable.
27 Race 1997, 114–15.
28 Boring 1979, 39.
29 According to the *Scholia on Aristophanes' Birds*, the fourth-century CE Roman author Symmachus also mentions this, an author not discussed by Kelly or West (*Scholia on Aristophanes Birds*, 1283–1284, ed. White 1914, 228).
30 Boring 1979, 41; Piccirilli 1981, 5; Sommerstein 1987, 283; Sommerstein 1990, 205; Sommerstein 2002; 236.
31 Aristophanes, *Lysistrata*, 985–991; Boring 1979, 41; Sommerstein 1987, 283; Sommerstein 1990, 205; Sommerstein 2002, 236.
32 Boring 1979, 41; Sommerstein 1990, 205. We also see this in Plutarch's second-century CE description of the *scytale*, where Plutarch discussed that the stick as well as the (official) dispatch bore the same name: '*scytale*' (*Life of Lysander*, 19.7).
33 Hornblower 2009, 64–5; Rankov 2007, 41. Later in the Roman army an *optio*, acting as deputy of a *centurion*, would also carry a stick with which to keep the troops in order.
34 Hornblower 2009, 61.
35 Eliade 1970, 20; Piccirilli 1981, 6. When used as a cryptographic device, *scytalae* indeed gave power to both the sender and the recipient, not clear visible power that

36 Boring 1979, 39.
37 Anderson 1970, 68; West 1988, 43–4. See also Michell 1952, 273–4; Leopold 1900, *passim*; Oehler 1927, 691–2; Sheldon 2003, 73.
38 Sheldon 2003, 73. According to Sheldon, a disadvantage to this method would be that the stick can only be used for the purpose of authentication once. It is indeed correct that one side would have both halves of the stick after the messenger had delivered his message. However, either of the halves could be sent back with him the next time he delivered a message.
39 Jeffery 1961, 57.
40 This idea of *scytalae* used for transport of messages can also be found in Nicophon's *Birth of Aphrodite* (*The Fragments of Attic Comedy* 1, Fragment 2), and Thucydides' *History of the Peloponnesian War* (1.131.1).
41 Plutarch and Gellius do not describe the measurements of the *scytale*. As long as the two sticks were the same length and diameter one had a workable method. Edouard Charton (writing in 1837) believes that a *scytale* was always 1.5 foot in length, and 3 inches in diameter (Charton 1837, 43).
42 Hammond 2009, 63; Smith 1919, 220–1.
43 Hammond 2009, 63; Smith 1919, 220–1.
44 Lattimore 1998, 63; Rhodes 2014, 161, 271.
45 Lattimore 1998, 63; Rhodes 2014, 161, 271. See also: Jeffery 1961, 57.
46 Gomme, Andrewes et. al 1981, 120.
47 '… οὐκ ἐς κόρακας τὼ χεῖρ᾽ ἀποίσεις ἐκποδὼν ἀπὸ τοῦ σκυταλίου < > καὶ τῆς διφθέρας᾽. See also Edmonds 1957, 935; Kassel and Austin 1989, 64.
48 Edmonds 1957, 935; Jeffery 1961, 57.
49 Storey 2011a, 401.
50 Or in this case the form '*σκυταλίου*' (*scytaliou*).
51 Kelly 1998, 248.
52 Aly 1943; Keaney 1974, 179–94; Sbordone 1950.
53 Keaney 1974, 179–80; Szedegy-Maszak 1981, 91–5.
54 Kelly 1998, 251; Stylianou 2013, 262–3.
55 Oldfather 1950, 425.
56 Diels 1914, 65; Oehler 1927, 691; Sheldon 2003, 75.
57 Kelly 1985, 143.
58 Luft 1952; Russell 1966; Flower 1988; Candau Morón 2000; Verdegem 2010; Schettino 2013.
59 On Theopompus as Plutarch's key source for his *Life of Lysander*, including his description of the Spartan *scytale*, see Luft 1952; Russell 1966; Flower 1988; Candau Morón 2000; Verdegem 2010; and Schettino 2013.

60 Like Plutarch, Photius wrote at a considerable distance in time (ninth century CE) from the time Theopompus lived (fourth century BCE), so we must be careful with this source. Yet, it is the only available biography on Theompompus.

61 This becomes clear from the fact that no less than 275 earlier Greek and Roman authors are mentioned in the work. These sources include literary figures like Homer and Hesiod (*Attic Nights*, 3.11), grammarians, including Fronto (2.26) and Publius Nigidius (3.12), and scholarly authors, including Pliny (3.16, 9.5, 9.16, 10.12, 17.15), and Varro (3.10; Rolfe 1927, xvi–xvii). For more on Aulus Gellius' sources, see Anderson 2004; Cavazza 2004 (esp. 66–8); Holford-Strevens 2003 (esp. 65–81); Holford-Strevens 2019a; Holford-Strevens 2019b (for the passage see especially p. 590); Holford-Strevens and Vardi 2004; Keulen 2004).

62 So important is Plutarch as a source for Aulus Gellius, that Gellius shows his indebtedness by making the word 'Plutarch' the very first word of his *Attic Nights* (1.1: 'Plutarch, in the book which he wrote on Hercules [...]'; Grafton, Most and Settis 2013, 748. See further on Gellius' sources: Leopold 1900, 365; Oikonomopoulou 2019; Howley 2018; Grafton, Most and Settis 2013; Cavazza 2004; Holford-Strevens 2003; Holford-Strevens 2019a; Holford-Strevens 2019b (especially p. 590); Holford-Strevens and Vardi 2004; Rolfe 1927, xvii.

63 See Oikonomopoulou 2019, 45.

64 Cavazza 2004, 66.

65 See Holford-Strevens 2003, 72–8 on Aulus Gellius' sources. Holford-Strevens dismisses the idea that there is only one identifiable source for each chapter of *Attic Nights* (2003, 77).

66 Holford-Strevens 2003, 78.

67 For example, Thucydides is an obvious source for a significant portion of the Greek history incorporated in *Attic Nights*. For more on Gellius' use of sources, see Holford-Strevens 2003, 246–7.

68 In *Attic Nights* 16.15, Aulus Gellius reports that Theopompus believed that the Bisaltian hare possessed two livers.

69 Cavazza 2004; Holford-Strevens 2003; Holford-Strevens 2019a; Holford-Strevens 2019b; Holford-Strevens and Vardi 2004; Rolfe 1927, xvii.

70 Xenophon argues that there was nothing more profitable in war than deception, since the greatest advantages in war were achieved in this way (*Hipparchicus*, 5.9–11). While deceiving your friends was wrong, deceiving your enemies was not such a problem, according to the author. See also Dvornik 1974, 41.

71 In fact, much of what is known today about Spartan society comes from Xenophon's works, including his works *Agesilaus* and the *Constitution of the Lacedaemonians*.

72 Brownson 1918, 223; Warner and Cawkwell 1979, 162.

73 Brownson 1921, 49; Warner and Cawkwell 1979, 268.

74 Ibid.

75 While the original Greek text provides us with the word 'ἐπιστολέως/ ἐπιστολή', Bearzot incorrectly mentions the word 'γράμματα' when discussing the passage (Bearzot 2014, 100).
76 Perrin 1916, 287; Poe 1841, 33.
77 Kahn 1967, 75–6; Mollin 2005, 9; Smith 1955, 16.
78 Jeffery 1961, 57; Sherwood 2006, 536–7.
79 Bauer 2007a, 382; Reinke 1962, 113; Singh 1999, 5.
80 Singh 1999, 7.
81 Plutarch gives examples of the specific contexts in which *scytalae* were used for secret communication (*Life of Lysander*, 19.1–20.7; *Life of Alcibiades*, 38.1–4; *Life of Artaxerxes*, 6.1–6; *Life of Agesilaus*, 10.1–6; 15.1–6), but Aulus Gellius simply discusses how the Spartans used a *scytale* as a cryptograph (*Attic Nights*, 17.9.6–16. Aulus Gellius and Ausoinus are two of the Roman authors discussed in chapter five who were certain that the Spartans used *scytalae* for secret communication.
82 Perrin 1916, 286–7.
83 See also Homer, *Iliad*, 6.166–170, 178 for the story of Bellerophon who carried his own death sentence in a message from Proetus to Iobates.
84 This example can be compared to Thucydides' story of the Spartan general Pausanias who was also summoned home by the *ephors* because of misbehaviour by means of a *scytale* message (*History of the Peloponnesian War*, 1.131.1).
85 Bauer 2013, 4; Singh 1999, 9.
86 Plutarch, *Life of Lysander*, 19.4–20.
87 Verdegem 2010, 339ff. For his *Life of Alcibiades,* Plutarch used a range of sources belonging to various genres, including Theopompus' *Hellenica* (*Life of Alcibiades*, 23.3–5, 27–39), Thucydides' *History of the Peloponnesian War* (6.3, 11.2, 13.4, 20.6), Xenophon's *Hellenica* (23.7–9, 27–39) and Ephorus' *Library of History* (27–39).
88 Perrin 1916, 113.
89 For this work Plutarch again used a range of sources, including works from Theopompus, Dinon, Ctesias and Xenophon (Soares 2007, 86).
90 Perrin 1926, 130.
91 For this work Plutarch relied heavily on Xenophon's *Agesilaüs*, *Anabasis*, and *Hellenica* (Plutarch, *Life of Agesilaus*, 4.1 = Xenophon, *Agesilaüs*, 6.4; 11.7 = 5.4–7; 14.1 = 5.7; 20.5 = 8.7; 36.1 = 2.28–31; Plutarch, *Life of Agesilaus*, 18.1 = Xenophon, *Anabasis* 5.3.6; Plutarch, *Life of Agesilaus*, 5.1 = Xenophon, *Hellenica*, 3.3.2; 6.6 = 3.4.3f.; 7.1 = 3.4.7; 9.4 = 3.4.15; 10.1 = 3.4.16; 10.5 = 3.4.27; 11.1 = 4.1.1; 11.3 = 3.4.20; 12.5 = 4.1.28–38; 13.3 = 4.1.39; 16.4 = 4.2.18–4.3.1; 16.5 = 4.3.9; 18.1 = 4.3.16; 21.1 = 4.5.5; 22.2 = 4.5.11–18; 22.3 = 4.5.8; 22.5 = 4.5.3–4.7.1; 23.1 = 4.8.10; 23.3 = 5.1.26ff.; 24.1 = 5.4.2–12; 24.2 = 5.3.13–25; 26.1 = 5.4.24–34; 26.2 = 5.4.35; 27.1 = 5.4.47–58; 27.3 = 6.3.3–20; 29.4 = 6.4.16; 30.5 = 6.5.10–21; 31.4 = 6.5.28; 33.8 = 6.5.50; 33.4= 7.1.28–32; 34.3 = 7.5.10; 34.6 = 7.5.12–14; 35.1 = 7.5.22–24. Again, Plutarch also used Theopompus (*Life of Agesilaus*, 10.5, 31.3, 32.8, 33.1).

92 Perrin 1917, 25, 41.
93 See also Shepherd 1793, 280. Shepherd, in his translation of the work, only used the word 'letter' for all the letters that were sent in the passage, and suggested that Pharnabazus simply wrote his second letter in private.
94 On the development of the *scytale* system into modern transposition ciphers, see chapter six.
95 D'Agapeyeff 1939, 15, 135; Churchhouse 2002, 13; Gardner 1983, 56; Mollin 2005, 5; Piper and Murphy 2002, 22; Sheldon 1986, 46–7; Smart 2018, 3; Walker 2008, 150.
96 '*Chiliades*' means 'thousands', referring to the number of lines in the work (over 12,000 lines of fifteen syllables). On Johannes Tzetzes' *Chiliades*, see e.g.: Abrantes 2017a; Abrantes 2017b; Alican 2012, 554; Pantelia 2022, 747.
97 This is also mentioned by the fourth-century CE Roman author Symmachus (*Scholia on Aristophanes Birds*, 1283–1284, ed. White 1914, 228).
98 The scholar probably mistook a snake for a fish. From Lucan and Isidore of Seville, we know of a snake known as the *scytale* (Isodore of Seville, *The Etymologies*, 12.4.19; Lucan, *Pharasalia*, 9.717-718).
99 Aulus Gellius only mentions a thin strip and does not clarify what material was used (Aulus Gellius, *Attic Nights*, 17.9.12–16).
100 Since Cardano does not describe the working of the *scytale* in *De Subtilitate*, Scaliger must have used Plutarch's and Gellius' earlier sources in his response to Cardano's work.
101 Tomokiyo 2014.
102 Gamer 2022, 137; Wolf 2004, 270.
103 Hulme 1898, 47; Tomikiyo 2020.
104 Unfortunately, Porta does not quote or refer to these other sources. Therefore, we cannot know with certainty which other scholars – before Porta – ascribed the *scytale* to Archimedes. See also Blair 1807, entry *cipher*; *Encyclopédie du dix-neuvième siècle*, entry *polygraphie*, 6–9.
105 Mpampiniotis (1998) entry κοντάκιο. A *kontakion* is a form of hymn performed in the Orthodox and the Eastern Catholic liturgical traditions. The text of the hymn could have been wrapped around a stick: Peltomaa 2021, 40. See, for example, on *kontakia* (pl. of *kontakion*) in the Greek Orthodox Church: Birkbeck 1922; Floros 2009; Floros and Moran 2015; Koder 2008; Lingas 1995; Range 2016; Skinner 2008; Trypanis 1968.
106 See Nicophon's *Birth of Aphrodite* (*The Fragments of Attic Comedy* 1, Fragment 2); Thucydides' *History of the Peloponnesian War* (1.131.1); Jeffery 1961, 57; Lattimore 1998, 63; Rhodes 2014, 161, 271.
107 For archives in the ancient Mediterranean world, see e.g.: Brosius 2003; Gagarin 2009; Snell 2008; Thatcher, Keith et al. (2017).

108 Thicknesse 1772, 99.
109 One possibility is that *kontakia* were written in the same way as ancient *scytale* messages, and were then unwrapped from the sticks to create partial and broken letters. This would make the text unreadable for everyone else but the priests who used the *kontakia*, scrolls, and sticks, and it would have increased the level of mysticism and power of the religious texts (see e.g. Caubet 2008, 421; Mollin 2005, 4–5; Pieprzyk, Hardjono and Seberry 2013, 6; Waldstein and Wisse 1995; Wisse 1979; 1980; 1981; 1982; 1983; 1989; 1990).
110 De Guilletiere 1676, 524–6.
111 Aquilino 1831, 36; Bonavilla and Aquilino 1821, 36; D'Alembert and Diderot 1751 (I), entry *chiffre*, 333–4; 1751 (II), entry *scytale*, 847; De Real de Curban 1762, 430–1; 1767, 569; *Dictionnaire Universel Des Sciences Morale* 1779, 626; *Dictionnaire Universel Francois et Latin* 1743, 65; Gallois 1677, 190–1; Griselini 1774, 176; Jacob 1858, 6–11 ; Klauer 1695, 27–8.
112 Bonavilla and Aquilino 1821, 36; Jacob 1858, 6–11.
113 Aquilino 1831, 36; Ball 1892, 1914, 402; Bonavilla and Aquilino 1821, 36; De la Torre 1946, 80–96; Delastelle 1902, 133; Farrow 1885, 435; Klüber 1809, 114–15; 127; Martin 1877, 1161–2 ; Walsh 1891, 536; 1892, 158.
114 Charton 1837, 43; Von Moshamm 1805, 421–2. Tomokiyo incorrectly states that Charton and Von Moshamm also believed that every letter became broken when the strip was unwrapped from the *scytale*, as did the other authors discussed in this section (Tomokiyo 2014).
115 Cario 1919, 322; Langie 1917, 405; 1922, 13–14.
116 Poe 1841, 33.
117 *Dictionnaire étymologique* 1803, 461.
118 De Guilletiere 1676, 524–6. In 1841, Edgar Allan Poe already argued that De Guilletiere's statement was incorrect (Poe 1841, 33). The early twentieth-century scholars Lange and Soudart also incorrectly presume the Spartans invented transposition ciphers (1925, 18).
119 Falconer 1685, section 5, p. 91. The authors of the nineteenth-century French *Encyclopédie du dix-neuvième siècle* also presume that *scytalae* were commonly used in ancient Greece in the fifth/fourth centuries BCE (*Encyclopédie du dix-neuvième siècle*, entry *polygraphie*, 6–9).
120 Toustain and Tassin 1750, 605.
121 Ibid., 605.
122 Anderson 1970, 68; West 1988, 43–5.
123 Panciroli 1660, 264; Forelius 1697, 12. Forelius' *Dissertatio academica de modis occulte scribendi & præsertim de scytala Laconica* is the second oldest study of the *scytale*, after Klauer's 1695 work *Disputatio historico-philologica de Scytala Lacedaemoniorum* (Sheldon 2003, 74).

124 Bazeries 1901, 7 ; Carmona 1894, 36; D'Alembert 1821, 490–3; D'Alembert and Diderot 1751 (III), entry *dechiffrer*, 666–8; Dallet 1877, 290; *Encyclopédie du dix-neuvième siècle*, entry *polygraphie* 1846, 6–11; 1852, 6–11; 1855, 6–11 1867, 6–11; Jacob 1858, 9–11; Marchal 1861, 207–9; 1866, 207–9 ; Panckoucke and Thevin 1782, 545–54; Plum 1882, 40.
125 Süß 1922, 142–75.
126 Kelly 1985, 162; Kelly 1998, 245; West 1988, 42
127 Kelly 1998, 245.
128 West 1988, 42.
129 Sheldon 1986, 44.
130 Sheldon 2003, 75.
131 Sheldon 2003, 73.
132 Strasser 2007, 278.
133 Coles and Landrum 2009, 7.
134 For examples of the *scytale* in popular studies and stories, see e.g.: Ohaver 1924; 1925; including a *scytale* puzzle to be solved and submitted to the magazine; Ohaver 1925, 1151–2, including the solution of the puzzle and the winners); De la Torre 1946, 80–96; Ranpo *Ni-Sen Doka* (Ranpo 1923).
135 D'Agapeyeff 1939, 15.
136 D'Agapeyeff 1939, 15, 135.
137 Gardner 1983, 56. Although Gardner mentions the *scytale* as being the earliest known code device used by the Spartans, he discusses it as nothing more than a 'toy' cipher.
138 Sheldon 1986, 46–7.
139 Walker 2008, 150.
140 Mollin 2005, 5.
141 Smart 2018, 3.
142 For these and all other meanings of the word '*scytale*', see: Liddell and Scott 2014, entry σκυτάλη; Montanari, Goh et al. 2015, entry σκυτάλις.
143 Anderson 1970, 68; Debidour 2019, 195–208.
144 West 1988, 43–5.
145 West 1988, 45. See also Fischer 2004, 14; Glassner 2003, 1.
146 One of the oldest known mnemonics is the so-called 'knot record'. People could make knots in a string whereby every knot stood for a word or message. In this way people could remember these messages. Knot-records are also seen as an early form of counting (Glassner 2003, 1; Fischer 2004, 14).
147 West 1988, 42.
148 A detailed engagement with ancient literacy and letter writing lies beyond the scope of this book, but see e.g. Adams 2003; Boring 1979; Cartledge 1978; Goody and Watt 1968; Harris 1989; Harvey 1966; Millender 1996; 1999; 2001; 2002; 2009; Street 1984; Woodard and Scott 2014.

149 Sheldon 2008, 11–14.
150 West 1988, 42.
151 Strasser 2007, 278; Whitehead 1990, 183–4.
152 Kahn 1967, 77; Mollin 2005, 11; Oriyano 2013, 56; Stewart, Chapple et al. 2012, 362; Stinson 1995, 4; Stinson 2002, 4.
153 Churchhouse 2002, 13; Gardner 1983, 56; Mollin 2005, 5; Piper and Murphy 2002, 22; Sheldon 1986, 46–7; Walker 2008, 150.
154 Luenberger 2012, 167; Raggo and Hosmer 2012, 9; Reinke 1962, 116; Singh 1999, 8–9. How the principle of the use of *scytalae* can still be found in modern transposition ciphers – particularly those used in warfare – will be discussed in chapter six.

4 Cryptography and Steganography in Aeneas Tacticus' *How to Survive Under Siege*

1 Strasser 2007, 278; West 1988, 42; Whitehead 1990, 183–4.
2 Whitehead 1990, 183 4.
3 Sheldon 1987, 45; West 1988, 42.
4 Aeneas Tacticus is often identified as Aineias of Stymphalos, an Arcadian general from the fourth century BCE who is mentioned in Xenophon's *Hellenica* (Xenophon, *Hellenica*, 7.3.1); Barends 1955, 171; Bliese 1994, 108; Brownson 1918, 281; Chaniotis 2013, 441; Dain and Bon 1967, vii, xii; David 1986a, 343; Delebecque, 1957, 430; Hug 1877, 28ff.; Hunter and Handford, 1927 ix–x, xxii, xxiv–xxv, 264; Millett 2013, 65; Oldfather 1923, 7; Rawlings 2007, 13; Starr 1957, 68; Vela Tejada 2004, 14162; Usher 1970, 210211; Whitehead 1990, 10112; Winterling 1991, 196. See also Vela Tejada 1991. It is likely that Aeneas wrote at least four other works on military strategy that have been lost. Three of the works are referred to in *How to Survive Under Siege*: a work on military preparations (7.4, 8.5, 21.1, 40.8); a work on procurement (14.2); and a work on encampment (21.2). Scholars presume that Aeneas also wrote a work on conducting siege operations (Aelian, *The Tactics*, 1.2, 3.4; Julius Africanus, *Kestoi*, 37).
5 Chaniotis 2013, 446; Jenkins 1999, 35; Moore 2013, 462; Vela Tejada 2004, 14112. See also Vela Tejada 1991.
6 Kelly 1985, 141–69; Sheldon 1987, 45; West 1988, 42; Whitehead 1990, 184.
7 Kelly 1985, 141–69; West 1988, 42; Whitehead 1990, 184. In a previous publication based on my research, I suggested sixteen different methods (Diepenbroek 2019). I have since identified a total of twenty-one different methods catalogued in Aeneas Tacticus' work. In D'Agapeyeff's work we see the name of the Roman Tacitus being connected to the invention of these methods of secret communication (D'Agapeyeff 1939, 16). D'Agapeyeff potentially confuses the names Aeneas Tacticus and Tacitus, an example of how some modern historians of cryptography seem to misinterpret the original sources.

8   Kelly 1985, 141–69; Sheldon 1987, 45; West 1988, 42; Whitehead 1990, 184.
9   David 1986a, 343; Spence 2010, 26; Whitehead 1990, 9,12.
10 In 31.14 of *How to Survive Under Siege* Aeneas Tacticus discussed Herodotus' story of Demaratus without mentioning any names or places. Aeneas simply stated that someone had once written under the wax of a wax tablet.
11 Bliese 1994, 108; Chaniotis 2013, 446; Hanson 2007b, 3; Hunter and Handford 1927, xii–xiii; Jenkins 1999, 35; Moore 2013, 462; Oldfather 1923, 4, 8–9; Vela Tejada 1991; Vela Tejada 2004, 14123; Rawlings 2007, 139; Whitehead 1990, 14 15; Vela Tejada 1991; Vela Tejada 2004, 14122.
12 Burliga 2008; Pretzler 2018a; Liddel 2018, 123; Rawlings 2007, 139; Spence 2010, 26; Shipley 2018; Whitehead 1990, 4, 2024; Williams 1904, 390.
13 Hunter and Handford discuss eighteen different methods, but they do not discuss the two variations of the *astragali* method (also known as the 'knucklebones method') separately. Instead, they see only one variation (Hunter and Handford 1927, 211). Yet, I believe this distinction to be crucial since the two variations are clearly different methods as becomes clear from Aeneas' work on the astragali and its variations (*How to Survive Under Siege*, 31.16–22).
14 The method of fire signalling – known from Polybius' work – also falls into the category of steganography (Polybius, *Histories*, 10.44–4); See also chapter six in this book, and Diepenbroek 2019, 63–76. Various methods that Aeneas Tacticus discusses can also be found in Julius Africanus' *Kestoi* (51–53).
15 Whitehead 1990, 183, 187.
16 Debidour 2006; Liddel 2018, 135; Rance 2018, 313.
17 Liddel 2018, 135.
18 Aeneas Tacticus, *How to Survive Under Siege*, 4.1–4, 5.1, 9.2, 10.6, 10.11, 10.18–19, 10.25–26, 11.3–6, 12, 18.3–6, 18.8–11 (see also Polyaenus, *Stratagems of War*, 2.36), 18.13–21, 20, 22.5, 22.7, 23.7–11, 29.3–10.
19 Aeneas Tacticus, *How to Survive Under Siege*, 31.14 = Herodotus, *Histories*, 7.239; Aeneas, *Siege*, 31.25–27 = *Histories*, 8.128; Aeneas, *Siege*, 31.28–29 = *Histories*, 5.35; Aeneas, *Siege*, 37.6 = *Histories*, 4.200; see also Aeneas, *Siege*, 2.3–6 = Thucydides, *History of the Peloponnesian War*, 2.2–6 (esp. 4); Aeneas, *Siege*, 27.11 = Xenophon, *Anabasis*, 2.2.20. On Aeneas' sources, see Bettalli 1990; Brown 1981; Dain and Bon 1967; David 1986a; David 1986b; Hunter and Handford 1927; Luraghi 1988; Vela Tejada 1991, 37H43; Vela Tejada and Garcia 1991; Whitehead 1990.
20 On examples of Aeneas Tacticus' personal experience, as discussed in *How to Survive Under Siege*, see Burliga 2008.
21 For a parallel from Roman times, see Herodian, *History of the Empire from the Death of Marcus*, 7.6.5. When using a source, Aeneas Tacticus did not literally quote it. Instead, he paraphrased his sources to bring out his own points in the clearest way,

22 Yet, the person has no name in Aeneas' text.
23 For a parallel from Roman times, see Frontinus, *Stratagems*, 3.13.5–8; Pliny, *Natural History*, 10.53 (37). A link can be made with the use of animals as secret messengers in the twentieth century. For the role of carrier pigeons in the Second World War, see e.g., O'Connor 2018.
24 To make sure that the hidden message was not affected by water and mud, Aeneas suggested that it be written on a piece of lead (31.4). Whitehead incorrectly presumes that Ovid suggested this same method in *Ars Amatoria*, 3.624 (Whitehead 1990, 184). However, Ovid simply mentioned that one could hide a letter in a sandal, amongst a selection of simple methods to communicate in secret quickly and easily (*Ars Amatoria*, 3.619–630).
25 This method could have been useful if one did not trust the messenger.
26 This is not an example of the use of invisible ink since the recipient simply had to pour out the oil to be able to read the text again. He did not have to use, for example, charcoal to make the text visible again. For the use of invisible ink in Antiquity, see Ausonius, *Epistles*, 28.21–22; Ovid, *Ars Amatoria*, 3.627–630; Philo, *Compendium of Mechanics*, D. 77 (102.31–36); Pliny the Elder, *Natural History* (26.39 (62)).
27 Bauer 2007a, 10; Kipper 2004, 42.
28 Aeneas Tacticus, *How to Survive Under Siege*, 4.1, 4.5–6, 6.1–7, 7.1–4, 10.25–26; Apollodorus, *Epitome*, 5.19; Aristotle, *On the Universe*, 398a; Aeschylus, *Agamemnon*, 7–9, 20–29, 278–350; Appian of Alexandria, *The Civil Wars*, 1.6.51, 12.66; Ibid., *The Spanish Wars*, 6.15.90–92; Caesar, *The Gallic War*, 2.33, 3.65–67, 7.3; Ibid., *The Civil War*, 3.65; Cicero, *The Verrine Orations*, 2.5.35; Diodorus Siculus, *Library of History*, 18.57.5, 19.17.7; Flavius Josephus, *Books of the History of the Jewish War against the Romans*, 4.10.5; Frontinus, *Stratagems*, 2.5.16; Herodotus, *Histories*, 6.115, 7.183, 9.3; Homer, *Iliad*, 4.275–276, 5.770–771, 18.203–214; Julius Africanus, *Kestoi*, 77; Livy, *History of Rome*, 22.19.6; Maurice, *Strategikon*, 7.2.10; Onasander, *The General*, 25.3; Pausanias, *Description of Greece*, 2.25.2; Pliny, *Natural History*, 35.48 (14); Polybius, *The Histories*, 1.19, 8.28–29, 10.42–47; Polyaenus, *Stratagems of War*, 4.19.2, 6.16.2; Simonides, *Elegies*, 130; Suetonius, *Tiberius*, 65; Thucydides, *History of the Peloponnesian War*, 1.63, 2.94, 3.22, 3.80, 4.42, 4.111, 8.95, 8.102; Vegetius, *The Military Institutions of the Romans*, 3.5.25l; Virgil, *Aeneid* 10.454, 11.526; Ibid., *The Eclogues*, 8, 59; Xenophon, *Hellenica*, 1.1.1–4, 2.1.27, 5.1.27, 6.2.33–34. See also: Aschoff 1984; Dvornik 1974, 31A3; Hyde 1915; Sheldon 1987, 135; Sheldon 2005, 127; Woolliscroft 2001, 159 71.
29 D'Agapeyeff 1939, 16 17; Dvornik 1974, 4213; Hunter and Handford 1927, 120, 122–3; Liddel 2018, 127d8; Oldfather 1923, 46,7; Rihll 2018, 28177.
30 See also Dvornik 1974, 56; Sheldon 1987, 28.

31 Woolliscroft 2001; Sheldon 2005, 205.
32 Woolliscroft 2001, 32, see already Hunter and Handford 1927, 120.
33 Kahn 1996a, 76–83; Mollin 2005, 9310; Mollin 2006, 89; Smith 1955, 16.
34 Bauer – based on Hunt 1929 – suggests that the ancient Greeks were familiar with the cryptographic principle of replacing letters with other letters (Bauer 2017, 96). See also Bengtson 1962, 460; Glotz and Cohen 1936, 41061; Dain and Bon 1967, 75; Oldfather 1923, 5,7; Von Gutschmid 1880, 588–90; Whitehead 1990, 191.
35 From *c.* 600–500 BCE, Hebrew scholars were already using a substitution system known as the *Atbash* cipher, and Aeneas Tacticus may have based his simple cipher on this model. See Strasser 2007, 278.
36 This method is also suggested by Cardano in his 1550 work *De Subtilitate* (17.1036–1037).
37 Aeneas' use of *astragali* is discussed for the first time in modern cryptographic scholarship by Hunter and Handford in 1927 (p. 209).
38 Olivetti 2015, 263.
39 It is plausible that Aeneas Tacticus tried out the method before putting it into practice. Namely, in passage 31.18, he discussed how to 'write' his own name by pulling a thread through the holes of the *astragalus*.
40 Hunter and Handford 1927, lxxxii; Whitehead 1990, 187.
41 Whitehead 1990, 87. If there is no actual writing involved in creating cryptographic messages, it is known as a semagram: Chatton 2010, 43; Lunde 2012, 42.
42 Diels 1914, 67.
43 Welskopf 1974, 44.
44 Sheldon 1987, 45; West 1988, 42; Whitehead 1990, 183W4.

5 Roman Views Towards the Spartan *Scytale*

1 Hanson 2007a and b.
2 Other examples of ancient military manuals include Xenophon's *Art of Horsemanship* and *Cavalry Commander*, and Roman examples such as Vegetius' *Military Institutions of the Romans* (Hanson 2007a, 3; Pretzler 2018a, 68–95). See also Burliga 2008, 92.101; Pretzler 2010, 85–107; 2018b, 146,65; Shipley 2018. Although military manuals like Aeneas Tacticus' work were intended as pragmatic guides to commanders in the field, Burliga is uncertain to what extent, if at all, Aeneas Tacticus' work served a useful purpose in real military circumstances (Burliga 2008, 95–6).
3 Stewart, Chapple et al. 2012, 362. See also Kahn 1967, 77; Mollin 2005, 11; Oriyano 2013, 56; Stinson 2002.
4 Freisenbruch 2007; Henderson 2007; Morello 2007.

5   Malherbe 1988.
6   Sarri 2017, 125.
7   In Greek sources, a variety of terms are used for an official messenger: ἄγγελοι (*angeloi*; 'messengers'), κήρυκες (*kerukes*; 'heralds'), ἡμεροδρόμοι (*hemerodromoi*; 'day-runners'), δρομοκήρυκες (*dromokerukes*; 'couriers') or δρομοκῆρυξ (*dromokerus*; 'runner herald').
8   Carey 1981, 23–4; Ceccarelli 2013, 10–11; Gibson and Morrison 2007, 6–7.
9   From the reign of Diocletian until the end of the Roman Empire, private letters even outnumber public letters/decrees (MacMullen 1982, 236).
10 Sarri 2017, 125; Sidebottom 2007, 9. See also Head 2009a; 2009b; Kolb 2001.
11 Sarri 2017, 125; Sidebottom 2007, 9.
12 Head 2009a and b.
13 On security problems and other issues that Cicero encountered when sending his letters, see Nicholson 1994.
14 Achtemeier 1990, 15, 17; Porter and Pitts 2013, 505.
15 Henderson 2007, 61.
16 Adkins and Adkins 2014, 209; Erdkamp 2011, 287; Jeffery 1961, 57; Lewis 2015, xxxix; Sherwood 2006, 536A7.
17 Strasser 2007; Swift 2019, 278.
18 Shackleton Bailey 1999, 155.
19 Other Roman letter writers used this practice of combining the Greek and Latin language as well: Butler 2012; Dunkel 2000; Hall 2009; Keeline 2018; Kelsey 2007; Poster and Mitchell 2007; Shackleton Bailey 1980; Ibid 1999 (all); Ibid 2004 (all) White 2010. On Graeco-Roman bilingual documents, see e.g.: Adams 2003; Dirkzwager 1976; Dunkel 2000; Elder and Mullen 2019; Kajanto 1980; Kramer 1983; Lietzmann 1968; Mullen and James 2012; Rea 1968; Rea 1970; Sarri 2017; Trapp 2003; Wouters 1976.
20 Shackleton Bailey 1999, 155.
21 Shackleton Bailey 1999, 155. See also Strasser 2007, 278.
22 Donderer 1995, 98–9. See also Nicholson 1994, 4798.
23 Rolfe 1929, 51; Watson 1886, 326 7.
24 Lewis and Short, entry '*clava*, give the following definitions for the term: 1: A knotty branch or stick, a staff, cudgel, club; 2: As a weapon for exercising, used by young men, and especially by soldiers, a foil; 3: As a badge of Hercules; 4: *clava Herculis*, a plant, otherwise called *nymphea*.
25 A discussion on the relationship between Ausonius and Paulinus lies beyond the scope of this book. On the topic see e.g.: Dräger 2002; Ebbeler 2007; Knight 2005; Trout 1999.
26 What other methods Ausonius was familiar with are unclear, since he does not discuss them in any of his surviving letters.

27 Green 1982, 272; McKeown 1989, 85–6.
28 Wax tablets seem to have been more commonly used among the Romans for writing: Adkins and Adkins 2014, 209; Erdkamp 2011, 287; Jeffery 1961, 57; Lewis 2015, xxxix; Sherwood 2006, 53657.
29 Goold 1977, 45.
30 The vitriol that makes the text visible again works as a reagent. A reagent is a substance or compound that is added to a system in order to bring about a chemical reaction or to see if a reaction occurs: Macrakis 2014, 11; McNaught and Wilkinson 1997, 149.
31 Karpenko and Norris 2001, 998.
32 Whitiak 2003, 1, 2.
33 Whitiak 2003, 1, 2
34 Khan 2007; Fiorentino and Zech-Matterne 2018.
35 Marks 2010, entry: 'Citrus'.
36 Khan 2007; Fiorentino and Zech-Matterne 2018.
37 Macrakis 2014, 138.
38 Here it echoes Herodotus' story of Histiaeus tattooing one of his slaves with a message to revolt against King Darius (Herodotus, *Histories*, 5.35; see also chapter two).
39 Moreover, Ovid's suggestions for lovers to communicate in secret once more refer to the idea of communication in the Roman world being more of a private matter than it was in the Greek world.
40 Sheldon 2004, 201. All references to these signals are related to warfare. We cannot find any references to, for example, commercial, or diplomatic purposes.
41 Sheldon 2004, 201.
42 For Roman signalling stations, see Cichorius 1900, 2; Sheldon 2004, 204; Webster 1994, 163; Woolliscroft 2001, 26.
43 During the day, signals by red flags replaced smoke signals, which seems to have been an improvement: Warry 2015.
44 Naval signalling was well known too, but there was always the chance that the enemy picked up the signals (Sheldon 2004, 201). Therefore, it is plausible that the meaning of these messages was discussed between communicating parties beforehand, making them, in a way, secret.
45 Merriam-Webster's Collegiate Dictionary (2003), entry: 'Sejanus'; Adams 1955.
46 On Ausonius' *Epistles*, see e.g.: Dräger 2002; Evelyn-White 1921; Knight 2005. On Ovid's influence on Ausonius, see e.g.: Guzmán and Martínez 2018; Fielding 2017; Martin 2004; Moroni 2010.
47 Evelyn-White 1921, 111. See also Dräger 2002; Knight 2005.
48 Mollin 2005, 11; Stinson 1995, 4.

49 See for example: Apelbaum 2007, 54; Bauer 2007a, 382; Salomon 2003, 59; Salomon 2006, 243.
50 Mollin 2005, 8, 11; Kahate 2013, 219; Stinson 2002, 4. For earlier substitution ciphers, see Strasser 2007, 278 (on the *Atbash* cipher used by Hebrew scholars *c.* 600–500 BCE); Aeneas Tacticus' *How to Survive Under Siege*, 31.30-31 (on replacing vowels by dots or other symbols, *c.* 350 BCE).
51 The exact difference between the two groups is uncertain. Sheldon simply presumes that *speculatores* were used both as spies and scouts (Sheldon 2008, 13, 84), while Ezov argues that *speculatores* gathered information through spying, while *exploratores* gathered information though patrols with much less secrecy (Ezov 1996, 93). See also Perkins 1953, 84; Russell 1999, 485; Sheldon 1987, 106.
52 Caesar, *The Gallic War*, 2.35, 5.11, 5.46, 5.48, 7.9, 7.49, 8.11; Ibid., *The Civil War*, 1.1, 1.9, 1.10, 2.13, 2.37, 3.25, 3.78; Ibid., *The Alexandrian War*, 34, 42, 51, 56; *The African War*, 4, 26, 32, 86.
53 Caesar, *The Gallic War*, 2.1, 2.10, 3.19, 4.5, 4.19, 4.37, 5.1, 5.6-7, 5.11, 5.18, 5.25, 5.40, 5.45-46, 5.47, 5.49, 7.6-7, 7.41, 7.67, 7.86, 8.1, 8.4, 8.19, 8.39, 8.46; Ibid., *The Civil War*, 1.7, 1.10, 1.18, 1.26, 1.39, 1.59, 3.18, 3.43, 3.106; Caesar, *The African War*, 1, 7, 31, 63, 65; Ibid., *The Spanish War*, 18-19.
54 Caesar, *The Gallic War*, 2.35, 4.38, 5.11, 5.46, 5.48, 7.9, 7.13, 7.49, 7.90, 8.11; Ibid., *The Civil War*, 1.1, 1.9, 1.10, 2.13, 2.37, 3.25, 3.78; Ibid., *The Alexandrian War*, 34, 42, 51, 56; Ibid., *The African War*, 4, 26, 32, 86. For references to messages sent to specific people, see Caesar, *The Gallic War*, 3.3, 3.19, 4.23, 4.25-26, 4.37, 5.1, 5.7, 5.52, 6.1, 7.49, 7.65, 8.27; Caesar, *The Civil War*, 1.8, 1.23, 1.25, 1.28, 1.82, 2.37, 3.2, 3.46, 3.62, 3.76, 3.78, 3.106-107; Ibid., *The Alexandrian War*, 1, 9, 13, 51; Ibid., *The African War*, 8, 12, 26, 31-32, 37, 40.
55 Caesar, *The Gallic War*, 1.10, 1.15, 1.24, 2.25, 2.35, 3.7, 3.10-11, 3.28, 4.7, 4.14, 4.18-19, 4.34, 4.38, 5.1-2, 5.8, 6.3, 6.5, 6.9, 6.32-33, 6.44, 7.9, 7.11, 7.40, 7.68, 7.80, 8.2, 8.38-39, 8.46; Ibid., *The Civil War*, 1.8, 1.15, 1.32, 1.41, 1.64, 1.72, 1.80, 1.87, 2.1, 2.22, 3.2, 3.6, 3.16, 3.52, 3.78, 3.106; Ibid., *The Alexandrian War*, 10, 11, 14, 33, 48, 66, 73, 78; Ibid., *The African War*, 1, 2, 9, 63, 86, 89, 98; Ibid., *The Spanish War*, 4, 40-42.
56 Caesar, *The Gallic War*, 1.21, 1.22, 1.24, 1.54, 2.17, 2.19-22, 2.26, 2.34-35, 3.1, 3.10-11, 3.16, 3.19, 3.28, 3.29, 4.14, 4.21-22, 4.32-33, 4.36, 4.38, 5.2, 5.10, 5.15, 5.24, 5.27, 6.1, 6.3, 6.5-6.7, 6.29, 6.33, 6.40-41, 7.34, 7.37, 7.45, 7.51, 7.56, 7.80, 7.87-88, 7.90, 8.2, 8.4, 8.5-7, 8.16-17, 8.19, 8.24-25, 8.43, 8.46, 8.52, 8.54; Ibid., *The Civil War*, 1.11-12, 1.18, 1.26, 1.30, 1.32, 1.36-37, 1.39, 1.43, 1.45, 1.63, 1.66, 1.72, 1.78, 1.87, 2.5, 2.19, 2.21, 2.23, 3.8, 3.19, 3.24, 3.26, 3.34, 3.42, 3.56-57, 3.62, 3.77-78, 3.89, 3.97, 3.101; Ibid., *The Alexandrian War*, 1, 9, 15, 17, 20, 21, 30, 31, 42; Ibid., *The African War*, 2, 8, 10, 17-18, 20, 31, 37, 43, 51, 54, 58, 60-62, 66, 77-78, 81, 86; Ibid., *The Spanish War*, 4, 26, 35, 39.

57 For references to letters sent during the civil war and situations in which secret letters could have been sent, see Caesar, *The Civil War*, 1.1, 1.7, 1.8, 1.9, 1.10, 1.11–12, 1.15, 1.18, 1.23, 1.25, 1.26, 1.28, 1.30, 1.32, 1.36–37, 1.39, 1.41, 1.43, 1.45, 1.59, 1.63, 1.64, 1.66, 1.72, 1.78, 1.80, 1.82, 1.87, 2.1, 2.5, 2.13, 2.19, 2.21, 2.22, 2.23, 2.37, 3.2, 3.6, 3.8, 3.16, 3.18, 3.19, 3.24, 3.25, 3.26, 3.34, 3.43, 3.43, 3.46, 3.52, 3.56–57, 3.62, 3.76, 3.77–78, 3.89, 3.97, 3.101, 3.106–107.

58 Cary and Foster 1914, 419.

59 Adams 2003, 329; Harris 1989, 182 3.

60 Pieprzyk, Hardjono and Sebbery 2013, 6.

61 Bauer 2017, 99, 148; Holmes 1911, 218119; Singh 1999, 10. For similar examples of Greek texts written phonetically with the Latin alphabet, and Latin texts written phonetically with the Greek alphabet, see e.g. *P. Oxy*.2.244, 36.2772; Adams 2003; Burrell 2009, 69395; Dirkzwager 1976; Kajanto 1980; Kramer 1983; Lietzmann 1968; Rea 1968; 1970; Wouters 1976.

62 Reinke 1962, 114.

63 Edwards 1917, 297.

64 Harris 1995, 14.

65 Mollin 2005, 11; Stinson 1995, 4.

66 Apelbaum 2007, 54; Bauer 2007a, 382; Salomon 2003, 59; Salomon 2006, 243.

67 Kahn 1974, 77; Oriyano 2013, 56; Van Tilborg 2006, 9.

68 Rolfe 1914, 109.

69 See also Figure 9 for encryption with the Caesar cipher, and Figure 10 for decryption with the Caesar cipher.

70 Cary and Foster 1914, 419; Rolfe 1914, 109.

71 If using the classical Latin alphabet for his cipher, Caesar had an alphabet of either twenty-one or twenty-three letters. According to Cicero, the alphabet of the late Republican period was composed of twenty-one letters (*On the Nature of the Gods*, 2.37): the letters 'J', 'U', 'W', 'Y' and 'Z' were not used. However, according to Sherwood, Nikolic, et. al. the Romans already added the Greek letters 'Y' and 'Z' to their alphabet after the conquest of Greece in 146 BCE (Sherwood, Nikolic et al. 2003, 525; see also Wallace 2015, 14, 16).

72 See, for example, Bauer 2013; Churchhouse 2002; Piper and Murphy 2002; Purnamaa and Rohayani 2015; Van Tilborg 2006, 9–10.

73 Stewart, Chapple et al. 2012, 362. See also Kahn 1967, 77; Mollin 2005, 11; Oriyano 2013, 56; Stinson 2002.

74 Augustus used the same principle as Caesar, yet with a right shift of one, hereby writing 'B' for 'A', 'C' for 'B', etc.: Cassius Dio, *Roman History*, 51.3.7; Suetonius, *The Deified Augustus*, 88. This right shift of one can again be seen in Viking texts (Bauer 2017, 118,20), and in the work of the fourteenth-century CE Greek scholar Georgius Chrysocossas, who used β for α, γ for β, and so on. A partial Latin translation of the

work of Georgius Chrysocossas can be found in various fifteenth- and sixteenth-century copies of a manuscript known as the *Expositio in Syntaxin Persarum* (Gardthausen 1911, 302).

6 The Development of the Principle of the Transposition Cipher System of the *Scytale* in Ciphers from the Renaissance to the Twenty-First Century

1 Dooley 2013, 12; Kahn 1967, 78; Saiber 2017, 23. See also Saltzman 2018 for a discussion of cryptography among early medieval English monks, an exception to the rule.
2 Caubet 2008, 421; Mollin 2005, 4 5; Pieprzyk, Hardjono and Seberry 2013, 6.
3 After the first century CE there is little extant evidence for the use of substitution ciphers like the Caesar cipher in the western part of the Roman empire. Christians – especially in the Eastern Roman Empire – continued to use Caesar ciphers in Greek, Coptic and Syriac, the three main languages used in Christian scripts from Late Antiquity until the Middle Ages: Darnell and Darnell 2002; Delattre 2008; Fronczak 2013; Wisse 1979.
4 Süß 1922, 142S75; see also Reinke 1962, 153.
5 Apelbaum 2007, 54; Bauer 2007a, 382; Salomon 2003, 59; Salomon 2006, 243.
6 Kahn 1967, 94 5.
7 Apelbaum 2007, 54; Bauer 2007a, 382; Salomon 2003, 59; Salomon 2006, 243.
8 Strasser 2007, 281; Kahn 1996b, 128; Lunde 2012, 73.
9 Strasser 2007, 281; Lunde 2012, 73. When discussing Alberti's disk, D'Agapeyeff incorrectly argues that cipher wheels always had to consist of an outer disk which had the letters of the alphabet in their usual order, and an inner disk containing the letters of the same alphabet in reversed order: D'Agapeyeff 1939, 119.
10 Piper 2002, entry 'cryptography'.
11 '*Tu idem in provincia interlegendum admonitus inventa maiuscula eam scies* [...].' De Componendis Cifris, 14.
12 Kahn 1967, 94.
13 In fact, with all the components needed to encipher and decipher messages involved, Alberti believed his system to be the most suitable way to send secret messages over a long distance: *De Componendis Cifris*, 16.
14 Compared to the modern twenty-six-letter alphabet the letters 'J' and 'U' are missing.
15 Bauer 2007b, 381,446.
16 Since Bellaso's manuscript is not easily available, the discussion of the working of his method is based on the work of modern scholars: Bauer 2007a and b; Couto 2006; Lunde 2012; Strasser 2007.

17 Piper 2002, entry 'cryptography'.
18 Compared to the modern twenty-six-letter alphabet, the letters 'J', 'K', 'V' and 'W' are missing.
19 For more on the working of Bellaso's system, see Bauer 2007a and b; Couto 2006; Lunde 2012; Strasser 2007.
20 Bauer 2007a and b; Couto 2006; Lunde 2012; Strasser 2007.
21 Kahn 1996a, 194; Luenberger 2012, 176.
22 Monticello/University of Viriginia 2023, entry 'Wheel Cipher'.
23 The device had certainly been used by Jefferson himself when he became America's minister to France (1784–89). In this period, adoption of codes was necessary. Codes were an essential part of Jefferson's correspondence because European postal workers routinely opened and read any suspect letters passing through their command (Monticello/University of Viriginia 2023, entry 'Wheel Cipher').
24 Kahn 1996a, 194; Luenberger 2012, 176.
25 Kahn 1996a, 194. Here one can see the principle of the key (the information needed to encrypt and decrypt a message) as discussed by Aeneas Tacticus, *How to Survive Under Siege*, 31.1.
26 Kahn 1996a, 194; Kahn 1996b Luenberger 2012, 176.
27 From the Greek word αὐτός and Latin *auto*, meaning 'self'.
28 For the use of cryptography during the American Civil War, see Barker, 1978, 87; Kahn, 1996a, 217–21; Reynard 1999, 28; Wrixon 1992, 32–3.
29 Kahn 1996a, 83; Kahn 1996b; Lunde 2012, 7819; Mollin 2006, 90.
30 Mollin 2006, 90; Lunde 2012, 78 9; Kahn 1996a, 83; Kahn 1996b.
31 Mollin 2005, 1; Reba and Shier 2015, 480.
32 Kahn 1996a, 83; Kahn 1996b; Lunde 2012, 78–9; Mollin 2006, 90; Van Tilborg 2006, 32.
33 Van Tilborg 2006, 32.
34 Childs 1919, 13; Dooley 2016, 65; Klima and Sigmon 2012, 55; Mollin 2005, 1; Reba and Shier 2015, 480.
35 The German alphabet has thirty letters: twenty-six letters as in the English alphabet and four more characters (ä, ö, ü and ß). These signs were left out in the Polybius square.
36 If Polybius had decided to change the order of letters on his tablets (regularly), the method would have become more secure. Yet, in this case, communicating parties would have had to send each other the key information on the changed order of letters.
37 It is relevant to mention here that the aforementioned step is only the first stage of ADFGX encryption. This is followed by columnar transposition before sending the message. The addition of this second element makes the system a combination of a transposition and a substitution cipher. For columnar transposition ciphers, see e.g.: Bauer 2013, 128 30, 136; Bauer 2017, 217222; Bishop 2003, 19; Childs 1919, 13;

Churchhouse 2003, 4526; Collard 2004; Dooley 2016, 6265; Kahn 1996, 535, 539; Stamp and Low 2007.
38 Klima and Sigmon 2012, 55S7.
39 Mollin 2000, 12.
40 Churchhouse 2002, 45 6; Kahn 1996b, 334; 535–9; Mollin 2000, 12.
41 Kahn 1996b, 413; Kopal 2018, 941; Kruh 1981, 197.
42 Bauer 2013, 205.
43 Kruh 1981, 195.
44 Dooley 2016, 62–5.
45 Bauer 2013, 128, 130, 136. See also Bauer 2017, 217122.
46 Perhaps the most famous ciphers that used a combination of transposition and substitution are the German ADFGX and ADFGVX ciphers, discussed previously in this chapter (Childs 1919, 13; Churchhouse 2002, 45-6; Diepenbroek 2019; Dooley 2016, 65; Kahn 1996b, 535, 539).
47 Bishop 2003, 19; Collard 2004; Stamp and Low 2007, 5.
48 Reinke 1962, 116.
49 Dooley 2013, 8; Klima and Sigmon 2012, 34S5.
50 Bauer 2013, 124.
51 Reinke 1962, 115–16.
52 Kahn 1996b, 413; Kopal 2018, 94l; Kruh 1981, 197.
53 Bauer 2017, 361–4; Dooley 2018, 137–8; Kruh 1981, 195; Salomon 2003, 422; Salomon 2006, 262.
54 Curley 2013, 25; Kruh 1981, 197.
55 Curley 2013, 25; Dooley 2018, 137–8; Kruh 1981, 193.
56 Kruh 1981, 193–4.
57 Kruh 1981, 194.
58 Kruh 1981, 194.
59 Bauer 2017, 361–4; Dooley 2018, 137–8; Kruh 1981, 195; Salomon 2003, 422; Salomon 2006, 262.
60 Kruh 1981, 193. See also Bauer 2003, 119.
61 Bauer 2003, 119; Kruh 1981, 195.
62 Bauer 2017, 361 4.
63 Kruh 1981, 196.
64 Kruh 1981, 196.
65 Kahn 1967, xi.
66 Boicea, Rădulescu et al., 2016, 2–6; Garg 2009, 387; NIST 2001, 1651. Shannon, in 1949, already showed that one needs to use both transposition and substitution to have decent security: Shannon 1949, 656–715.
67 Churchhouse 2002, 42.
68 Army Security Agency 1948, 39.

Conclusion

1. Connor 1988, 18; Detienne 1968, 123; Krentz 1997 (*passim*); 2002, 23; Mitchell 1996, 87–105; De Romilly 1968, 211; Sage 1996, xvii; Van Wees 2000; Vernant 1968, 21.
2. Krentz, 1997; Krentz 2002; Pritchett 1971; Van Wees 2000.
3. Gerolymatos 1986, 13.
4. However, it must be kept in mind that Diodorus Siculus and Polyaenus may be referring to Tyrtaeus' writing in the seventh century BCE.
5. Boicea, Rădulescu et al., 2016, 2e6; Garg 2009, 387; NIST 2001, 1651.
6. Bauer 2017, 99.
7. For example, in 1921, the first serious attempts were made to decipher the Voynich manuscript: a late medieval work in code. Newbold had already stated that this work would never be deciphered (Bird 1921, 494). Today, about a hundred years later, this work has still not been deciphered: Goldstone and Goldstone 2005; Kennedy and Churchill 2005.
8. Macrakis 2014, 301.
9. Bauer 2007b, 100.
10. Bauer 2007b, 100.

Bibliography

Abrantes, M. C. (2017a). *Explicit Sources of Tzetzes Chiliades*. Scotts Valley: CreateSpace Independent Publishing Platform.

Abrantes, M. C. (2017b). *Explicit Sources of Tzetzes Chiliades – Second Edition*. Scotts Valley: CreateSpace Independent Publishing Platform.

Achtemeier, P. J. (1990). Omne Verbum Sonat: The New Testament and the Oral Environment of Late Western Antiquity. *Journal of Biblical Literature,* 109 (1): 3–27.

Adams, F. (1955). The Consular Brothers of Sejanus. *The American Journal of Philology,* 76 (1): 70–6.

Adams, J. N. (2003). *Bilingualism and the Latin Language.* Cambridge: Cambridge University Press.

Africa, T. W. (1968). Cleomenes III and the Helots. *California Studies in Classical Antiquity,* 1: 1–11.

Aitkenhead, D. (2012). The Fugitive: An Interview with Julian Assange – 8 December. Online resource. Retrieved from: *The Guardian Online,* http://www.theguardian.com/media/2012/dec/07/julian-assange-fugitive-interview (Accessed date: 14-05-2023).

Adkins, L. and Adkins, R. (2014). *Handbook to Life in Ancient Rome.* New York: Facts on File.

Al-Kadi, I. A. (1992). Origins of Cryptology: The Arab Contributions. *Cryptologia,* 16 (2): 97–126.

Alican, N. F. (2012). *Rethinking Plato: A Cartesian Quest for the Real Plato.* Amsterdam/New York: Rodopi.

Aly, W. (1943). *Fragmentum Vaticanum de Eligendis Magistratibus: e Codice bis Rescripto Vat. Gr. 2306.* Vatican City: Biblioteca apostolica Vaticana.

Amyx, D. A. (1988). *Corinthian Vase Painting of the Archaic Period.* Berkeley/Los Angeles/London: University of California Press.

Anderson, G. (2004). Aulus Gellius as a Storyteller. In: Holford-Strevens, L. and Vardi A. (eds), *The Worlds of Aulus Gellius.* Oxford: Oxford University Press, 105–17.

Anderson, J. K. (1970). *Military Theory and Practice in the Age of Xenophon.* Berkeley/Los Angeles: University of California Press.

Anderson, C. T. (2016). *Intelligence by Design: Power of the Hebrew Alphabet.* New York: BookPatch LLC.

Andrewes, A. (1956). *The Greek Tyrants.* London: Hutchinson.

Anochin, V. A. and Rolle, R. (1998) Griechische Schleuderbleie bei den Mauern von Olbia. In: Rolle, R. and Schmidt K. (eds), *Archäologische Studien in Kontaktzonen der antiken Welt,* Göttingen: Vandenhoeck und Ruprecht, 837–49.

Apelbaum, Y. (2007). *User Authentication Principles, Theory and Practice*. Second Edition. Pewaukee: Fuji Technology Press.

Aquilino, B. (1831). *Dizionario etimologico di tutti vocaboli usati nelle scienze: arti e mestieri che traggono origine dal greco, Tomo IV*. Milan: G. Pirola.

Ashey, J. R. (2004). *The Macedonian Empire: The Era of Warfare Under Philip II and Alexander the Great, 359–323 B.C.* Jefferson/London: McFarland.

Aschoff, V. (1984). *Geschichte der Nachrichtentechnik: Beiträge zur Geschichte der Nachrichtentechnik von ihren Anfängen bis zum Ende des 18. Jahrhunderts*. Berlin/Heidelberg/New York/Tokyo: Springer-Verlag.

Army Security Agency (1948). *The History of Army Strip Cipher Devices (July 1934–October 1947)*. SRH-366. Washington DC: US Army Security Agency.

Augustyn, A. (2022). Herodotus. *Encyclopaedia Britannica*. Online resource. Retrieved from: https://www.britannica.com/biography/Herodotus-Greek-historian (accessed date 01-05-2023).

Babbitt, F. C. (1931). Plutrach, Moralia III: Saying of the Spartan Women. In: *Volume III: Sayings of Kings and Commanders. Sayings of Romans. Sayings of Spartans. The Ancient Customs of the Spartans. Sayings of Spartan Women. Bravery of Women*. Loeb Classical Library 245. Cambridge, Massachusetts: Harvard University Press, pp. 451–69.

Ball, W. W. R. (1892). *Mathematical Recreations and Essays – First Edition*. London: MacMillan and Co.

Ball, W. W. R. (1914). *Mathematical Recreations and Essays – Sixth Edition*. London: MacMillan and Co.

Barends, D. (1955). *Lexicon Aeneium: A Lexicon and Index to Aeneas Tacticus' Military Manual 'On the Defence of Fortified Positions'*. Assen: Van Gorcum.

Barley, S., Lewis, W., Beach, J. and Berghof, O. (2006). *The Etymologies of Isidore of Seville*. Cambridge: Cambridge University Press.

Bartlett, J. (2002). *The Ease of Steganography and Camouflage*. SANS Information Security White Papers, No. 762. Online Resource. Retrieved from: https://sansorg.egnyte.com/dl/4sRdRhVeLE (accessed date: 14-05-2023) *The Ease of Steganography and Camouflage*. SANS Institute InfoSec Reading Room.

Bar-Kochva, B. (1973). *The Seleucid Army: Organization and Tactics in the Great Campaigns*. Cambridge: Cambridge University Press.

Bauer, C. P. (2013). *Secret History: The Story of Cryptology*. Boca Raton/London/New York: CRC Press – An Imprint of Taylor and Francis Group.

Bauer, C. P. (2017). *Unsolved! The History and Mystery of the World's Greatest Ciphers from Ancient Egypt to Online Secret Societies*. New Jersey/Woodstock: Princeton University Press.

Bauer, F. L. (2007a). *Decrypted Secrets: Methods and Maxims of Cryptology*. Berlin/Heidelberg/New York: Springer-Verlag.

Bauer, F. L. (2007b). Rotor Machines and Bombs. In: De Leeuw, K. and Bergstra, J. A. (eds), *The History of Information Security: A Comprehensive Handbook*. Amsterdam/

Boston/Heidelberg/London/New York/Oxford/Paris/San Diego/San Francisco/Singapore/Sydney/Tokyo: Elsevier, 381–446.

Bauer, F. L. (2013). *Decrypted Secrets: Methods and Maxims of Cryptology.* Berlin/Heidelberg: Springer-Verlag.

Bausi, A., Brockmann, C., Friedrich, M. and Kienitz, S., eds (2018). *Manuscripts and Archives: Comparative Views on Record-Keeping.* Berlin/Boston: Walter de Gruyter GmbH and Co KG.

Baynes, T. S. and Robertson Smith, W., eds (1887). *Encyclopaedia Britannica: A Dictionary of Arts, Sciences and General Literature – Ninth Edition.* Edinburgh: Adam and Charles Black.

Bazeries, E. (1901). *Les Chiffres Secrets Dévoilés: Étude historique sur les chiffres, les chiffres, appuyée de documents inédits tirés des différents dépôts d'archives.* Paris: Charpentier et Fasquelle.

Bellamy, R. (1989). Bellerophon's Tablet. *The Classical Journal,* 84 (4): 289–307.

Bengtson, H. (1962). Die griechische Polis bei Aeneas Tacticus. *Historia: Zeitschrift für Alte Geschichte,* 11 (4): 458–68.

Bengtson, H., ed. (1975). *Die Staatsverträge des Altertums: Die Verträge der griechisch-römischen Welt von 700 bis 338 v. Chr.* 2nd edn. Munich/Berlin: C. H. Beck.

Bennett, C. E. and McElwain, M. (1925). *Frontinus: Stratagems – Aqueducts of Rome.* Loeb Classical Library 174. Cambridge, Massachusetts: Harvard University Press.

Benson, J. L. (1989). *Earlier Corinthian Workshops: A Study of Corinthian Geometric and Protocorinthian Stylistic Groups.* Amsterdam: Allard Pierson Museum.

Bettalli, M. (1990). *Enea Tattico, la difesa di una città assediata (Poliorketika). Introduzione, traduzione e commento.* Pisa: ETS editrice.

Bird, J. M. (1921). The Roger Bacon Manuscript: Investigations into Its History, and the Efforts to Decipher It. *Scientific American Monthly,* 3 (6): 492–6.

Birkbeck, R. K. G. (1922). *Life and Letters of W. J. Birkbeck.* London: Longmans, Green and Co.

Bishop, D. (2003). *Introduction to Cryptography with Java Applets.* Surbury/Boston/Toronto/London/Singapore: Jones and Bartlett Publishers.

Blamire, A. (1959). Herodotus and Histiaeus. *The Classical Quarterly,* 9 (2): 142–54.

Blair, W. (1807). Cipher. In: Rees, A. *The Cyclopædia; Or Universal Dictionary of Arts, Sciences, and Literature Volume 8.* London: Longman, Hurst, Rees, Orme and Brown.

Bliese, J. R. (1994). Rhetoric Goes to War: The Doctrine of Ancient and Medieval Military Manuals. *Rhetoric Society Quarterly,* 23 (3–4): 105–30.

Blome, D. A. (2020). *Greek Warfare Beyond the Polis: Defense, Strategy, and the Making of Ancient Federal States.* Ithaca/London: Cornell University Press.

Blösel, W. (2018) Herodotus' Allusions to the Sparta of his Day. In: Harrison, T. and Irwin, E. (eds), *Interpreting Herodotus.* Oxford: Oxford University Press, 243–64.

Bodel, J. P. (2001). *Epigraphic Evidence: Ancient History from Inscriptions.* London: Routledge – An Imprint of Taylor and Francis Group.

Boedeker, D. (1987). The Two Faces of Demaratus. *Arethusa*, 20 (1): 185–201.
Boicea, A., Rădulescu, F., Truică, C.-O. and Grigore, E. (2016). New Scytale – Improving Encryption Techniques. In: Research Paper, presented at *International Business Information Management Association Conference on Visio 2020: Sustainable Growth, Economic Development, and Global Competitiveness*, 1–6. Oline resource. Retrieved from: https://www.academia.edu/32203059/New_Scytale_Improving_Encryption_Techniques.
Bonavilla, M. and Aquilino, B. (1821). *Dizionario etimologico di tutti i vocaboli usati nelle scienze arti e mestieri che traggono origine dal greco, Tomo V*. Milan: Gi. Pirola.
Boring, T. A. (1979). *Literacy in Ancient Sparta*. Leiden: Brill.
Bowden, H. (1993). Hoplites and Homer: Warfare, Hero Cult and the Ideology of the Polis. In: Rich, J. and Shipley, G. (eds), *War and Society in the Greek World*. London/New York: Routledge – An Imprint of Taylor and Francis Group.
Bowie, A. (2013). 'Baleful Signs': Letters and Deceit in Herodotus. In: Hodkinson, O., Rosenmeyer, P. and Bracke, E. (eds), *Epistolary Narratives in Ancient Greek Literature*. Leiden: Brill, 71–83.
Bowie, A. M. (2007). *Histories: Book VIII*. Cambridge/New York: Cambridge University Press.
Bowie, E. (2019). Alcaeus' *stasiotica*: Catulland and Horation Readings. In: Currie, B. and Rutherford, I. (cds), *The Reception of Greek Lyric Poetry in the Ancient World: Transmission, Canonization and Paratext*. Leiden/Boston: Brill, 279–94.
Bowie, E. (2021). *Essays on Ancient Greek Literature and Culture – Volume 1: Greek Poetry before 400 BC*. Cambridge: Cambridge University Press.
Bowman, A. K. (1975). The Vindolanda Writing Tablets and the Development of the Roman Book Form. *Zeitschrift für Papyrologie und Epigraphik*, 18: 237–52.
Bowra, C. M. (1972). *Homer*. London: Duckworth.
Bradford, A. S. (2011). *Leonidas and the Kings of Sparta: Mightiest Warriors, Fairest Kingdom*. Santa Barbara/Oxford: ABC-CLIO.
Brandt, P. (1963). *P. Ovidi Nasonis: Amores Libri Tres*. Hildesheim: Georg Olms Verlagsbuchhandlung.
Briant, P. (2002). *From Cyrus to Alexander: A History of the Persian Empire*. Winona Lake, Indiana: Eisenbrauns.
Brock-Utne, A. (1945). Der Feind – Die alttestamentliche Satansgestalt im Lichte der sozialen Verhältnisse des nahen Orients. *Klio* 28: 219–27.
Brosius, M., ed. (2003). *Ancient Archives and Archival Traditions: Concepts of Record-keeping in the Ancient World*. Oxford: Oxford University Press.
Brown, T. S. (1981). Aeneas Tacticus, Herodotus and the Ionian Revolt. *Historia: Zeitschrift für Alte Geschichte*, 30 (4): 385–93.
Brownson, C. L. (1918). *Xenophon: Hellenica*. Books 1–4. Loeb Classical Library 88. Cambridge, Massachusetts: Harvard University Press.
Brownson, C. L. (1921). *Xenophon: Hellenica*. Books 5–7. Loeb Classical Library 89. Cambridge, Massachusetts: Harvard University Press.

Burkert, W. (1983). Oriental Myth and Literature in the Iliad. In: Hägg, R. (ed), *The Greek Renaissance of the Eighth Century BC: Tradition and Innovation*. Stockholm: Svenska Institutet in Athen, 51-6.
Burliga, B. (2008). Aeneas Tacticus between History and Sophistry: The Emergence of the Military Handbook. In: Pigon J., *The Children of Herodotus. Greek and Roman Historiography and Related Genres*. Newcastle: Cambridge Scholars Publishing, 92-101.
Burn, A. R. (1972). *Herodotus: The Histories*. London: Penguin Classics.
Burrell, B. (2009). Reading, Hearing, and Looking at Ephesos. In: Johnson, W. and Parker, H. *Ancient Literacies: The Culture of Reading in Greece and Rome*. Oxford: Oxford University Press, 69-95.
Butler, S. (2012). *The Hand of Cicero*. London: Routledge – An Imprint of Taylor and Francis Group.
Campbell, D. B. (2006). *Besieged: Siege Warfare in the Ancient World*. Oxford/New York: Osprey Publishing.
Campbell, D. B. (2012). *Spartan Warrior 753-331 BC*. London: Bloomsbury Publishing.
Campbell, D. B. (2014). How Long was the Macedonian Sarissa? *Ancient Warfare Magazine* 8 (3): 48-52.
Candau Morón, J. M. (2000). Plutarch's *Lysander* and *Sulla*: Integrated Characters in Roman Historical Perspective. *American Journal of Philology* 121: 453-78.
Cardano, G. (1550). *De Subtilitate Rerum*. Nuremberg: Petreius.
Carey, C. (1981). *A Commentary on Five Odes of Pindar*. New York: Arno Press.
Cario, L. (1919). Cryptographie. *Mercure de France*, 132: 319-23.
Carmona, J. G. (1894). *Tratado de Criptografia con Aplicacion especial al Ejercito*. Madrid: Est. Tip. Sucesores de Rivadeneyra.
Carras, C. (2013). Identity. In: Wilson, N. (ed.), *Encyclopedia of Ancient Greece*. New York/London: Routledge – An Imprint of Taylor and Francis Group, 375-6.
Carruthers, B. (2014). *War in Ancient Greece*. Barnsley: Pen and Sword Military.
Cartledge, P. (1978). Literacy in the Spartan Oligarchy. *Journal of Hellenistic Studies* 98: 25-37.
Cartledge, P. (2001). *Spartan Reflections*. London: Duckworth.
Cartledge, P. (2002). *Sparta and Lakonia. A Regional History 1300 to 362 BC*. New York: Routledge – An Imprint of Taylor and Francis Group.
Cartledge, P. (2003a). *The Spartans: The World of the Warrior-Heroes of Ancient Greece, from Utopia to Crisis and Collapse*. New York: Vintage Books.
Cartledge, P. (2003b). *Spartan Reflections*. Berkeley: University of California Press.
Cartledge, P. (2006). *Thermopylae: The Battle That Changed the World*. New York: The Overlook Press.
Cartledge, P. (2009). *Ancient Greek Political Thought in Practice*. Cambridge: Cambridge University Press.
Cartledge, P. (2013). *Sparta and Lakonia: A Regional History 1300-362 BC*. London/New York: Routledge – An Imprint of Taylor and Francis Group.

Cartledge, P. (2015). Aristomenes (1), Traditional Messenian Hero. In: Whitmarch, T. (chief ed.). *Oxford Classical Dictionary Online*. Online resource. Retrieved from: https://oxfordre.com/classics/view/10.1093/acrefore/9780199381135.001.0001/acrefore-9780199381135-e-760 (accessed date: 14-05-2023).

Cary, E. and Foster, B. (1914). *Dio Cassius: Roman History*. Books 36–40. Loeb Classical Library 53. Cambridge, Massachusetts: Harvard University Press.

Caspers, C. (2022). Astragaloi. *Hermeneus – Tijdschrift voor antieke cultuur*, 94 (4): 32–7.

Castleden, R. (2008). *Conflicts that Changed the World*. London: Canary Press Ebooks Limited.

Catling, H. W. and Cavanagh, H. (1976). Two Inscribed Bronzes from the Menelaion, Sparta. *Kadmos*, 15: 145–57.

Caubet, A. (2008). Vitreous Materials. In: Aruz, J, Benzel, B. and Evans, J. (eds), *Beyond Babylon: Art, Trade, and Diplomacy in the Second Millennium B.C.* New York/New Haven/London: The Metropolitan Museum of Art/Yale University Press, 419–34.

Cavazza, F. (2004). Gellius the Etymologist. In: Holford-Strevens, L and Vardi, A. (eds), *The Worlds of Aulus Gellius*. Volume 1. Oxford: Oxford University Press, 65–104.

Cawkwell, G. (1978). *Philip of Macedon*. London: Faber and Faber.

Ceccarelli, P. (2013). *Ancient Letter Writing: A Cultural History (600 BC–150 BC)*. Oxford: Oxford University Press.

Ceccarelli, P. (2019a). *Athenaios (166)*. In: Worthington, I. (ed.), *Brill's New Jacoby Online Second Edition*. Online resource. Retrieved from: http://dx.doi.org.bris.idm.oclc.org/10.1163/1873-5363_bnj2_a166 (accessed date 14-05-2023).

Ceccarelli, P. (2019b). *Autokrates (297)*. In: Worthington, I. (ed.), *Brill's New Jacoby Online Second Edition*. Online resource. Retrieved from: http://dx.doi.org.bris.idm.oclc.org/10.1163/1873-5363_bnj_a297 (accessed date 14-05-2023).

Chadwick, J. (1976). *The Mycenaean World*. Cambridge: Cambridge University Press.

Chadwick, J. (1987). *Linear B and Related Scripts*. Berkeley: University of California Press.

Champion, C. B. (2019). *Timonides von Leukas (561)*. In: Worthington, I. (ed.), *Brill's New Jacoby Online Second Edition*. Online resource. Retrieved from: https://scholarlyeditions.brill.com/reader/urn:cts:greekLit:fgrh.0561.bnjo-2-comm1-eng:1/(accessed date 14-05-2023).

Champion, C. B. (2019). *Timaios von Tauromenion (566)*. In: Worthington, I. (ed.), *Brill's New Jacoby Online Second Edition*. Online resource. Retrieved from: https://scholarlyeditions.brill.com/reader/urn:cts:greekLit:fgrh.0566.bnjo-2-comm2-eng:1/(accessed date 14-05-2023).

Chaniotis, A. (2005). *War in the Hellenistic World: A Social and Cultural History*. Malden/Oxford/Victoria: Blackwell Publishing.

Chaniotis, A. (2013). Greeks Under Siege: Challenges, Experiences, and Emotions. In: Campbell, B. and Tritle, L. (eds), *The Oxford Handbook of Warfare in the Classical World*. Oxford/New York: Oxford University Press, 438–56.

Chaniotis, A., Pleket, H. W., Stroud, R. S. and Strubbe, J. H. S. (2003). *Supplementum Epigraphicum Graecum*. Volume 50. Amsterdam: Giebe.

Chapman, G. A. (1972). Herodotus and Histiaeus' Role in the Ionian Revolt. *Historia: Zeitschrift für Alte Geschichte,* 21 (4): 546–68.

Charton, E. (1837). De la Cryptographie. *Le magasin pittoresque,* 5: 43–4.

Charzelis, G. and Harris, J. (2017). *A Tenth-Century Byzantine Military Manual: The Sylloge Tacticorum.* London/New York: Routledge – An Imprint of Taylor and Francis Group.

Chatton, B. (2010). *Using Poetry Across the Curriculum: Learning to Love Language.* Santa Barbara: ABC-CLIO LLC.

Cherry, C. (1962) On Communication Before the Days of Radio. In: *Proceedings of the IRE. Section 17: Information Theory,* 1143–5.

Cheshire Library Science (2013). *Caesar Cipher Encryption and Decryption tables.* Online resource. Retrieved from: https://cheshirelibraryscience.wordpress.com/category/codes-and-ciphers/(accessed date 14-05-2023).

Childs, J. R. (1919). *War Department Office of the Chief Signal Officer, Washington: German Military Ciphers from February to November 1918. Technical Paper of the Intelligence Section War Plans and Training Division.* Online resource. Retrieved from NSA Online Database: https://www.nsa.gov/Portals/75/documents/news-features/declassified-documents/friedman-documents/correspondence/ACC39301/41782529082158.pdf (accessed date 14-05-2023).

Christesen, P. (2017). Sparta and Athletics. In: Powell, A. (ed.), *A Companion to Sparta.* Oxford/Chichester: John Wiley and Sons Limited, 534–64.

Christidis, A. F., Arapopoulou, M. and Chriti, M. (2001). *A History of Ancient Greek: From the Beginnings to Late Antiquity.* Cambridge: Cambridge University Press.

Churchhouse, R. F. (2002). *Codes and Cipher: Julius Caesar, the Enigma and the Internet.* Cambridge: Cambridge University Press.

Cichorius, C. (1900). *Die Reliefs der Traianssäule – herausgegeben und historisch erklärt von Conrad Cichorius. Zweiter Textband.* Berlin: Georg Reimer.

Clanchy, M. T. (1979). *From Memory to Written Record: England, 1066–1307.* Cambridge, Massachusetts: Cambridge University Press.

Cluzan, S. (2008). Cyprus: An International Nexus of Art and Trade. In: Aruz, J, Benzel, B. and Evans, J. (eds), *Beyond Babylon: Art, Trade, and Diplomacy in the Second Millennium B.C.* New York/New Haven/London: The Metropolitan Museum of Art/Yale University Press, 371–86.

Coles, M. and Landrum, R. (2009). *Expert SQL Server 2008 Encryption.* New York: Apress.

Collard, B. (2004). *Les Languages secrets dans l'Antiquité Gréco-Romaine. Introduction Générale, Plan et Bibliographie par Brigitte Collard.* Folia Electronica Classica (Louvain-la-Neuve) – Numéro 7 janvier – juin 2004. Online resource. Retrieved from: http://bcs.fltr.ucl.ac.be/FE/07/CRYPT/Intro.html (accessed date 14-05-2023).

Coldstream, J. N. (2005). *Geometric Greece: 900–700 BC.* London: Routledge – An Imprint of Taylor and Francis Group.

Connolly, P. (2006). *Greece and Rome at War – New Edition*. London: Greenhill Books.

Connor, W. R. (1988). Early Greek Land Warfare as Symbolic Expression. *Past and Present* 119: 3–28.

Cox, I. J., Kalker, T. and Ro, Y. M. (2004). *Digital Watermarking: Second International Workshop, IWDW 2003, Seoul, Korea, October 20–22, 2003, Revised Papers*. Berlin/Heidelberg/New York: Springer-Verlag.

Cox, I., Miller, M., Bloom, J., Fridrich, J. and Kalker, T. (2008). *Digital Watermarking and Steganography*. 2nd edn. Amsterdam/Boston/Heidelberg/London/New York/Oxford/Paris/San Diego/San Francisco/Singapore/Sydney/Tokyo: Morgen Kaufman Publishers – An Imprint of Elsevier.

Crell, L. C. (1697). *De scytala laconica inclytæ philosophorum facultatis benevolo indultu, pro loco in ea olim obtinendo, d. 13. Martii 1697 secundum disputabit m. Ludovicus Christianus Crellius, schol. nic. sen. con-r.* Leipzig: Literis Fleischerianis.

Crowley, J. (2012). *The Psychology of the Athenian Hoplite: The Culture of Combat in Classical Athens*. Cambridge: Cambridge University Press.

Cummins, J. (2010). *Why Some Wars Never End: The Stories of the Longest Conflicts in History*. Beverly, Massachusetts: Fair Wind Press.

Curley, R. (2013). *Cryptography: Cracking Codes*. New York: Britannica Educational Publishing.

D'Agapeyeff, A. (1939). *Codes and Ciphers – A History of Cryptography*. Oxford /London /New York/Toronto: Oxford University Press.

D'Alembert, J. L. R. and Diderot, D., eds (1751a). *Encyclopédie, ou Dictionnaire raisonné des sciences, des arts et des métiers. Tome Troisième*. Paris: Briasson.

D'Alembert, J. L. R. and Diderot, D., eds (1751b). *Encyclopédie, ou Dictionnaire raisonné des sciences, des arts et des métiers. Tome Quatrième*. Paris: Briasson.

D'Alembert, J. L. R. and Diderot, D., eds (1751c). *Encyclopédie, ou Dictionnaire raisonné des sciences, des arts et des métiers. Tome Quatorzième*. Paris: Briasson.

D'Alembert, J. L. R. (1822). *Oeuvres de d'Alembert. Tome Quatrième – Première Partie*. Paris: A. Belin.

Dain, A. and Bon, A. (1967). *Énée le Tacticien: Poliorcétique*. Paris: Les Belles Lettres.

Dallet, G. (1877). Les écritures chiffrées et leurs applications. *La Revue Scientifique (Revue Rose). Troisième Série*, 14 (10): 289–97.

Damon, C. (2016). *Caesar: Civil War*. Loeb Classical Library 39. Cambridge, Massachusetts: Harvard University Press.

Danilov E. S. (2007). Boevoi klich drevnosti: istoriko-psikhologicheskii exkurs. *Yaroslavskii psikhologicheskii vestnik*, 22: 175–6.

Darnell, J. C. and Darnell, D. (2002). Opening the Narrow Doors of the Desert: Discoveries of the Theban Desert Road Survey. In: Friedman, R. F. (ed), *Egypt and Nubia: Gifts of the Desert*. London: The British Museum Press, 132–55.

David, E. (1986a). Aeneas Tacticus, 11.7–10 and the Argive Revolution of 370 BC. *Amercian Journal of Philology*, 107 (3): 343–9.

David, E. (1986b). The Oligarchic Revolution in Argos, 417 B.C. *L'Antiquité Classique* 55: 113–24.

Davis, N. and Wrenn, C. L. (1962). *English and Medieval Studies: Presented to J.R.R. Tolkien on the Occasion of His Seventieth Birthday*. London: Allen and Unwin.

Davis, P. (1999). *100 Decisive Battles*. Oxford: Oxford University Press.

De Forest Allen, F., Burnet, J., Pomeroy Parker, C. and Greene, W. (1938). *Scholia Platonica*. Haverford: Societas Philologica Americana.

De Romilly, J. (1968). Guerre et paix entre cités. In: Vernant, J. P. (ed.), *Problèmes de la guerre en Grèce ancienne*. Paris/The Hague: Mouton and Co., 207–29.

Debidour, M. (2006). Le secret et les messages secrets dans la poliorcétique d'Enée le Tacticien. In: Olivier, H., Giovannelli-Jouanna, P. and Bérard, F. (eds), *Ruses, secrets et mensonges chez les historiens grecs et latins*. Lyon: Université Jean Moulin-Lyon 3, 213–41.

Debidour, M. (2019). Le secret de l'information et la cryptographie dans le monde gréco-romain. In: Brun, P. and Denécé, E. (eds), *Renseignement et espionnage pendant l'Antiquité et le Moyen-Âge*, Paris, Ellipses Édition, 195–208.

De Guilletiere, G. G. (1676). *Lacédémone ancienne et nouvelle, où l'on voit les moeurs et les coûtumes des Grecs modernes, des Mahométans et des Juifs du pays, . . . par le sieur de La Guilletière*. Paris: C. Barbin

De la Torre, L. (1946). The Stolen Christmas Box. *Ellery Queen's Mystery Magazine*, January 1946, 80–96.

De Real de Curban, G. (1762). *La science du gouvernement: le traite de politique. Tome Sixieme*. Paris: Les Libraires Associés.

De Real de Curban, G. (1767). *Die Staatskunst, oder, Vollständige und gründliche Anleitung zu Bildung kluger Regenten, geschickter Staatsmänner und rechtschaffener Bürger. Sechster und Letzter Theil*. Frankfurt/Leipzig: Gobhardtischen Buchhandlung.

De Saint-Priest, A., ed. (1846). *Encyclopédie du dix-neuvième siècle: répertoire universel des sciences, des lettres et des arts, avec la biographie et de nombreuses gravure. Tome Vingtième*. Paris: Bureau de l'Encyclopédie du XIXe Siècle.

De Saint-Priest, A., ed. (1852). *Encyclopédie du dix-neuvième siècle: répertoire universel des sciences, des lettres et des arts, avec la biographie et de nombreuses gravure. Tome Septième*. Paris: Bureau de l'Encyclopédie du XIXe Siècle.

De Saint-Priest, A., ed. (1855). *Encyclopédie du dix-neuvième siècle: répertoire universel des sciences, des lettres et des arts, avec la biographie et de nombreuses gravure. Tome Neuvième*. Paris: Bureau de l'Encyclopédie du XIXe Siècle.

De Saint-Priest, A. ed. (1867). *Encyclopédie du dix-neuvième siècle: répertoire universel des sciences, des lettres et des arts, avec la biographie et de nombreuses gravure. Troisième Edition – Tome Dixième*. Paris: Bureau de l'Encyclopédie du XIXe Siècle.

Delattre, A. (2008). Inscriptions Grecques et Coptes de la montagne thébaine relatives au culte de Saint Ammônios. In: Delattre, A. and Heilporn, P. (eds), *Et maintenant ce* ne sont plus que des villages ... Thèbes et sa région aux époques hellénistique, romaine et byzantine. Actes de colloque tenu à Bruxelles les 2 et 3 décembre 2005, Bruxelles: Association Égyptologique Reine Élisabeth, 183–8.

Delebecque, E. (1957). Essai sur la vie de Xénophon. *Revue des Études Anciennes Année*, 60 (3): 429–36.

De Ste. Croix, G. E. M. (1972). *The Origins of the Peloponnesian War*. London: Duckworth.

De Ste. Croix, G. E. M. (1977). Herodotus. *Greece and Rome*, 24 (2): 130–48.

De Souza, P. (2003). *The Greek and Persian Wars, 499–386 BC*. Oxford: Osprey Publishing.

Delastelle, F. (1902). *Traité élémentaire de cryptographie: mathematiques appliquées*. Paris: Gauthier-Villars.

Demand, N. (1994). *Birth, Death, and Motherhood in Classical Greece*. Baltimore/London: Johns Hopkins University Press.

Detienne, M. (1968). La phalange: problèmes et controverses. In: Vernant, J. P. (ed.), *Problèmes de la guerre en Grèce ancienne*. Paris/The Hague: Mouton and Co., 119–42.

Dewald, C. (1993). Reading the World: The Interpretation of Objects in Herodotus' Histories. In: Rosen, R. and Farrell, J. (eds), *Nomodeiktes: Greek Studies in Honor of Martin Ostwald*. Ann Arbor: University of Michigan Press, 55–70.

Dewald, C. (2003). Form and Content: The Question of Tyranny in Herodotus. In: Morgan, K. A. (ed.), *Popular Tyranny: Sovereignty and Its Discontents in Ancient Greece*. Austin: University of Texas Press, 29–58.

Dewing, H. B. (1935). *Procopius. The Anecdota or Secret History*. Loeb Classical Library 290. Cambridge, Massachusetts: Harvard University Press.

Diels, H. (1914). *Antike Technik. Sechs Vorträge*. Leipzig/Berlin: Teubner.

Diepenbroek, M. L. M. (2015). Enigma: Secret Communication in Greco-Roman Warfare. MA diss. Free University Amsterdam/University of Amsterdam.

Diepenbroek, M. L. M. (2019). From Fire Signals to ADFGX: A Case Study in the Adaptation of Ancient Methods of Secret Communication. *KLEOS – The Amsterdam Bulletin of Ancient Studies and Archaeology*, 2: 63–76.

Diepenbroek, M. L. M. (2021). The Spartan *Scytale*. *Ancient Warfare Magazine*, 14 (3): 44–7.

Diepenbroek, M. L. M. (2022). Hiding Secrets in Greek Siegecraft: Why Did Aeneas Tacticus Never Discuss the Spartan *Scytale*? *Ancient History Bulletin*, 36 (3–4): 145–65.

Dimovski, A. and Gligoroski, D. (2003). Attacks on the Transposition Ciphers using Optimization Heuristics. *Proceedings of ICEST 2003*, 1–4.

Dirkzwager, A. (1976). Latijns Grieks. *Hermeneus – Tijdschrift voor Antieke Cultuur*, 48 (2): 125–9.

Donderer, M. (1995). Merkwürdigkeiten im Umgang mit Griechischer und Lateinischer Schrift in der Antike. *Gymnasium*, 102: 97–122.

Dooley, J. F. (2013). *A Brief History of Cryptology and Cryptographic Algorithms*. Cham/Heidelberg/New York/Dordrecht/London: Springer.

Dooley, J. F. (2016). *Codes, Ciphers and Spies: Tales of Military Intelligence in World War I*. New York: Copernicus Books – An imprint of Springer Nature.

Dooley, J. F. (2018). *History of Computing*. Cham: Springer.

Doran, T. (2018). *Spartan Oliganthropia*. Leiden/Boston: Brill.

Douglas Olson, S. (2009). *Athenaeus: The Learned Banqueters*. Books 10.420e-11. Loeb Classical Library 274. Cambridge, Massachusetts: Harvard University Press.

Dräger, P. (2002). *D. Magnus Ausonius, Mosella, Bissula, Briefwechsel mit Paulinus Nolanus*. Düsseldorf/Zürich: Artemis and Winkler.

Ducat, J. (1990). Les Hilotes. *Suppléments au Bulletin de Correspondance Hellénique*, 20. Athens: École Française d'Athènes, 1–150.

Ducat, J. (2006). *Spartan Education: Youth and Society in the Classical Period*. Swansea: Classical Press of Wales.

Ducat, J. (2009). Perspectives on Spartan Education in the Classical Period. In: Hodkinson, S. and Powell, A. (eds), *Sparta: New Perspectives*. Swansea: The Classical Press of Wales, 43–66.

Dunbabin, T. J. and Robertson, M. (1953). Some Protocorinthian Vase Painters. *Annual of the British School at Athens*, 48: 172–81.

Dunkel, G. E. (2000). Remarks on Code-switching in Cicero's Letters to Atticus. *Museum Helveticum*, 57 (2), 122–9.

Dunstan, W. E. (2000). *Ancient Greece*. Orlando: Harcourt Incorporated.

DuBois, P. (1988a). Inscription, the Law and the Comic Body. *Mètis: Anthropologie des mondes grecs anciens*, 3 (1–2): 69–84.

DuBois, P. (1988b). *Sowing the Body: Psychoanalysis and Ancient Representations of Women*. Chicago: University of Chicago Press.

DuBois, P. (1991). *Torture and Truth*. New York/London: Routledge – An Imprint of Taylor and Francis Group.

DuBois, P. (2003). *Slaves and Other Objects*. Chicago: University of Chicago Press.

DuBois, P. (2007). The Coarsest Demand: Utopia and the Fear of Slaves. *Actes du Groupe de Recherches sur l'Esclavage depuis l'Antiquité*, 29: 435–44.

DuBois, P. (2010). *Out of Athens: The New Ancient Greeks*. Cambridge, Massachusetts: Harvard University Press.

Dvornik, F. (1974). *Origins of Intelligence Services: The Ancient Near East, Persia, Greece, Rome, Byzantium, the Arab Muslim Empires, the Mongol Empire, China, Muscovy*. New Brunswick/New Jersey: Rutgers University Press.

Eastaugh N., Walsh, V., Chaplin, T. and Siddall, R., eds (2004). *The Pigment Compendium: A Dictionary of Historical Pigments*, vol. 1. Amsterdam/Boston/Heidelberg/London/New York/Oxford/Paris/San Diego/San Francisco/Singapore/Sydney/Tokyo: Elsevier Butterworth-Heinemann.

Ebbeler, J. (2007). Mixed Languages: The Play of Epistolography Codes in Two Late Antique Latin Correspondences. In: Morello, R. and Morrison, A. D. (eds), *Ancient*

Letters: Classical and Late Antique Epistolography. Oxford: Oxford University Press, 301–24.

Edmonds, J. M. (1957). *The Fragments of Attic Comedy: After Meineke, Bergk and Kock. Augmented, Newly Edited with their Contexts, Annotated, and Completely Translated into English Verse by John Maxwell Edmonds*, vol. 1. Leiden: Brill.

Edwards, H. J. (1917). *Caesar: The Gallic War*. Loeb Classical Library 72. Cambridge, Massachusetts: Harvard University Press.

Elder, O. and Mullen, A. (2019). *The Language of Roman Letters: Bilingual Epistolography from Cicero to Fronto*. Cambridge: Cambridge University Press.

Eliade, M. (1970). *De Zalmoxis a Gengis-Khan: études comparatives sur les religions et le folklore de la Dacie et de l'Europe orientale*. Paris: Payot.

Elliott, S. (2021). *Ancient Greeks at War: Warfare in the Classical World from Agamemnon to Alexander*. Oxford: Casemate Publishers.

Elliott, S. (2022). *Alexander the Great Versus Julius Caesar: Who was the Greatest Commander in the Ancient World?* Philadelphia: Pen and Sword Military.

Erasmus, D. and Mynors, R. (1991). *Adages*. Collected works of Erasmus 33: IIi1 to IIvi100. Toronto/Buffalo: University of Toronto Press.

Erasmus, D. and Mynors, R. (1992). *Adages*. Collected Works of Erasmus 34: IIvii1 to IIIiii100. Toronto/Buffalo: University of Toronto Press.

Erbse, H. (1971). *Scholia Graeca in Homeri Iliadem (scholia vetera) Recensuit Hartmut. Erbse: 2. Scholia ad libros E – I continens*. Berlin: De Gruyter.

Erdkamp, P. (2011). *A Companion to the Roman Army*. Malden: Wiley-Blackwell.

Esposito, G. (2020). *Armies of Ancient Greece circa 500–338 BC: History, Organization and Equipment*. Philadelphia: Pen and Sword Military.

Evans, J. A. (1976). Herodotus and the Ionian Revolt. *Historia: Zeitschrift für Alte Geschichte,* 25 (1): 31–7.

Evelyn-White, H. G. (1921). *Ausonius, Paulinus Pellaeus. Volume II: Books 18–20. Paulinus Pellaeus: Eucharisticus*. Loeb Classical Library 115. Cambridge, Massachusetts: Harvard University Press.

Ezov, A. (1996). The 'Missing Dimension' of C. Julius Caesar. *Historia: Zeitschrift für Alte Geschichte,* 45 (1): 64–94.

Fabule, D. K. (2011). *Information-gathering and the Strategic Use of Culture in Herodotus*. Stellenbosch: University of Stellenbosch.

Facultad de Informática (2018). Facultad de Informática de la Universidad de Las Palmas de Gran Canaria: Leon Battista Alberti. Online resource. Retrieved from: http://serdis.dis.ulpgc.es/~ii-cript/PAGINA%20WEB%20 CLASICA/CRIPTPLOGIA/alberti (accessed date 14-05-2023).

Falconer, J. (1685). *Cryptomenysis patefacta: or The Art of Secret Information Disclosed Without a Key. Containing Plain and Demonstrative Rules for Deciphering All Manner of Secret Writing*. London: Daniel Brown.

Farrington, E. (2019). *Men of Bronze: Ancient Greek Hoplite Battles*. Oxford/New York: Bloomsbury Publishing.

Farrow, E. S. (1885). *Farrow's Military Encyclopedia; A Dictionary of Military Knowledge, Illustrated with Maps and about Three Thousand Wood Engravings,* vol. 1. New York: The Author.
Feemster Jashemski, W. and Meyer, F. G., eds (2002). *The Natural History of Pompeii.* Cambridge: Cambridge University Press.
Ferrill, A. (1978). Herodotus on Tyranny. *Historia: Zeitschrift für Alte Geschichte,* 27 (3): 385–98.
Fielding, I. (2017). *Transformations of Ovid in Late Antiquity.* Cambridge/New York: Cambridge University Press.
Figueira, T. J. (2006). The Spartan Hippeis. In: Hodkinson, S. and Powell, A. (eds), *Sparta and War.* Swansea: The Classical Press of Wales, 57–84.
Figueira, T. (2018). Helotage and the Spartan Economy. In: Powell, A. (ed), *A Companion to Sparta.* Hoboken. New Jersey/Chichester: Wiley Blackwell, 565–95.
Fink, D. (2014). *The Battle of Marathon in Scholarship: Research, Theories and Controversies Since 1850.* Jefferson: McFarland and Company Inc. Publishers.
Fine, J. V. A. (1983). *The Ancient Greeks: A Critical History.* Cambridge, Massachusetts: Harvard University Press.
Fiorentino, G. and Zech-Matterne, V. (2018). *Agrumed: Archaeology and History of Citrus Fruit in the Mediterranean.* Naples: Publications du Centre Jean Bérard.
Fischer, S. (2004). *A History of Writing.* London: Reaktion Books Limited.
Fisher, N. R. E. (1993). *Slavery in Classical Greece.* London: Bristol Classical Press/Duckworth.
Flaceliere, R. and Chambry, E. (1971). *Plutarque: Vies. Volume VI, Pyrrhos-Marius/Lysandre-Sylla.* Paris: Les Belles Lettres.
Flensted-Jensen, P (2000). *Further Studies in the Ancient Greek Polis.* Stuttgart: Franz Steiner Verlag.
Floros, C. and Moran, N. K. (2009). *The Origins of Russian Music – Introduction to the Kondakarian Notation. Revised, Translated, and with a Chapter on Relationships between Latin, Byzantine and Slavonic Church Music by Neil K. Moran.* Frankfurt-am-Main: Peter Lang.
Floros, C. (2015). *Das mittelbyzantinische Kontaktienrepertoire. Untersuchungen und kritische Edition Volume 1–3.* Hamburg Universität Hamburg: Habilitation 1961.
Flower, M. A. (1988). Agesilaus of Sparta and the Origins of the Ruler Cult. *The Classical Quarterly,* 38 (1): 123–34.
Forelius, H. (1697). *Dissertatio academica de modis occulte scribendi & præsertim de scytala Laconica, quam ex consensu amplissimi collegii philosophici in regia academia Upsaliensi, præside ... dn. Hemmingo Forelio ... pro solitis in philosophia honoribus ad publicum examen defert Martinus Solander Ang. In auditorio Gustav: maj: VI Octob. an. M DC XCVII.* Stockholm: B. Billingsley.
Forster Smith, C. (2010). *A Study of Plutarch's Life of Artaxerxes – With Especial Reference to the Sources.* Morrisville: Lulu.com (Online Publishing Company). First

published as: Forster Smith, C. (1881). *A Study of Plutarch's Life of Artaxerxes with Especial Reference to the Sources, a Dissertation.* Leipzig: Metzger und Wittig.

Forrest, W. G. (1979). Motivation in Herodotos: The Case of the Ionian Revolt. *The International History Review,* 1 (3): 311–22.

Forrester, J. M. and Henry, J. (2013). *The Subtilitate of Girolamo Cardano in Two Volumes.* Tempe: The Arizona Centre for Medieval and Renaissance Studies.

Fowler, H. N. (1926). *Plato: Cratylus. Parmenides. Greater Hippias. Lesser Hippias.* Loeb Classical Library 167. Cambridge, Massachusetts: Harvard University Press.

France, R. T. (2007). *The New International Commentary on the New Testament: The Gospel of Matthew.* Michigan/Cambridge: Wm. B. Eerdmans Publishing.

Frazer, J. G. (1921). *Apollodorus: The Library, Volume I: Books 1–3.9.* Loeb Classical Library 121. Cambridge, Massachusetts: Harvard University Press.

Freisenbruch, A. (2007). Back to Fronto: Doctor and Patient in his Correspondence with an Emperor. In: Morello, R. and Morrison, A. (eds), *Ancient Letters: Classical and Late Antique Epistolography.* Oxford: Oxford University Press, 235–56.

Fronczak, M. (2013). Atbah-Type Ciphers in the Christian Orient and Numerical Rules in the Construction of Christian Substitution Ciphers. *Cryptologia,* 37 (4): 338–44.

Furetiere, A., ed. (1743). *Dictionnaire universel français et latin, contenant la signification et la définition tant des mots de l'une & de l'autre langue, avec leurs différens usages . . . vulgairement appelé Dictionnaire de Trévoux /Avec des remarques d'érudition et de critique . . . Dedié à . . . Monseigneur Prince Souverain de Dombes.* Paris: La Veuve Delaune.

Gabriel, R. A. (2001). *Great Captains of Antiquity.* London: Greenwood Publishing Group.

Gaebel, R. (2002). *Cavalry Operations in the Ancient Greek World.* Norman: University of Oklahoma Press.

Gagarin, M., ed. (2009). *The Oxford Encyclopedia of Ancient Greece and Rome,* vol. 1. Oxford: Oxford University Press.

Galland, J. S. (1945). *An Historical and Analytical Bibliography of the Literature of Cryptology.* Evanston: North Western University Press.

Gallois, J. (1677). *Le Journal des Scavans de l'an M.DC.LXXVI.* Amsterdam: Pierre Le Grand.

Gamer, M. (2022). *Die Polygraphia des Johannes Trithemius nach der handschriftlichen Fassung (Band 1): Edition, Übersetzung und Kommentar.* Leiden: Brill.

Gardner, C. A. M. (2019). The Origins and Evolution of Ancient Spartan Identity in the Mani Peninsula, Greece. *Thersites,* 10: 177–208.

Gardner, M. (1983). *Codes, Ciphers and Secret Writing.* New York: Dover Publications Incorporated.

Gardthausen, V. E. (1911). *Griechische Paleographie,* vol. 2: *Die Schrift, Unterschriften und Chronologie im Altertum und im Byzantinischen Mittelalter.* Leipzig: Veit und Comp.

Garfield, S. (2013). *To the Letter: A Celebration of the Lost Art of Letter Writing.* Reprinted Edition. New York: Penguin Publishing Group.

Garg, P. (2009). Genetic Algorithms, Tabu Search and Simulated Annealing: A Comparison between Three Approaches for the Cryptanalysis of Transposition Cipher. *Journal of Theoretical and Applied Information Technology,* 5 (4): 387–92.

Gauthier, P. (1972). *Gauthier symbola: les étrangers et la justice dans les cités grecques.* Annales de l'Est, Mémoire 42. Nancy: Université de Nancy II.

Georges, P. (1994). *Barbarian Asia and the Greek Experience.* Baltimore: Johns Hopkins University Press.

Gerber, D. E. (1997). Elegy. In: Gerber, D. E. (ed.), *A Companion to the Greek Lyric Poets.* Leiden/New York/Cologne: Brill, 89–132.

Gerber, D. E. (1999a). *Tyrtaeus, Solon, Theognis, Mimnermus: Geek Elegian Poetry: From the Seventh to the Fifth Centuries BC.* Loeb Classical Library 258. Cambridge, Massachusetts: Harvard University Press.

Gerber, D. E. (1999b). *Archilochus, Semonides, Hipponax: Greek Iambic Poetry: From the Seventh to the Fifth Centuries BC.* Loeb Classical Library 259. Cambridge, Massachusetts: Harvard University Press.

Gerolymatos, A. (1986). *Espionage and Treason.* Amsterdam: J. C. Gieben Publisher.

Gibson, R. and Morrison, A. (2007). Introduction: What is a Letter? In: Morello, R. and Morrison, A. (eds), *Ancient Letters: Classical and Late Antique Epistolography.* Oxford: Oxford University Press, 1–16.

Gillespie, A. (2013). *The Causes of War,* vol. 1: *3000 BCE to 1000 CE.* Oxford: Hart Publishing Limited.

Glassner, J. (2003). *The Invention of Cuneiform: Writing in Sumer* (Originally published as: *Ecrice a Sumer: L'Invention du Cunéiforme.* Paris: Éditions de Seuil). Baltimore: Johns Hopkins University Press.

Glotz, G. and Cohen, R. (1936). *Histoire Grecque Tome III: La Grèce au IVe siècle; la Lutte pour L'Hégémonie* (404–336). Paris: Les Presses universitaires de France.

Godley, A. D. (1920). *Herodotus: The Persian Wars.* Volume 1: Books 1–2. Loeb Classical Library 117. Cambridge, Massachusetts: Harvard University Press.

Godley, A. D. (1922). *Herodotus: The Persian Wars.* Volume 3: Books 5–7. Loeb Classical Library 119. Cambridge, Massachusetts: Harvard University Press.

Godley, A. D. (1925). *Herodotus: The Persian Wars.* Volume 4: Books 8–9. Loeb Classical Library 120. Cambridge, Massachusetts: Harvard University Press.

Golden, M. (2019). *Sex and Difference in Ancient Greece and Rome.* Edinburgh: Edinburgh University Press.

Goldstone, L. and Goldstone, N. (2005). *The Friar and the Cipher: Roger Bacon and the Unsolved Mystery of the Most Unusual Manuscript in the World.* New York: Crown/Archetype Publishing.

Goldsworthy, A. K. (1997). The Othismos, Myths and Heresies: The Nature of Hoplite Battle. *War in History,* 4 (1): 1–26.

Gomme, A., Andrewes, A. and Dover, K. (1981). *A Historical Commentary on Thucydides.* Oxford: Clarendon Press.

González-Wippler, M. (1988). *The Complete Book of Spells, Ceremonies, and Magic.* St. Paul: Llewellyn Publications.

Goody, J. (1986). *The Logic of Writing and the Organisation of Society.* Cambrigde: Cambridge University Press.

Goody, J. and Watt, I. (1968). The Consequences of Literacy. In: Goody, J. (ed.), *Literacy in Traditional Societies.* Cambridge: Cambridge University Press, 27–86.

Goold, G. P., ed. (1977). *Ovid In Six Volumes I: Heroides and Amores.* Loeb Classical Library 41. Trans. G. Showerman. Cambridge, Massachusetts: Harvard University Press.

Gould, J. P. (1989). *Herodotus. Historians on Historians.* London: George Weidenfeld and Nicolson.

Gould, J. P. (2012). Herodotus (1). In: Hornblower, S., Spawforth, A. and Eidinow, E. (eds), *The Oxford Classical Dictionary.* Oxford: Oxford University Press, 674–6.

Graf, F. (2005). Rolling the Dice for an Answer. In: Iles Johnston, S. and Struck, P. (eds), *Mantikè: Studies in Ancient Divination.* Leiden: Brill, 51–97.

Grafton, A., Most, G. W. and Settis, S. (2013). *The Classical Tradition.* Cambridge, Massachusetts/London: The Belknap Press of Harvard University Press.

Grant, R. G. (2017). *1001 Battles That Changed the Course of History.* New York: Chartwell Books.

Gray, V. (1995). Herodotus and the Rhetoric of Otherness. *The American Journal of Philology,* 116 (2): 185–211.

Green, P. (1982). *Ovid: The Erotic Poems.* London: Penguin Classics.

Green, P. (1996). *The Greco-Persian Wars.* Berkeley: University of California Press.

Griselini, F. (1774). *Dizionario delle arti e de mestieri, compilato da Francesco Griselini, Tomo Decimosesto.* Venice: Appresso Modesto Fenzo.

Grossman, D. (1996). *On Killing: The Psychological Cost of Learning to Kill in War and Society.* London/New York: Open Road Media.

Gura, N. (2015). *Divine Wisdom and Warning: Decoded Messages from God.* Lanham/Boulder/New York/Toronto/Plymouth: Hamilton Books.

Guthrie, K. S. and Fideler, D. (1987). *The Pythagorean Sourcebook and Library: An Anthology of Ancient Writings Which Relate to Pythagoras and Pythagorean Philosophy.* Grand Rapids: Phanes Press.

Guzmán A. and Martínez, J., eds (2018). *Animo Decipiendi? Rethinking Fakes and Authorship in Classical, Late Antique, and Early Christian Works.* Groningen: Barkhuis.

Hall, E. (1989). *Inventing the Barbarian: Greek Self-Definition through Tragedy.* Oxford: Clarendon Press.

Hall, J. M. (2007). *A History of the Archaic Greek World, ca. 1200–479 BCE.* Chichester/Oxford: Wiley Blackwell.

Hall, J. M. (2009). *Politeness and Politics in Cicero's Letters.* Oxford: Oxford University Press.

Hall, J. M. (2013). *A History of the Archaic Greek World, ca. 1200–479 BCE.* 2nd edn. Chichester/Oxford: Wiley Blackwell.

Hamel, D. (2012). *Reading Herodotus: A Guided Tour through the Wild Boars, Dancing Suitors, and Crazy Tyrants of The History*. Baltimore: Johns Hopkins University Press.

Hammond, M. (2009). *The Peloponnesian War: A New Translation by Martin Hammond*. Oxford: Oxford University Press.

Hanink, J. (2014). *Lycurgan Athens and the Making of Classical Tragedy*. Cambridge: Cambridge University Press.

Hannig, R. (2003). *Ägyptisches Wörterbuch: Altes Reich und Erste Zwischenzeit*. Darmstadt: Verlag Philipp von Zabern.

Hanson, A. E. (1994). A Division of Labor: Roles for Men in Greek and Roman Birth. *Thamyris*, 1 (2): 157–202.

Hanson, V. D. (1991). *Hoplites: The Classical Greek Battle Experience*. London/New York: Routledge – An Imprint of Taylor and Francis Group.

Hanson, V. D. (2007a). *Carnage and Culture: Landmark Battles in the Rise to Western Power*. New York: Anchor Book

Hanson, V. D. (2007b). The Modern Historiography of Ancient Warfare. In: Sabin, P., Van Wees, H. and Whitby, M. (eds), *The Cambridge History of Greek and Roman Warfare*, vol. 1: *Greece, the Hellenistic World, and the Rise of Rome*. Cambridge: Cambridge University Press, 3–21.

Haralick, R. M. (1995). *Inner Meaning of the Hebrew Letters*. Lanham: Rowman and Littlefield Publishers Inc.

Harris, R. (1995). *Enigma*. London: Arrow Books.

Harris, S. L. and Platzner, G. (2012). *Classical Mythology Images and Insights – Sixth Edition*. New York: McGraw-Hill.

Harper, R. F. (1892–1914). *Assyrian and Babylonian Letters*. Chicago: University of Chicago Press.

Harris, W. V. (1989). *Ancient Literacy*. Cambridge, Massachusetts: Harvard University Press.

Harvey, F. D. (1966). Literacy in the Athenian Democracy. *Revue des Études Grecques*, 79: 585–635.

Havelock, E. (1963). *Preface to Plato*. Cambridge, Massachusetts: Harvard University Press.

Havelock, E. A. (1971). *Prologue to Greek Literacy*. Cincinnati: University of Cincinnati Press.

Havelock, E. A. (1982). *The Literate Revolution in Greece and Its Cultural Consequences*. Princeton: Princeton University Press.

Head, P. M. (2009a). Letter-Carriers in the Ancient Jewish Epistolary Material. In: Evans, C. and Zacharias, H. (eds), *Jewish and Christian Scripture as Artifact and Canon*, 203–219

Head, P. M. (2009b). Named Letter-Carriers among the Oxyrhynchus Papyri. *Journal for the Study of the New Testament*, 31 (3): 279–99.

Henderson, J. (2000). *Aristophanes: Birds. Lysistrata. Women at the Thesmophoria*. Loeb Classical Library 179. Cambridge, Massachusetts: Harvard University Press.

Henderson, J. (2007)....when who should walk into the room but...': Epistoliterarity in Cicero, Ad Qfr. 3.1. In: Morello, R. and Morrison, A. (eds), *Ancient Letters: Classical and Late Antique Epistolography*. Oxford: Oxford University Press, 37–86.

Herman, G. (1987). *Ritualised Friendship and the Greek City*. Cambridge: Cambridge University Press.

Heubeck, A. (1979). *Archaeologia Homerica, Band 3, Kapitel X*. Göttingen: Vandenhoeck and Ruprech.

Hodges, A. (1985). *Alan Turing: The Enigma*. New York: Vintage Books.

Holford-Strevens, L. (2003). *Aulus Gellius: An Antonine Scholar and his Achievement*. Oxford: Oxford University Press.

Holford-Strevens, L. (2019a). *Aulus Gellius: Attic Nights: Preface and Books 1–10*. Oxford: Oxford University Press.

Holford-Strevens, L. (2019b). *Aulus Gellius: Attic Nights: Books 11–20*. Oxford: Oxford University Press.

Holford-Strevens, L. and Vardi, A. (2004). *The Worlds of Aulus Gellius*. Oxford: Oxford University Press.

Hodkinson, S. (2022). Agoge. In: Hornblower, S. (ed.), *Oxford Classical Dictionary Online*. Oxford: Oxford University Press. Online resource. Retrieved from: https://www.oxfordreference.com/view/10.1093/acref/9780198606413.001.0001/acref-9780198606413-e-201 (accessed date 10-05-2023).

Holland, T. (2006). *Persian Fire: The First World Empire and the Battle for the West*. London: Abacus.

Holland, T. and Cartledge, P. (2013). *Herodotus The Histories*. London: Penguin Classics.

Hollmann, A. (2005). The Manipulation of Signs in Herodotus' Histories. *Transactions of the American Philological Association (1974–2014)*, 135 (2): 279–327.

Hollmann, A. (2011). *The Master of Signs: Signs and the Interpretation of Signs in Herodotus' Histories*. Washington: Center for Hellenic Studies.

Holmes, T. R. (1911). *Caesar's Conquest of Gaul*. 2nd edition. Oxford: Clarendon Press.

Hondius, J. J. E. and Woodward, A. M. (1919/20–1920/21). Laconia I Inscriptions. *The Annual of the British School at Athens* 24 (supplement): 88–143.

Hornblower, S. (1996). *A Commentary on Thucydides*. Oxford: Clarendon Press.

Hornblower, S. (2009). Sticks, Stones, and Spartans: The Sociology of Spartan Violence. In: Van Wees, H. (ed.), *War and Violence in Ancient Greece*. London/Swansea: Gerald Duckworth/The Classical Press of Wales, 57–82.

Hornblower, S. (2010). *A Commentary on Thucydides*. 2nd edn. Oxford: Oxford University Press.

Hornung, E. (1999). *The Ancient Egyptian Books of the Afterlife*. Ithaca: Cornell University Press.

How, W. W. and Wells, J. (1928). *A Commentary on Herodotus*. 2 vols. Oxford: Oxford University Press.

Howley, J. A. (2018). *Aulus Gellius and Roman Reading Culture: Text, Presence, and Imperial Knowledge in the Noctes Atticae*. Cambridge: Cambridge University Press.

Hoyos, D. (2015). *Mastering the West: Rome and Carthage at War*. Oxford/New York: Oxford University Press.

Hug, A. (1877). *Aeneas von Stymphalos, ein Arkadischer Schriftsteller aus Klassischer Zeit: Gratulationsschrift der Universität Zürich an die Universität Tübingen zu deren vierhundertjähriger Stiftungsfeier vom VIII. – XI. August MDCCCLXXVII*. Zürich: Zürcher & Furrer.

Hulme, E. (1898). *Cryptography, or, The History, Principles, and Practice of Cypher-Writing*. London: Ward, Lock and Co. Limited.

Hunt, A. S. (1929). A Greek Cryptogram. *Proceedings of the British Academy*, 15: 127–34.

Hunt, L. A. (1995). *The Challenge of the West: Peoples and cultures from the stone age to 1640*. Lexington: D.C. Heath.

Hunt, P. (2007). Military Forces. In: Sabin, P., Van Wees, H. and Whitby, M. (eds), *The Cambridge History of Greek and Roman Warfare* (Volume II: The Hellenistic World and the Roman Republic). Cambridge: Cambridge University Press, 325–67.

Hunter, L. and Handford, S. (1927). *Aineiou Poliorkētika: Aeneas on Siegecraft*. Oxford: Clarendon Press.

Huxley, G. L. (1983). Herodotos on Myth and Politics in Early Sparta. *Proceedings of the Royal Irish Academy: Archaeology, Culture, History, Literature*, 83C: 1–16.

Hyde, W. W. (1915). The Mountains of Greece. *The Bulletin of the Geographical Society of Philadelphia* 13: 1–16, 47–64, 110–26.

Illinois Greek Club (1928). *Aeneas Tacticus, Asclepiodotus, and Onasander*. Loeb Classical Library 156. Cambridge, Massachusetts: Harvard University Press.

Immerwahr, H. R. (1985). Herodotus. In: Easterling P. E. and Knox B. M. W. (eds), *Greek Literature: The Cambridge History of Classical Greek Literature*, vol. 1. Cambridge: Cambridge University Press, 426–41.

Immerwahr, H. R. (1990). *Attic Scripts, A Survey*. New York/Oxford: Oxford University Press.

Jacob, P. L. (1858). *La cryptographie, ou, L'art d'écrire en chiffres: les secrets de nos pères recueillis par le bibliophile Jacob*. Paris: Adolphe Delahays.

Jacobson, H. (1974). *Ovid's Heroides*. Princeton: Princeton University Press.

Jacoby, F., Bollansée, J., Bonnechere, P. and Radicke, J. (1969). *Die Fragmente der Griechischen Historiker – Volume 3B: Geschichte von Städten und Völkern (Horographie und Ethnographie); b. Kommentar zu Nr. 297–607; Text*. Berlin: Weidmann.

Jeanmaire, H. (1913). La cryptie lacédémonienn. *Revue des études grecques*, 26 (117): 121–50.

Jebb, R., ed. (1976). *Antigone*. Cambridge: Cambridge University Press.

Jeffery, L. H. (1961). *The Local Scripts of Archaic Greece: A Study of the Origin of the Greek Alphabet and Its Development from the Eighth to the Fifth Centuries B.C.* Oxford: Clarendon Press.

Jenkins, T. E. (1999). *Intercepted Letters: Epistles and Their Readers in Ancient Literature*. Cambridge, Massachusetts: Harvard University Press.

Jestin, C. and Katz, P. (2000). *Ovid: Amores, Metamorphoses Selections*, 2nd edn. Illinois: Bolchazy-Carducci Publishers.

Johnson, N., Duric, Z. and Jajodia, S. (2001). *Information Hiding: Steganography and Watermarking-Attacks and Countermeasures*. Norwell: Kluwer Academic Publishers.

Johnson, W. and Parker, H. (2009). *Ancient Literacies: The Culture of Reading in Greece and Rome*. Oxford: Oxford University Press.

Jones, C. P. (1987). Stigma: Tattooing and Branding in Graeco-Roman Antiquity. *The Journal of Roman Studies* 77: 139–55.

Jones, C. P. (2000). Stigma and Tattoo. In: Caplan, J. (ed.), *Written on the Body: The Tattoo in European and American History*. Princeton: Princeton University Press, 1–16.

Jones, W. H. and Andrews, A. (1980). *Pliny: Natural History*. Volume VII: Books 24–7. Loeb Classical Library 393. Cambridge, Massachusetts: Harvard University Press.

Jones, N. F. (2008). *Politics and Society in Ancient Greece*. Westport: Prager.

Jones, R. T. (2016). Hegemon, Hegominia. In: Phang, S. E., Spence, I., Kelly D. and Londey P. (eds), *Conflict in Ancient Greece and Rome: The Definitive Political, Social, and Military Encyclopedia*, 3 vols. Santa Barbara: ABC-CLIO LLC, 294–95.

Kagan, D. (2004). *The Peloponnesian War*. New York: Penguin Books.

Kahate, A. (2013). *Cryptography and Network Security*. Porur (Chennai): McGraw Hill Education.

Kahn, D. (1967). *The Codebreakers: The Story of Secret Writing*. London: Weidenfeld and Nicolson.

Kahn, D. (1974). *The Codebreakers, abridged version* 2nd edn. London: Weidenfeld and Nicolson.

Kahn, D. (1996a). *The Codebreakers: The Comprehensive History of Secret Communication from Ancient Times to the Internet*. 3rd edn. London: Weidenfeld and Nicolson.

Kahn, D. (1996b). The History of Steganography. In: Anderson, R. (ed.), *Information Hiding: First International Workshop, Cambridge, U.K., May 30 – June 1, 1996. Proceedings*, vol. 1. Cambridge: Springer-Verlag, 1–6.

Kajanto, I. (1980). Minderheiten und ihre Sprachen in der Hauptstadt Rom. In: Neumann, G. and Untermann J. (eds), *Die Sprachen im Römischen Reich der Kaizerzeit: Kolloquium vom 8. bis 10. April 1974*. Cologne: Rheinland, 83–101.

Kamen, D. (2010). A Corpus of Inscriptions: Representing Slave Marks in Antiquity. *Memoirs of the American Academy in Rome*, 55: 95–110.

Karpenko, V. and Norris, J. A. (2001). Vitriol in the History of Chemistry. *Chemické listy-The Official Journal of the Czech Chemical Society*, 96: 997–1005.

Kartalopoulos, S. V. (2009). *Security of Information and Communication Networks*. Hoboken: Wiley-Blackwell.

Kassel, R. and Austin, C. (1983). *Poetae Comici Graeci*, vol. 2: *Menander: Testimonia et Frangmenta apud scriptores servata*. Berlin/New York: De Gruyter.

Kassel, R. and Austin, C. (1986). *Poetae Comici Graeci*, vol. 5: *Damoxenus – Magnes*. Berlin/Boston: De Gruyter.

Kassel, R. and Austin, C. (1989). *Poetae Comici Graeci*, vol. 7: *Menecrates – Xenophon*. Berlin/Boston: De Gruyter.

Kaufman, R. (1884). *Our Young Folks' Plutarch.* London: W. H. Allen and Co.

Kasten, J. (2001). One Fish, Two Fish, Red Fish, Blowfish: A History of Cryptography and Its Application in Society. *Sans Institute InfoSec Reading Room*. Online resource. Retrieved from: https://www.sans.org/reading-room/whitepapers/vpns/fish-fish-red-fish-blowfish-history-cryptography-its-application-soci-726 (accessed date 10-05-2023).

Keaney, J. J. (1974). Theophrastus on Greek Judicial Procedure. *Transactions of the American Philological Association*, 104: 179–94.

Keeline, T. J. (2018). *The Reception of Cicero in the Early Roman Empire: the Rhetorical Schoolroom and the Creation of a Cultural Legend.* Cambridge: Cambridge University Press.

Keightley, T. (1856). *The Mythology of Ancient Greece and Italy: for the Use of Schools.* New York: D. Appleton and Company.

Keightley, T. (1859). *The Mythology of Ancient Greece and Italy: for the Use of Schools.* 2nd edn. New York: D. Appleton and Company.

Kelley, D. (2011). *The Gospel of Numbers and Letters in Scripture.* Morrisville: Lulu.com (Online Publishing Company).

Kelly, T. (1970). Did the Argives Defeat the Spartans at Hysiai in 669 BCE? *American Journal of Philology*, 91: 31–42.

Kelly, T. (1985). The Spartan Scytale. In: Eadie, J. W. and Ober, J. (eds), *The Craft of the Ancient Historian: Essays in Honor of Chester G. Starr*. Lanham: University Press of America, 141–69.

Kelly, T. (1998). The Myth of the Skytale. *Cryptologia,* 22 (3): 253–60.

Kelsey, F. W. (2007). *Select Orations and Letters of Cicero.* Eugene: Wipf and Stock.

Kennedy, G. and Churchill, R. (2005). *The Voynich Manuscript: The Unsolved Riddle of an Extraordinary Book Which Has Defied Interpretation for Centuries*. London: Orion Publishing.

Kennell, N. M. (2010). *Spartans: A New History*. Malden/Oxford/Chichester: John Wiley and Sons.

Keulen, W. (2004). Gellius, Apuleius, and Satire on the Intellectual. In: Holford-Strevens, L. and A. Vardi (eds), *The Worlds of Aulus Gellius*. Oxford: Oxford University Press, 223–46.

Klauer, G. C. (1695). *Disputatio historico-philologica de scytala lacedaemoniorum.* Altdorf: Kohlesius.

Klüber, J. L. (1809). *Kryptographik: Lehrbuch der Geheimschreibekunst (Chiffrir- und Dechiffrirkunst) in Staats- und Privatgeschäften*. Tübingen: J. G. Cottsachen Buchhandlung.

Khan, I. A. (2007). *Citrus Genetics, Breeding and Biotechnology*. Wallingford: CABI.

Kidd, S. E. (2017). How to Gamble in Greek – The Meaning of *Kubeia. Journal of Hellenic Studies*, 137: 119–34.

Kipper, G. (2004) *Investigator's Guide to Steganography*. Boca Raton: Auerbach (a CRC Press company).

Kirk, G. S. (1962). *The Songs of Homer*. Cambridge: Cambridge University Press.

Klima, R. and Sigmon, N. (2012). *Cryptology: Classical and Modern with Maplets*. Boca Raton/London/New York: Chapman and Hall/CRC.

Knight, G. R. (2005). Friendship and Erotics in the Late Antique Verse-Epistle: Ausonius to Paulinus Revisited. *Rheinisches Museum für Philologie Neue Folge,* 148 (3–4): 361–408.

Köchly, H. (1835). *Commentatio de Lacedaemoniorum cryptia*. Leipzig: Opuscula philologica.

Koder, J. (2008). Imperial Propaganda in the Kontakia of Romanos the Melode. *Dumbarton Oaks Papers*, 62: 275–91.

Kolb, A. (2001). Transport and Communication in the Roman State: the Cursus Publicus. In: Adams, C. and Laurence, R. (eds), *Travel and Geography in the Roman Empire*. London/New York: Routledge – An Imprint of Taylor and Francis Group, 95–105.

Kolbe, W. (1913). Inscriptiones Graecae V.1: Laconiae et Messeniae. Berlin: Reimer.

Konstan, D. (1987). Persians, Greeks and Empire. *Arethusa,* 20*: Herodotus and the Invention of History*: 59–73.

Koon, S. (2010). *Infantry Combat in Livy's Battle Narratives*. BAR International Series 2071. Oxford: Archaeopress.

Kopal, N. (2018). *Secure Volunteer Computing for Distributed Cryptanalysis*. Kassel: Kassel University Press.

Kovacs, D. (1995). *Euripides. Children of Heracles. Hippolytus. Andromache. Hecuba*. Loeb Classical Library 484. Cambridge, Massachusetts: Harvard University Press.

Kovacs, D. (1998). *Euripides. Suppliant Women. Electra. Heracles*. Loeb Classical Library 9. Cambridge, Massachusetts: Harvard University Press.

Kramer, J. (1983). *Glossaria Bilinguia in Papyris et Membranis Reperta*. Bonn: Habelt.

Krentz, P. and Wheeler, E. L (1994). *Polyaenus: Stratagems of War*. Chicago: Ares.

Krentz, P. (2002). Fighting by the Rules: The Invention of the Hoplite Agôn. *Hesperia*, 71: 23–39.

Krentz, P. (2009). Deception in Archaic and Classical Greek Warfare. In: Van Wees, H. (ed.), *War and Violence in Ancient Greece*. Swansea: The Classical Press of Wales, pp. 167–200

Kruh, L. (1971). The Genesis of the Jefferson/Bazeries Cipher Device. *Cryptologia* 5 (4): 193–208.

Kuzewizc, C. (2021). The War Dead in Archaic Sparta. In: Konijnendijk, R., Kucewizc, C. and Lloyd, M. (eds), *Brill's Companion to Greek Land Warfare Beyond the Phalanx*. Leiden/Boston: Brill, 83–121.

Ladner, G. (1979). Mediaeval and Modern Symbolism, a Comparison. *Speculum,* 54: 223–56.

Lafayete, G. (1877). Astragalus/Tali. In: Daremberg, C. V. and Saglio, E. *Dictionnaire des antiquités grecques et romaines, d'après les textes et les monuments*, vol. 5. Paris: Hachette, 475.

Laks, A. and Most, G. W. (2016). *Early Greek Philosophy*. Volume IX: Sophists, Part 2. Loeb Classical Library 532. Cambridge, Massachusetts: Harvard University Press.

Lane Fox, R. (2006). *The Classical World*. New York: Basic Books.

Landwehr, C. E., Bull, A. R., McDermott, J. P. and Choi, W. S. (1993). A Taxonomy of Computer Program Security Flaws, with Examples. *Information Technology Division, Code 5542, Naval Research Laboratory, Washington, D.C. 20375-5337*, 1–37. Online resource. Retrieved from: https://apps.dtic.mil/sti/pdfs/ADA465587.pdf (accesssed date 10-05-2023).

Lang, M. (1967). Scapegoat Pausanias. *Classical Journal*, 63: 79–85.

Lang, M. (1968). Herodotus and the Ionian Revolt. *Historia: Zeitschrift für Alte Geschichte*, 17 (1): 24–36.

Lang, M. (1984). *Herodotean Narrative and Discourse*. Cambridge, Massachusetts: Harvard University Press.

Lange, E. and Soudart, E.-A. (1925). *Traité de Cryptographie*. Paris: Librairie Félix Alcan.

Langie, A. (1917). De la Cryptographie. *Bibliothèque universelle et Revue Suisse*, 87: 187–97, 404–17.

Langie, A. (1922). *Cryptography, A Study on Secret Writings*. London/Bombay/Sydney: Constable and Company Limited.

Lateiner, D. (1989). *The Historical Method of Herodotus*. Toronto: University of Toronto Press.

Lateiner, D. (1990). Deceptions and Delusions in Herodotus. *Classical Antiquity*, 9 (2): 230–46.

Lattimore, S. (1998). *The Peloponnesian War: Thucydides – Translated, with Introduction and Notes*. Indianapolis/Cambridge: Hackett Publishing Company Incorporated.

Law, G. R. (2010). *Identification of Darius the Mede*. Pfafftown: Ready Scribe Press.

Lazenby, J. F. (1993). *The Defence of Greece 490–479 BC*. Liverpool: Liverpool University Press/Aris and Phillips Classical Texts.

Lazenby, J. F. (2012). *The Spartan Army*. Mechanicsburg: Stackpole Books.

Lebow, R. N. (2008). *A Cultural Theory of International Relations*. New York: Cambridge University Press.

Leopold, J. H. (1900). De scytala Laconica. *Mnemosyne*, 28: 365–91.

Lendering, J. (2019). *Xerxes in Griekenland: De mythische oorlog tussen Oost en West*. Utrecht: Uitgeverij Omniboek.

Lévy, E. (2003). *Sparte: histoire politique et sociale jusqu'à la conquête romaine*. Paris: Le Seuil.

Levy, Y. B. A. (2006). *Yeshua: The Lion of Juda*. Maitland: Xulon Press.

Leighton, A. C. (1969). Secret Communication among the Greeks and Romans. *Technology and Culture*, 10 (2): 139–54.

Lewis, K. M. (2015). *How John Wrote the Book of Revelation: From Concept to Publication*. Lorton: Kim Mark Lewis.

Lewis, C. T. and Short, C. (2019). *A Latin Dictionary Online*. Online resource. Retrieved from: http://www.perseus.tufts.edu/hopper/text?doc=clava&fromdoc= Perseus%3Atext%3A1999.04.0059 (accessed date 10-05-2023).

Liddel, P. (2018). Writing and Other Forms of Communication in Aineias' Poliorketita. In: Pretzler, M. and Barley, N. (eds), *Brill's Companion to Aineias Tacticus*. Leiden/Boston: Brill, 123–45.

Liddell, H. and Scott, R. (2014). ἄχνυμαι. In: *Greek-English Dictionary*. Online resource. Retrieved from: http://stephanus.tlg.uci.edu/lsj/#eid=19173 (accessed date 10-05-2023).

Liddell, H. and Scott, R. (2014). ξίφος. In: *Greek-English Dictionary*. Online resource. Retrieved from: https://www.perseus.tufts.edu/hopper/text?doc=Perseus:text:1999.04.0057:entry=ci/fos (accessed date 10-05-2023).

Liddell, H. and Scott, R. (2014). σκῠτάλη *(scytale)*. In: *Greek-English Dictionary*. Online resource. Retrieved from: http://stephanus.tlg.uci.edu/lsj/#eid=98117 (accessed date 10-05-2023).

Lietzmann, H. (1968). *Kleine Texte für Vorlesungen und Übungen, 17–18. Begründet von Hans Lietzmann. Herausgegeben von Kurt Aland*. Berlin: Verlag Walter de Gruyter and Co.

Lingas, A. (1995). The Liturgical Place of the Kontakion in Constantinople. In: Akentiev, C. C. (ed). *Liturgy, Architecture and Art of the Byzantine World*, vol. 1. St Petersburg: Byzantinorossica: publications of the St. Petersburg Society for Byzantine and Slavic Studies, 50–7.

Lods, A. (1939). Les origines de la figure de Satan, ses fonctions à la cour celeste. In: Dussaud, R. (ed.), *Mélanges syriens offerts à Monsieur René Dussaud, secrétaire perpétuel de l'Académie des Inscriptions et Belles-Lettres par ses amis et ses élèves*, vol. 2. Paris: Librairie orientaliste Paul Geuthner, 649–66.

Low, P. (2006). Commemorating the Spartan War-Dead. In: Hodkinson, S. and Powell, A. (eds), *Sparta and War*, 85–110.

Lloyd, A. (2004). *Marathon: The Crucial Battle that Created Western Democracy*. London: Souvenir Press.

Luenberger, D. G. (2012). *Information Science*. Princeton: Princeton University Press.

Luft, H. M. (1952). *An Examination of the Sources of Plutarch's Lives of Nicias and Lysander*. Durham: Durham University E-Theses. Online resource. Retrieved from: http://etheses.dur.ac.uk/9656/2/9656_6445-vol2.PDF (accessed date 10-05-2023).

Lunde, P. (2012). *The Secrets of Codes: Understanding the World of Hidden Messages*. San Francisco: Weldon Owen.

Luraghi, N. (1988). Polieno come fonte per la Storia di Dionisio il Vecchio. *Prometheus*, 14: 164–80.

Luschan, F. and Andrae, W. (1943). *Ausgrabungen in Sendschirli*, vol. 5: *Die Kleinfunde von Senschirli*. Mittheilungen aus den orientalischen Sammlungen 15. Berlin: De Gruyter.

Maas, G. S. (2012). Perseus and Bellerophon. In: Gagarin, M. (ed.), *The Oxford Encyclopedia of Ancient Greece and Rome*, vol. 1. Oxford: Oxford: University Press, 215–17.

MacMullen, R. (1982). The Epigraphic Habit in the Roman Empire. *The American Journal of Philology,* 103 (3): 233–46.

Macrakis, K. (2014). *Prisoners, Lovers, and Spies: The Story of Invisible Ink from Herodotus to Al-Qaeda*. New Haven/London: Yale University Press.

Malherbe, A. J. (1988). *Ancient Epistolary Theorists*. Atlanta: Scholars Press.

Mallowan, M. E. (1966). *Nimrud and Its Remains I*. London: Collins.

Manville, P. B. (1977). Aristagoras and Histiaios: The Leadership Struggle in the Ionian Revolt. *The Classical Quarterly*, 27 (1): 80–91.

Markle, M. M. III (1977). The Macedonian Sarrissa, Spear and Related Armor. *American Journal of Archaeology – Archaeological Institute of America*, 81 (3), 323–339.

Markle, M. M. III (1982) Macedonian Arms and Tactics under Alexander the Great. *Studies in the History of Art,* vol. 10, Symposium Series 1: *Macedonia and Greece in Late Classical and Early Hellenistic Times*, 86–111.

Marks, G. (2010). *Encyclopedia of Jewish Food*. Boston: Houghton Mifflin Harcourt Company.

Marshal, C. (1861). *Dictionnaire universel d'éducation*. Paris: T. Lefèvre.

Marshal, C. (1866). *Dictionnaire universel d'éducation*, vol. 2. Paris: Achille Faure.

Martin, A. (1877). Scytale. In: Daremberg, C. V. and Saglio, E. (eds), *Dictionnaire des antiquités grecques et romaines, d'après les textes et les monuments*, vol. 4. Paris: Hachette, 1161–2.

Martin, C. (2004). *Metamorphoses*. New York: Norton.

Martin, T. R. (2013). *Ancient Greece: From Prehistoric to Hellenistic Times*. 2nd edn. New Haven/London: Yale University Press.

McNab, C. (2018). *Greek Hoplite vs Persian Warrior: 499–479 BC*. New York: Osprey Publishing.

McKeown, J. C. (1989). *Ovid: Amores. Text, Polegomena and Commentary*. Leeds: F. Cairns.

McNaught, A. D. and Wilkinson, A., eds (1997). *IUPAC. Compendium of Chemical Terminology*. 2nd edn. Oxford: Blackwell Scientific Publications.

McNeese, T. (1999). *Ancient Greece II: The Golden Age to the Hellenistic Era*. Oxford: Lorenz Educational Press.

Melville, S. and Melville, D. (2008). Observations on the Diffusion of Military Technology: Siege Warfare in the Near East and Greece. In: Ross, M. (ed.), *From the Banks of the Euphrates: Studies in Honor of Alice Louise Slotsky*. Warsaw, USA: Eisenbrauns, 145–68.

Merriam-Webster's collegiate dictionary (2003). Sejanus. Online Resource. Retieved from https://www.merriam-webster.com/dictionary/Sejanus (access date 09-05-2023)

Michell, H. (1952). *Sparta. To krypton tēs politeias tōn Lakedaimoniōn*. Cambridge: Cambridge University Press.

Millender, E. G. (1996). *'The Teacher of Hellas': Athenian Democratic Ideology and the 'Barbarization' of Sparta in Fifth-Century Greek Thought*. Philadelphia: University of Pennsylvania Press.

Millender, E. G. (1999). Athenian Ideology and the Empowerd Spartan Woman. In: Hodkinson, S. and Powell, A (eds), *Sparta: New Perspectives*. Swansea: The Classical Press of Wales, 355–91.

Millender, E. G. (2001). Spartan Literacy Revisited. *Classical Antiquity*, 20 (1): 121–64.
Millender, E. G. (2002). Herodotus and Spartan Despotism. In: Hodkinson, S. and Powell, A. (eds), *Sparta: Beyond the Mirage*. Swansea: The Classical Press of Wales, 1–61.
Millender, E. G. (2009). The Spartan Dyarchy: A Comparative Perspective. In: Hodkinson, S. and Powell, A. (eds), *Sparta: Comparative Approaches*. Swansea: The Classical Press of Wales, 1–67.
Miller, W. I. (2002). *The Mystery of Courage*. Cambridge, Massachusetts: Harvard University Press.
Miller, W. (1914). *Xenophon: Cyropaedia*. Volume II: Books 5–8. Loeb Classical Library 52. Cambridge, Massachusetts: Harvard University Press.
Millett, P. (2013). Writers on War: Part 1 Greece: Winning Ways of Warfare. In: Campbell, B. and Tritle, L. (eds), *The Oxford Handbook of Warfare in the Classical World*. Oxford/New York: Oxford University Press, 46–73.
Mintz, A. I. (2018). Sparta, Athens, and the Surprising Roots of Common Schooling. *Philosophy of Education Yearbook 2018*, 74: 105–16. Online resource. Retrieved from: educationjournal.web.illinois.edu (Accessed date: 14-05-2023).
Mitchell, S. (1996). Hoplite Warfare in Ancient Greece. In: Lloyd, A. B. (ed.), *Battle in Antiquity*. London: Duckworth/Classical Press of Wales, 87–105.
Mollin, R. A. (2000). *An Introduction to Cryptography*. Boca Raton/London/New York/Washington: Chapman and Hall/CRC.
Mollin, R. A. (2005). *Codes: The Guide to Secrecy From Ancient to Modern Times*. Boca Raton/London/New York/Singapore: Chapman and Hall/CRC – An Imprint of Taylor and Francis Group.
Mollin, R. A. (2006). *An Introduction to Cryptography*. 2nd edn. Boca Raton/London/New York/Washington: Chapman and Hall/CRC – An Imprint of Taylor and Francis Group.
Moller, D. W. (1695). *Disputatio historico-philologica de Scytala Lacedaemoniorum, quam . . . sub praesidio . . . Dan. Guil. Molleri . . . d. [] junii 1695 . . . eruditorum examini exponet Georgius Casparus Klauer, . . ." of Georg Caspar Klauer*. Altdorfii: Lteris Kohlesianis.
Montanari, F., Goh, M. and Schroeder, C. (2015). *The Brill Dictionary of Ancient Greek*. Leiden/Boston: Brill.
Montanari, F. (2022). *History of Ancient Greek Literature*, vol. 1: *The Archaic and Classical Ages*. Berlin/Boston: Walter de Gruyter Gesellschaft mit beschränkter Haftung (GmbH).
Montgomery, B. (1983). *A History of Warfare: Field-Marshal Viscount Montgomery of Alamein*. New York: William Morrow and Company.
Monticelli and the University of Virginia in Charlottesville – Thomas Jefferson Foundation (2023). Wheel Cipher. Online Resource derived from: https://www.monticello.org/research-education/thomas-jefferson-encyclopedia/wheel-cipher/ Accessed date: 14-05-2023.

Moore, R. (2013). Generalship: Leadership and Command. In: Campbell, B. and Tritle, L. (eds), *The Oxford Handbook of Warfare in the Classical World*. Oxford/New York: Oxford University Press, 457–73.

Morello, R. (2007). Confidence, Inuidia, and Pliny's Epistolary Curriculum. In: Morello, R. and Morrison, A. (eds), *Ancient Letters: Classical and Late Antique Epistolography*. Oxford: Oxford University Press, 169–90.

Morin, J.-B. (1803). *Dictionnaire étymologique des mots françois dérivés du Grec, et usités principalement dans les sciences, les lettres et les arts*. Paris: B. Warée.

Moroni, B. (2010). I Tristia di Ausonio. Pater ad filium. *Annali della Facoltà di Lettere e Filosofia*, 63: 75–96.

Mozley, J. H. (1929). *Ovid: Art of Love. Cosmetics. Remedies for Love. Ibis. Walnut-tree. Sea Fishing. Consolation.* Revised edn by G. P. Goold. Loeb Classical Library 232. Cambridge, Massachusetts: Harvard University Press.

Mpampiniotis, G. (1998). *Lexiko tis neas ellinikis glossas* (Dictionary of the Modern Greek Language). Athens: Kentro lexikologias. Online resource. Retrieved from: https://www.greek-language.gr/greekLang/modern_greek/tools/lexica/triantafyllides/search.html?lq=%CE%BA%CF%8C%CE%BD%CF%84&dq= (accessed date 10-05-2023).

Mullen, A. and James, P. (2012). *Multilingualism in the Graeco-Roman Worlds*. Cambridge: Cambridge University Press.

Munari, F. (1959). *Amores testo, introduzione, traduzione e note*. Firenze: La Nuova Italia.

Mure, W. (1854). *A Critical History of the Language and Literature of Ancient Greece*, vol. 3. London: Longman, Brown, Green, and Longmans.

Müri, W. (1976). *Griechische Studien. Ausgewählte Wort- und Sachgeschichtliche Forschungen zur Antike.* Basel: Friedrich Reinhardt.

Murray, A. T. and Wyatt, W. F. (1924). *Homer: Iliad*. Volume I: Books 1–12. Revised edn by William F. Wyatt. Loeb Classical Library 170. Cambridge, Massachusetts: Harvard University Press.

Murray, A. T. and Wyatt, W. F. (1925). *Homer: Iliad*. Volume II: Books 13–24. Revised edn by William F. Wyatt. Loeb Classical Library 171. Cambridge, Massachusetts: Harvard University Press.

Murray, A. T. and Wyatt, W. F. (1999). *Homer: Iliad*. Volume II: Books 13–24. Revised edn by William F. Wyatt. Loeb Classical Library 171. 2nd edn. Cambridge, Massachusetts: Harvard University Press.

Murray, O. (1986). Greek Historians. In: Boardman, J., Griffin, J. and O. Murray, O. (eds), *The Oxford History of the Classical World*. Oxford: Oxford University Press, 186–203.

Murray, O. (1993). *Early Greece*. Cambridge, Massachusetts: Harvard University Press.

Mylonas Shear, I. (1998). Bellerophon Tablets from the Mycenaean World? A Tale of Seven Bronze Hinges. *The Journal of Hellenic* Studies, 118: 187–9.

Naiden, F. S. (2017). Military Communications: The Case of the Classical Battlefield. In: Naiden, F. S. and Talbert, R. J. A. (eds), *Mercury's Wings: Modes of Communication in the Ancient World*. Oxford: Oxford University Press, 62–84.

Naiden, F. S. (2021). The Organization of Greek Armies. In: Heckel, W., Naiden, F. S., Edward Garvin, E. and Vanderspoel, J. (eds), *A Companion to Greek Warfare*. Hoboken: Wiley Blackwell, 119–38.

Nafissi, M. (2018). Lykourgos the Spartan 'Lawgiver': Ancient Beliefs and Modern Scholarship. In: Powell, A. (ed.), *A Companion to Sparta*. Oxford/Chichester: John Wiley and Sons Limited, 93–123.

Nemet-Nejat, K. R. (1998). *Daily Life in Ancient Mesopotamia*. Westport/London: Greenwood Press.

Nettleship, H. (1883). The Noctes Atticae of Aulus Gellius. *American Journal of Philology*, 4 (1): 391–415.

Nicholson, J. (1994). The Delivery and Confidentiality of Cicero's Letters. *The Classical Journal*, 90 (1): 33–63.

National Institute of Standards and Technology (2001). Announcing the Advanced Encryptoin Standard (AES). Online resource. Retrieved from: https://csrc.nist.gov/csrc/media/publications/fips/197/final/documents/fips-197.pdf (accessed date 10-05-2023)

Novokhatko, A. (2015). Greek Scholarship from its Beginning to Alexandria. In: Motanari, F., Matthaios, S. and Rengakos, A. (eds), *Brill's Companion to Ancient Greek Scholarship*. Leiden: Brill, 3–59.

NSA Picture Gallery Online (2008). Online resource. Retrieved from: http://www.nsa.gov/gallery/thumbs/thumb00050.jpg (accessed date 09-05-2023).

Oehler, J. (1927). Scytale. In: *Pauly-Wissowa Realencyclopädie der classischen Altertumswissenschaft – Band III A-1*. Stuttgart: Metzler, 691.

O'Halloran, B. (2018). *The Political Economy of Classical Athens: A Naval Perspective*. Leiden/Boston: Brill.

O'Connor, B. (2018). *Bletchley Park and the Pigeon Spies*. Morrisville: Lulu.com (Online Publishing Company).

Ohaver, M. E. (1924). Solving Cipher Secrets. *Flynn's* 13 December: 138–40.

Ohaver, M. E. (1925). Solving Cipher Secrets. *Flynn's* 17 January: 1151–2.

Oikonomopoulou, K. (2019). Plutarch in Gellius and Apuleius. In: Oikonomopoulou, K. and Xenophontos, S. (eds), *Brill's Companion to the Reception of Plutarch*. Leiden: Brill, 37–55.

Oldfather, C. H. (1950). *Diodorus Siculus: Library of History*. Volume V: Books 12.41V13. Loeb Classical Library 384. Cambridge, Massachusetts: Harvard University Press.

Oldfather, W. A. (1923). Introduction and Notes. Illinois Greek Club (ed.), *Aeneas Tacticus, Asclepiodotus, Onasander*. Loeb Classical Library 156. Cambridge, Massachusetts: Harvard University Press, 1–25 (introduction; notes: passim).

Oliensis, E. (2019). *Loving Writing/Ovid's Amores*. Cambridge/New York: Cambridge University Press.

Olivetti, L. (2015). *Atlas of Imaging Anatomy*. Cham /Heidelberg/New York/Dordrecht / London: Springer International Publishing Switzerland.

Olsen, D. W. (2013). *Celestial Sleuth: Using Astronomy to Solve Mysteries in Art, History and Literature*. New York/Heidelberg/Dordrecht/London: Springer Science and Business Media.

Oppenheim, A. L. (1968). The Eyes of the Lord. *Journal of the American Oriental Society*, 88 (1): 173–80.

Oriyano, S.-P. (2013). *Cryptography InfoSec Pro Guide*. New York/Chicago/San Francisco: McGraw Hill Education.

Osborne, R. (2000). *Classical Greece, 500–323 BC*. Oxford: Oxford University Press.

Osborne, R. (2011). *The History Written on the Classical Greek Body*. Cambridge: Cambridge University Press.

O'Sullivan, N. (1995). Written and Spoken in the First Sophistic. *Mnemosyne*, 157: 115–27.

O'Toole, J. M. (1991–92). Herodotus and the Written Record. *Archivaria: The Journal of the Association of Canadian Archivists*, 33: 148–60.

Pallartly, R. (2022). *Semaphore*. Online resource. Retrieved from: Encyclopaedia Brittanica Online: https://www.britannica.com/technology/distortion-communications (accessed date 08-05-2021).

Panciroli, G. (1660). *Guidonis Pancirolli Rerum memorabilium sive Deperditarum pars prior (liber secundus)*. Frankfurt: Schönwetter.

Panckoucke, C.-J. and Thevin, J. (1782). *Encyclopédie méthodique. Grammaire et littérature: dédiée et présentée a Monsieur le Camus de Néville, maître des requêtes, directeur général de la librairie. Tome Premiere*. Paris: Panckoucke.

Pantelia, M. C. (2022). *Thesaurus Linguae Graecae: A Bibliographic Guide to the Canon of Greek Authors and Work*. Oakland: University of California Press.

Parke, H.W. and Wormell D. E. W. (1956). *The Delphic Oracle*. 2 vols. Oxford: Blackwell.

Paton, W., Walbank, F. and Habicht, C. (2011). *Polybius: The Histories*. Volume IV: Books 9–15. Loeb Classical Library 159. Cambridge, Massachusetts: Harvard University Press.

Pébarthe, C. (2006). *Cité, démocratie et écriture. Histoire de l'alphabétisation d'Athènes à l'époque classique*. Culture et Cité 3. Paris/Brussels: De Boccard/Université Libre de Bruxelles, Centre de Recherche sur la Cité Grecque.

Pechatnova, L. G. (2001). *A History of Sparta (Archaic and Classic periods)*. Saint Petersburg: Academy of the Humanities.

Peek, W. (1974). Ein neuer spartanischer Staatsvertrag. Abhandlungen der Sächsischen Akademie der Wissenschaften zu Leipzig. *Philologisch-historische Klasse*, 65: 3–15.

Pelling, C. (2002). Speech and Action: Herodotus' Debate on the Constitutions. *Proceedings of the Cambridge Philological Society*, 48: 123–58.

Peltomaa, L. M. (2021). *The Image of the Virgin Mary in the Akathistos Hymn*. Leiden: Brill.

Perkins, E. J. (1953). The Military Staff – Its History and Development. *Military Review*, 33 (6): 81–8.

Perrin, B. (1914). *Plutarch: Lives*. Volume I: Theseus and Romulus. Lycurgus and Numa. Solon and Publicola. Loeb Classical Library 46. Cambridge, Massachusetts: Harvard University Press.

Perrin, B. (1916). *Plutarch: Lives*. Volume IV: Alcibiades and Coriolanus; Lysander and Sulla. Loeb Classical Library 80. Cambridge, Massachusetts: Harvard University Press.

Perrin, B. (1917). *Plutarch: Lives*. Volume V: Agesilaus and Pompey. Pelopidas and Marcellus. Loeb Classical Library 87. Cambridge, Massachusetts: Harvard University Press.

Perrin, B. (1926). *Plutarch: Lives*. Volume XI: Aratus. Artaxerxes. Galba. Otho. General Index. Loeb Classical Library 103. Cambridge, Massachusetts: Harvard University Press.

Phang, S. E., Spence, I., Kelly D. and Londey P. (2016). *Conflict in Ancient Greece and Rome: The Definitive Political, Social, and Military Encyclopedia*, 3 vols. The Definitive Political, Social, and Military Encyclopedia. Santa Barbara: ABC-CLIO LLC.

Phiher, M. (2012). *A Handbook of Military Strategy and Tactics*. New Delphi: Vij Books India.

Piccirilli, L. (1981). Licurgo e Alcandro Monoftalmia e Origine dell' 'Agoge' Spartana. *Historia: Zeitschrift für Alte Geschichte,* 30 (1): 1–10.

Pieprzyk, J., Hardjono, T. and Seberry, J. (2013). *Fundamentals of Computer Security*. Berlin: Springer Science and Business Media.

Piper, F. (2002). Cryptography. In: Marciniak, J. J. (ed.), *Encyclopedia of Software Engineering*. Oxford/Chichester: John Wiley and Sons. Online resource. Retrieved from: https://onlinelibrary.wiley.com/doi/book/10.1002/0471028959 (accessed date 07-11-2016).

Piper, F. and Murphy, S. (2002). *Cryptography: A Very Short Introduction*. Oxford: Oxford University Press.

Plum. W. R. (1882). *The Military Telegraph During the Civil War in the United States With an Exposition of Ancient and Modern Means of Communication, and of the Federal and Confederate Cipher Systems; Also a Running Account of the War Between the States*, vol. 1. Chicago: Jansen, McClurg and Company Publishers.

Poe, E. A. (1841). A Few Words on Secret Writing. *Graham's Magazine,* 19: 33–8.

Poe, E. A. (1843). *The Gold-Bug*. Philadelphia: Philadelphia Dollar Newspaper.

Pomeroy, S. (2002). *Spartan Women*. Oxford: Oxford University Press.

Porter, S. E. and Pitts, A. W. (2013). *Christian Origins and Hellenistic Judaism: Social and Literary Contexts for the New Testament*. Leiden: Brill.

Poster, C. and Mitchell, L. (2007). *Letter-writing Manuals and Instruction from Antiquity to the Present: Historical and Bibliographic Studies.* Columbia: University of South Carolina Press.

Powell, A. (2017). *A Companion to Sparta*. Hoboken, New Jersey/Chichester: Wiley Blackwell.

Powell, A. (2021). *Athens and Sparta: Constructing Greek Political and Social History from 478 BC*. Oxford: Routledge – An Imprint of Taylor and Francis Group.

Powell, B. B. (1997). Homer and Writing. In: Morris, I. and Powell B. B. (eds), *A New Companion to Homer*. Leiden/New York/Cologne: Brill, 3–32.

Pretzler, M. (2010). Polyaenus the Historian? Stratagems and the Use of the Past in the Second Sophistic. In: Brodersen K. (ed.), *Polyaenus. New Studies.* Berlin: Verlag Antike, 85–107.

Pretzler, M. (2018a). Aineias and History: The Purpose and Context of Historical Narrative on the Poliorketika. In: Pretzler, M. and Barley, N. (eds), *Brill's Companion to Aineias Tacticus*. Leiden/Boston: Brill, 68–95.

Pretzler, M. (2018b). The Polis Falling Apart: Aineias Tacticus and Stasis. In: Pretzler, M. and Barley, N. (eds), *Brill's Companion to Aineias Tacticus*. Leiden/Boston: Brill, 146–65.

Pritchard, D. M. (2018). *Athenian Democracy at War*. Cambridge: Cambridge University Press.

Pritchard, D. M. (2018). The Archers of Classical Athens. *Greece and Rome*, 65 (1): 86–102.

Pritchett, W. K. (1971). *Ancient Greek Military Practices*. Berkeley: University of California Press.

Pritchett, W. K. (1985). *The Greek State at War: Part IV*. Berkeley/Los Angeles/London: University of California Press.

Pulak, C. (1998). The Uluburun [1] Shipwreck: An Overview. *The International Journal of Nautical Archaeology*, 27 (3): 188–224.

Purnamaa, B. and Rohayani, A. H. (2015). A New Modified Caesar Cipher Cryptography Method With Legible. *Procedia Computer Science*, 59: 195–204.

Race, W. H. R. (1997). *Pindar*. Loeb Classical Library 56. Cambridge, Massachusetts: Harvard University Press.

Raggo, M. T. and Hosmer, C. (2012). *Data Hiding: Exposing Concealed Data in Multimedia, Operating Systems, Mobile Devices and Network Protocols*. Burlington: Elsevier Science.

Ranpo, E. (1923). Ni-sen Doka. *Shinseinen*, 4 (5): 244–53.

Ramsey S. (2016). *Tools of War: History of Weapons in Ancient Times*. New Delphi: Vij Books India.

Rance, P. (2018). The Reception of Aineias' Poliorketika in Byzantine Military Literature. In: Pretzler, M. and Barley, N. (eds), *Brill's Companion to Aineias Tacticus*. Leiden/Boston: Brill, 290–374.

Range, M. (2016). *British Royal and State Funerals: Music and Ceremonial since Elizabeth I*. Woodbridge: Boydell Press.

Rankov, B. (2007). Military Forces. In: Sabin, P., Van Wees, H. and Whitby, M. (eds), *The Cambridge History of Greek and Roman Warfare*, vol. 2: *Rome from the Late Republic to the Late Empire*. Cambridge: Cambridge University Press, 30–75.

Rawlings, L. (2007). *The Ancient Greek at War*. Manchester/New York: Manchester University Press.

Rawling, L. (2009). Alternative Agonies. In: Van Wees, H. (ed.), *War and Violence in Ancient Greece*. London/Swansea: Gerald Duckworth/The Classical Press for Wales, 233–59.

Rawlinson, G. (1859). *The History of Herodotus*, vol. 1. New York: D. Appleton and Company.

Ray, F. E. Jr. (2011). *Land Battles in 5th Century BC Greece: A History and Analysis of 173 Engagements*. Jefferson/London: McFarland.

Rea, J. (1968). Oxyrhynchus Papyri 2660/2660(a). In: Parsons, P., Rea, J. and Turner, E. (eds), *The Oxyrhunchus Papyri*, vol. 33. London: The Egypt Exploration Society, 77–9.

Rea, J. (1970). Oxyrhynchus Papyri 2772: Instructions to a Banker. In: Coles, R., Foraboschi, D., Soliman El-Mossalamy, A., Rea, J. and Schlag, U. (eds), *The Oxyrhynchus Papyri*, vol. 36. London: The Egypt Exploration Society, 63–5.

Reba, M. A. and Shier, D. R. (2015). *Puzzles, Paradoxes, and Problem Solving: An Introduction to Mathematical Thinking*. London/New York/Boca Raton: CRC Press – An Imprint of Taylor and Francis Group.

Reinke, E. C. (1962). Classical cryptography. *The Classical Journal*, 58 (3): 113–21.

Rhodes, P. J. (2014). *Thucydides: History*. Oxford: Oxbow.

Ribbeck, O. (1962). *Comicorum Romanorum Fragmenta: Praeter Plautum et Terentium*. Hildesheim: Olms.

Richardson, D. P. (1984a). *Greek Mythology for Everyone: Legends of the Gods and Heroes*. New York: Avenel Books.

Richardson, D. P. (1984b). *Great Zeus and All His Children: Greek Mythology for Adults*. Upper Saddle River: Prentice-Hall.

Richardson, E. (2017). *Alexander the Great*. New York: Cavendish Square Publishing LLC.

Richer, N. (2017). Spartan Education in the Classical Period. In: Powell, A. (ed.), *A Companion to Sparta*. Oxford/Chichester: John Wiley and Sons Limited, 525–42.

Richmond, J. A. (1998). Spies in Ancient Greece. *Greece and Rome* 45 (1): 1–18.

Rihll, T. E. (2018). Technology in Aineias Tacticus: Simple and Complex. In: Pretzler, M. and Barley, N. (eds), *Brill's Companion to Aineias Tacticus*. Leiden/Boston: Brill, 265–89.

Ritter, T. (1991). Transposition Cipher with Pseudo-random Shuffling: The Dynamic Transposition Combiner. *Cryptologia*, 15 (1): 1–17.

Robbins, E. (1883). *Grecian History: Adapted to the Use of Schools and Young Persons: Illustrated by Maps and Engravings*. New York: Roe Lockwood.

Robinet, J. B., ed. (1779). *Dictionnaire universel des sciences morale, économique, politique et diplomatique; ou bibliotheque de l'homme-d'état et du citoyen: au temps & à la vérité*, vol. 11. London: Les Libraires Associés.

Robinson, E. W. (2011). *Democracy Beyond Athens: Popular Government in the Greek Classical Age*. Cambridge: Cambridge University Press.

Rodríguez, H. U. (2012). *Prácticas rituales, iconografía vascular y cultura material en Libisosa (Lezuza, Albacete): nuevas aportaciones al ibérico final del sudeste*. Alicante: Universidad de Alicante/Cajasol Obra Social.

Roisman, J. (1993). *The General Demosthenes and His Use of Military Surprise*. Stuttgart: Franz Steiner Verlag.

Rolfe, J. C. (1914). *Suetonius: Lives of the Caesars*. Volume I: Julius. Augustus. Tiberius. Gaius. Caligula. Loeb Classical Library 31. Cambridge, Massachusetts: Harvard University Press.

Rolfe, J. C. (1927). *Aulus Gellius: Attic Nights*. Volume I: Books 1–5. Loeb Classical Library 195. Cambridge, Massachusetts: Harvard University Press.

Rolfe, J. C. (1929). *Cornelius Nepos: On Great Generals. On Historians.* Loeb Classical Library 467. Cambridge, Massachusetts: Harvard University Press.

Rolfe, J. C. (1946). *Gellius: Attic Nights.* Volume III: Books 14–20. Loeb Classical Library 212. Cambridge, Massachusetts: Harvard University Press.

Rolfe, J. C. (1950). *Ammianus Marcellinus: History.* Volume I: Books 14–19. Loeb Classical Library 300. Cambridge, Massachusetts: Harvard University Press.

Romm, J. (1998). *Herodotus.* New Haven: Yale University Press.

Rosenmeyer, P. A. (2001). *Ancient Epistolary Fictions: The Letter in Greek Literature.* Cambridge/New York: Cambridge University Press.

Rosenstein, N. (2015). Italy: Economy and Demography after Hannibal's War. In: Hoyos, D. (ed.), *A Companion to the Punic Wars.* Chichester: Wiley Blackwell, 412–29.

Rösler, W. (2009). Books and Literacy. In: Boys-Stones, G., Graziosi, B. and Vasunia, P. (eds), *The Oxford Handbook of Hellenic Studies.* Oxford: Oxford University Press, 432–41.

Ross, B. D. (2012). Krypteia: A Form of Ancient Guerrilla Warfare. *Grand Valley Journal of History,* 1 (4): 1–10. Online resource. Retrieved from: http://scholarworks.gvsu.edu/gvjh/vol1/iss2/4 (accessed date 10-05-2023).

Rücker, N. (2012). *Ausonius an Paulinus von Nola: Textgeschichte und Literarische Form der Briefgedichte 21 und 22 des Decimus Magnus Ausonius.* Göttingen: Vandenhoeck and Ruprecht.

Rundle Clark, R. T. (1959). *Myth and Symbol in Ancient Egypt.* New York: Thames and Hudson.

Russell, D. A. (1966). On Reading Plutarch's Lives. *Greece and Rome* 13 (2): 139–54.

Russell, F. S. (1999). *Information Gathering in Classical Greece.* Ann Arbor: University of Michigan Press.

Ruzicka, S. (2012). *Trouble in the West: Egypt and the Persian Empire, 525–332 BC.* Oxford: Oxford University Press.

Saiber, A. (2017). *Measured Words: Computing and Writing in Renaissance Italy.* Toronto: University of Toronto Press.

Salmon, J. (1977). Political Hoplites? *The Journal of Hellenic Studies,* 97: 84–101.

Salomon, D. (2003). *Data Privacy and Security: Encryption and Information Hiding.* New York: Springer.

Salomon, D. (2006). *Coding for Data and Computer Communications.* New York: Springer.

Saltzman, B. A. (2018). Vt hkskdkxt: Early Medieval Cryptography, Textual Errors, and Scribal Agency. *Speculum: A Journal of Medieval Studies,* 93 (4): 975–1009.

Sarri, A. (2017). *Material Aspects of Letter Writing in the Graeco-Roman World: 500 BC – AD 300.* Berlin: De Gruyter.

Saunders, L. J. (2007). *Lecture History 223: Ancient Greece: The Messenian Wars.* Montreal: Concordia University.

Savard, J. (1998/99). *The Bifid, the Trifid, and the Straddling Checkerboard.* Online resource. Retrieved from: http://www.quadibloc.com/crypto/pp1322.htm (accessed date 10-05-2023).

Sacks, D., Murray, O. and Brody, L. R., eds (2014). *Encyclopedia of the Ancient Greek World*. New York: Facts on File Inc.

Sbordone, F. (1950). Le Pergamene Vaticane 'De Eligendis Magistratibus'. *La Parola del Passato*, 3: 269–90.

Scaliger, J. C. (1557). *Exotericarum Exercitationes liber quintus decirnus de subtilitate ad Hieronymum Cardanum*. Paris: Michele Viscosani.

Scanlon, T. F. (2002). *Eros and Greek Athletics*. New York: Oxford University Press.

Schaathun, H. G. (2012). *Machine Learning in Image Steganalysis*. Chichester: John Wiley and Sons Limited.

Schaeder, H. H. (1934). *Iranica: 1: Das Auge des Königs – 2: Fu-Lin*. Abhandlungen der Akademie der Wissenschaften in Göttingen. Philologisch-historische Klasse, 3 (Band 10). Berlin: Weidmann.

Schettino, M. T. (2013). The Use of Historical Sources. In: Beck, M. (ed.), *A Companion to Plutarch*. Oxford: Blackwell, 417–36.

Schmidt, N. (1920). Bellerophon's Tablet and the Homeric Question in the Light of Oriental Research. *Transactions and Proceedings of the American Philological Association*, 5: 56–70.

Schrader, H. (2011). *Leonidas of Sparta: A Peerless Peer*. Tucson: Wheatmark.

Schwab, G. (2011). *Gods and Heroes of Ancient Greece*. New York: Knopf Doubleday Publishing Group.

Scott, A. G and Figueira, T. J. (2012). Helots. In: *The Encyclopedia of Ancient History Online*. Online resource. Retrieved from: https://onlinelibrary.wiley.com/doi/abs/10.1002/9781444338386.wbeah06161 (accessed date 10-05-2023).

Sebag-Montefiore, H. (2004). *Enigma: The Battle for the Code*. London: Weidenfeld and Nicholson.

Sekunda, N. (1998). *The Spartan Army*. Oxford: Osprey Publishing.

Sekunda, N. (2000). *Greek Hoplite 480–323 BC*. Oxford: Osprey Publishing.

Seyfarth, W. (1970). *Ammianus Marcellinus, Römische Geschichte. Lateinisch und Deutsch und mit einem Kommentar versehen von Wolfgang Seyfarth* (Römische Geschichte Zweiter Teil – Buch 18–21). Berlin: Akademie-Verlag.

Shackleton Bailey, D. R. (1980). *Cicero: Select Letters*. Loeb Classical Library 31. Cambridge, Massachusetts: Harvard University Press.

Shackleton Bailey, D. R. (1999). *Cicero: Letters to Atticus*. 4 vols. Loeb Classical Library 7, 8, 97, 491. Cambridge, Massachusetts: Harvard University Press.

Shackleton Bailey, D. R. (2001). *Cicero: Letters to Friends*. 3 vols. Loeb Classical Library 205, 216, 230. Cambridge, Massachusetts: Harvard University Press.

Shackleton Bailey, D. R. (2004a). *Cicero: Epistulae ad Quintum fratrem et M. Brutum*. Cambridge/New York: Cambridge University Press.

Shackleton Bailey, D. R. (2004b). *Cicero's Letters to Atticus*. 7 vols. Cambridge: Cambridge University Press.

Shahbazi, A. S. (2012). The Achaemenid Persian Empire (550–330 BCE). In: Daryaee, T. (ed.), *The Oxford Handbook of Iranian History*. Oxford: Oxford University Press, 120–41.

Shannon, C. (1949). Communication Theory of Secrecy Systems. *Bell System Technical Journal*, 28 (4): 656–715.

Sheldon, R. M. (1986). Tradecraft in Ancient Greece. *Studies in Intelligence,* 20 (1): 39–47.

Sheldon, R. M. (1987). *Tinker, Tailor, Caesar, Spy: Espionage in Ancient Rome.* Ann Arbor: UMI Dissertation Information Service.

Sheldon, R. M. (2003). *Espionage in the Ancient World: An Annotated Bibliography of Books and Articles in Western Languages.* Jefferson/ London: McFarland and Company Incorporated Publishers.

Sheldon, R. M. (2004). *Intelligence Activities in Ancient Rome: Trust in the Gods, but Verify*. London/New York: Routledge – An Imprint of Taylor and Francis Group.

Sheldon, R. M. (2005). *Intelligence Activities in Ancient Rome: Trust in the Gods, but Verify*. London: Frank Cass.

Sheldon, R. M. (2008). *Espionage in the Ancient World: An Annotated Bibliography of Books and Articles in Western Languages. Second Edition*. Jefferson/ London: McFarland and Company Incorporated Publishers.

Shenef, Y. D. (2021). *Practical Introduction to the Hebrew Script: Learn to Read and Write Hebrew Quickly by Using Familiar Names and Vocabulary Already Known before the Language Study, with Tables and Easy Explanations of Hebrew and Yiddish*. Norderstedt: Books On Demand.

Shepherd, R. (1793). *Polyænus's Stratagems of War; Translated from the Original Greek, by R. Shepherd, F. R. S.* London: George Nicol.

Sherwood, A. N. (2006). Papyrus and Parchment. In: Wilson, N. G. (ed.), *Encyclopedia of Ancient Greece*. New York/London: Routledge – An Imprint of Taylor and Francis Group, 535–7.

Sherwood, A. N., Nikolic, M., Humphrey, J. W. and Oleson, J. P. (2003). *Greek and Roman Technology: A Sourcebook: Annotated Translations of Greek and Latin Texts and Documents*. London/New York: Routledge – An Imprint of Taylor and Francis Group.

Shipley, D. G. J. (2018). Aineias Tacticus in His Intellectual Context. In: Pretzler M. and Barley. N. (eds), *Brill's Companion to Aineias Tacticus*. Leiden/Boston: Brill, 49–67.

Shipley, G. (2002). Laconia Survey Inscriptions Catalogue. Online resource. Retrieved from: http://archive.csad.ox.ac.uk/Laconia/catalogue.html (accessed date 10-05-2023).

Shipley, G., Cavanagh, W. G., Crouwel, J. H, Crowther, C. and Landuyt, F. (2007). *The Laconia Survey Project*. Online resource. Retrieved from: https://archaeologydataservice.ac.uk/archives/view/laconia_ba_2004/(accessed date 10-05-2023).

Sickinger, J. P. (1994). Inscriptions and Archives in Classical Athens. *Historia* 43: 286–96.

Sickinger, J. P. (2018). *Public Records and Archives in Classical Athens*. Chapel Hill: University of North Carolina Press.

Sidebottom, H. (2007). International Relations. In: Sabin, P., Van Wees, H. and Whitby, M. (eds), *The Cambridge History of Greek and Roman Warfare*, vol. 2: *Rome from the Late Republic to the Late Empire*. Cambridge: Cambridge University Press, 1–29.

Silva, A. L. (2019). *A Key to the Hebrew Alphabet and Numbers*. Morrisville: Lulu.com (Online Publishing Company).

Sinclair, T. A. (1967). *A History of Greek Political Thought*. London: Routledge – An Imprint of Taylor and Francis Group.

Singh, S. (1999). *The Code Book: The Science of Secrecy from Ancient Egypt to Quantum Cryptography*. London: Fourth Estate.

Skinner, M. (2008). *What We Did For the Russians*. Morrisville: Lulu Press (Online Publishing Company).

Smart, N. (2018). *CyBOK Cryptography Knowledge Area Issue*. London: The National Cyber Security Centre. Online resource. Retrieved from: https://www.cybok.org/media/downloads/Cryptography-issue-1.0.pdf (accessed date 10-05-2023).

Smith, W., ed. (1870). *Dictionary of Greek and Roman Antiquities*. London: John Murray.

Smith, C. F. (1919). *Thucydides: History of the Peloponnesian War*. Volume I: Books 1–2. Loeb Classical Library 108. Cambridge, Massachusetts: Harvard University Press.

Smith, L. D. (1955). *Cryptography: The Science of Secret Writing: History and Modern Use of Codes and Ciphers, Together with 151 Problems and their Solutions*. Mineola: Courier Corporation: Business and Economics/Dover Publications.

Smith, W. (2000). *A Smaller History of Ancient Greece* (eBook). Online resource. Retrieved from: http://www.ellopos.net/elpenor/greek-texts/ancient-greece/history-of-ancient-greece-4-668.asp?pg=10 (accessed date 10-05-2023).

Snell, D. C., ed. (2008). *A Companion to the Ancient Near East*. Oxford/Carlton: Blackwell Publishing.

Snodgrass, A. M. (1965). The Hoplite Reform and History. *The Journal of Hellenic Studies*, 85: 110–22.

Soares, C. (2007). Rules for a Good Description: Theory and Practice in the 'Life of Artaxerxes' (§§ 1–19). *Hermathena*, 182: 85–100.

Sommerstein, A. H. (1987). *Aristophanes Birds*. Wiltshire: Aris and Phillips Limited.

Sommerstein, A. H. (1990). *Aristophanes Lysistrata*. Wiltshire: Aris and Phillips Limited.

Sommerstein, A. H. (2002). *The Comedies of Aristophanes: Volume 12*. Warminster: Aris and Philips

Sommerstein, A. H. (2008). *Aeschylus: Oresteia: Agamemnon. Libation-Bearers. Eumenides*. Loeb Classical Library 146. Cambridge, Massachusetts: Harvard University Press.

Sosin, J. D. (2018). '*Scytale (σκυτάλη)' (I)*. Online resource. Retrieved from: https://dcthree.github.io/photios/entry#urn_cts_greekLit_tlg4040_lexicon_dc3_%CF%83_389 (accessed date 10-05-2023).

Sosin, J. D. (2018). *'Scytale (σκυτάλη)' (II)*. Online resource. Retrieved from: https://dcthree.github.io/photios/entry#urn_cts_greekLit_tlg4040_lexicon_dc3_%CF%83_390 (accessed date 10-05-2023).

Spar, I. and Jursa, M. (2014). *Cuneiform Texts in The Metropolitan Museum of Art*, vol. 4: *The Ebabbar Temple Archive and Other Texts from the Fourth to the First Millenium B.C.* New York/Indiana: The Metropolitan Museum of Art/Eisenbrauns Incorporated.

Spence, I. G. (2010). *The A to Z of Ancient Greek Warfare*. Lanham/Toronto/Plymouth: The Scarecrow Press Incorporation.

Sprawski, S. (2011). The Early Temenid Kings to Alexander the Great. In: Roisman, J. and Worthington, I. (eds), *A Companion to Ancient Macedonia*. Malden: Wiley-Blackwell, 125–44.

Stamp, M. and Low, R. M. (2007). *Applied Cryptanalysis: Breaking Ciphers in the Real World*. San Jose: Wiley Interscience.

Starr, C. G. (1957). Review of: *Lexicon Aeneium. A Lexicon and Index to Aeneas Tacticus' Military Manual 'On the Defence of Fortified Positions'* by D. Barends. *Classical Philology*, 52 (1): 68.

Starr, C. G. (1974). *Political Intelligence in Classical Greece*. Leiden: Brill.

Steiner, D. T. (1994). *The Tyrant's Writ: Myths and Images of Writing in Ancient Greece*. Princeton: Princeton University Press.

Stewart, J., Chapple, M. and Gibson, D. (2012). *CISSP: Certified Information Systems Security Professional Study Guide*. Hoboken: John Wiley and Sons Incorporation.

Stillwell, R., MacDonald, W. L. and Holland McAllister, M., eds (1976). *The Princeton Encyclopedia of Classical Sites*. Princeton: Princeton University Press.

Stinson, D. R. (1995). *Cryptography: Theory and Practice*. Boca Raton/New York/Washington DC: CRC Press.

Stinson, D. R. (2002). *Cryptography: Theory and Practice*. 2nd edn. Boca Raton/London/New York/Washington DC: Chapman and Hall – An Imprint of CRC Press Company.

Storey, I. C. (2011a). *Fragments of Old Comedy*. Volume II: Diopeithes to Pherecrates. Loeb Classical Library 514. Cambridge, Massachusetts: Harvard University Press.

Storey, I. C. (2011b). *Fragments of Old Comedy*. Volume III: Philonicus to Xenophon. Adespota. Loeb Classical Library 515. Cambridge, Massachusetts: Harvard University Press.

Strasser, G. F. (2007). The Rise of Cryptology in the European Renaissance. In: De Leeuw, K. and Bergstra, J. A. (eds), *The History of Information Security: A Comprehensive Handbook*. Amsterdam/Boston: Elsevier, 277–325.

Street, B. V. (1984). *Literacy in Theory and Practice*. Cambridge: Cambridge University Press.

Stylianou, P. J. (2013). Ephorus. In: Wilson, N. (ed.), *Encyclopedia of Ancient Greece*. New York/London: Routledge – An Imprint of Taylor and Francis Group, 262–3.

Süß, W. (1922). Über Antike Geheimschriftenmethoden und ihr Nachleben. *Philologus: Zeitschrift für antike Literatur und ihre Rezeption /A Journal for Ancient Literature and its Reception*, 78 (1–2): 142–75.

Svenbro, J. (2018). *Phrasikleia: An Anthropology of Reading in Ancient Greece*. Ithaca/London: Cornell University Press.

Swift, L. (2019). *Archilochus: The Poems. Introduction, Text, Translation, and Commentary*. Oxford: Oxford University Press.

Swiggers, P. (1996). Transmission of the Phoenician Script to the West. In: Daniels, P. and Bright, W. (eds), *The World's Writing Systems*. Oxford: Oxford University Press, 261–70.

Szedegy-Maszak, A. (1981). *The Nomoi of Theophrastus*. New York: Arno Press.

Talbert, R. (1989). The Role of the Helots in the Class Struggle at Sparta. *Historia*, 38 (1): 22–40.

Taylor, R. (2021). *The Greek Hoplite Phalanx: The Iconic Heavy Infantry of the Classical Greek World*. Philadelphia: Pen and Sword Military.

Teitelbaum, E. G. (2022). Polybian Views on Tactics: The Problem of Traditions and Innovations. *Vestnik Drevnei Istorii*, 82 (2): 329–45.

Thatcher, T., Keith, C., Raymond F., Person Jr. R. F. and Stern, E. R. (2017). *The Dictionary of the Bible and Ancient Media*. London: Bloomsbury Publishing.

Thévenot, M., Boivin, J. and de La Hire, P. (1693). *Veterum Mathematicorum Athenæi, Apollodori, Philonis, Bitonis, Heronis, et Aliorum Opera: Græce et Latine pleraque nunc primum edita. Ex Manuscriptis Codicibus Bibliothecæ Regiæ*. Paris: Ex Typographa Regia.

Thicknesse, P. (1772). *A Treatise on the Art of Decyphering, and of Writing in Cypher With an Harmonic Alphabet*. London: W. Brown.

Thomas, C. G. (1995). Wingy Mysteries in Divinity. *Mnemosyne*, 157: 179–94.

Thomas, R. (1989). *Oral Traditon and Written Record in Classical Athens*. Cambridge: Cambridge University Press.

Thomas, R. (2002). *Herodotus in Context: Ethnography, Science and the Art of Persuasion*. Cambridge/New York: Cambridge University Press.

Thomas, R. (2009). Writing, Reading, Public and Private 'Literacies'. In: Johnson, W. and Parker, H. (eds), *Ancient Literacies: The Culture of Reading in Greece and Rome*. Oxford: Oxford University Press, 13–45.

Thureau-Dangin, F. (1922). Nouvelles Lettres d'El-Amarna. *Revue d'Assyriologie et d'archéologie orientale*, 19: (2): 91–108.

Tigerstedt, E. N. (1965). *The Legend of Sparta in Classical Antiquity*. Stockholm: Almqvist and Wiksell.

Tod, M. N. (1911). Apella. In: Chisholm, H. (ed.), *Encyclopædia Britannica*, vol. 2. 11th edn. Cambridge: Cambridge University Press, 160.

Tod, M. N. (1933). *A Selection of Greek Historical Inscriptions*. Oxford: Clarendon Press.

Tomokiyo, S. (2020). Scytale Not As a Transposition Cipher (Summary Version). *Cryptiana: Articles on Historical Cryptography*. Online resource. Retrieved from: http://cryptiana.web.fc2.com/code/scytale.htm (accessed date 10-05-2023).

Tonini, T. A. (1975). Il problema dei neodamodeis nell'ambito della società spartana. *Rendiconti dell'Instituto Lombardo*, 109: 305–16.

Torzcyner, H. (1937). How Satan Came into the World. *Bulletin of the Hebrew University*, 4: 14–20.

Too, L. (2001). *Education in Greek and Roman Antiquity*. Leiden/Boston: Brill.

Toustain, C. and Tassin, R. (1750). *Nouveau traité de diplomatique, par deux religieux Bénédictins de la congrégation de s. Maur R.P. Tassin, C.F. Toustain et J.B. Baussonnet*. Paris: G. Desprez and P.-G. Cavelier.

Trapp, M. (2003). *Greek and Latin Letters: An Anthology with Translation*. Cambridge: Cambridge University Press.

Trendall, A. D. (1952). Paestan Pottery: A Revision and a Supplement. *Proceedings of the British School in Rome*, 52: 1–53.

Treu, M. (1956). Der Stratege Demosthenes. *Historia: Zeitschrift für Alte Geschichte*, 5 (4): 420–47.

Trithemius, J. (1518). *Polygraphiae Libri Sex, Ioannis Trithemii Abbatis Peapolitani, Qvondam Spanheimensis, Ad Maximilianvm Caesarem*. Basel: Haselberg.

Tritle, L. (2013). *The Greek World in the Fourth Century: From the Fall of the Athenian Empire to the Successors of Alexander*. London/New York: Routledge – An Imprint of Taylor and Francis Group.

Trout, D. E. (1999). *Paulinus of Nola: Life, Letters, and Poems*. Berkeley: University of California Press.

Trypanis, C. A. (1968). *Fourteen Early Byzantine Cantica*. Vienna: Herman Böhlaus Nachf.

Turner, E. G. (1952). *Athenian Books in the Fifth and Fourth Centuries B.C.* London: H. K. Lewis.

Turner, E. G. (1973). *The Papyrologist at Work*. Durham, North Carolina: Duke University.

Untila, A., Berkowitz, G., Ramiotis, K., Dogani, V., Alexander, J., Fadhlurrahman, M. F., Silva, O. and Giallousis, N. (2015). *John Tzetzes' Chiliades in English*. Mitologia em Português/The Theoi Classical Texts Library. Online resource. Retrieved from: https://www.theoi.com/Text/TzetzesChiliades9.html (accessed date 10-05-2023).

Usher, S. (1970). Review of: *Aeneas Tacticus. Poliorcétique*, edited by A. Dain, translated by A.-M. Bon. *The Journal of Hellenic Studies*, 90: 210–1.

Van Oldenburg Ermke, F. (1959). *Homeros: Ilias en Odyssea*. Retie: Kempische Boekhandel.

Van Tilborg, H. C. (2006). *Fundamentals of Cryptology: A Professional Reference and Interactive Tutorial by Henk C. A. van Tilborg, Eindhoven University of Technology, The Netherlands*, 2nd edn. Boston/Dordrecht/London: Kluwer Academic Publishers.

Van Wees, H. (2000). The Development of the Hoplite Phalanx: Iconography and Reality in the 7th Century. In: Van Wees, H. (ed.), *War and Violence in Ancient Greece*. London/Swansea: Gerald Duckworth/The Classical Press for Wales, 57–82.

Van Wees, H. (2017). Luxury, Austerity and Equality in Sparta. In: Powell, A. (ed.), *A Companion to Sparta*. Oxford/Chichester: John Wiley and Sons Limited, 202–35.

Vaughn, P. (1993). The Identification and Retrieval of the Hoplite Battle-Dead. In: Davis Hanson, V. (ed.), *Hoplites: The Classical Battle Experience*. London: Routledge – An Imprint of Taylor and Francis Group, 38–62.

Vela Tejada, J. (1991). *Estudio sobre la Lengua de la Poliorcética de Eneas el Tactico.* Zaragoza: Departamento de Ciencias de la Antigüedad de la Universida Zaragoza.

Vela Tejada, J. (2004). Warfare, History and Literature in the Archaic and Classical periods: The Development of Greek Military Treatises. *Historia: Zeitschrift für Alte Geschichte,* 53 (2): 129–46.

Vela Tejada, J. and García, F. M. (1991). *Eneas el Táctico: Poliorcética. Polieno, Estratagemas.* Madrid: Gedros.

Verdegem, S. (2010). *Plutarch's Life of Alcibiades: Story, Text and Moralism.* Leuven: Leuven University Press.

Vernant, J. P. (1968). Introduction. In: Vernant, J. P. (ed.), *Problèmes de la guerre en Grèce ancienne.* Paris/The Hague: Mouton and Co., 10–30.

Von Gutschmid, H. A. (1880). Review of: *Aeneas von Stymphalos: Ein Arkadischer Schriftsteller aus Klassischer Zeit,* by A. Hug. *Literarsiches Zentralblatt 1880*: 588–90.

Von Moshamm, F. X. (1805). *Europäisches Gesandschaftsrecht.* Landshut: Franz Seraph Hagen.

Von Fritz, K. (1941). Theopompus the Historian. *The American Historical Review,* 46: 765–87.

Von Pauly, A. F., Walt, C. and Teuffel, S. (1839). *Real-Encyclopädie der classischen Altertumswissenschaft in alphabetischer Ordnung,* vol. 1. Stuttgart: Metzler.

Von Pauly, A. F. (1842). *Paulys Real-Encyclopädie der classischen Altertumswissenschaft in alphabetischer Ordnung.* Stuttgart: Metzler.

Von Pauly, A. F. (1864). *Paulys Real-Encyclopadie der classischen Altertumswissenschaft: 1.1 A-Apollinopolis,* vol. 1. Stuttgart: Metzler.

Von Pauly, A. F. (1920). *Paulys Real-Encyclopädieder classischen Altertumswissenschaft. 2. Reihe R-Z,* vol. 1. Stuttgart: Metzler.

Wachsmuth, W. (1844–6). *Hellenische Altertumskunde aus dem Geschichtpunkt des Staates (Teil 1 und 2).* Halle: C.A. Schwetschke und Sohn.

Waldstein, M. and Wisse, F. (1995). *The Apocryphon of John: Synopsis of Nag Hammadi Codices II, 1, III, 1, and IV, 1, with BG 8502, 2.* Leiden: Brill.

Walker, C. H. (2008). Document Security in the Ancient World. In: Quigley, M. (ed.), *Encyclopedia of Information Ethics and Security.* Hershey/London: IGI Global, 150–6.

Wallace, R. E. (2015). Language, Alphabet, and Linguistic Affiliation. In: Bell, S. and Carpino, A. (eds), *A Companion to the Etruscans.* Chichester: Wiley Blackwell, 203–24.

Wallon, H. (1850). *Explication d'un passage de Plutarque sur une loi de Lycurgue nommée la Cryptie (fragment d'une Histoire des Institutions politiques de la Grèce).* Paris: Dupont.

Walsh, W. S. (1891). Secret Correspondence. *The Illustrated American,* 8 (89): 536.

Walsh, W. S. (1892). *Handy-book of Literary Curiosities.* Philadelphia: J. B. Lippencott Company.

Warner, R. and Cawkwell, G. (1979). *A History of My Times (Hellenica).* London: Penguin.

Warry, J. (2015). *Warfare in the Classical World: War and the Ancient Civilisations of Greece and Rome*. London: Batsford.
Waterfield, R. (2018). *Creators, Conquerors, and Citizens: A History of Ancient Greece*. Oxford: Oxford University Press.
Waters, K. H. (1972). Herodotos and Politics. *Greece and Rome,* 19 (2): 136–50.
Waters, K. H. (1985). *Herodotus the Historian: His Problems, Methods and Originality*. London: Croom Helm.
Waters, M. (2014). *Ancient Persia: A Concise History of the Achaemenid Empire, 550–330 BCE*. Cambridge: Cambridge University Press.
Watson, J. S. (1853). *Marcus Junianus Justinus: Epitome of the Philippic History of Pompeius Trogus*. D. Camden (ed.), Online resource. Retrieved from: http://www.forumromanum.org/literature/justin/english/trans2.html#10 (accessed date 10-05-2023).
Watson, J. S. (1866). *Cornelius Nepos: Lives of Eminent Commanders, Translated, with Notes, by the Reverend John Selby Watson*. R. Pearse (ed.), Online resource. Retrieved from: http://www.tertullian.org/fathers/nepos.htm (accessed date 10-05-2023).
Way, A. G. (1955). *Caesar: Alexandrian War. African War. Spanish War*. Loeb Classical Library 402. Cambridge, Massachusetts: Harvard University Press.
Webber, C. (2011). *The Gods of Battle: The Thracians at War, 1500 BC – 150 AD*. Barnsley: Pen and Sword Military.
Webster, G. (1994). *The Roman Imperial Army of the First and Second Centuries AD*. Norman: University of Oklahoma Press.
Welskopf, E. A. (1974). *Hellenische Poleis: Krise, Wandlung, Wirkung*, vol. 4. Darmstadt: Wissenschaftliche Buchgesellschaf.
West, S. (1988). Archilochus' Message Stick. *Classical Quarterly,* 38: 42–8.
Whately, C. (2021). *Procopius on Soldiers and Military Institutions in the Sixth-Century Roman Empire*. Leiden/Boston: Brill.
Whisker, J. B. and John R. Coe, J. R. (2021). *The Citizen-Soldier in War and Peace: An Introduction to the History and Evolution of Citizen Armies and Militias*. Irvine/Boca Raton: Universal-Publishers.
White, J. W. (1914). *The Scholia on the Aves of Aristophanes with an Introduction on the Origin, Development, Transmission, and Extant Sources of the Old Greek Commentary on his Comedies*. Hildesheim/New York: Georg Olms Verlag.
White, P. (2010). *Cicero in Letters: Epistolary Relations of the Late Republic*. New York: Oxford University Press.
Whitehead, D. (1990). *Aineias the Tactician: How to Survive Under Siege*. Oxford: Clarendon Press.
Whitiak, D. A. (2003). *The Art of Steganography*. Global Information Assurance Certification Paper, SANS Institute 2003. Online resource. Retrieved from: http://www.giac.org/paper/gsec/2944/art-steganography/104 (accessed date 10-05-2023).
Whittaker, C. R. (1970). *Herodian: History of the Empire*. Volume II: Books 5–8. Loeb Classical Library 455. Cambridge, Massachusetts: Harvard University Press.

Wilkins, J. (1641). *Mercury or the Secret and Swift Messenger.* London: I. Norton.
Williams, K., March, L. and Wassell, S. R. (2010). *The Mathematical Works of Leon Battista Alberti.* Basel: Birkhäuser.
Williams, T. H. (1904). The Authorship of the Greek Military Manual Attributed to 'Aeneas Tacticus'. *American Journal of Philology,* 25 (4): 390–405.
Willetts, R. F. (1959). The Servile Interregnum at Argos. *Hermes* 87 (4): 495–506.
Willock, M. M. (1978). *The Iliad of Homer.* London: Macmillan Education.
Winterling, A. (1991). Polisbegriff und Stasistheorie des Aeneas Tacticus. Zur Frage der Grenzen der Griechischen Polisgesellschaften im 4. Jahrhundert vor Christus. *Historia: Zeitschrift für Alte Geschichte,* 40 (2): 193–229.
Wisse, F. (1979). Language Mysticism in the Nag Hammadi Texts and in Early Coptic Monasticism I: Cryptography. *Enchoria: Zeitschrift für Demotistik und Koptologie,* 9: 101–20.
Wisse, F. (1980). Textual Restorations in 'On the Origin of the World' (CG II,5). *The Bulletin of the American Society of Papyrologists,* 17 (1–2): 87–91.
Wisse, F. (1981). The Opponents in the New Testament in light of the Nag Hammadi Writing. In: Barc B. (ed.), *Colloque international sur les textes de Nag Hammadi: Québec, 22–25 août 1978.* Québec/Louvain: Presses de l'Université Laval/Editions Peeters, 99–120.
Wisse, F. (1982). *The Profile Method for the Classification and Evaluation of Manuscript Evidence, as Applied to the Continuous Greek Text of the Gospel of Luke.* Grand Rapids: Eerdmans.
Wisse, F. (1983). Prolegomena to the Study of the New Testament and Gnosis. In: Logan, A. and Weddeburn, A. (eds), *The New Testament and Gnosis: Essays in Honour of Robert McL. Wilson.* Edinburgh: T&T Clark, 138–45.
Wisse, F. (1989). The Nature and Purpose of Redactional Changes in Early Christian Texts: The Canonical Gospels. In: Petersen, W. (ed.), *Gospel Traditions in the Second Century: Origins, Recensions, Text, and Transmission.* Notre Dame: University of Notre Dame Press, 39–53.
Wisse, F. (1990). Pseudo-Liberius, Oratio Consolitaria de morte Athanasii. *Le Muséon,* 103 (1–2): 43–65.
Wolicki, A. (2018). *Spartan Symmachy in the Sixth and Fifth Centuries* BCE. Warsaw: Wydawnictwa Uniwersytetu Warszawskiego.
Wolf, J. (2004). *Humanism, Machinery, and Renaissance Literature.* Cambridge: Cambridge University Press.
Woodard, R. and Scott, D. (2014). *The Textualization of the Greek Alphabet.* Cambridge: Cambridge University Press.
Woodcock, E. C. (1928). Demosthenes, Son of Alcisthenes. *Harvard Studies in Classical Philology* (39): 93–108.
Woolliscroft, D. I. (2001). *Roman Military Signalling.* Stroud: Tempus.
Worley, L. J. (1994). *Hippeis: The Cavalry Of Ancient Greece.* New York: Routledge – An Imprint of Taylor and Francis Group.

Wouters, A. (1976). 'Latijns Grieks' en 'Grieks Latijn', over Translitteraties en hun Bedoeling. *Hermeneus – Tijdschrift voor Antieke Cultuur,* 48 (4): 179–91.

Xanthippos, D. (2003). The Second Messenian War. In: *Ancient Worlds LLC* (2002–2022). Online resource. Retrieved from: https://ancientworlds.net/aworlds_direct/app_main.php?pageData=Post/157630 (accessed date 10-05-2023).

Yagel, J. (2020). *Hebrew Alphabet Letters and their Spiritual Meanings: Symbolic Meanings of Hebrew Letters AlefBet, Symbols and Numerical Values Gematria, Biblical Hebrew Book that Shows the Secrets of the Hebrew Alphabet . . ., Christians, Jewish and Kabbalah Mysticism.* Seattle: Amazon Digital Services LLC.

Youtie, H. C. (1971). Βραδέως γράφων: Between Literacy and Illiteracy. *Greek, Roman, and Byzantine Studies,* 12 (2): 239–61.

Zafeiropoulou, F. and Agelarakis, A. (2005). Warriors of Paros. *Archaeology,* 58 (1): 30–5.

Zapechnikov, S., Tolstoy, A. and Nagibi, S. (2015). History of Cryptography in Syllabus on Information Security Training. *9th IFIP World Conference on Information Security Education (WISE).* Berlin/Heidelberg: Springer-Verlag, 146–57.

Zavaliy, A. G. (2020). *Courage and Cowardice in Ancient Greece: From Homer to Aristotle.* Cham: Springer Nature Switzerland.

Index

A Composition of Ciphers (work) 122
    see Alberti; De Componendis Cifris
A Few Words on Secret Writing 63, 76
    see Poe, Edgar Allan
A Treatise on the Art of Decyphering, and of Writing in Cypher (work) 74, 75
    see Thicknesse, Philip
absolute ruler 36
    see tyrannos
Achaeus of Eretria 49
Acharnenses (work) 17
    see Aristophanes
Acrisius 27
Adages (work) 72, 104, 105
    see Erasmus
addressee (of message) 103
ADFGVX cipher 134, 135, 136, 181
ADFGX cipher 6, 134, 135, 136, 180, 181
admiral 61, 62
Advanced Encryption Standard (AES) 143
Aegean Sea 12
Aelian 51, 164, 171
Aeneas Tacticus 5, 6, 11, 2, 6, 9, 10, 13, 62, 83, 85, 86, 87, 88, 89, 90, 91, 92, 93, 94, 95, 96, 97, 98, 99, 101, 102, 103, 110, 111, 112, 147, 159, 161, 171, 172, 173, 174, 177, 180
Aeneid (work) 15, 8, 145, 173
    see Virgil
Aeschines 9
Aeschylus 11, 37, 38, 92, 93, 160, 162, 173
Against Alcibiades (work) 51
    see Lysias
Against Catiline (work) 102
    see Cicero
Against Ctesiphon (work) 9
    see Aeschines
Against Leocrates (work) 50
    see Lycurgus
Agamemnon 93
Agamemnon (work) 11, 92, 173
    see Aeschylus

agents (secret) 9, 87, 89, 92, 97, 147
Agesilaus 20, 44, 47, 60, 69, 70, 86, 166, 167
Agesilaus (work) 50
    see Xenophon
agrammatos 44
aide-mémoire (for messenger) 49
Aineias of Stymphalos 171
Aineias the Tactician 86
    see Aeneas Tacticus
Alberti 6, 11, 122, 123, 124, 125, 126, 128, 131, 132, 179
Alcibiades 20, 59, 67, 105, 167
Alexander (work) 51
    see Plato
Alexander the Great 153
alliance(s) 7, 12, 13, 14, 15, 16, 18, 23, 33, 61, 145
allies 15, 17, 18, 19, 30, 61, 111
    Cretan 156
alphabet 6, 25, 95, 96, 98, 113, 114, 116, 117, 118, 119, 124, 126, 128, 129, 131, 132, 140, 141, 157, 178, 179, 180
    ancient Greek 117, 178
    German 134, 180
    Greek 96
    Italian 122, 124, 127
    Latin 122, 125
Amasis 159
Amazons (tribe) 28
ambush 23
American War of Independence 129
Ammianus Marcellinus 11
Amores (work) 12, 102, 103, 107, 108
    see Ovid
ampersand (symbol on cipher disk) 122, 124
An Historical and Analytical Bibliography of the Literature of Cryptology 4
Anabasis (work) 14, 16, 51, 68, 153, 154, 155, 167, 172
    see Xenophon
anagram 128, 132, 136, 137, 139

Anatolia 25, 28
ancient
    code 27
    communication security 8
    cryptography 8, 5, 84, 148
    Mediterranean world 31, 168
    Near East, see Near East
Andocides 51
Annals (work) 111
    see Tacitus
Anteia 24, 27
Antiquity 8, 3, 4, 9, 25, 26, 38, 45, 57, 64, 78, 81, 82, 83, 85, 88, 102, 114, 136, 140, 148, 149, 152, 173, 179
anti-Spartan sentiment 5, 23, 34, 41, 43
apella 19, 156
Apollodorus 11, 26, 27, 28, 29, 173
Apollonius, see Apollonius of Rhodes
Apollonius of Rhodes 48, 49, 50, 79
Apology 29, 43
    see Plato
Apophthegmata Laconica (work) 14
    see Plutarch
Appian 110, 173
Apsis (work) 51
    see Menander
arcana notis 108
archaeological record 27
Archaic (period) 7, 9, 10, 23, 26, 54, 92, 145, 146, 159
archers 14
Archilochus of Paros 11, 48, 49, 50, 52, 79, 82, 102, 164
Archimedes 74, 168
Argives 51
Argos 11, 18
Aristagoras 32, 33, 34, 35, 36, 39, 40, 41, 90
Aristarchus 11, 25
Aristarchus of Samothrace 25
Aristides (work) 12, 14
    see Plutarch
aristocratic culture (Roman) 102
Aristophanes 11, 17, 33, 41, 43, 47, 50, 51, 52, 53, 56, 71, 78, 81, 102, 164
Aristotle 38, 44, 50, 56, 57, 58, 154, 173
armour 14, 17, 19, 91, 112, 153
army
    ancient Greek 15, 5, 7, 10, 11, 12, 14, 18, 19, 20, 154

British 133
German 136
Spartan 18, 19, 20, 69, 156
United States 136, 140, 141, 142
Ars Amatoria (work) 12, 102, 103, 107, 108, 109, 157, 161, 173
    see Ovid
Art of Horsemanship (work) 174
    see Xenophon
Artabazus 35, 36, 40, 41, 159
Artaphernes 12
Artaxerxes II 68
Artaxerxes II 68
Asclepiodotus 153
ash 109
Asia 18, 30, 32, 33, 36, 60, 69, 87, 105
Asia Minor 18, 30, 32, 33, 36, 60, 87
aspis 153
Assyria 37
astragali 89, 97, 98, 172, 174
    see knucklebones
astragalus 98, 99, 174
    see *astragali*; knucklebones
Astyages 31, 32, 40
Athenaeus, see Athenaeus of Naucratis
Athenaeus of Naucratis 11, 9, 47, 48, 49, 59, 78
Athenian Constitution (work) 50
    see Aristotle
Athenian sources (on Sparta) 21, 23, 24, 34, 43, 44, 148
Athenian-Persian fleet 20
Athenians 5, 9, 11, 12, 15, 18, 23, 30, 41, 42, 44, 45, 52, 53, 57, 67, 79, 145, 154
Athens 12, 15, 17, 18, 20, 23, 29, 36, 41, 42, 43, 44, 50, 52, 53, 60, 61, 154, 155
attaches (military) 142
Attic Nights (work) 11, 3, 10, 20, 47, 48, 57, 59, 60, 61, 62, 63, 64, 65, 66, 68, 70, 71, 72, 73, 75, 76, 77, 80, 81, 90, 101, 104, 106, 114, 146, 166, 167, 168
    see Aulus Gellius
Attica 42, 44
Atticus 105
Augustus (Roman emperor) 178
Aulon 60
Aulonians 61

Aulus Gellius 3, 5, 10, 20, 21, 42, 47, 48, 57, 58, 59, 60, 61, 62, 63, 64, 65, 66, 68, 70, 71, 72, 73, 74, 75, 77, 79, 80, 81, 84, 85, 90, 100, 101, 104, 106, 107, 110, 114, 119, 128, 137, 144, 145, 146, 166, 167, 168
Ausonius 8, 11, 73, 101, 103, 104, 106, 107, 108, 109, 112, 113, 157, 173, 175, 176
authentication system 54
autocrat 31
autocratic ruler 32
autokey 131
   see key
auxiliaries 19
Axis and Allied powers (Second World War) 137

Balbus 114
banquets 107
barbarians (non-Greeks) 41, 44
barbaric, see barbarian
battle 11, 12, 13, 14, 15, 17, 19, 30, 50, 51, 56, 153, 154, 164
battle cries 14
Battle of Aegospotami 18
Battle of Cnidus 20
Battle of Coronea 12
Battle of Cunaxa 154
Battle at Koroneia 50
Battle of Leuctra 18, 20, 58, 145
Battle of Marathon 11, 12, 13
Battle of Naxos 156
Battle of Olynthus 154
Battle of Plataea 13
Battle of Salamis 15, 34
Battle of Sepeia 11, 153
battlefield 3, 8, 10, 13, 14, 15, 28, 49, 50, 51, 54, 56, 92, 110, 145, 146, 147, 154, 164
battlefield signalling 10
Bazeries, Etienne 78, 136, 140
beacon signals 93, 95
Bellaso, Giovan Battista 7, 126, 127, 128, 129, 130, 131, 132, 136, 179, 180
Bellerophon 23, 24, 25, 26, 27, 28, 105, 159, 167
betrayal 32, 33, 35, 36, 39, 40
bias (in source material) 38
biblia, see *biblion*

biblion 63
Birds (work) 41, 47, 52, 53, 71, 78, 164
   see Aristophanes
bladder 91, 112
blockades 18, 45
Boer War 133, 136
Book of Histories in Political Verse 70
   see *Chiliades*; Johannes Tzetzes
Books of the History of the Jewish War against the Romans (work) 173
   see Flavius Josephus
borders (of Roman empire) 110
British Army 136
   Special Operations Executive (SOE) 137
Bronze Age 26
Brutus 112
bureaucratic autocracy 36
Byzantine Empire 121
Byzantine encyclopaedia (Suda) 31
   see Suda
Byzantine encyclopedia 56
Byzantium 68

Caesar, Julius 6, 8, 11, 3, 83, 84, 101, 103, 110, 113, 114, 115, 116, 117, 118, 119, 121, 122, 124, 126, 148, 173, 177, 178, 179
Caesar cipher 6, 8, 3, 83, 84, 101, 113, 114, 115, 116, 117, 118, 119, 121, 122, 148, 178, 179
Capri 111
Cardano 11, 73, 168, 174
Cardano, Gerolamo 72
cardboard 80, 126
Carian pirates 28
Carneia 154
carrier pigeons 112, 173
Carthaginian(s) 94, 110
   see Carthaginian
Cassius Dio 11, 113, 114, 115, 117, 178
cavalry 7, 11, 13, 14, 19, 93, 154, 155, 156
   Syracusan 155
Cavalry Commander (work) 174
   see Xenophon
cavalrymen 14, 19, 154
Chigi vase 11
Children of Heracles (play) 8
   see Euripides

Chiliades 12, 70, 71, 72, 168
  see Tzetzes, Johannes
  see *Book of Histories in Political Verse*;
    Johannes Tzetzes
Chimaera 28
Chios 58, 59
Cicero 11, 44, 101, 102, 103, 104, 105, 113,
  115, 173, 175, 178
Cicero, Marcus Tullius 105
Cicero, Quintus 116
Cinadon 60
Cinesias 53
cipher
  cryptography 6, 7, 8, 2, 4, 5, 48, 49, 65,
    70, 80, 81, 84, 97, 99, 103, 113, 114,
    115, 116, 117, 118, 119, 121, 122,
    123, 124, 126, 128, 129, 130, 134,
    135, 136, 137, 140, 141, 142, 143,
    144, 148, 168, 170, 174, 177, 178,
    179, 180
  disk 122, 123, 126
  machine 128, 130, 136, 141, 142
  machine (electromechanical) 142
  monoalphabetic 122
  polyalphabetic 122
ciphertext 2, 3, 65, 66, 113, 116, 117, 118,
  121, 122, 123, 124, 125, 126, 128,
  131, 132, 134, 135, 139, 141
  alphabet 3, 113, 116, 117, 122, 125, 126,
    128, 131, 132
city walls 87, 89
city-state(s) 10, 12, 13, 14, 15, 16, 17,
  18, 44
Civil War (American) 131, 132, 180
Civil War (Roman) 115, 178
Classical Greece 9, 10
Classical period 1 5, 7, 10, 19, 23, 44, 45, 79,
  145, 146
Classical world
  see Classical period
clava 105, 106, 175, 205
Clearchus 20, 68, 70
Cleomenes I (king of Sparta) 11
client-king 36
cloak 17, 53, 56
closed societies (non-Greek) 38
clothing 91, 107, 109, 112
Clytaemnestra 92
code 55

cryptography 8, 2, 25, 26, 27, 75, 108,
  109, 124, 135, 142, 170, 182
  Morse 134
codebook 124, 125
cohesion (maintaining within troops) 12,
  13, 14
column
  in square 135, 139
  in table 64, 132, 133, 134, 139, 140
columnar transposition 142, 180
commander (army) 16, 19, 20, 35, 54, 62,
  63, 69, 136, 154, 159
commanders 7, 9, 14, 15, 16, 20, 52, 58, 60,
  69, 71, 101, 129, 145, 174
communication 8, 9, 14, 15, 2, 4, 5, 6, 7, 8, 10, 12,
  13, 14, 15, 16, 17, 18, 19, 20, 21, 23, 24, 25,
  26, 27, 28, 29, 30, 33, 36, 38, 39, 42, 43, 47,
  48, 50, 52, 53, 54, 55, 56, 57, 58, 61, 62, 67,
  68, 69, 71, 72, 73, 76, 77, 78, 79, 80, 81, 82,
  83, 85, 86, 87, 88, 89, 90, 92, 94, 97, 98, 99,
  101, 102, 103, 104, 105, 107, 108, 109,
  110, 111, 112, 113, 116, 118, 119, 121,
  122, 125, 128, 132, 136, 137, 142, 145,
  146, 147, 148, 152, 167, 171, 176
  breakdown 154
  military 83
  network 7, 16, 20, 145
  official 107
  security 8, 4, 5, 6, 8, 20, 73, 78, 80, 86,
    121, 122, 128, 147, 148
  security systems 6, 20, 122, 128
  written forms 29
  vertical in network 16
Comparison of Lycurgus and Numa 44
  see Plutarch
Compendium of Mechanics (work) 12, 91,
  108, 173
  see Philo of Byzantium
computer systems 143
Concerning Military Matters (work) 110
  see Vegetius
confidante 108
confidential
  communication 8, 15, 8, 9, 20, 24,
    30, 47, 50, 66, 68, 69, 81, 114, 115,
    116, 125, 128, 137, 142, 143, 145,
    152, 157
  information 8, 15, 8, 24, 47, 69, 81, 152,
    157

congress (of Corinth) 15
Constitution of the Itacans (work) 58
   see Aristotle
Constitution of the Lacedaemonians
   (work) 11, 15, 17, 19, 166
   see Xenophon
contract (record keeping) 58
contractual processes (record keeping) 56
coordinate (in square) 132, 133, 134
copper ore deposits 108
Corinth 15, 18
Corinthian War 18, 20, 155
Cornelius Nepos 12, 67, 101, 104, 105, 106
correspondence
   handwritten 143
   military 102
   official governmental 102
coup d'état 31
covert messaging 23
Crell 74
Crete 14
cryptanalyst 140, 142
cryptogram 2
cryptographic
   device 3, 4, 5, 47, 49, 50, 52, 53, 55, 57,
      58, 59, 66, 77, 78, 79, 80, 82, 83, 85,
      86, 87, 101, 104, 107, 144, 146, 147,
      148, 164
   see cryptography
cryptography 1, 2, 3, 4, 5, 6, 8, 10, 12, 14, 15,
   16, 18, 20, 23, 24, 26, 27, 28, 30, 32,
   34, 36, 38, 40, 43, 44, 46, 48, 50, 52,
   54, 56, 58, 60, 62, 64, 66, 67, 68, 70,
   72, 73, 74, 76, 77, 79, 80, 81, 82, 83,
   84, 85, 86, 87, 88, 89, 90, 91, 92, 93,
   94, 95, 96, 97, 98, 99, 100, 101, 1–2,
   104, 106, 107, 108, 110, 112, 114,
   116, 117, 118, 119, 121, 122, 123,
   124, 126, 130, 132, 134, 136, 138,
   140, 142, 143, 144, 146, 147, 148,
   149, 151, 152, 154, 157, 171, 179, 180
   historians of 8, 23, 24, 81, 84, 85, 86,
      96, 148
   to increase level of mysticism in
      religious practices 81, 157, 169
Cryptomenysis Patefacta (work) 74
   see Falconer, John
Ctesias 15, 167
cuneiform 157

cursus publicus 102
cylinders (*scytalae*) 72, 140
cylindrical cipher device 140
Cyprus 108
Cyropaedia (work) 37, 38
   see Xenophon
Cyrus 31, 32, 35, 36, 37, 38, 39, 40, 41, 43,
   68, 154

Damasistratus 59
Darius I 32
Darius the Great 12
Dark Ages 10
Datis 12
De Componendis Cifris (work) 11, 122,
   179
   see Alberti
De Falsa Legatione (work) 56
   see Demosthenes (author)
de Guilletiere, Georges Guillet 75
De la Cryptographie (work by Cario and
   Langie) 76
De la Cryptographie (work by Charton) 76
De Occultis Literarum Notis (work) 74
   see Porta, Giovan Battista
De Subtilitate 11, 72, 73, 168, 174
   see Cardano
deceit (in warfare) 15, 8, 21, 24, 28, 30, 36,
   37, 145, 159
deception (in warfare) 8, 9, 30, 37, 41, 166
Deioces 38
Delian League 17
Delos 71
Demaratus 24, 33, 34, 35, 36, 38, 40, 41, 45,
   46, 68, 69, 90, 146, 159, 160, 161, 172
democratic Athens 43
democratic state (in Greece) 36
Demosthenes 9, 10
Demosthenes (author) 56
Description of Greece (work) 19, 27, 28, 29,
   163, 173
   see Pausanias
despatch 102, 104, 105, 106
   see dispatch
despotic
   leader 37
   regimes 31, 32
device
   cryptography 102, 137

for secret communications 8, 9, 2, 3, 5, 6, 20, 45, 53, 58, 60, 61, 63, 66, 71, 77, 79, 80, 81, 82, 83, 85, 86, 87, 97, 99, 101, 104, 105, 119, 124, 128, 129, 135, 136, 140, 141, 142, 146, 147, 148, 152, 164, 170, 180
diameter (of *scytale*-stick) 54, 71, 80, 93, 106, 119, 123, 125, 130, 140, 142, 165
Dictionnaire étymologique (work) 76, 169
Didymus 52, 71
Diodorus Siculus 12, 15, 47, 49, 50, 51, 56, 57, 68, 78, 146, 173, 182
Diomedes 9, 28
Dion (work) 15
　see Plutarch
Dioscorides 57, 108
diplomacy 34
disk 6, 98, 99, 122, 123, 124, 125, 126, 128, 129, 130, 131, 136, 140, 141, 179
　cryptographic device 179
dispatch 53, 55, 57, 61, 63, 66, 67, 68, 69, 77, 140, 164
diversification (of joined Greek forces) 15, 17
Dizionario etimologico 75
dog collar 91, 112
Dolon 152
doru 153
dots
　for marking 2, 97, 119, 177
　for markings in text 97

Early Modern (period) 5, 122
earrings 91, 99, 112
Ecclesiazusae (work) 56
　see Aristophanes
economic warfare 18
education (in ancient world) 35, 44
Egypt 17, 24, 25, 37, 77, 81, 121, 157, 159, 161
Egyptians 17, 24, 43
ekklesia 19, 156
Elegies (work) 173
　see Simonides
elegists (Augustan) 107
encrypted text 6, 65, 66, 116, 133
　see ciphertext
encryption 7, 8, 3, 56, 57, 62, 66, 80, 81, 84, 92, 97, 104, 113, 114, 116, 118, 119, 121, 123, 124, 126, 128, 129, 130, 131, 132, 133, 134, 135, 136, 137, 140, 142, 143, 144, 178, 180
　monoalphabetic 117
Encyclopedia Britannica 75
enemy 15, 7, 8, 9, 10, 11, 12, 13, 17, 18, 23, 30, 32, 51, 52, 62, 63, 72, 78, 88, 97, 114, 115, 145, 149, 154, 164, 176
　territory 111
Enigma machine 6, 136, 137, 138, 142
enōmotarches 19
enōmotia 19
envoy(s) 62, 71
ephoroi 162
ephors 47, 57, 60, 61, 62, 63, 66, 67, 68, 69, 71, 74, 105, 111, 144, 167
Ephorus 56, 57, 167
Epirus 91, 112
Epistles (work) 73, 101, 104, 106, 108, 109, 113, 157, 173, 176
　see Ausonius
epistoleos 61
Epitome of the Philippic History (work) 12, 29, 38, 90, 160, 173, see Justin
Erasmus 72, 104, 105
Ethiopica (work) 71
　see Heliodorus of Emessa
Euripides 12, 8, 27, 43
Europäisches Gesandschaftsrecht (work) 76
Europe 109, 121
Europe (Western) 121
Excerpta Constantiniana (work) 49, 56, 57
Exercitationes (work) 73, 78
　see Scaliger, Julius Caesar
exile 33, 36, 60, 68
exile (of commanders) 68
exploratores 114, 177
Expositio in Syntaxin Persarum (work) 179
　see Georgius Chrysocossas

Fables (work) 28
　see Hyginus
Falconer, John 74, 76, 169
Farrow's Military Encyclopedia 75
feathers of arrows (hidden message) 35
financial processes (record keeping) 56
finger-bone 81
　scytale 71
fire signalling 86, 87, 92, 93, 94, 95, 96, 110, 132

first Persian invasion of Greece 12
First World War 134, 135, 136, 137, 140, 143, 164
fish (*scytale*) 71, 168
Flavius Josephus 173
flax 108
fleet 15, 18, 20, 154, 156
    Spartan 156
folded tablet (writing) 26
folk-tale motifs 29, 41
footwear 91, 112
France 142, 180
frontal assault 11
Frontinus 12, 17, 111, 112, 173
Fronto 166
funeral rites 50

Gallic War 115
gallnuts 108, 109
Gaul(s) 114, 115, 116
general (military) 4, 10, 12, 18, 31, 35, 36, 55, 57, 62, 63, 66, 67, 68, 72, 74, 84, 104, 105, 110, 114, 115, 147, 167, 171
Georgius Chrysococcas 178, 179
glass-making (recipe) 157
Glaucus 28
glue 91, 92
goat's lettuce 109
    see Mediterranean spurge
Gorgo 33, 34, 161
Graeco-Persian 7, 12, 17, 20, 33, 145
    wars 7, 12, 15, 17, 20, 145
Graeco-Roman literature 8
Great Rhetra, *see* Spartan constitution
Greater Hippias (work) 42
    see Plato
Greek
    commanders 16
    language 6, 2, 26, 28, 29, 34, 36, 48, 49, 56, 74, 79, 80, 81, 95, 96, 98, 103, 104, 106, 115, 116, 118, 125, 126, 159, 175, 178, 180
    military communications 7
    military history 9
    military protocols 8
    soldiers 7, 16, 17
    victory 15
grid (cryptography) 6, 135, 137, 138, 139

Griechische Paleographie (work) 4
guest friendship 24, 27, 28, 158
    see *xenia*; hospitality
Gylippus 57

Halicarnassus 31
handwriting 108
Handy-book of Literary Curiosities (work) 75
hare (message in) 31, 166
Harpagus 31, 32, 35, 36, 39, 40, 41, 160
Hebrew scholars 174, 177
Hecataeus 39, 40
hegemony 18, 20, 145
    Spartan 18, 20, 145, 155
Heliodorus of Emessa 71
Hellanicus 29
Hellenica (work) 13, 8, 11, 12, 13, 14, 15, 17, 18, 19, 47, 60, 61, 69, 154, 155, 167, 171, 173
    see Xenophon
Hellenica (work) 58
    see Theopompus
Hellespont 18
helots 19, 61, 156
Herennius Philo 49, 146
hero's plaque 90
Herodian 12, 112, 172
Herodotus 12, 4, 5, 8, 10, 11, 12, 14, 15, 21, 23, 24, 28, 29, 30, 31, 32, 33, 34, 35, 36, 37, 38, 39, 40, 41, 43, 45, 46, 47, 56, 68, 77, 79, 89, 90, 95, 97, 102, 146, 152, 154, 155, 158, 159, 160, 162, 172, 173, 176, 204
Heroides (work) 12, 107, 108
    see Ovid
Hesiod 28, 166
hieroglyphs 121
himation 56
hippagretai 156
Hipparchicus (work) 9, 166
    see Xenophon
hippeis 14, 19, 156
Hippias of Elis 42
Hippocrates 61
Hirtius 112
Histiaeus 32, 33, 34, 35, 36, 39, 40, 41, 90, 160, 176

historicity (of ancient sources) 30
Histories (work) 8, 2, 8, 10, 11, 12, 13, 14, 15, 21, 23, 24, 28, 29, 30, 31, 33, 36, 37, 38, 40, 41, 43, 45, 47, 56, 68, 86, 87, 89, 90, 92, 93, 94, 95, 96, 102, 110, 146, 152, 154, 155, 159, 162, 172, 173, 176
  see Herodotus
Histories (work) 13, 14, 87, 92, 94, 110, 172
  see Polybius
historiography 38
history of cryptography 4, 5, 81, 149
History of Rome (work) 154, 173
  see Livy
History of the Empire from the Death of Marcus (work) 112, 172
  see Herodian
History of the Peloponnesian War (work) 13, 8, 12, 13, 14, 15, 19, 41, 42, 44, 47, 51, 55, 102, 105, 152, 155, 160, 161, 165, 167, 168, 173
  see Thucydides
Hitt, Parker 140
Homer 8, 12, 15, 5, 8, 9, 21, 23, 24, 25, 26, 27, 28, 29, 39, 41, 51, 77, 79, 105, 145, 152, 158, 159, 166, 167, 173
hoplite 8, 10, 11, 12, 13, 14, 15, 17, 18, 19, 50, 51, 145, 153, 154, 156
  army 11, 15, 153
  battles 153
  phalanx 11, 13
hoplites 10, 11, 12, 13, 14, 16, 17, 19, 93, 153, 154
hoplon 153
hospitality 24
  see *xenia*; guest friendship
How to Survive Under Siege (work) 5, 11, 2, 9, 10, 13, 62, 83, 85, 86, 87, 88, 89, 90, 92, 97, 99, 101, 102, 112, 147, 159, 161, 171, 172, 173, 177, 180
  see Aeneas Tacticus
hub and spokes (communication network) 16
hybris 40, 41
Hyginus 28
hymn 76, 168
Hysiai 163

identification
  of the dead on a battlefield 50
  tags 3, 50, 51, 164
identity (of sender of messages) 54, 81, 108, 142
Iliad (work) 11, 9, 21, 23, 24, 25, 26, 27, 28, 51, 105, 152, 158, 159, 167, 173
  see Homer
illiteracy 34, 42, 43, 44, 46, 61, 80, 145, 146
image (writing) 4, 2, 25, 65, 90
India 37, 213
infantry 10, 11, 14, 19, 93, 156
ink 2, 33, 91, 92, 108, 109, 173
intelligence 15, 8, 9, 10, 37, 60, 111, 145
  agency 37
  American military 142
  German military 134, 135, 137
  networks 15
interception
  of confidential information 8, 15
  of messages 62
international (internationalisation of armies) 7
internationalisation (of Greek warfare) 27, 28
invisible ink 106, 108, 109, 113, 173
Iobates (king) 24, 25, 26, 27, 28, 167
Ionia 18, 30, 32, 60
Ionian Revolt 32, 33, 38, 160
Ionian states 32
Ionians 30, 43, 158
Irish Republican Army 137
iron sulphate 108
Isidore of Seville 12, 168
Isocrates 9, 44
Italy 142

Jefferson wheel cipher 131, 140
  see Jefferson, Thomas; Jefferson's cipher machine
Jefferson, Thomas 129, 180
Jefferson's cipher machine 129, 131
  see Jefferson, Thomas
jewellery 91, 99, 112
judicial procedures (in Sparta) 56
Julius Africanus 12, 90, 91, 171, 172, 173
Justin 12, 38, 90, 160

Karneios 154
katalogos 50
Kenchreai 163

Kestoi (work) 90, 91, 171, 172, 173
   see Julius Africanus
key
   cryptography 13, 62, 86, 105, 119, 123, 124, 126, 127, 128, 131, 132, 133, 134, 139, 165, 180
   phrase 127, 128, 131
keyword 126, 128, 131, 139
King's Eyes and Ears 37, 38, 42
kings 19, 27, 38, 40, 53
   of Sparta 19, 42, 43, 156, 162
knot record 170
knucklebones 89, 97, 98, 172
   see astragali
kontakia, *see kontakion*
kontakion 74, 75, 168–9
krypteia 38, 41, 42, 43
Kryptographik Lehrbuch der geheimschreibe kunst 75

La Cifra del Sig. Giovan Battista Bellaso (work) 126
   see Bellaso, Giovan Battista
La cryptographie 75
Lacedaemon 17, 42
Lacedaemonians 17, 34, 62, 63
Lacédémone ancienne et nouvelle (work) 75
   see de Guilletiere, Georges Guillet
Laches 13
lakōnismos 59
lambda 17
language 2, 14, 28, 39, 49, 113, 116, 175
   Greek 115
Latin 104, 105, 106, 108, 113, 116, 117, 118, 122, 132, 169, 175, 178, 180
Latin America 137
Laws (work) 3, 38, 42, 50
   see Plato
lead (as material for earrings) 8, 19, 91, 99, 112, 121, 173
lead (material) 112
leather 34, 54, 62, 64, 72, 80, 106, 129
legend 26, 40
lemon 109
   juice 109
   juice as invisible ink 109
Leonidas (king of Sparta) 34
Leontiades 61
Les Chiffres Secrets Dévoilés (work) 78
   see Bazeries, Etienne

letter
   symbol in wiritng 6, 17, 24, 26, 27, 28, 30, 33, 34, 35, 36, 45, 46, 55, 61, 63, 64, 66, 67, 69, 72, 75, 76, 77, 91, 95, 96, 97, 98, 99, 101, 102, 103, 104, 105, 106, 107, 108, 109, 113, 114, 115, 116, 117, 123, 124, 125, 126, 127, 129, 131, 132, 134, 135, 137, 139, 146, 158, 159, 160, 161, 164, 168, 169, 170, 173, 175, 179, 180
   writing 6, 24, 28, 46, 101, 102, 103, 108, 158, 159, 170
letters (written texts) 6, 2, 3, 24, 25, 26, 29, 33, 34, 35, 44, 55, 62, 63, 64, 65, 66, 67, 69, 73, 75, 76, 77, 78, 80, 95, 96, 97, 98, 99, 102, 103, 106, 108, 109, 112, 113, 114, 115, 116, 117, 118, 119, 122, 123, 124, 125, 126, 127, 128, 129, 131, 132, 133, 134, 135, 136, 137, 139, 140, 141, 142, 147, 152, 158, 159, 168, 169, 175, 178, 179, 180
Letters to Atticus (work) 101, 103, 104
   see Cicero
Letters to Brutus (work) 102
   see Cicero
Letters to Friends (work) 102, 103
   see Cicero
Letters to Quintus (work) 103
   see Cicero
letter-writing 26, 104, 159
lexicon 106
Lexicon (work) 47, 57, 58, 59, 71
   see Photius
Library (work) 4, 12, 15, 26, 27, 28, 47, 68, 78
   see Apollodorus
Library of History 15, 47, 49, 50, 51, 56, 57, 68, 78, 146, 167, 173
   see Diodorus Siculus
Life of Aemilius Paulus (work) 17
   see Plutarch
Life of Agesilaus (work) 20, 44, 47, 69, 86
   see Plutarch
Life of Alcibiades (work) 20, 47, 67, 167
   see Plutarch
Life of Artaxerxes (work) 20, 47, 68, 167
   see Plutarch
Life of Cleomenes (work) 38, 42
   see Plutarch

Life of Lycurgus (work) 38, 42, 44, 45
    see Plutarch
Life of Lysander (work) 18, 20, 47, 59, 66, 69, 70, 71, 74, 77, 86, 106
    see Plutarch
Life of Pythagoras (work) 157
    see Porphyry of Tyre
linguistic
    signs 27
    steganography 2
literacy 26, 29, 34, 35, 43, 44, 45, 46, 82, 158, 159, 170
    skills 34, 45, 46
Livy 154, 173
lochagos 19
lochos 19
long-distance communication 10, 20, 29, 36, 47, 85, 87, 88, 94, 124, 128, 136, 144, 147
Louis XV 75
love
    affair (secret) 106
    elegy (Roman) 161
lovers (communicating in secret) 102, 107, 108, 109, 176
Lycia 24, 25, 27, 28
Lycurgus 3, 11, 17, 19, 38, 42, 44, 45, 50, 164
Lycurgus (work), see Plutarch
Lygdamis 31, 32
Lysander 3, 18, 20, 47, 48, 57, 58, 59, 61, 62, 63, 64, 65, 66, 67, 68, 69, 70, 71, 72, 74, 75, 76, 77, 81, 86, 146, 164, 165, 167, 206
Lysias 51, 154
Lysistrata (work) 47, 53, 78, 102, 164
    see Aristophanes

M-138-A strip cipher 6, 141, 142, 143
M-138 strip cipher 141
M-94 cipher cylinder 6, 136, 137, 140, 141, 144
Macedon 12
Macedonian (hoplites) 153
malum medicum 109
manoeuvres 15
manual (military) 86, 101
manuscript 10, 80, 179
Marathon 12
marble masons 71
Mardonius 12

Mark Anthony 104, 105
markings (in text) 51, 97
Mathematical Recreations and Essays 75
Mauborgne, Joseph O. 140
Maurice 173
Medea (work) 27
    see Euripides
Medes 31
Median 31, 32
Medical Compendium in Seven Books (work) 71
    see Paul of Aegina
Mediterranean Spurge 108
    see goat's lettuce
Memorabilia (work) 44
    see Xenophon
Menander 51
Menelaion 46
mercenaries 7, 14, 18, 68
mercenary 60, 68
Mercury or the Secret and Swift Messenger (work) 73, 74
    see Wilkins, John
Mesopotamia 24, 25, 81, 157
message under wax of wax tablet 33
messaging 15, 3, 6, 21, 23, 30, 31, 39, 40, 41, 46, 47, 48, 49, 50, 52, 53, 54, 74, 76, 77, 78, 79, 81, 82, 83, 86, 89, 97, 100, 104, 107, 109, 111, 112, 113, 119, 125, 126, 146
messenger 30, 46, 49, 52, 53, 54, 77, 82, 83, 91, 97, 102, 103, 111, 112, 164, 165, 173, 175
    trustworthiness 102
messenger-stick 49, 52, 102
Metamorphoses (work) 103
    see Ovid
Middle Ages 4, 70, 121, 179
Middle East 109
Miletus 32, 33, 39, 90
military communication 5, 7, 9, 11, 13, 15, 17, 19, 21, 152
military
    dress (Spartan) 17, 155
    history 15
    institutions (Greek) 10
    protocols 60
Military Institutions of the Romans (work) 174
    see Vegetius

milk 106, 108, 109, 113
Miltiades (work) 12
   see Cornelius Nepos
missives (secret) 108
mnemonic, *see* mnemonic tools
mnemonic tools 82
mobilis 122
modern transposition cipher 70
Moller 74
monopoly (on battlefield) 51
mora 19, 156
moral (in stories) 29, 41
Moralia (work) 42, 45, 51, 59, 164
   see Plutarch
muster roll 50
Mycenaean 26, 154
   see Mycenae
myth 39, 40, 45, 104, 152
mythology 39, 45

Nabis 156
narrative 31, 36, 38, 39, 40, 162
Natural History (work) 108, 109, 157, 173
   see Pliny
navarch 156
navy 14, 15, 18, 20, 69, 162
Near East 9, 23, 26, 28, 29, 32, 33, 35, 36, 38, 43, 47, 49, 77, 79, 92, 159, 161
Near Eastern kingdoms 9, 43
neodamodeis 156
Nestor 51
New Scytale algorithm 143, 144, 148
Nicophon 12, 47, 55, 56, 165, 168
Nitocris 158
Nomoi (work) 47
   see Theophrastus
non-democratic (societies) 38
'non-Greek' (Spartans) 13, 23, 36, 43, 56, 160, 161
non-verbal 15
North Africa 109
Northern Africa 31
Nouveau traité de diplomatique (work) 77, 151
   see Toustain, C. F. and Tassin, R. P.
Numantia 110
numbers (in cryptography) 3, 7, 12, 37, 44, 105, 118, 122, 124, 129, 130, 132, 133, 164

Odysseus 9, 28
Odyssey (work) 15, 8, 9, 28, 145
   see Homer
officer (army) 16, 154
oil 49, 91, 92, 173
   linseed 109
oil-flask 49, 91
Olympian Odes (work) 12, 47, 52, 102, 146
   see Pindar
On Benefits (work) 44
   see Seneca the Younger
On Customs (work) 57
   see Dioscorides
On Great Generals (work), *see* Cornelius Nepos
On the Crown (work) 9
   see Demosthenes (author)
On the Defence of Fortified Positions (work), *see* Aeneas Tacticus; *How to Survive Under Siege* (work)
On the Different Meanings of Words (work) 49, 146
   see Herennius Philo
On the Mysteries (work) 51
   see Andocides
On the Orator (work) 44
   see Cicero
On the Universe (work) 38, 173
   see Aristotle
Onasander 173
Onomasticon (work) 27
   see Pollux
open code 2
Oppius 114
oral
   communication 29, 40, 41, 79, 82, 89, 102, 158
   histories 29, 41
   poetry 29, 41
   society 29, 79
Ovid 12, 102, 103, 107, 108, 109, 113, 157, 161, 173, 176

Panathenaicus (work) 44
   see Isocrates
paper 56, 66, 107, 109, 113, 126, 140, 141, 143
papyrus 3, 20, 34, 63, 64, 66, 103, 106, 109, 129, 147

parchment 3, 20, 54, 55, 56, 62, 63, 64, 66, 72, 74, 103, 106, 147
Paros 11
partial and broken letters (in *scytale* message) 137, 142
Paul of Aegina 71
Paulinus 106, 113, 175
Pausanias 19, 20, 27, 28, 29, 55, 67, 101, 104, 105, 106, 163, 167, 173
Peace (work) 50, 51
see Aristophanes
Peisetairos 52
pellets (slingshot) 17
Peloponnese 87
Peloponnesian League 17
Peloponnesian War 5, 7, 8, 12, 13, 14, 15, 17, 18, 19, 20, 21, 23, 34, 41, 42, 43, 44, 47, 51, 55, 58, 61, 87, 102, 105, 145, 147, 152, 155, 156, 160, 165, 167, 168, 172
peltasts 154
pentēkontēr 19
pentēkostys 19
Pericles 59
perioikoi 19
Persia 12, 15, 32, 33, 34, 36, 37, 41, 43, 60, 68, 159
Persian fleet 15, 20
Persian Wars 12, 17
see Graeco-Persian Wars
Persians 12, 13, 15, 17, 18, 30, 31, 32, 34, 37, 38, 41, 43, 68, 146, 155, 160
Persica (work) 15
see Ctesias
personal advantage (gaining) 36
Petronius 33
Phaedrus (work) 29, 30
see Plato
phalanx 10, 11, 12, 13
pharaoh 162
Pharnabazus 66, 67, 69, 74, 168
Philo of Byzantium 12, 91, 108
phoinikis 17
Photius 12, 47, 57, 58, 59, 70, 71, 166
pictorial images (writing) 25
Pindar 12, 46, 47, 52, 102, 146
pipes (used for signalling on battlefield) 15
plaintext 2, 3, 65, 66, 113, 114, 116, 117, 118, 122, 124, 125, 126, 128, 130, 131, 132, 134, 137, 140, 160

Plataea 12, 15, 45
Plataicus (work) 9
see Isocrates
Plato 12, 3, 9, 13, 29, 30, 38, 42, 43, 50, 51, 196
Playfair 144
Pliny the Elder 12, 103, 108, 109, 157, 166, 173
Plutarch 12, 3, 5, 11, 12, 14, 15, 17, 18, 19, 20, 21, 38, 42, 44, 45, 47, 48, 51, 54, 57, 58, 59, 60, 61, 62, 63, 64, 65, 66, 67, 68, 69, 70, 71, 72, 73, 74, 75, 76, 77, 78, 79, 80, 81, 83, 84, 85, 86, 87, 99, 100, 105, 106, 107, 110, 119, 128, 137, 142, 144, 145, 146, 163, 164, 165, 166, 167, 168
Poe, Edgar Allan 63, 76, 151, 167, 169
poetry 109
poetry (oral) 29
poleis, see polis
polemarchos 19
polis 10, 43, 87, 88, 89, 92, 147, 162
political treachery 37
Pollux 27
Polyaenus 12, 3, 10, 17, 47, 49, 50, 51, 57, 67, 69, 87, 90, 94, 102, 110, 146, 159, 160, 172, 173, 182
polyandrion 11
Polybius 6, 12, 2, 13, 14, 86, 87, 92, 93, 94, 95, 96, 110, 132, 133, 134, 135, 136, 172, 173, 180
square 6, 96, 132, 133, 134, 135, 136, 180
Polybius' tablets 132
Polycrates of Samos 159
Polygraphia (work) 74, 125, 127
see Trithemius, Johannes
Porphyry of Tyre 12, 157
Porta, Giovanni Battista 74, 168
postal system 102
post-Herodotean sources (on Sparta) 21, 41
Potidaea 35
prearranged
codes 16
messages 95, 96, 110
prehistory 82
Procopius 12, 9
Procopius of Caesarea 9

Proetus 24, 25, 26, 27, 28, 159, 167
Propertius 107, 161
provisionary troops (military) 19
psiloi 14, 154
psychological motivation (of soldiers) 14
public gatherings 107
Publius Nigidius 166
punishment (in armies) 14, 154

raiding parties 16
reading
  culture 29
  and writing (in ancient world) 44, 80, 146
real semagram 2, 92
  see semagram
rebellion 18, 33, 34
recipient (of message) 54, 64, 69, 72, 89, 90, 91, 97, 98, 102, 103, 106, 123, 124, 130, 131, 133, 134, 140, 141, 142, 164, 165, 173
recovery of the dead (from the battlefield) 50
Renaissance 5, 4, 119, 121, 122, 125, 148, 179
Republic (period in Roman history) 110
Republic (work) 9, 44, 51
  see Plato
resistance 36, 39
  groups (modern) 137
Rhesos (work) 8
  see Euripides
risk
  of discovery of secret messages 14, 35, 87, 92
  of discovery (of secret communication) 35
rod (*scytale*) 54, 57, 66, 71, 72, 74, 77, 80, 93, 94, 104, 119, 123, 125, 126, 128, 129, 132, 136, 137
Roman Empire (Eastern) 121
Roman Empire (Western) 121
Roman History (work), see Ammianus Marcellinus
Roman History (work) 113, 114, 115, 117, 178
  see Cassius Dio
Roman period 26, 44
row (in table) 64, 98, 125, 128, 130, 131, 132, 133, 134, 135, 139, 141

Royal Air Force 137
Russia 142

sandal(s) 91, 107, 173
sarissa 153
Satyricon (work) 33
  see Petronius
Scaliger, Julius Caesar 73, 78, 168
sceptres 53
Scholia on Aristophanes' Birds (work) 164, 168
  see Symmachus
Scholia to the Iliad (work), see Aristarchus
Scione 35
Scionians 35, 159
Scipio Aemilianus 110
scouting parties 19
scouts 114, 177
scytale 3, 5, 6, 8, 9, 15, 3, 4, 5, 6, 19, 20, 21, 23, 38, 42, 46, 47, 48, 49, 50, 51, 52, 53, 54, 55, 56, 57, 58, 59, 60, 61, 62, 63, 64, 65, 66, 67, 68, 69, 70, 71, 72, 73, 74, 75, 76, 77, 78, 79, 80, 81, 82, 83, 84, 85, 86, 87, 88, 89, 92, 96, 99, 100, 101, 102, 103, 104, 105, 106, 107, 110, 111, 112, 113, 116, 119, 121, 123, 124, 125, 126, 128, 129, 130, 131, 132, 136, 137, 140, 142, 143, 144, 145, 146, 147, 148, 149, 152, 163, 164, 165, 167, 168, 169, 170, 171
scytalida 56
Scythians 32
sealed tablet 27
  see folded tablet
sealing of messages 108
second Persian invasion of Greece 12, 15
Second Philippic Oration Against Marcus Antonius (work) 103
  see Cicero
Second World War 109, 134, 136, 137, 142, 143, 156, 173
secrecy (in messaging) 23, 30, 41, 42, 46, 81, 101, 105, 108, 110, 113, 177
secret 29
  communication 8, 9, 4, 7, 20, 21, 23, 26, 27, 28, 42, 48, 52, 53, 54, 55, 56, 57, 58, 61, 67, 68, 72, 79, 81, 82, 83, 85, 86, 87, 88, 89, 92, 94, 98, 101, 104, 107, 113, 116, 136, 146, 147, 148, 167

communication (mystical) 121
hidden communication 21
letter(s) 35, 46, 91, 116, 159
messaging 6, 47, 50, 53, 77, 78, 109, 146
service (ancient) 37, 38
Secret History (work) 9,
   see Procopius
secretive Spartans 21, 34, 42
Sejanus 111, 176
Seleucia on the Tigris 157
semagram(s) 2, 92, 174
semi-literate 41, 163
sender (of messages) 13, 65, 91, 98, 108,
   123, 124, 130, 134, 141, 142, 164, 165
Seneca the Elder 44
Seneca the Younger 44
settings (of cipher disk) 123, 124
shield 11, 17, 153
shipwreck 26
short distance communication 10
Sicyon 17
Sicyonians 17
siege (siege warfare) 18, 35, 45, 85, 87, 88,
   89, 90, 92, 99
Siege of Plataea 45
sieges 18, 86, 87, 89, 90, 147, 159
sign (writing) 4, 2, 25, 35
signalling 6, 10, 87, 92, 93, 94, 96, 110, 135,
   172, 176
signals (secret) 107
signs (secret) 14, 24, 25, 26, 30, 105, 107,
   109, 180
Simonides 173
skin (as writing material) 56, 72, 112
slave(s) 9, 10, 32, 33, 35, 90, 97, 107, 108,
   158, 160, 176
Socrates 29, 30, 42
soldier(s) 3, 8, 11, 14, 15, 16, 28, 31, 35, 42,
   49, 50, 51, 106, 111, 112, 126, 146,
   152, 155, 164, 175
Solymi 28
sources
   Greek 4, 5, 8, 23, 24, 37, 38, 41, 47, 48,
     62, 67, 101, 103, 104, 107, 146, 147,
     175
   Roman 4, 5, 24, 67, 80, 101, 104, 109,
     112, 113, 147
Spanish Wars (work) 110, 173
   see Appian

Sparta 5, 3, 12, 15, 17, 18, 19, 20, 23, 24, 25,
   27, 29, 31, 33, 34, 35, 36, 37, 38, 39,
   41, 42, 43, 44, 45, 47, 50, 51, 52, 54,
   56, 57, 58, 59, 60, 61, 63, 67, 68, 69,
   71, 74, 85, 87, 110, 111, 144, 147,
   156, 157, 159
Spartan(s) 3, 5, 6, 8, 11, 12, 13, 15, 17, 18,
   19, 20, 21, 23, 24, 33, 34, 35, 36, 41,
   42, 43, 44, 45, 46, 47, 48, 49, 51, 52,
   53, 54, 55, 56, 57, 58, 59, 60, 61, 67,
   68, 69, 71, 72, 73, 76, 77, 78, 79, 80,
   83, 84, 85, 86, 87, 90, 96, 100, 101,
   104, 111, 113, 122, 123, 125, 128,
   132, 136, 137, 142, 143, 144, 145,
   146, 148, 149, 152, 154, 156, 160,
   161, 163, 164, 167, 169, 170
   inscriptions 34
   lack of culture (according to
     Athenians) 44, 45
   message-staff 49
   navy 18, 20
   written documents 34
Spartan Constitution 44
   see Great Rhetra
Spartiates 19, 156
spear 11, 46, 153
speculatores 114, 177
Speeches (work) 154
   see Lysias
spy 9, 10, 15, 28, 37, 38, 43, 114, 145, 160,
   177
spying, *see* spies
spying and eavesdropping (on one's
   subordinates) 38
square table 125
   see Trithemius, Johannes; *tabula recta*
stabilis 122
staff 52, 53, 54, 55, 56, 57, 62, 63, 74, 79, 81,
   83, 106, 107, 115, 148, 175
steganogram 2
Steganographia (work) 151
   see Trithemius, Johannes
steganography 5, 8, 15, 2, 4, 23, 24, 30, 31,
   32, 36, 43, 73, 77, 83, 85, 86, 87, 88,
   89, 91, 92, 93, 95, 97, 99, 106, 107,
   109, 111, 121, 147, 149, 151, 157,
   171, 172
stereotype 34, 45, 46, 54, 61
stereotypical ideas 44

stick (literal meaning of 'scytale') 8, 20, 49, 52, 53, 54, 55, 56, 57, 63, 64, 66, 71, 72, 73, 74, 75, 76, 77, 79, 80, 81, 83, 91, 102, 104, 106, 107, 116, 123, 148, 164, 165, 168, 175
story-telling 29, 41
Straits of Salamis 15
stratagems (use in war) 4, 41, 85, 87, 92, 99, 107, 112
Stratagems (work) 1 2, 3, 10, 17, 67, 90, 94, 102, 110, 111, 112, 173
  see Frontinus
Stratagems of War (work) 1 2, 3, 10, 17, 47, 49, 50, 51, 57, 67, 69, 87, 94, 110, 146, 159, 160, 173
  see Polyaenus
strategies of attrition 18
Strategikon (work) 173
  see Maurice
strategos 35, 159
strip
  cipher 141, 142
  of writing material 6, 20, 54, 63, 64, 65, 66, 72, 73, 74, 75, 76, 77, 78, 80, 106, 112, 125, 126, 128, 129, 131, 132, 136, 137, 140, 141, 142, 168, 169
structure (of Greek army) 5, 7, 8, 9, 10, 11, 13, 15, 17, 18, 19, 20, 21, 40, 152
substitution 6, 8, 2, 3, 88, 97, 113, 116, 117, 118, 119, 122, 124, 125, 137, 174, 177, 179, 180, 181
  see substitution cipher
substitution cipher 2, 3, 88, 97, 116, 118, 124, 137, 141, 177, 179, 180
  see substitution
Suda (work) 3, 31, 50
Suesoriae (work) 44
  see Seneca the Elder
Suetonius 13, 102, 110, 111, 113, 114, 115, 117, 173, 178
Suppliant Women (play) 8, 38
  see Euripides
surprise attacks 23
Susa 32
sword 46, 153
symbol 27
symbol(s) 3, 26, 118, 177
  writing 2, 17, 25, 97, 122, 124
Symmachus 164, 168

Symposium (work) 153
  see Xenophon

tablet
  boxwood 90
  writing 24, 25, 26, 27, 28, 33, 89, 90, 95, 96, 107, 109, 147, 157, 159, 161, 172
  see writing tablet
tabula recta 125, 126, 131
  see Trithemius, Johannes; square table
Tacitus 111, 171
tactics 14, 15, 19, 62, 86, 93
Tactics (work) 153, 171
  see Asclepiodotus
tattoo (secret message on slave's head) 32
tattooing 160, 176
  of slaves 33
taxiarch 50
technical steganography 2
Teleutias 154
text semagram 2
  see semagram
The African War (work) 11, 177
  see Caesar, Julius
The Alexandrian War (work) 177
  see Caesar, Julius
The Ancient Customs of the Spartans (work) 45
  see Plutarch
The Birth of Aphrodite (work) 47, 55, 165, 168
  see Nicophon
The Book on the Great Generals of Foreign Nations (work) 67, 101, 104, 105
  see Cornelius Nepos
The Civil War (work) 11, 110, 173, 177, 178
  see Caesar, Julius
The Civil Wars (work) 173
  see Appian
The Codebreakers 4
The Constitution of the Athenians (work) 154
  see Aristotle
The Deified Augustus (work) 102, 178
  see Suetonius
The Deified Julius (work) 13, 114, 115, 117
  see Suetonius
The Eclogues (work) 173
  see Virgil

The Etymologies (work)
    see Isidore of Seville
The Gallic War (work) 11, 110, 114, 115, 116, 118, 173, 177
    see Caesar, Julius
The General (work) 173
    see Onasander
The History of Animals (work) 44
    see Aristotle
The Knights (work) 50
    see Aristophanes
The Learned Banqueters (work) 9, 47, 48, 49, 59, 78
    see Athenaeus of Naucratis
The Library (work) 11
    see Apollodorus
The Military Institutions of the Romans (work) 173
    see Vegetius
The Persians (work) 162
    see Aeschylus
The Spanish War (work) 11, 177
    see Caesar, Julius
The Stolen Christmas Box 76
The Verrine Orations (work) 173
    see Cicero
Theban army 12
Thebans 18, 61
Thebes 18, 61
Themistocles 15, 30, 59, 158
Theogony (work) 28
    see Hesiod
Theophrastus 13, 47, 56, 57
Theopompus 42, 58, 59, 60, 70, 165, 166, 167
theoretical transposition cipher (*scytale*) 47, 48, 62, 78
Thessaly 91, 112
Thicknesse, Philip 74, 75, 169
third party 36
Thrace 12
thread (for sewing through *astragali*) 98, 99, 174
Thucydides 13, 8, 12, 13, 14, 15, 19, 41, 42, 43, 44, 47, 51, 55, 102, 105, 106, 152, 155, 160, 161, 165, 166, 167, 168, 172, 173
Tiberius 111
Tiberius (work) 13, 110, 111, 173
    see Suetonius

Tibullus 107, 161
Timocratem (work) 56
    see Demosthenes (author)
Timoxenus 35, 36, 39, 40, 41, 159
Tiryns 27
token 25, 27, 28
    identification 51
torch 93, 96
Toustain, C. F. and Tassin, R. P. 77, 82, 151, 169
toxotai 14
toy (cipher) 4, 48, 70, 80, 81, 84, 144, 148, 170
tragic poets (tragedy) 40
Traité élémentaire de cryptographie 76
traitor 35
transcript 97
transport (of messages by messenger) 54, 55, 75, 165
transposition 8, 9, 2, 3, 5, 6, 20, 47, 48, 62, 66, 70, 77, 78, 84, 85, 88, 98, 117, 119, 121, 122, 124, 126, 137, 139, 140, 143, 144, 149, 163, 168, 169, 171, 180, 181
    columnar 139, 140, 180
    cipher 9, 2, 3, 5, 6, 20, 47, 48, 62, 66, 70, 77, 78, 85, 98, 119, 122, 137, 142, 144, 149
    cipher (theoretical) 20, 121, 148
treachery 35, 89, 159
    from within the city during sieges 87, 88
treason 35
Treatise on Archilochus (work) 48, 49
    see Apollonius of Rhodes
trickery (in warfare) 15, 8, 21, 24, 27, 28, 30, 36, 37, 111, 145, 159
trireme 20, 156
Trithemius, Johannes 7, 74, 125, 126, 127, 131, 132, 136, 151
Trojan horse 15, 8, 21, 28, 145, 152
Trojans 8, 9, 28
Troy 9, 28, 93, 152
trumpets (used in battle) 14
tyrannical autocrat 31
    see autocrat
tyrannos 36
    see absolute ruler
tyrant 32, 36

Tyrtaeus 13, 3, 11, 50, 56, 182
Tzetzes, Johannes 70, 71, 72, 73, 74

Uluburun 26
uncivilised (Spartans, according to Athenians) 41, 44, 46, 54
uniforms 17
United States Army Security Agency 144
United States National Institute of Standards and Technology (NIST) 143
units (army) 7, 14, 16, 18, 19, 117, 122, 142, 156
unwritten rules 7, 8, 15, 145
of Greek warfare 7, 8, 145
urine (as invisible ink) 109

Various History (work) 51, 164
see Aelian
Varro 166
Vegetius 110, 173, 174
verbal (communication) 15
Vigenère, Blaise de 7, 131, 132, 133, 136
Vigenère
cipher 131
table 7, 131, 132, 133
Virgil 15, 8, 145, 173
vitriol 108, 109, 176
vowels 97, 177
Voynich manuscript 182

walking stick 52
warfare (Greek) 15, 7, 8, 9, 10, 11, 12, 13, 17, 18, 20, 21, 23, 24, 27, 28, 34, 60, 69, 85, 87, 94, 97, 108, 109, 126, 128, 132, 136, 137, 142, 145, 151, 157, 159, 171
watchtowers (Roman) 110
watchwords 16
water clock 6, 94, 95

wax 33, 34, 89, 90, 103, 108, 109, 147, 159, 172
tablet 103
Western Asia 31
wheel (cipher machine) 128, 140, 141
whip 57
scytale 70
whistles (used in battle) 14
Wilkins, John 73, 74
wood 34, 62, 80, 98, 164
wooden, *see* wood
writing under wax of wax tablet 89
written communication 25, 29

xenia 24
see hospitality; guest friendship
Xenophon 13, 8, 9, 11, 12, 13, 14, 15, 16, 17, 18, 19, 37, 38, 44, 47, 50, 51, 60, 61, 62, 68, 69, 81, 153, 154, 155, 166, 167, 171, 172, 173, 174, 203
Xerxes 12, 15, 24, 30, 33, 34, 36, 38, 40, 41, 68
Xerxes' invasion of Greece 24, 30, 33, 68
xiphos 153

Zenodotus of Ephesus 25

βιβλιά 69
see biblion; biblia
βιβλίον 63
see biblion
ἐπιστολέως 61, 167
see epistoleos
ἱμάτιον 56
see himation
ὁπλίτης 153
see hoplon
ὅπλον 153
see hoplon
σκυτάλη 47, 52, 57, 58, 61, 63, 69, 71, 79, 104, 106, 170

www.ingramcontent.com/pod-product-compliance
Lightning Source LLC
Chambersburg PA
CBHW071824300426
44116CB00009B/1423